Kitchener and the Dardanelles Campaign: A Vindication

George H. Cassar

Wolverhampton Military Series No. 38

Helion & Company

**To Tom Calkin and to the memory of Walt Learning,
Peter Cale, Bill Spray and Lou Gimelli**

Helion & Company Limited
Unit 8 Amherst Business Centre
Budbrooke Road
Warwick
CV34 5WE
England
Tel. 01926 499 619
Email: info@helion.co.uk
Website: www.helion.co.uk
Twitter: @helionbooks
Visit our blog at blog.helion.co.uk

Published by Helion & Company 2022
Designed and typeset by Mach 3 Solutions (www.mach3solutions.co.uk)
Cover designed by Paul Hewitt, Battlefield Design (www.battlefield-design.co.uk)

Text © George H. Cassar 2022
Images © as individually credited
Maps © George Cassar 2022
Cover image: Lord Kitchener inspecting Anzac Cove, November 1915. (Open source)

Every reasonable effort has been made to trace copyright holders and to obtain their permission for the use of copyright material. The author and publisher apologize for any errors or omissions in this work and would be grateful if notified of any corrections that should be incorporated in future reprints or editions of this book.

ISBN 978-1-915113-75-7

British Library Cataloguing-in-Publication Data.
A catalogue record for this book is available from the British Library.

All rights reserved. No part of this publication may be reproduced, stored in a retrieval system, or transmitted, in any form, or by any means, electronic, mechanical, photocopying, recording or otherwise, without the express written consent of Helion & Company Limited.

For details of other military history titles published by Helion & Company Limited contact the above address or visit our website: http://www.helion.co.uk.

We always welcome receipt of book proposals from prospective authors.

Contents

List of Illustrations	iv
List of Maps	vi
Abbreviations	vii
Acknowledgements	viii
Series Editor Preface, The Wolverhampton Military Studies Series	x
Preface	xii
Introduction	xvii
1 Supreme War Lord	27
2 Pulled by the Undertow of the Dardanelles	44
3 The Changing Character of the Naval Operation	63
4 From the Navy to the Army	86
5 The Last Throw of the Dice	104
6 The Darkening Scene	130
7 The End of the Ill-Fated Expedition	153
Conclusion: General Review and Reflections on the Dardanelles Campaign	173
Appendix: Assessing the Charges Against Kitchener	177
Bibliography	196
Index	202

List of Illustrations

1. H.H. Asquith. A brilliant parliamentarian and orator possessing exceptional intellectual qualities, he was more of a conciliator than a war leader. (Library of Congress) ... i
2. David Lloyd George. An opportunist with no fixed principles, he had no compunction about resorting to gutter tactics against anyone who opposed him or stood in his way. (Open source) ... i
3. Winston Churchill. Intelligent, energetic, resolute but impulsive, opinionated and self-absorbed, his personal concern in 1915 overrode national interests. (Open source) ... i
4. Edward Grey. If the quality of his work sometimes drew criticism, no one had reason to question his sense of duty, personal conduct and integrity. (Open Source) ... i
5. Kitchener clad in civilian clothes, leaves the War Office to attend his first cabinet meeting where his unexpected disclosures startled his colleagues. (*Illustrated London News*) ... ii
6. Maurice Hankey. The brilliant ex-Royal Marine provided sound advice as well as indispensable service as secretary to the inner councils of war. (Library of Congress) ... ii
7. The most iconic recruiting poster, contrary to long held common belief, was not a vital factor in rousing young men to enlist. (Open source) ... ii
8. In a typical scene throughout Britain on Parliament's declaration of war against Imperial Germany, crowds of young men from all social classes form long queues outside Whitehall recruiting station to join the colours. (IWM) ... iii
9. Field Marshal Sir John French. The former cavalry officer was hopelessly out of his depth as BEF C-in-C. (Open source) ... iii
10. Postcard depicting Kitchener inspecting what appears to be a guard of Royal Marines. (Open source) ... iii
11. Kitchener and Hankey after attending a conference, Paris September 1914. (Open source) ... iv
12. Kitchener arriving at the War Office during the political crisis of May 1915. (*Manchester Guardian History of the War*, vol. 2) ... iv
13. General Joffre acknowledges the cheers of the crowds on leaving the War Office with Lord Kitchener during his visit to London at the end of October 1915. (*Illustrated London News*) ... iv

14. Hamilton is chatting with General Henri Gouraud, the fearless and talented French commander he much admired and respected. Several days after this picture was taken, Gouraud was critically wounded by a shell fired from a gun on the Asiatic shore and was transported back to France. (*Illustrated London News*)	iv
15. Kitchener (with a walking stick) following an inspection at Mudros on 11 November 1915. Monro is speaking to him. Immediately behind is Maxwell. (Australian War Memorial)	v
16. Kitchener walking through the ruins of Sedd-el-Bahr fortress on Cape Helles. To his right are abandoned Turkish shells. (Australian War Memorial)	v
17. Lieutenant General Francis Davies, VIII Corps commander, leading his small party to survey enemy positions at Cape Helles. At the moment he is pointing towards Achi Baba. Next to Kitchener are Generals Birdwood and Maxwell. (Picryl)	vi
18. Kitchener shaking hands with General Maurice Bailloud who had succeeded Gouraud. Hamilton's relations with Bailloud were strained as he was not nearly as competent as his predecessor. (Australian War Memorial)	vi
19. Australians watching the arrival of Kitchener at Anzac. (Australian War Memorial).	vi
20. Birdwood introduces Kitchener to Australian officers. (Australian War Memorial)	vii
21. Kitchener chatting with a group of Australian soldiers. (Australian War Memorial)	vii
22. Kitchener and Birdwood observing the Turkish position from Russel's Top at Anzac. (Australian War Memorial)	vii
23. Kitchener was at the time this photograph was taken, actually within 30 yards of an enemy trench manned by hundreds of Turks who were unaware of his presence. Maxwell is on the right of Kitchener and nearest to the camera. (Australian War Memorial)	viii
24. Kitchener's farewell salute after visiting Anzac. (Australian War Memorial)	viii
25. Kitchener in late 1915. His worn out appearance was caused by an enormous workload, constant stress imposed by the war and sharp differences with his colleagues, mainly over strategic policies. (Library of Congress)	viii

List of Maps

1	The Sudan Campaign, 1896-1898.	xxi
2	The Turkish Empire in 1914.	40
3	The Allied Naval Attack at the Dardanelles, 18 March 1915.	88
4	Theatre of Operations.	96
5	The British Landing on 25 April.	99
6	The British Landing on 6 August.	125
7	The Balkan States in 1915.	137

Abbreviations

ADC	Aide de Camp
ANZAC	Australian and New Zealand Corps
BEF	British Expeditionary Force
BMF	British Mediterranean Force
CIGS	Chief of the Imperial General Staff
C-in-C	Commander in Chief
DMO	Director of Military Operations
GHQ	General Headquarters (British Army Headquarters)
FO	Foreign Office
GHQ	*Grand Quartier Général* (French Army Headquarters)
HMSO	His Majesty's Stationary Office
IWM	Imperial War Museum
K	Kitchener
LHCMA	Liddell Hart Centre for Military Archives
MEF	Mediterranean Expeditionary Force
NA	National Archives
WO	War Office

Acknowledgements

As historical scholarship is a collaborative endeavour, it is a pleasure to acknowledge once more the help and support I received from many people and institutions. I must begin by thanking Lieutenant Colonel Edward Erickson, a leading expert on the Ottoman army, for faithfully replying to my many question. I am also indebted to Dr Mesut Uyar, formerly a colonel in the Turkish army, for his assistance and advice. William Spencer, a friend of long standing and now retired from his position as Principal Military Specialist at the National Archives in Kew, kindly returned to his former place of employment several times to track down documents that had eluded my attention while I was doing research there. Whenever I contacted Dr Christopher Bell to ask a question about specific material in his most recent book (*Churchill and the Dardanelles*), he graciously took the time to provide me with lengthy explanations.

As I am not able to work at home because of the distractions, I am extremely grateful to Dr James Smith, President of Eastern Michigan, for allowing me to keep an office at the university after I retired from teaching. I am also obliged to colleagues and friends for advice, assistance and forbearance while my work was in progress: Dr John McCurdy put up with repeated interruptions to act as my sounding board; Dr Jonathon Marvil, with whom I discussed this project at various stages, for his thoughtful suggestions; Dr Roger Long gave me the benefit of his expertise on the pre-war nationalist movement in India; Dr Jesse Koffman shared his extensive naval knowledge with me; and I turned to Dr Steven Ramold whenever I required to discuss military issues. Dr Mehmet Yaya, a native of Turkey and currently head of the economic department at Eastern, took the time to locate remote towns mentioned in the text for my maps as well as worked out the distances between some of the places; George Contis, my student assistant over four decades ago, performed a similar task with regard to Greece where he grew up and returns periodically to see relatives and friends; Given my lack of computer savvy, David Zylstra, College Technology Specialist, led me through the publisher's list of instructions and requests before I submitted my manuscript; Rachelle Marshall, the senior Department secretary, attended to my many requests, often going beyond the call of duty. Mrs Rachel Trudell-Jones made sense out of my rough sketches to produce the excellent maps.

My project owes much to the personnel in the libraries and archives where I carried on my research. Thanks are due to the staff at the Clark Library at the University of Michigan; the Halle Library at Eastern Michigan University; the National Archives; the Imperial War Museum; the British Library; the National Army Museum; Churchill College in Cambridge; Bodleian Library in Oxford; Liddell Hart Centre for Military Archives, King's College. I am grateful to the above British libraries and archival institutions for permission to examine and quote from papers in their possession. Crown copyright material in the British National archives is reproduced by permission of the Controller of Her Majesty's Stationary Office. My sincere apologies are due to the holder of any copyright I may have infringed upon inadvertently.

As always my greatest debt is to my wife Mary who tolerated my absences while I was engaged in lengthy research in the United Kingdom or in my university office for days on end battling through the writing process. Furthermore she worked through many drafts of my manuscript, saving me from numerous grammatical pitfalls and suggesting a more suitable alternative to awkwardly or ambiguously expressed phrases.

The Wolverhampton Military Studies Series
Series Editor Preface

As series editor, it is my great pleasure to introduce the *Wolverhampton Military Studies Series* to you. Our intention is that in this series of books you will find military history that is new and innovative, and academically rigorous with a strong basis in fact and in analytical research, but also is the kind of military history that is for all readers, whatever their particular interests, or their level of interest in the subject. To paraphrase an old aphorism: a military history book is not less important just because it is popular, and it is not more scholarly just because it is dull. With every one of our publications we want to bring you the kind of military history that you will want to read simply because it is a good and well-written book, as well as bringing new light, new perspectives, and new factual evidence to its subject.

In devising the *Wolverhampton Military Studies Series*, we gave much thought to the series title: this is a *military* series. We take the view that history is everything except the things that have not happened yet, and even then a good book about the military aspects of the future would find its way into this series. We are not bound to any particular time period or cut-off date. Writing military history often divides quite sharply into eras, from the modern through the early modern to the mediaeval and ancient; and into regions or continents, with a division between western military history and the military history of other countries and cultures being particularly marked. Inevitably, we have had to start somewhere, and the first books of the series deal with British military topics and events of the twentieth century and later nineteenth century. But this series is open to any book that challenges received and accepted ideas about any aspect of military history, and does so in a way that encourages its readers to enjoy the discovery.

In the same way, this series is not limited to being about wars, or about grand strategy, or wider defence matters, or the sociology of armed forces as institutions, or civilian society and culture at war. None of these are specifically excluded, and in some cases they play an important part in the books that comprise our series. But there are already many books in existence, some of them of the highest scholarly standards, which cater to these particular approaches. The main theme of the *Wolverhampton Military Studies Series* is the military aspects of wars, the preparation for wars or their prevention, and their aftermath. This includes some books whose main theme is the technical details of how armed forces have worked, some books on wars and battles, and some books that re-examine the evidence about the existing stories, to show in a different light what everyone thought they already knew and understood.

As series editor, together with my fellow editorial board members, and our publisher Duncan Rogers of Helion, I have found that we have known immediately and almost by instinct the kind of books that fit within this series. They are very much the kind of well-written and challenging books that my students at the University of Wolverhampton would want to read. They are books which enhance knowledge and offer new perspectives. Also, they are books for anyone with an interest in military history and events, from expert scholars to occasional readers. One of the great benefits of the study of military history is that it includes a large and often committed section of the wider population, who want to read the best military history that they can find; our aim for this series is to provide it.

Stephen Badsey
University of Wolverhampton

Preface

A large library already existed on the subject of the Dardanelles campaign when I began my professional career in 1968 and it has continued to grow practically on a yearly basis. Given that many of the recent historical works have not added much to our understanding of the ill-fated expedition, it is reasonable to ask whether another investigation is warranted. My response would be that it depends on the nature of the study. For over a century the vast majority of writers focused entirely on the military and naval engagements and only a handful showed any interest in coming to grips with the issue of high policy. Among the few who had written about the "war behind the war" none in my view related the story accurately or explored the vital areas of my interest.

I had previously written two books on Kitchener that analyzed his record during the two years that he served as Secretary of State for War. They covered a host of topics and in the limited amount of space I had to work with I could not delve into the details of his role in the complex and controversial Dardanelles operation. Through my research on the period, I was always convinced that he became a convenient scapegoat for his political enemies in the cabinet, not only because they found him secretive and difficult to work with, but, perhaps more importantly, they needed to conceal their mistakes by blaming someone in authority who was no longer around to defend his action. I have thought about writing this book for a long time and what finally drove me to make that commitment was the way writers have continued to view Kitchener as principally culpable for the debacle in the Dardanelles. The list is long but a few examples will suffice. In *Gallipoli: The End of the Myth,* Robin Prior concludes that "Churchill's responsibility is great but of a lesser order than Kitchener's."[1] Elsewhere he writes that "Kitchener must bear a great deal of the responsibility in all this."[2] In a more recent study Eugene Rogan maintains in *The Fall of the Ottomans,* that the moving spirit behind the naval attack was Kitchener, not Churchill. He writes: "From the outset Kitchener advocated a naval operation against the Turks."[3] And again: "It is ironic that, to this day, Churchill takes the blame for Gallipoli when Kitchener was so clearly the campaign's most influential decision maker."[4]

In all fairness it is useful to remember that those who concentrated on describing and analyzing the military and naval action were not authorities on the higher direction of the campaign. They accepted as the last word the dubious claims of the leading political participants. Consequently

---

1 Robin Prior, *Gallipoli: The End of The Myth* (New Haven: Yale University Press, 2009), p. 71.
2 Ibid., p. 248.
3 Eugene Rogan, *The Fall of the Ottomans* (New York: Basic Books, 2015), p. 130.
4 Ibid., p. 189.

they echoed the popular version of events that Kitchener wielded arbitrary power and that he completely dominated the decision-making process in the cabinet and in the inner councils of war. My object in undertaking this project was to arrive as closely as possible to the truth. To that end it was necessary to peel off layers of myths and misconceptions firmly embedded in the story of the disastrous operation.

As the architect of the naval plan to force the Dardanelles, Churchill had expected an easy victory in which he would establish his reputation as a talented war leader and gifted strategist. However, he disregarded the elementary principles of war, driven as he was by wishful thinking and imagined benefits with the result that the campaign never had a chance of succeeding. Churchill came under increasing attack in the press for the poorly conceived naval assault and some newspapers even claimed without evidence, that he was also responsible for the more costly military operation (which turned out to be true). As a vital step in rebuilding his political career he had to reshape public perception of his part in the campaign. Accordingly, he wrote a defence of his strategy in volume 2 of *The World Crisis* in 1923. Churchill's claims could not be verified against the facts as official records were then inaccessible to the public and would be until the mid 1960s. While Churchill has few apologists nowadays, it is curious that even among the vast majority of writers who have condemned his scheme, there is a tendency to accept his version of the events uncritically. But *The World Crisis* is not an accurate account of what occurred behind the scenes. Rather it is Churchill's attempt to rewrite the history of the campaign.

Early in my career I believed Churchill's explanation in his memoirs that the plan to force the Dardanelles by ships alone was sound and that its failure was due to events beyond his control. After all Churchill's legacy had grown to mythical proportions and his justification for initiating the campaign seemed credible and persuasive. As I gained more experience in my field and could better assess what really happened, my perception of Churchill's scheme tilted sharply in the opposite direction, and my criticism focused on his poor judgement, excessive optimism and lack of technical skill. As it happened, it was only the beginning of his failings.

During the course of my research, I suspected that Churchill had made factual mistakes and therefore I began comparing his narrative in *The World Crisis* to the official minutes of the War Council meetings. To my surprise and dismay, I discovered that Churchill had a habit, not merely of bias and stretching the truth, but of lying and fabricating or distorting evidence to exculpate himself from what had turned out to be a futile and costly sideshow.

By far Churchill's most serious gaffe was his responsibility in ensuring that the land campaign on Gallipoli flowed inevitably from the unsuccessful naval assault. He had won the approval of the War Council in January 1915 to carry out the naval attack on condition that, if resistance turned out to be stronger than anticipated, the attack would be broken off and, to avoid loss of face in the Muslim world, an announcement would be made that the bombardment was in fact a feint for a landing elsewhere. It was important that no publicity should attend the naval action in case the ships had to be recalled. It was feared that the appearance of defeat would likely trigger serious nationalist outbreaks in Egypt and India which could only be suppressed with troops at the expense of hindering, perhaps fatally, the war effort against Germany on the western front. A day after the ships opened a heavy bombardment against the Turkish forts, Churchill, certain of victory and eager to claim the lion's share of the credit, went back on his word by issuing a press release which drew world attention on the attack in the Dardanelles and the perceived objective. In so doing he foreclosed the option that the operation would be terminated in case the ships ran into unforeseen difficulties. Thus even before the naval attack miscarried a month later (18 March), British authorities had accepted the idea of sending in the army if necessary to avoid the stigma of defeat.

In hindsight Churchill obviously recognized the catastrophic consequences of his selfish act though he never acknowledged it. He omitted any mention of his announcement to the media in the doctored version of his account as he would have had to explain that he deliberately broke faith with his colleagues in which case he could hardly have tried to distance himself from the devastating military defeat in the Dardanelles. By distorting the evidence, he lessened his culpability which allowed him to make a case that it was Kitchener who, on his own, had ordered the army to land on the Gallipoli Peninsula. A detailed analysis in this study will set the record straight, show how Churchill was unwittingly responsible for escalating the operation; and prove conclusively that by sending the army to invade Gallipoli, Kitchener was acting, not on his own, but in concert with the overriding sentiment in the War Council.

In fact given the scarcity of manpower in Britain, the last thing that Kitchener wanted was to be dragged into a land campaign. But he and the other members of the War Council felt they had no other option after Churchill made his colossal blunder. The worst part is that the chances the army could take control of the Gallipoli Peninsula were practically non-existent, as the Turks had been forewarned, enjoyed superior numbers, occupied the high ground and were further aided by strong defensive fortifications. The landings were checked on both occasions after which the French, as junior partners, offered to significantly increase the number of their divisions with the object of finishing the job. Their proposed expedition to the Dardanelles was suddenly diverted to the Balkans to try to help Serbia which was in danger of being crushed between the Austro-Germans and Bulgarians. The French had made the commitment without consulting London which was expected to supply half the troops. On learning of the French move, the British hesitated to follow suit as their resources were already stretched to the breaking point and they simply could not afford to become involved in another theatre of war. London, however, was eventually forced to comply to avoid a French political crisis which might have strained, if not split, the alliance. The upshot was that the British government could no longer sustain the Dardanelles front and thereupon ordered its forces to withdraw.

A greater accepted version of the events, but no less flawed than *The World Crisis, was* the report of the Dardanelles Commission, a body set up by Parliament in 1916 to examine the inception and conduct of the naval and military campaign. As a government organ with the authority to question participants and examine evidence inaccessible to the public, it was taken for granted that it would fulfil its task thoroughly and without prejudice. Unfortunately it did neither. Weighing against the objectivity of the Commission was that one of its appointed members nursed an undisguised hatred of Kitchener. As he was the only military expert among his associates, one can only speculate the extent of his influence on them but it had to be significant. That may explain why the judgements of the Commission did not always reflect the range of opinions it had heard. On top of this, the Commission had a tendency to accept at face value the testimony of participants, some of whom had good reason to shield their mistakes or had colluded behind the scenes to avoid incriminating or contradicting one another, instead of seeking to arrive at the truth. Too often they censored Kitchener without providing corroborating evidence of wrong doing.

There were others in the Asquith cabinet who joined Churchill in assailing Kitchener's judgement. Although the politicians were intellectually brilliant, they had no experience in shaping war policy, not to mention they lacked good judgement. As an example they had pledged to assist in the fight against Germany but had not prepared the nation to meet its formidable commitment. Kitchener, who took over the War Office in August 1914, made arrangements for a conflict that would last at least three years and happily he was a master improviser. Given that the members of the cabinet were intimidated by Kitchener's reputation in the early months of the war, they gave him carte blanche to run the war as he saw fit. It was during this period that Britain made the greatest contribution to the allied war effort.

Kitchener's political ascendency started to wane after a deadlock set in on the western front. With no solution in sight for the impasse, the leading politicians, unhappy at the costly offensives which netted no gains, began to take an active role in trying to find a novel approach to the conflict. Prior to 1914 none had shown any interest in the study of military history but they came to believe that the recipe to win inexpensive victories and accelerate an end to the war lay in attacking Germany's allies. As a start it was seen that the defeat of Turkey, the weakest members of the Central Powers, would sap Germany's strength and bring about its collapse.

They were unaware that it was Germany who sustained its allies, not the other way around. They flitted from one half-baked scheme to another without understanding the importance of such relevant factors as logistics, the nature of the terrain, interior versus exterior lines, probable enemy response and whether the necessary troops were available. They were blind to the fact that there was no short cut to victory. They ignored Kitchener's often-repeated claim that the war could only be won on the western front and that the price of beating the Germans would be tragically high.

The cabinet's adoption of a peripheral strategy, even if the operations in the Dardanelles and in other secondary theatres had been conducted successfully, would have had no bearing on the final outcome of the war, yet tied down hundreds of thousands of troops who could have been used more effectively elsewhere. Kitchener often felt in 1915 that he was waging a war simultaneously on two fronts, one against the Germans and the other against his silver-tongue colleagues against whom he was no match in debate. As differences deepened over the government's strategic direction of the war, Kitchener's isolation from the other members of the cabinet grew increasingly until his influence had all but disappeared. Admittedly Kitchener had a difficult time expressing himself clearly, was inflexible, distrusted politicians and his methods were sometimes open to question; but overall his leadership during the early months of the war when he did not have to defend his policies had paid enormous dividends. After the politicians insisted on taking control of the war effort, the nation's fortunes spiraled downward. Nevertheless they were quick to point an accusatory finger at Kitchener in their testimony to the Dardanelles Commission, in their memoirs or in accounts passed on to journalists whenever there were war-related shortages or setbacks on the battlefield over which he had little or no control. They found Kitchener to be a convenient scapegoat because he was no longer able to answer his critics. The most scathing among Kitchener's political critics was Lloyd George who blamed him for practically everything that went wrong in the war and of course minimized or ignored his achievements. The Welshman hated Kitchener with whom he had often clashed, especially for standing in the way of implementing his strategy which was based on gut instinct rather than military logic. Given his lack of scruples, he had no qualms about spreading disinformation to sully Kitchener's reputation. It is interesting that Lloyd George and other key cabinet ministers who led the lesser lights in the cabinet down the primrose path, none except Churchill, suffered any harm to their career, but at least they are identified here.

I will not deny that there is much in this account that is controversial. It is mainly for that reason I consider it probably the most difficult and challenging subject that I have ever undertaken. Although I greatly admired the war leader who stood in defiance of Nazi Germany and changed the course of the Second World War, he bore only slight resemblance to the flawed individual who launched the Dardanelles operation a quarter of a century earlier. In holding the younger Churchill as the villain of the piece, I based my reasoning on the following factors: that he imposed a hurriedly conceived and defective naval plan on the War Council; that to enhance his flagging reputation he deliberately attracted world attention to the naval attack and, in so doing, broke the agreement with his colleagues, ultimately leaving them with no choice but to sanction a land campaign that was virtually unwinnable; that he indulged in fabrications, deceptions and lies in his written account to cover his mistakes; and that he was relentless in his efforts to blame others for the disaster that he had created.

Whilst many of the recurring criticism that have been levelled against Kitchener over the years are distorted, exaggerated or simply wrong, it would be idle to pretend that he made no mistakes. In describing Kitchener's leadership in the conduct of the military campaign I have not omitted or glossed over his errors in judgement. It is only when all the facts are laid out that he can be fairly evaluated.

This study went beyond the original limits of trying to correct the misimpressions about Kitchener's role in the Dardanelles operation. It became necessary to afford Churchill much more space than I had intended when I discovered damning evidence that was far more serious than his abortive naval plan to force the Dardanelles. As a result of his malfeasance to bolster his political standing, he became accountable, albeit inadvertently, for initiating the land campaign and the terrible consequences that ensued. The new material uncovered compelled me to digress, not only to introduce documentation to substantiate my disclosure about Churchill, but to correct critical errors which inevitably changed the trajectory of the traditional narrative of the campaign. This text also questions whether the politicians in Asquith's cabinet, given their sorry record in 1915, were qualified to manage the war. Finally this work seeks to place the story of the Dardanelles in the context of the war as a whole, helping to explain such issues as to why reinforcements were sometimes unavailable or how political factors sometimes induced the British to give due consideration to requests from one or more of their allies.

In summary, by bringing new perspective to long-standing controversies, while consigning others to the dustbin, I would like to think that I have produced a more accurate version of the history of the Dardanelles expedition, as well as dispelled the most serious charges against Kitchener. Whether my claims have merit is for others to judge.

Introduction

Born near Listowel, Ireland on 24 June 1850, Horatio Herbert Kitchener grew up in modest circumstances, the third child and second son of British parents, Lieutenant Colonel Henry Horatio Kitchener, a retired army officer, and his first wife, Frances Anne.[1] The first of his given names was borrowed from his father who was named after Lord Nelson, the hero of Trafalgar, although the family always called him Herbert. The Colonel had no faith in public schools and until the age of thirteen Herbert's education was haphazard, dependent on a succession of transient governesses and tutors. Herbert had his heart set on obtaining an army commission and, since he had educational deficiencies, was coached by a crammer before he succeeded in entering the Royal Military Academy at Woolwich in 1868. Nicknamed "the Shop," the Academy trained cadets to serve as officers in the royal engineers and royal artillery. Kitchener found the work grueling and he struggled to keep up with his classmates. While his academic record was undistinguished, he passed out of Woolwich and was gazetted into the royal engineers in January 1871.

Kitchener welcomed the break from the dull routine service at home when he was lent to the Palestine Exploration Fund, which had been founded to conduct a detailed survey of Palestine and to methodically identify the landmarks referred to in the Bible in order to refute the onslaught by contemporary scientists upon the foundations of orthodox religion. Here he developed leadership skills, established work habits, learned Arabic and became a talented diplomat through his constant dealings with local officials. Kitchener completed the survey of western Palestine within four years, a remarkable feat considering much of the work was conducted under circumstances of extreme difficulty. As a testament to the quality of the finished product, it has had a lasting effect on the Middle East. Archaeologists and geographers working in the southern Levant, regularly consult the data compiled by Kitchener and his team. Another result was the establishment of the border between Israel and Lebanon at a point where Kitchener's survey stopped.

The Fund highly praised Kitchener for his zeal, energy, thoroughness and keeping expenditures below the sum allocated in the budget. On the day that Kitchener submitted his finished

---

1   Unless otherwise indicated the material for this section was drawn from the following sources: Sir George Arthur, *Life of Lord Kitchener* (London: Macmillan, 1920), vols. 1-2; Philip Magnus, *Kitchener: Portrait of an Imperialist* (New York: E.P. Dutton, 1959); George H. Cassar, *Kitchener: Architect of Victory* (London: William Kimber, 1977); Trevor Royle, *The Kitchener Enigma* (London: Michael Joseph, 1985); John Pollock, *Kitchener: Architect of Victory, Artisan of Peace* (New York: Carroll and Graf, 1998); C. Brad Faught, *Hero and Anti-Hero* (London: I.B. Tauris, 2016).

work to the Fund (10 September 1877), the Foreign Office appointed him to survey and triangulate Cyprus, then a new British Protectorate. A brief stint as military vice consul at Kastamanu in northern Anatolia followed before he was posted to Egypt, recently occupied by the British to protect their interest in the Suez Canal.

Promoted major in the newly established Egyptian army under the command of Sir Evelyn Wood, Kitchener was selected to train the single cavalry regiment and, after a year, found more congenial work as an intelligence officer. Taking advantage of Kitchener's knowledge of Arabic, Wood assigned him to gather information on the Sudan where there was currently an uprising against Egyptian rule, led by Mohammed Ahmed who claimed to be the Mahdi (the expected one) and a descendant of the prophet Mohammed. The movement quickly assumed the strength of a hurricane and within a year the Mahdi had extended his control over the southern part of the country. The Gladstone government, already far more deeply committed in Egypt than it intended, had no desire to add the Sudan to its responsibilities. Its solution was to despatch world-renowned Major General Charles "Chinese" Gordon to the Sudan to evacuate the Egyptian garrison and their families. Once in Khartoum, Gordon disobeyed his orders. The idea of cutting his losses and abandoning a people who looked to him for their salvation was absolutely alien to his nature. Thus he vowed to remain in Khartoum until help came or the city fell. By the spring of 1884, the Mahdi's forces had begun the investment of Khartoum. Gladstone remained indifferent to Gordon's urgent need for help and it was only after intense public protest that he finally gave way and in August authorized a relief force to march southwards from Egypt to lift the siege of Khartoum. Kitchener was assigned as an intelligent officer to the expedition which was commanded by General Garnet Wolseley.

Riding well ahead of the relief column, Kitchener questioned passers-by or town locals to try to interpret the designs of the Mahdists, tested the loyalty of the tribes, selected camp sites and maintained a lifeline with Gordon. Wolseley was more cautious that he ought to have been in view of Gordon's urgent circumstances. By the time the relief force came within sight of Khartoum on 28 January 1886, it was met by artillery fire and Gordon's flag was no longer flying over the palace, sure signs that the city had fallen. Two days earlier Mahdist forces had overwhelmed the exhausted and half-starved defenders and during the orgy of rape and murder that followed, Gordon had been killed. Nothing more could be done so the relief force turned back. Kitchener was in Gadkul, located north of Khartoum, when he learned of Gordon's death on 2 February. He was so devastated that a month later it still weighed heavily on his mind. "The shock of the news was dreadful, and I can hardly realise it yet," he admitted in a letter to his father. "I feel that now he is dead, the heart and soul of the Expedition is gone."[2]

Kitchener was one of the few soldiers who emerged from that unhappy episode with his reputation enhanced. He was promoted to the rank of lieutenant colonel and Wolseley, in reports, lavished praise on him for the quality of his service. British newspapers, through their correspondents, had published articles about his exploits and commended him highly for his exceptional courage and initiative. In the summer of 1885 Kitchener, sickened by the Gladstone's government refusal to avenge the death of Gordon, which he considered a stain on the country's honour, resigned his commission in the Egyptian army and sailed for England.

---

2   Cited in Pollock, *Kitchener*, p. 73.

Kitchener spent the summer in England attending public dinners and other social gatherings as well as taking advantage of his growing fame to make useful political connections. In November 1885, he was selected as the British member of the Zanzibar Boundary Commission, which also included French and German representatives. The object of the Commission was to investigate the Sultan's claims to exercise sovereignty over territory on the mainland opposite his island. Kitchener's own work was completed some ten months later and he was on his way back home when he received a message to proceed to Suakin to take up his new duties as governor of the Eastern Sudan and Red Sea Littoral. Notwithstanding the grandiose title, Kitchener's authority extended only a few miles beyond the port. Suakin was the last remaining town held by the Egyptians in the Sudan and was constantly harried by dervish forces who owed their allegiance to the late Mahdi's successor, Abdullahi Ibn Muhammed, a brutal and debauched despot known as the Khalifa. Kitchener spent his time trying to regain the loyalty of Arab tribes by disbursing subsidies or bribes, fortifying the town, and adopting an aggressive policy against Osman Digna, the talented Khalifa's commander in the area. On 17 January 1888, Kitchener led a dawn attack against Handub, a village 15 miles north of Suakin, in the hope of catching Digna at his base and scattering his forces. The raid missed capturing Digna but killed some 200 Mahdists while Kitchener's losses were only 19. The action had to be broken off when Kitchener was struck by a bullet which pierced his jaw and embedded itself in his neck. Kitchener was taken to Cairo for medical treatment and during his convalescence was hailed by the press and by his superiors for his gallant behavior – presumably his retreat was understood to have been no fault of his own. He was promoted brevet colonel and Queen Victoria appointed him an aide-de-camp

Kitchener was back on the job before he was fully recovered. A few months later he returned to England on leave during which he was often the welcomed guest at the homes of prominent politicians. The highlight of his social activities was an invitation to stay at Hatfield House, the country seat of Lord Salisbury, the Prime Minister, who offered him the post of adjutant–general of the Egyptian army. Kitchener accepted and had barely settled in his new headquarters in Cairo when in December 1888 he was sent with Sir Francis Grenfell, the sirdar (commander) of the Egyptian army, and two of his brigades to defend Suakin. While Kitchener was in England, the troublesome Osman Digna had laid siege to Suakin. In charge of a brigade, Kitchener played a prominent role in a spirited action that inflicted a punishing defeat on Digna's forces outside the walls of the town. Grenfell later complimented Kitchener, saying that he had led his men with coolness and gallantry and well sustained his previous reputation.

In the summer of 1889 Kitchener was again called upon to take the field, this time to assist Grenfell to beat back a dervish army under Wad-el-Nejumi, one of the Khalifa's most able and fanatical lieutenants. The encounter occurred near the village of Toski, a short distance inside Egypt. Up against withering and disciplined rifle fire, plus an intense artillery barrage, the dervish army was cut to pieces and its leader was killed. In command of the cavalry, Kitchener's action headed off the dervish army and lured it to its destruction. Kitchener's vital role in the victory was acknowledged and he was awarded a CB.

During the autumn of 1889 Kitchener spent a few week's leave in India, touring some of the principal attractions and visiting his younger brother Walter, an army captain in the West Yorkshire Regiment. On returning to Cairo, he was summoned by the British consul-general, Sir Evelyn Baring, and asked to combine temporarily the post of inspector-general of the Egyptian police with his current job. Baring wanted a firm and trusted hand to reorganize the police force which for years had been plagued by lax discipline, corruption and bribery. Kitchener was reluctant to accept the position less because of the daunting nature of the work than fear that it would jeopardized his chances to succeed Grenfell someday. However, Kitchener yielded to Baring's appeal when assured that, on the contrary, his odds to become sirdar would be enhanced if he took on the additional assignment. In a little over a year, Kitchener's policies exceeded expectations, reducing serious crime by half and doubling the number of convictions.

Grenfell resigned as sirdar in April 1892 and Baring urged London to appoint Kitchener in his place. Kitchener was trained as an engineer and there were other British officers in Egypt who, at least on the surface, had a better claim to the office in view of their greater experience in battle. Baring, however, had an eye on the eventual liberation of the Sudan, an undertaking that would depend more on planning and solving the problems of transport and supply than on the gift of exercising battlefield control. Besides Kitchener knew the country, the people and their language. He was immensely painstaking and thorough with a reputation of rising above the most difficult challenges and his driving concern for strict economy was essential in view of the impoverished condition of the Egyptian treasury. Both Grenfell and Salisbury agreed with Baring that Kitchener was the best man for the task and he was duly appointed in April 1892 with the rank of major general.

Foremost in Kitchener's mind was the conviction that he had a duty to avenge Gordon and liberate the Sudan from the grasp of Mahdism, but it was unclear how long he would have to wait before the Egyptian treasury could afford the huge outlay for such an operation. During the years that followed Kitchener spent much of his time making preparations for the future campaign and improving the training and efficiency of the Egyptian army. The moment that he longed for came unexpectedly on 13 March 1896, when he was authorized to advance into northern Sudan to relieve pressure on the Italians who had been badly defeated by the Abyssinians at Adowa a fortnight earlier. From his base at Wadi Halfa, he moved forward in a series of bounds scattering resistance along the way and, once the nature of his mission was extended, eventually arrived within sight of Omdurman, the Mahdist capital, on 1 September 1898. The next day the Khalifa assembled his army of about 60,000 strong outside the city and advanced towards Kitchener's camp. Worried that he would have to attack the Mahdists, electing to fight behind the walls of their capital, Kitchener could hardly believe his good fortune. He therefore arranged his 18,000-man Anglo-Egyptian army in a semicircle resting on the Nile while the drum beats of the approaching horde could be heard. Shortly after dawn the Mahdists struck, but under the concentrated fire of Kitchener's modern weapons the fight turned into a massacre as wave after wave of the faithful collapsed in heaps. Kitchener's victory was achieved at the low cost of 48 killed while no fewer than 11,000 Mahdists littered the battlefield and thousands more were taken prisoners. The Khalifa escaped with a handful of adherents but they were eventually hunted down and he was killed in the skirmish.

Returning home for a well-deserved rest Kitchener, now a lieutenant general, was given a tumultuous welcome at Dover on 27 October 1898 and an even greater reception after his train pulled into Victoria Station that same day. It was a sign of things to come as a wildly excited public wanted to express its gratitude to the hero who had captured their hearts and redeemed the nation's honour. Cities competed with one another to shower him with gifts and several universities awarded him honorary degrees. He was raised to the peerage as "Lord Kitchener of Khartoum and Aspall." His portrait appeared in public places and on commercial goods as if he was the symbol of the nation's virility and righteousness. Parliament expressed its thanks and

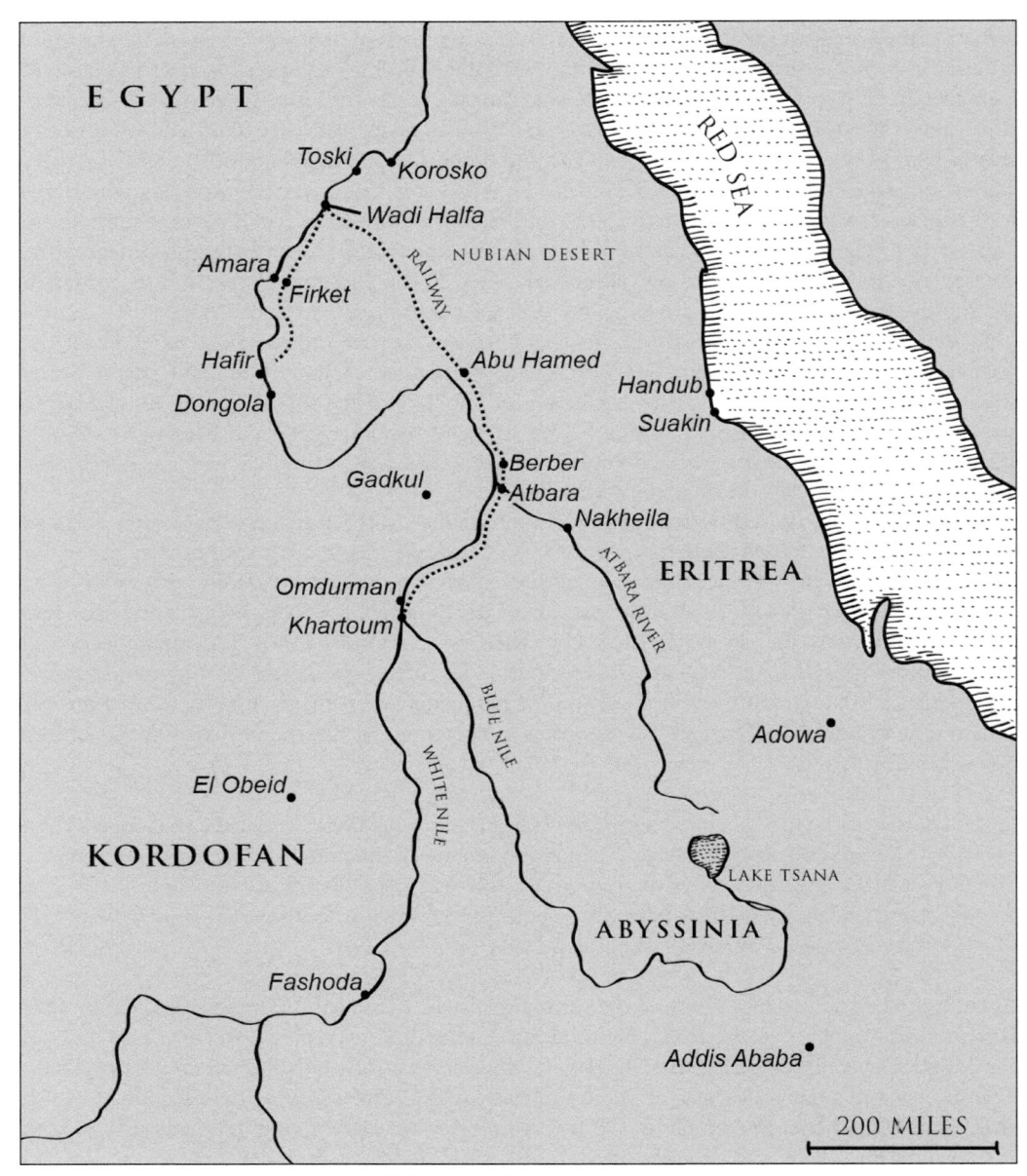

Map 1 The Sudan Campaign, 1896-1898.

awarded him a grant of £30,000. Omdurman not only made Kitchener a household name but would contribute significantly to the creation of his legend.

During a visit to Hatfield House, Salisbury informed Kitchener that he would be appointed governor-general of the Sudan, in addition to retaining his post as sirdar. The task that awaited Kitchener on his return to Khartoum (where he had set up his headquarters after the clash at Omdurman) at the end of December 1898 was daunting to say the least. There was a shortage of funds and staff to govern a territory of nearly one million square miles in extent. The first priority was to pacify the country and reestablish law and order. Despite the death of the Khalifa, there were tribes who remained loyal to Mahdism. The next step was to fix the economy which was in shambles. The root cause lay partly in the outbreak of a famine in certain parts of the country and partly by the turbulence of the Mahdist years, during which normally large grain-growing areas were allowed to remain fallow. Kitchener stayed in the Sudan for a year and succeeded in getting the country to move again when he received a call to serve in South Africa.

In October 1899, a conflict had broken out between Britain and the Boer republics of the Transvaal and Orange Free State in South Africa. British forces under General Redvers Buller were poorly trained, inadequate in numbers and unprepared for war, resulting in a series of embarrassing defeats. Salisbury responded by replacing Buller with Field Marshal Frederick Roberts, the nation's most acclaimed field commander, and appointing Kitchener as his chief of staff. The public greeted the changes with relief.

Kitchener hurriedly left Khartoum on 18 December 1899 and eight days later reached Gibraltar where he joined Roberts on board the *Dunottar Castle* and together they sailed for Cape Town. On the way over the two soldiers devised a simple but effective war-winning strategy. The plan called for a full scale invasion of the Boer republics, disposing of any opposing forces attempting to bar the way. Throughout their association in South Africa Kitchener and Roberts worked well together, notwithstanding wide differences in temperament and experience. Indeed Roberts expressed high praise for Kitchener when his part in the campaign was over and he was back in England. Viscount Esher, then secretary to the Office of Works, jotted down Roberts' remarks:

> Of Kitchener he has no words to express his high commendation. "Kitchener's self-possession, his eagerness to undertake all the hardest and most difficult work, his scorn of notoriety, and his loyalty, were beyond all praise. He was the only officer who shrank from no responsibility and no task however arduous." From start to finish, he says, not a cloud between them, not a difference of opinion.[3]

Roberts opened the second phase of the campaign on 12 February 1900 and shortly after alert British forces trapped a large Boer column under General Piet Cronje on the northern bank of the Modder river at Vendutie Drift. The battle, however, was officially named after Paardeberg, a prominent hill a few miles west of Vendutie Drift. As Roberts was lying in bed with a feverish chill, he left Kitchener in command. On the assumption that it was vital to win a quick victory and resume the advance, Kitchener decided to launch an attack. It was an unwise decision as

---

[3] Maurice V. Brett (ed.), *Journals and Letters of Reginal Viscount Esher*, vol. 1 (London: Ivor, Nicholson & Watson Ltd., 1934), vol. 1, p. 273.

Cronje could not escape, and under relentless bombardment would have been forced to surrender before very long. As for the assault on Cronje's laager, inadequate reconnaissance, poor coordination of units and unclear orders to key subordinates resulted in its repulse. The abortive operation had cost British forces a total of 1270 casualties, including 303 killed. It is interesting that Roberts never chided Kitchener, not even mildly, for ordering the attack or the manner in which he had conducted the battle.

The day after the battle, Roberts was back on his feet and resumed command of the operation. After he conferred with his commanders, he elected to bombard the laager and wait for the effect of investment. Eight days later, Cronje, with no way out and his camp subjected to bombardment around the clock, hoisted the white flag on the 27 February.

Almost immediately, Roberts resumed his march into the Orange Free State, sweeping away a Boer force at Poplar Grove and entering Bloemfontein in triumph on 13 March. Here an outbreak of enteric fever imposed a six weeks' delay but at the beginning of May Roberts pushed northwards into the Transvaal with an overwhelming force that covered the whole of the country from east to west. Roberts occupied Johannesburg on 12 May, then after ejecting a Boer force west of the town a fortnight later, resumed the march and rode into Pretoria on 5 June. With the Boer capitals and much of their territory in British hands, their armies scattered into fragments and their leaders on the run, Roberts concluded that the war was over except for mopping up operations. He handed over command in South Africa to Kitchener and returned to England to take up new duties.

The British, however, underestimated the tenacity and resilience of the Boers. Determined not to submit to British rule, they abandoned orthodox warfare in favour of guerilla tactics at which they excelled. Operating in their home areas, Boer commandos struck where they were least expected, seizing British supplies, cutting railway lines, and ambushing small army units before disappearing into the vastness of the veld or melting back into the general population. Kitchener's response to the changing nature of the war was to revise his strategy. To deprive the Boers of local support he extended Robert's scorched earth policy in the troublesome areas, systematically destroying farms, slaughtering livestock, burning crops and poisoning wells. As families (mostly women and children) could not be abandoned without food or shelter, they were taken to what was then called concentration camps, where regrettably many died because of endemic contagious diseases caused by poor diet, unsanitary conditions, overcrowding and inadequate medical arrangements. The other aspect of Kitchener's policy was to limit the mobility of Boer fighters. A system of blockhouses was constructed, each garrisoned by half a dozen men and linked by barbed wire, crisscrossed the war zone, dividing the vast veld into smaller districts. Within the compartmentalized zones, organized drives often caught small Boer units or drove them like wild animals against the blockhouses. These drastic measure gradually wore down the Boers and compelled them to accept peace terms in May 1902.

Sailing from Cape Town in South Africa, Kitchener arrived at Southampton on 12 July 1902, and in the weeks that followed was greeted everywhere he went with the same high level of jubilation as had occurred two years earlier after his return from the Sudan. The Prince of Wales was among the dignitaries on hand to welcome him as soon as he stepped down from the train at Paddington. On the way to St. James Palace, the streets were lined with cheering crowds, eager to pay homage to the man acknowledged to be the foremost soldier of the Empire. After lunch he was driven to Buckingham Palace where the new monarch, Edward VII, appointed him to the newly founded Order of Merit. Later honours included elevation to viscount, promotion to full general and the thanks of Parliament to which was attached a grant of £50,000 – a huge sum that would make him financially independent for the remainder of his life.

While still in South Africa Kitchener had accepted, as his next assignment, an enticing offer from Lord Curzon, the Viceroy of India, to command and reform the country's army. On arriving in India, Kitchener's aim was to reorganize the army to meet possible external aggression, not internal rebellion as had been previously the main concern. In the course of implementing the reforms, Kitchener clashed with Curzon when he insisted that all military decision-making power should be concentrated in the hands of the commander. The deepening dispute was referred to London which supported Kitchener's position, prompting Curzon to resign. Kitchener found Lord Minto, Curzon's successor, more compliant and content to leave him in control of army policy. Kitchener relinquished his post in September 1909 and was immediately gazetted field marshal. In the span of seven years, he had transformed a semi-obsolete system into one that was rational and highly effective. Indeed without Kitchener's thorough overhauling of the military system, the Indian army could not have served the Empire to the extent that it did during the Great War.

Back in England Kitchener was approaching 60 but he still possessed abundant energy and had to face the possibility that, if no suitable employment could be found, he would be forced to retire. During the next two years Kitchener spent his leisure time travelling to different parts of the world, purchasing a home called Broome Park near Canterbury and supervising its massive renovation, and serving as a member of the Committee of Imperial Defence (CID), a body established in 1903 as the cabinet's advisory and consultative body on matters relating to home and Imperial defence.

In July 1911 Sir Elton Gorst, the Proconsul of Egypt, was ill with advanced cancer from which he died shortly after his return to England. Gorst's tenure was considered to have been a failure, not the least was his mishandling of the economy and his refusal to clamp down on growing nationalist agitation which was inching closer to open rebellion. To succeed Gorst, the Foreign Office deemed Kitchener the obvious choice to restore order and guide the country towards a brighter era. He spoke Arabic, had spent many years in Egypt, appreciated its culture, and, as the conqueror of the dervishes and the Boers, was revered by the native population.

Kitchener was delighted with the appointment. He had spent more time in Egypt than anywhere else and regarded it as his spiritual home. One of the main reasons he was sent to Egypt was to stifle the troublesome activities of the nationalists. Accordingly he cracked down on centres of agitation and either imprisoned the leaders or drove them into exile. Dealt a crippling blow, the nationalists ceased to be a disruptive element in Egyptian society throughout Kitchener's term in office.

Although an ardent imperialist, Kitchener considered it a moral obligation to devise and carry out paternalistic policies to assist all peoples occupied by Britain for its own benefit. Since Egypt was an agricultural country dependent heavily on the export of cotton, Kitchener took great pains to improve and protect the condition of the fellahin (peasants). He was happy to exert himself on their behalf for he had great affection for them since the time they had formed the greater part of his Egyptian army command, not to mention that they constituted the backbone of the Egyptian economy. Riding roughshod over entrenched moneyed classes which had profited from the existing system, he passed laws that prohibited moneylenders from charging more than three percent interest per annum and protected the small peasant who owned five feddans (slightly over five acres) or less against expropriation for debt. On top of this, he provided centres where peasants could weigh and store their cotton, set up law courts in rural areas, enlarged irrigation areas, undertook land reclamation projects and made midwives available in remote villages. Grateful that Kitchener was on their side, the peasants turned their backs on the blandishments of the extreme nationalists.

Kitchener's firm hand in restoring political stability and creating conditions that bolstered the economy put the country in such good financial shape that it permitted him to carry out a wave of other creative and beneficial reforms. He introduced latrines in the cities, preserved ancient Egyptian monuments and financed a water filtration system, in addition to the construction of roads, bridges, railways and hospitals. All in all, his accomplishments in the sphere of domestic reform have rarely, if ever, been matched in any other comparable period in Egypt's history.[4]

The relationship between Britain and Egypt was better at the end of Kitchener's tenure than at any other time since the Occupation in 1882. On 17 June 1914, Kitchener received word from home that in recognition of his services to the Empire an earldom would be conferred upon him, an honour that pleased him immensely. The next day he left to spend his usual summer leave in England. Little did he realize that he would never set foot on Egyptian soil again.

---

4   George H. Cassar, *Kitchener as Proconsul in Egypt, 1911-1914* (London: Palgrave Macmillan, 2016), especially Chapter 5. Kitchener exercised such hold over the people of Egypt and the Middle East that many could not believe that he had perished at sea in June 1916. Mark Sykes, an official known for his brilliant work in the Middle East, related to Hankey an interesting episode on the subject. While on one of his frequent trips to the east, Sykes informed an Arab sheik that Kitchener had died, only to be met with disbelief and the reply that, "Lord Kitchener can never die." See *The Supreme Command*, vol. 2 (London: Allen and Unwin, 1960), p. 509.

1

Supreme War Lord

Kitchener's ship docked at Dover on 23 June and the next day he motored to London and stayed with his good friend Pandeli Ralli at 17 Belgrave Square. Four days later the Archduke Francis Ferdinand, the presumptive heir to the Austro-Hungarian throne, and his wife were assassinated in the Bosnian town of Sarajevo, setting members of the opposing alliances on a collision course. Europe had weathered a number of crisis in the decade before 1914 and on several occasions narrowly avoided warfare but for the latest incident no solution could be found. With Europe inching closer to the precipice, the Foreign Office on 31 July ordered all heads of mission on leave abroad to return to their posts. Kitchener made last minute calls or wrote letters bidding farewell to friends before spending the weekend at Broome Park. From there he intended to begin his journey back to Egypt.[1]

On Monday 3 August, Kitchener left for Dover to take the channel steamer to Calais. While waiting for the boat to leave, a message arrived from H.H. Asquith, the Prime Minister, requesting that he return to London. On reaching 17 Belgrade Square, Kitchener found a note from Asquith, apologizing for interrupting his journey but adding that in view of the deteriorating conditions in Europe, "I was anxious that you should not get beyond the reach of personal consultation and assistance."[2] Kitchener dreaded the thought of remaining in London in an advisory capacity without defined responsibilities. He waited anxiously for twenty-four hours, but when he did not receive the expected telephone call from the Prime Minister, sent him a note. Concealing his irritation, he requested permission to make arrangements to leave for Egypt on Friday. Asquith's secretary replied by telephone on 4 August, saying that he was to remain in London because, if war was declared, the Prime Minister would want to see him alone before a council of war convened the next day. The meeting took place in the evening between 7 and 8 pm at 10 Downing Street. Neither man left notes so we do not know precisely what was said, but Margot Asquith has an entry in her diary based on a conversation with her husband after Kitchener left.[3] Apparently the two men discussed the office of Secretary for

---

1   George H. Cassar, *Kitchener's War: British Strategy from 1914 to 1916* (Washington, DC: Potomac Books, 2004), pp. 19-20; Arthur, *Lord Kitchener,* vol. 3, p. 2.
2   Cited in Magnus, *Kitchener,* p. 277.
3   Michael and Eleanor Brock (eds.), *Margot Asquith's Great War Diary, 1914-1916* (Oxford: Oxford University Press, 2014), p. 14.

War which the Prime Minister was holding on a temporary basis after Jack Seely was forced to resign in March 1914 over the Curragh incident.[4] Asquith seemed surprised that Kitchener, when sounded out, "did not fancy" taking on the duties of the Secretary for War, even though, as he told his wife, "every detail of our war plan had been made."[5] Nothing was settled that evening, however. Asquith had to convince Grey to release Kitchener from his work in Egypt as well as persuade some of his colleagues to accept a soldier in a cabinet post normally held by a civilian. Kitchener had no interest in the position, not the least because he had his heart set on succeeding Sir Charles Hardinge as Viceroy of India at the expiration of his term in 1915.[6] Besides he was aware of his strengths and limitations. He could lead men and execute policy but he was not a team player. Apart from the fact that he disliked politicians with whom he had frequently clashed in the past, he was deficient in the arts of oral expression and no match for them in the swift give and take of cabinet deliberations.

The next day Britain was at war and Asquith reached a fateful decision after discussions with his colleagues. He concluded that a strong man was needed at the War Office to lead the country. He invited Kitchener to his residence and formally asked him to serve in the cabinet as Secretary for War. Initially the offer was not accepted but Asquith overcame Kitchener's reluctance by appealing to his sense of duty, a clever line of argument that was bound to resonate with a soldier who had spent his entire adult life in the service of his country. Asquith admitted at the time that Kitchener was "to do him justice, not at all anxious to come in, but when it was presented to him as a duty he agreed."[7]

The public and the press greeted news of Kitchener's appointment with ecstatic enthusiasm and relief. Kitchener's presence in a leadership capacity dissipated the anxiety that had gripped the nation after the government had declared war on Germany the previous day. To the ordinary man on the street he was a national hero and could do no wrong. His military record was impeccable, his resolve and devotion to duty unquestioned and there was unbridled confidence that in his sure and methodical way he would devise a way to defeat Britain's enemies. Standing like an immovable rock, enhanced by his imposing physical size (6'2") and single-mindedness, he became a symbol of the state's might and guarantor of victory.

Kitchener had no illusions about the sharp and undesirable turn his professional life was about to take. Accustomed to holding all the reins of power in his own hands, he now had to adapt to the concept of collective responsibility. Taciturn and shy by nature, he hated the thought of attending cabinet meetings during a hard day's work at the War Office to explain the reasons for arriving at his conclusions, or to engage in debates with men whose exceptional oratory

---

[4] When Home Rule for Ireland was on the verge of becoming official in 1914, the predominately Protestant population of Ulster swore that they would never submit to it. In March a sizeable group of cavalry officers stationed at Camp Curragh announced that they would accept dismissal rather than obey an order to march against their co-religionists in Ulster. Jack Seely, the Secretary for War, gave a written assurance that the forces of the crown would never be used to crush the opponents of Home Rule. The government kept its promise but an angry Asquith was unforgiving and demanded Seely's resignation. With the outbreak of the war, the government decided to postpone implementation of Home Rule until general peace was restored.

[5] Brock and Brock (eds.), *Margot Asquith's Great War Diary*, p. 14.

[6] Magnus, *Kitchener*, p. 277.

[7] Michael and Eleanor Brock, (eds.), *H.H. Asquith: Letters to Venetia Stanley* (Oxford: Oxford University Press, 1882), p. 157.

concealed their poor military judgement. On the morning of 6 August, while eating breakfast at 17 Belgrave Square, Kitchener remarked to Percy Girouard, his old comrade from the Sudan campaign who was sitting across the table: "May God preserve me from the politicians."[8]

Kitchener had good reason to be wary of joining a cabinet containing some of the most brilliant politicians in British history. H. H. Asquith began his career practicing law before turning to national politics where his rare intellectual gifts and talent as a public speaker, quickly allowed him to make a significant impression in the House. He held several cabinet positions before succeeding Henry Campbell-Bannerman as Prime Minister in 1908 and his record up to 1914 was impressive by any standard. His many social reforms earned him recognition as the father of the welfare state, quite apart from grappling with a series of difficult political issues – such as Irish Home Rule, Parliament Bill, labour unrest and women's suffrage – with calm, courage and magisterial skill. He did not live and breathe politics like some members of his cabinet and could readily cast aside the cares of his office to indulge in social pursuits. The drawn-out and bloody conflict that broke out in 1914, however, would expose his limitations as a war leader. His tendency to act as a mediator among his single-minded ministers, postpone contentious matters and allow peacetime leisurely discussion in the cabinet when quick decisions were necessary, had a detrimental effect on the conduct of the war.

A Welsh nationalist, David Lloyd George became the youngest member of parliament when he won a by-election for Caernarvon Boroughs at the age of twenty-seven in 1890, a seat he would retain for 55 years. A leading figure in the radical wing of the Liberal party, he gained notoriety when he spoke out against Britain's involvement in the Boer War. He was first appointed President of the Board of Trade in 1905 and three years later under Asquith, became Chancellor of the Exchequer. In his new capacity he helped lay the foundations of the welfare state, and because of a sharp increase in government spending, devised the highly controversial People's Budget in 1909 which imposed higher taxes on the wealthy. Although quick-witted, industrious, and charming on the surface, he was also egocentric, unscrupulous and an opportunist with no fixed principles except to eventually succeed Asquith. His nimble mind and verbal dexterity, masked to all but close associates his lack of formal education, culture and general knowledge. One astute political observer wrote that Lloyd George, for all his abilities, didn't have "a clue about geography … didn't know distances … didn't know logistics" and when it came to having an idea he might have one that sounded brilliant, but the practical application was absolutely fatal"[9] The Welshman opposed Britain's entry in the war, but unlike a few similarly minded ministers who resigned after the cabinet had made its decision, clung to his post.

Born into a life of privilege, Winston Churchill gave up a career as a junior officer in the army at the age of 26 to enter the House of Commons as a Unionist (or Conservative) in 1900. He aroused controversy and distrust practically from the start. In 1905 he crossed the floor of the House and joined the ranks of the Liberal party. He possessed a brilliant mind, imagination, exceptional energy and formidable powers of persuasion. As his career advanced rapidly, he created a legion of enemies by his mania for self-advertisement, exaggerated sense of his own ability, dogmatism, and unconcealed conviction that he expected to become prime minister someday. He served as President of the Board of Trade and Home Secretary before he was

---

8   Cited in Cassar, *Kitchener*, p. 177.
9   Robert Rhodes James (ed.), *Memoirs of a Conservative: J. C. C. Davidson's Memoirs and Papers, 1910-1937* (London: Weidenfeld and Nicolson, 1969), pp. 52-53.

appointed First Lord of the Admiralty (1911) where, to his credit, he implemented modern changes in the navy and ensured that it was ready when the war broke out.

Foreign Secretary since 1905, Sir Edward Grey was deeply respected throughout Europe for his integrity and decency. He was an unconventional foreign secretary in that he disliked travelling and preferred to conduct business through foreign ambassadors at home. He did not especially like his job and only a strong sense of duty induced him to remain in office for as long as he did when he would have preferred to live in the country and enjoy fly fishing, hiking and bird watching. Before the war he pursued a cautious, moderate policy which fitted his temperament but he showed little imagination, boldness or ability to command men and events. Consequently his conduct has drawn criticism from scholars, especially the role he played during the July crisis in 1914 – that is the period following the assassination of the Archduke Francis Ferdinand. It has been maintained by more than a few writers that if he had clearly stated Britain would support France and Russia in the event of a war, Germany might have convinced Austria-Hungary to settle differences with Serbia rather than attack it. After the outbreak of war, British foreign policy was less active, constrained as it was by military considerations, plus Grey's failing eyesight and deteriorating health caused by overwork.

For all its talents, the one vital area the Liberal government was deficient in was common sense. It had committed the nation to assist in the war against Germany, the strongest military power on the continent, without bothering to determine whether it had on hand the necessary human and material resources. In the years before 1914 Britain had good reason to be wary of Germany. The Kaiser's government had created a huge army, announced the expansion of a naval program aimed at challenging Britain's domination of the seas, pursued an aggressive foreign policy to expand the nation's empire and in the process, came perilously close to plunging Europe into a general war on several occasions. Germany's behavior should have alerted the Liberal government that it ought to at least make basic preparations in case war should break out. However during the pre-1914 period the staggering cost of social programs and naval construction left little funding to meet the army's needs which, at any rate, was not deemed a high priority. The Liberal politicians seemed to regard readiness for war as being inconsistent with democratic and religious principles and believed that differences between nations could be resolved amicably through diplomatic negotiations.

It is not surprising, therefore, that a government which had neglected to make even elementary preparations for war would have no machinery in place to coordinate the activities of the fighting services and to formulate the nation's strategy with speed and consistency. The decision-making system that developed during the opening months of the Great War was inefficient and cumbersome. A cabinet of 21 members was too large and often ill-informed to provide clear and timely direction on a multitude of diverse issues. Asquith could have created a permanent body of army and naval experts to coordinate policy with a cabinet committee, but he preferred to leave strategy and the conduct of operations in the hands of the two service ministers with himself as coordinator and arbiter. The lack of formal oversight suited Kitchener as it allowed him to advance his own agenda without delay and lengthy discussions.

For Kitchener things went remarkably well in the beginning. His colleagues, in awe of his legendary reputation and bewildered by the first stirrings of war, were thankful to leave the decision-making process in his capable hands. No criticism of his methods or proposals could be heard: "When he gave a decision," Churchill later declared with only slight exaggeration, "it was invariably accepted as final. He was never to my belief overruled … in any military matter, great or small ... Scarcely anyone ever ventured to argue with him in Council. All powerful, imperturbable, reserved, he dominated absolutely our counsels at the time."[10]

Consistent with the habit of an engineer, Kitchener instinctively looked at the broad picture when confronted by a problem and he had the uncanny ability to judge accurately what needed to be done. He appreciated that Germany was totally ready for war, had a large population, great resources and possessed self-confidence to the point of arrogance, all of which meant that it would not abandon the struggle until it had exhausted the last vestige of men and material. His own experience in the Sudan and South Africa, as well as a careful study of the American Civil War, reinforced his conviction that the conflict would be long and that victories would be won by superior numbers.

The cabinet entered the European conflict without expecting to fundamentally depart from the strategic doctrine laid down before 1914. It naively intended to wage war with comparatively little cost to Britain. The idea was to confine the country's part to supplying money and war material to its allies, impose a blockade of Germany and send a token force to France. The main burden of the fighting on land would be left to France and Russia. If France fared badly in the opening battles, the British Expeditionary Force (BEF) would retreat to the coast and be evacuated.[11] Implicit in Britain's policy of limited liability was its willingness to risk an Entente defeat.

At his first cabinet meeting, Kitchener gave notice that the war would be neither brief nor won on the sea. He pointed out that hostilities were likely to continue for at least three years and that Germany's capitulation would come, not after a few land battles but only when its manpower had been exhausted by a slow process of attrition. As Britain's miniature army would fall considerably short of tipping the balance in favor of the Entente, he explained that in order to discharge its obligation, the government must be prepared to place and maintain an army of 1,000,000 men (70 divisions) in the field.

The ministers were stunned by Kitchener's statement. Grey would later recall that Kitchener's prediction of a war lasting three years "seemed to most of us unlikely, if not incredible."[12] To the members of the cabinet, like virtually every high level politician and soldier in the country, the conflict was expected to be over in a matter of a few months, well before the million-man army could be assembled, trained and equipped. That being the case, it seemed to them a frightful waste of effort and treasure. Yet the ministers accepted Kitchener's plan to raise 70 divisions meekly and without discussion.[13] Lord Beaverbrook, hardly an admirer of Kitchener, wrote in his study *Politicians and the War 1914-1916:* "No other Secretary of State would have imagined it [the scope and duration the war], and so no other would have prepared for it; certainly no other man could have induced his colleagues to act on his conclusions or the public to accept them."[14]

10   Cited in Martin Gilbert, *Winston S. Churchill, The Challenge of War 1914-1916*, vol. 3 (Boston: Houghton Mifflin, 1971), p. 313.
11   David French, *British Strategy & War Aims 1914-1916* (London: Allen & Unwin, 1986), p. 20.
12   Viscount Grey of Fallodon, *Twenty-Five Years 1892-1916*, vol. 2 (New York: Frederick A. Stokes Co., 1925), p. 71.
13   Winston S. Churchill, *The World Crisis*, vol. 1 (New York: Charles Scribner's Sons, 1923), p. 253. When Asquith sent a summary of the day's cabinet meeting to George V, as was customary, he made no mention of Kitchener's crucial measure to raise an army of 70 divisions. Asquith to George V, 6 August 1915, CAB 41/35/26.
14   Lord Beaverbrook, *Politicians and the War, 1914-1916* (London: Oldbourne, 1960), p. 173.

By permitting Kitchener to transform Britain into a nation of arms, the cabinet had taken the most far-reaching policy decision of the entire war.

It was one thing for Kitchener to spell out the requirements necessary for the country to sustain its end in a war against a powerful coalition that he expected would be of long duration, quite another to achieve that objective. When Kitchener took stock of the nation's available resources for the conflict, he realized that the challenge ahead was much greater than he had anticipated. He told Lord Rosebury, the former Liberal prime minister, that the cabinet "deserved the Victoria Cross for its courage to declare war" with the nation in such a state of unpreparedness.[15] There was no plan for the rapid expansion of the army, for attending to its needs, or for industrial mobilization. Well might Kitchener complain to his private secretary George Arthur that he had no army and no munitions and, to make matters worse, lacked the means to make either. Since practically everything had to be built from the ground up, it was indeed a godsend that Kitchener was an outstanding improviser, perhaps the greatest in the annals of the British army prior to the nuclear age.

As Britain alone among the European powers had not embraced conscription before 1914, the New Armies, which popularly bore Kitchener's name, were necessarily built through voluntary enlistment.[16] By lending his name in the drive for recruits, Kitchener cast an aura of respectability on a profession regarded formerly by the general public as the last refuge of the riff raff and unemployed. Beginning on the opening days of the war, recruiting posters were placarded all over the country. For many decades it was believed that none was more effective than the call "Your Country Needs You," depicting above the caption Kitchener's imposing face, bristling mustache, outstretched finger and piercing eyes glaring directly at the onlooker. A recent investigation, however, contends that the design by Alfred Leete, did not appear in poster form until the end of September after the signing-up process peaked. Thus it would seem that the popular poster's influence on recruitment has been exaggerated. At any rate young men from all walks of life rushed to join the long queues that formed outside virtually all recruiting centres in the nation. So great was the surge of patriotic enthusiasm that during the first 18 months of the war – before conscription was introduced – nearly 2,500,000 men enlisted, forming hitherto the largest volunteer army in the history of any country.

The peacetime recruiting apparatus had to be thoroughly overhauled as it was not designed to handle the flood of men who came forward. It was vital to find additional officers and NCOs in abundant numbers to train the recruits. No less important the War Office had to arrange suitable accommodation for the men, feed them and supply them with equipment, uniforms and arms. Among Kitchener's greatest hurdle was to acquire munitions beyond the nation's current suppliers who could not begin to meet the demands of Britain's vastly expanding army. Already overburdened, he took on the additional duty of negotiating and placing contracts, of inspecting firms and the quality of production and constantly searching for new sources of supply. The

---

15   Robert Rhodes James, *Rosebery: A Biography of Archibald Philip, fifth Earl of Rosebery* (London: Weidenfeld and Nicolson, 1963), p. 426.
16   For the full story of Kitchener and his creation of the New Armies see Peter Simkins' excellent study, *Kitchener's Army: The Raising of the New Armies 1914-1916* (Manchester: Manchester University Press, 1988).

colossal task of creating the New Armies and their infrastructure in the midst of a great war, to use Churchill's words, "must certainly rank among the wonders of the time."[17]

Long used to professional independence, Kitchener had always circumvented the army's institutional systems and operated a one-man show. It had cut through red tape and eliminated unnecessary delays, upgraded the level of work, and generally functioned well in the past and in the early months of the war. Nevertheless, the increase in the volume of work resulting from the stalemate in the west and the extension of the war, far transcended anything that he had previously faced. Kitchener never shied away from hard work but there were limits to what even he could achieve. At the age of 64 he was still fit and able to work long hours each day with comparatively little sleep, but he combined in his own person the functions of four major departments. Besides administrating the War Office, he took on the responsibility of raising and providing the infrastructure for the New Armies, procuring armaments and munitions for the rapidly expanding army, and assuming the duties of the Imperial General Staff. It was a herculean load that no one man could carry out effectively.

Kitchener could have lightened his immense burdens if he had made greater use of the general staff at the War Office. It is true that most of the talented staff officers had left with the BEF for France and their places were taken by their deputies or retired soldiers – uncharitably called "dug-outs" – recalled to duty. Some of these officers were competent and energetic and could have proven their worth if given an opportunity. A case in point was Major General Charles Callwell who returned in August 1914 to serve as the Director of Military Operations at the War Office. A general staff built around keen and capable men could have supplied Kitchener with vital information he had no time to acquire on his own. Unfortunately Kitchener had a habit of taking into his confidence only subordinates he knew or had personally tested. Consequently the staff officers at the War Office were essentially reduced to clerks.

Kitchener had inherited as the Chief of the Imperial General Staff (CIGS), Sir Charles Douglas, a hard-working but unimaginative officer whom Asquith had appointed a few months earlier. Douglas remained at his post in a nominal capacity with Kitchener directing him to discharge a variety of tasks but never to formulate war plans. Douglas was in poor physical condition when the war broke out and the long hours that he spent carrying out his assignments may have contributed to his early death in October 1914. Thereupon Kitchener bypassed the claims of several prominent soldiers recommended by acquaintances, including Field Marshal Sir William Nicholson, a former CIGS, who was reputed to be headstrong and possess a sharp tongue, and instead selected Lieutenant General James Wolfe-Murray, a pathetic incompetent lacking whatsoever in personal conviction – Churchill nicknamed him "Sheep Murray." Aware of Wolfe-Murray's limitations, Kitchener made his appointment temporary, until supposedly he found someone "with first-hand knowledge of warfare."[18] In truth Kitchener did not exert himself to find a more gifted replacement, preferring to act as his own chief of staff as he had done in the Sudan and South Africa.

Kitchener would pay a huge price for neglecting to appoint a competent and seasoned soldier as CIGS, someone who understood the function of a general staff and could have transformed the inexperienced staff officers at the War Office into an efficient body. It was vital that the

---

17   Churchill, *World Crisis*, vol. 1, p. 254.
18   Creedy testimony, 3 April 1917, Dardanelles Commission Report, CAB 19/33.

Secretary for War should have all possible information on which to base a military decision. By practically effacing the general staff, it meant that he confronted new problems as they surfaced with haphazard improvisation rather than prearranged plans. No less critical was the damage done to his leadership in the cabinet. Without the reasoned arguments of an active general staff to buttress his case in the cabinet where he invariably had difficulty expressing himself, he opened the way for the ideas of amateur strategists to gain an ascendancy over professional judgement.

As Britain had no war plan of its own, arrangements had been made prior to 1914 to align the BEF on the left flank of the French army. The BEF was commanded by Field Marshal Sir John French, a 62-year-old former cavalry officer whose exploits in the South African War, culminating in his famous charge to clear the road to Kimberly, had made him a national hero. However, he was ill-suited for his new role. He was by all accounts a brave man and enjoyed a close rapport with the rank and file, inspiring their affection and respect. On the debit side was his inexperience in staff work and handling large bodies of troops, lack of mental acuity, massive insecurity, and mercurial disposition as he alternated between extremes of exuberance at one moment and of depression the next. Before long it would become apparent that he had neither the intellectual nor psychological qualities to cope with the new conditions of warfare.

The British high command wanted the staging area of its forces to take place at Maubeuge, near the Belgian frontier, to harmonize with French strategic designs. Kitchener was not a good tactician but conversely he was a first-rate strategist. He stood out against such a deployment which he maintained would place the BEF in great peril. In a crucial discussion with army leaders, he predicted that the Germans would make a wide sweep through northern Belgium and warned that the BEF would be overwhelmed if it concentrated at Maubeuge. He recommended Amiens, 70 miles to the rear, where the BEF would be in a better position to react to the German outflanking movement which he anticipated. He emphasized that Germany would not have invaded Belgium at the cost of driving the British into the war unless it intended to exploit its advantage to deliver a rapid knockout blow to France.[19] However Kitchener had been absorbed in the east for decades and could not claim that his conclusions were based on his active involvement in, or careful study of the complex problem of Continental strategy. Moreover he had made no exact calculation of the strength of the German forces or their probable distribution. The debate lasted three hours and with neither side giving ground, the matter was ultimately referred to Asquith who came down on the side of the nation's military leaders.[20]

As it frequently happened, Kitchener's military instinct and logic proved correct. On 23 August the German army, attempting a wide sweep around the allied left flank, ran headlong into the BEF near Mons. Although small, the BEF was highly disciplined, well equipped and organized. British riflemen, trained to fire fifteen aimed shots a minute, exacted a terrible toll on advancing Germans units and at day's end had held the field. Even so with the French in full retreat, the BEF had no option but to follow suit. Kitchener's anxiety over the BEF's retreat from Mons turned to alarm when Sir John French informed him that he proposed to leave the battle line and head southwest behind the Seine.[21] As far as Kitchener was concerned, the flight of the British army to Le Havre was not an option for such a move would split the alliance

19 Magnus, *Kitchener*, pp. 280-81.
20 Cassar, *Kitchener*, pp. 228-31.
21 Cassar, *Kitchener's War*, pp. 88-89.

and, without unity of purpose, defeat was inevitable. Kitchener would never have accepted a humiliating peace with Germany. He had made it clear from the moment he entered the War Office that he did not intend to withdraw the BEF from France until the Germany army had been crushed.[22]

Kitchener's overriding concern in his diplomatic and military dealings with the French, and occasionally Russians, was to avoid taking any action that would divide or strain the allied coalition. It was abundantly clear to him that close cooperation among the Entente partners was critical to an eventual victory. To that end there were instances when in yielding to the French position he had to sacrifice British interests. As frustrated as he must have felt in such circumstances, he understood, if it sometimes eluded his colleagues, that it was the inevitable cost of holding the alliance together. By establishing the course that Britain adopted to maintain good relations with its partners, he ensured that the alliance with France, despite sharp differences at times, would endure until the end of the war.

Late on the evening of 31 August the Prime Minister, at Kitchener's request, summoned a meeting of such ministers as could be assembled at short notice. Kitchener read Sir John's grim telegram after which he explained the political and military consequences that would flow from leaving the French in the lurch. It would have a disastrous effect on the solidarity of the alliance and almost certainly lead to the capitulation of France which, in effect, would mean that Britain would also lose the war.

There were several ministers who had assumed from the outset that if France faced defeat, the BEF could retreat to the coast and be evacuated. They argued that it would be inconsistent with tradition to deny the commander-in-chief freedom of action in the execution of his duties. Kitchener, backed by the Prime Minister, insisted that Britain could not desert France in its greatest hour of need and his argument carried the day.[23] Authorized to go over to France to deal with the emergency, Kitchener immediately hurried over to Dover and took a fast cruiser to Le Havre where he boarded a special train for Paris, arriving shortly before lunch. A meeting was arranged with Sir John French at the British Embassy on 1 September. There followed a stormy interview, the details of which are unknown, but in the end Sir John, presumably under the threat of dismissal, agreed to conform to the plans of General Joseph Joffre, the French commander.[24] This opened the way for the BEF to participate in the Battle of the Marne which halted the German juggernaut and irreparably dislocated the Schlieffen plan. Forced to fight on two fronts and outnumbered numerically, the Germans would be at a clear disadvantage if the war dragged on long enough.

In the wake of the Battle of the Marne the opposing armies were unable to advance and tried to outflank one another to the north, but only succeeded in extending the battle line towards the English channel. With the war likely to last longer than expected, both sides looked to add to their strength by enlisting neutral states. The Germans made the first notable acquisition when they induced the Ottoman Empire to fight on their side at the start of November 1914.

---

22 Kitchener to Gen. Hunter's sister-in-law cited in Archie Hunter, *Kitchener's Sword-Arm: The Life and Campaigns of General Sir Archibald Hunter* (Staplehurst: Spellmount, 1996), p. 220. See also Kitchener's views, as noted by Lieut. Gen. Sir Archibald Murray (then French's chief of staff) before he left for France, in Cassar, *Kitchener*, p. 231.
23 George H. Cassar, *Asquith as War Leader* (London: Hambledon Press, 1994), pp. 46-48.
24 Cassar, *Kitchener's War*, pp. 91-92.

The Germans, with their dominant standing in Constantinople during the prewar period, had concluded a secret treaty with the Ottoman Empire on 2 August 1914. Under its terms, the Ottomans committed themselves to join the Central Powers one day after Germany declared war on Russia. There were sharp divisions within the Turkish cabinet, however, for a number of ministers were not informed of the alliance and it was uncertain whether the government would ultimately act on it. The Germans in the beginning did not exert pressure on the Turks to enter into the fray. They did not anticipate a prolonged struggle, negating the need to escalate the conflict and in the process of contracting additional obligations.

The Entente powers were unaware of the secret alliance and hoped to keep Turkey neutral. Nevertheless relations deteriorated rapidly after Churchill, looking to reinforce the Royal Navy with the prospect of war likely, commandeered two modern battleships on 3 August which the Turkish government had ordered from British shipyards and paid for them by popular subscription. The arbitrary action was roundly condemned in Constantinople and strengthened the pro-German clique within the Ottoman government. While the Turks vacillated, two German warships, the heavily armed battleship *Goeben* and lighter cruiser *Breslau*, eluded British squadrons in the Mediterranean and headed eastwards. On reaching Turkish territorial waters on 10 August they were allowed to sail up the Dardanelles Straits towards Constantinople. To disguise what was clearly a breach of neutrality, the two ships were turned over to the Turkish authorities through a fictitious sale. The two warships, complete with German crews who wore the Turkish fez on their heads to disguise their identity, were renamed and became part of the Ottoman naval task force. A German Admiral (Wilhelm Souchon) was appointed to command the Ottoman navy, a move that increased the chances that the alliance would be implemented in the near future. The British responded by sending a naval squadron to blockade the Dardanelles with orders to intercept and destroy either ship attempting to pass into the Mediterranean.

Even at this late hour, Kitchener retained a slim hope that war with Turkey could be avoided or, failing that, postponed as long as possible. He could not spare any troops from France to defend the vital Suez Canal and sometime must elapse before Empire forces could reach Egypt. Thus every week's delay in keeping Turkey out of the conflict meant a corresponding increase in Britain's military strength. Moreover Kitchener considered it essential that, if the peace was shattered, the conflict must be seen as having been initiated by the unprovoked action of Turkey. Thus he urged that the cabinet avoid taking any measure against Turkey that might be construed as provocative lest it antagonized the Muslim population within the British Empire. In following such a policy, the Asquith administration often overlooked the Ottoman government's flagrant breeches of neutrality.

On 19 August the Greek government offered to place its military and naval resources at the disposal of the Entente. Kitchener met with Churchill on the 31st to consider the Greek proposal. Churchill, still smarting from the escape of the *Goeben* and *Breslau*, was eager to launch a strike against Turkey, setting his sights, in particular, against the Gallipoli Peninsula which reportedly was weakly defended. Such an operation, in his view, would not only lead to the defeat of the Ottomans but induce the neutral Balkan states to join the allies as a united bloc. The two men agreed that staff officers from the Admiralty and the War Office should meet the next day to work out a plan that would allow a Greek army of sufficient strength to seize the Gallipoli Peninsula and open a passage for a British fleet to enter the Sea of Marmara. Churchill wanted the two sides to get together immediately reasoning, as he would tell Douglas on 1 September, that "the matter is urgent as Turkey might make war on us at any moment."²⁵ The idea, as far as Kitchener was concerned, was to make a preliminary investigation, not lay plans to attack Turkey. Still, if Turkey could not be persuaded to remain neutral, there were distinct military advantages to be in a position to strike first. If a successful landing on the Gallipoli Peninsula could be effected, Turkey might capitulate, removing the threat to Egypt and the Suez Canal.

On the evening of 1 September, the meeting to discuss the possibility of a landing on Gallipoli took place at the Admiralty with Major General Callwell and Colonel Milo Talbot, a staff officer, representing the War Office. Callwell made it clear to Admiralty officials that, given "the strength of the Turkish garrison & the large force already mobilized in European Turkey, he did not regard it as a feasible military operation, & that he believed this to be the War Office view."²⁶ Churchill was evidently displeased by the results of the meeting for on 2 September he asked Callwell to return to the Admiralty for further talks. To what extent Churchill's pressing arguments and the weight of his position influenced Callwell to somewhat alter his opinion cannot be determined.²⁷ Churchill makes reference in *The World Crisis* to the second meeting at which he was present but omits the one on the previous day.

The matter was thrashed out again and this time Callwell was less rigid in his appraisal. He laid down his views on paper which he submitted to both Kitchener and Churchill on 3 September. The normal Turkish garrison on the Peninsula was estimated to number some 27,000 men, with further reinforcements nearby, and he stressed that a force of no less than 60,000 would be required to mount an attack on the Peninsula. Even then he warned that the undertaking "is likely to prove an extremely difficult operation of war." He drew attention to the fact that the matter had often been considered by the general staff in the past, as well as examined by the Committee of Imperial Defence in 1906 and the conclusion had always been that such an operation was risky and unlikely to achieve decisive results.²⁸ Callwell remarked in hindsight, that his exposition was "intended to be dissuasive," but Churchill interpreted its contents as suggesting that the operation was deemed viable.²⁹ On 4 September the First Lord telegraphed the chief of the British naval mission at Athens, Rear Admiral Mark Kerr, and instructed him to open discussions with Greek military and naval authorities on the issue "of the right war policy to be pursued if Great Britain and Greece are allies in a war against Turkey."³⁰ It so happened that the Greek offer of intervention was contingent on a simultaneous attack on Turkey by Bulgaria. To make matters worse, the Greek King Constantine, who had pro-German leanings, not the least because the Kaiser was his brother-in-law, extended the stipulation by declaring that Greece would not go to war unless it was first attacked by Turkey.

There was no further discussion in London on the question of operations against the Dardanelles until after the Turks committed a clear act of belligerency. In the meantime it

25 Churchill, *World Crisis*, vol. 1, pp. 531-32.
26 Cited in Gilbert, *Winston S. Churchill*, vol. 3, p. 202.
27 Ibid., pp. 202-3.
28 Callwell's memorandum can be seen in its entirety in Martin Gilbert (ed.), *Companion*, part 1 (London: Heinemann, 1972), pp. 81-83. This work contains documents relating to vol. 3 of the author's official biography of Churchill.
29 Maj. Gen. C.E. Callwell, *Experiences of a Dug-Out 1914-1918* (London: Constable, 1920), p. 90; Churchill, *World Crisis*, vol. 1, p. 532.
30 Gilbert, *Winston S. Churchill*, vol. 3, p. 204.

became important for the Germans to shake the Turks out of their neutral status so as to lessen pressure on its forces on the eastern front. At the end of October, Enver Pasha, the powerful Turkish War Minister, apparently without consulting the rest of the cabinet, consented during the last week in October to allow Souchon to take the Ottoman fleet into the Black Sea and bombard Russian sea ports. The Russians reacted by declaring war against Turkey on 2 November and its western allies, France and Britain, followed suit three days later.

On the last day of October, Churchill, convinced that war with Turkey was unavoidable, sought to give a demonstration of British sea power. Accordingly, on his orders, the British squadron covering the entrance of the Dardanelle, with the assistance of two French ships, opened fire at a range of about seven miles on the outer forts on 3 November.[31] The bombardment lasted only about twenty minutes and enjoyed astonishing success as a lucky shot hit the powder magazine at Sedd-el-Bahr, damaging or destroying the forts and dislocating all the heavy guns. Still the naval action undertaken by the Allies did not serve any political or strategic purpose but did have the effect of putting the Turks on the alert. Prodded by the Germans, the Turks accelerated the pace of their work in improving their defences. While they saw no merit in strengthening the forts (once rebuilt) at the entrance of the Dardanelles, reasoning that they could be demolished by the long-range fire of British guns, they concentrated instead on protecting the inner defences, laying new rows of mines and placing large numbers of howitzers and mobile guns on both sides of the Straits which could be concealed by the mountainous terrain.[32]

The growing stalemate on the western front and the expanding nature of the war, resulted in a change in Britain's structure of supreme command. It became obvious that the existing cabinet system, which lacked professional advice, a systematized contact between the armed services, and overall direction to anticipate events or prepare plans to deal with such emergencies as might arise, was wholly inadequate. Consequently late in November Asquith set up a special cabinet committee, known as the War Council, to assume responsibility for overseeing the conflict as a whole. The new body was initially composed of Asquith, Kitchener, Lloyd George, Churchill, Grey, Admiral Sir John Fisher (First Sea Lord), Wolfe-Murray and Arthur Balfour, a prominent member of the loyal opposition, with Maurice Hankey as secretary. Although not an elected member of the government, Hankey took part in the discussions in the War Council and frequently circulated papers containing his views on a variety of subjects. He began his career as an officer in the Royal Marine Artillery and in 1902 was appointed to the naval intelligence department. He left the marines in 1908 to become assistant secretary to the CID and rose to become its secretary four years later. He was a gifted linguist and could speak five languages – Greek, Spanish, German, Italian and French – possessed a formidable memory, an inordinate capacity for work, and was trusted by those wielding political power for his brilliant mind, discretion and ability to keep secrets. He was one of the few people in the government

---

31 Ibid., p. 218.
32 Brig. Gen. C. F. Aspinall-Oglander, *Military Operations: Gallipoli*, vol. 1 (London: William Heinemann, 1929), pp. 34-35; Edward J. Erickson, *Gallipoli: The Ottoman Campaign* (Barnsley, S. Yorkshire: Pen & Sword, 2015), p. 9.

that Kitchener trusted and confided in. Hankey's influence and reputation would grow as the war progressed.[33]

As it turned out, the War Council was not much of an improvement over the system it replaced. Between 1 December and 10 March four more cabinet ministers became regular members as did Admiral Arthur Wilson, so that the disadvantages in too large a directing authority reoccurred. Before the decisions of the War Council were implemented, they were referred for approval to the full cabinet where another discussion took place, causing unnecessary delays and hampering secrecy. The service experts held what amounted to secondary status for their opinion was not always solicited or accepted. The War Council did not work to an agenda and met only when the Prime Minister deemed it necessary. In short the War Council was not an instrument to supervise the day-to-day fluctuations of the war which remained in the hands of the service ministers in consultation with the prime minister, but rather a supplement to the cabinet for dealing with emergencies or exploring larger questions of policy.[34] No less glaring than the inherent flaws of the War Council was the failure of Asquith to set up a mechanism to coordinate military and naval planning with the result that the two services framed their plans without reference to one another. It should have been foreseen that this omission was bound in the long run to create serious problems.

Asquith called the first meeting of the War Council on 25 November at which the defence of Egypt was discussed, an issue of some concern now that Turkey had actively aligned itself with the Central Powers. Churchill maintained that the best way to preempt an invasion of Egypt was to undertake a combined naval and military operation against the Gallipoli Peninsula. If successful it would mean control of the Dardanelles, enabling Britain to dictate terms to Turkey. He conceded that the operation might be deemed impractical as it would be difficult and require a large force. A less ambitious alternative was to make a feint at Gallipoli and actually land at Haifa, or at another point on the Syrian coast. Kitchener expressed his opinion that it might eventually become necessary to attack Turkey but thought that the moment had not yet arrived. The requisite trained troops were unavailable at home and the army being built in Egypt was neither large enough nor sufficiently prepared to engage in an operation on a vast scale in the Mediterranean.[35]

Kitchener rarely revealed to his colleagues, none of whom he knew intimately, everything that was on his mind. In fact once military means were available he preferred to carry out his own plan which he had discussed on several previous occasions with Lieutenant General Sir John Maxwell, commander of the British troops in Egypt, for a landing at Alexandretta, located opposite Ayas Bay.[36] The area in and around Alexandretta was lightly defended and its occupation would have severed Turkey's main rail communication to the south and severely crippled its war effort in Syria and Egypt. It would have been extremely difficult for the Turks to mount

---

33   The material in the paragraph sketching Hankey's prewar activity and personal qualities was drawn from Stephen Roskill, *Hankey: Man of Secrets*, vol. 1 (London: Collins, 1970).
34   Maurice Hankey, *The Supreme Command 1914-1918*, vol. 1 (London: Allen and Unwin, 1961), pp. 237-39; Great Britain, *First Report of the Dardanelles Commission* (London: HMSO, 1917), pp. 5-6; H.H. Asquith, *Memories and Reflections*, vol. 2 (London: Cassell, 1928), pp. 87-88.
35   Minutes of the War Council, 25 November 1914, CAB 42/1/1; Hankey, *Supreme Command*, vol. 1, pp. 242-43; Aspinall-Oglander, *Gallipoli*, p. 44.
36   Sir George Arthur, *General Sir John Maxwell* (London: John Murray, 1932), p. 153.

Map 2 The Turkish Empire in 1914.

Supreme War Lord 41

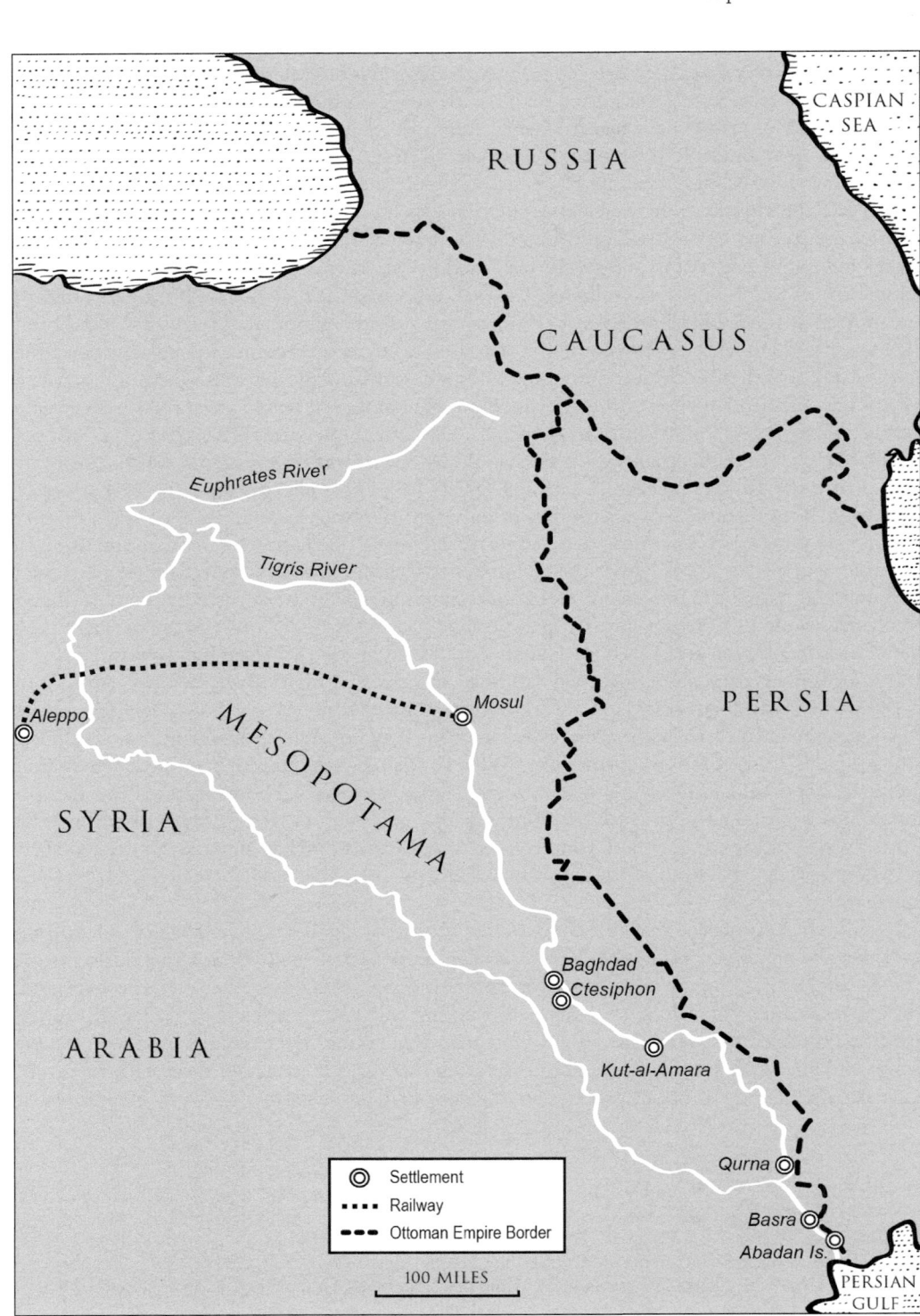

an effective counterattack because the railway through the mountain ranges to the north and south of the port were still unfinished in 1914. To arrive on the scene, a Turkish force moving in either direction would have had to operate from railheads beyond the mountains and across 80 miles of road and hilly track unfit for wheeled traffic. Without mechanized transportation the Ottomans would have been hard pressed to supply their army and it is certain they would have received little help from the local population which was composed mostly of Armenians.[37]

Kitchener turned to Callwell, on whom he would rely increasingly as he became aware of his ability and sound judgement, to carefully explore the possibility of an expedition to Alexandretta comprising of troops drawn from Egypt. Callwell discussed the proposal with the general staff, one of the few times early in the war its opinion was solicited and invited the views of Admiral Sir Henry Jackson who was involved with planning overseas operations. The conclusion of the general staff was that the Alexandretta operation was quite practicable and would not require a large force. The benefits, apart from offering protection to Egypt, would assist the Russians who were experiencing some difficulty in Armenia. All in all the seizure of Alexandretta with the perceived threat to the Dardanelles, which would tie down large enemy forces, was the best way to deal with the Turkish menace. According to Callwell, it was also the opinion of Kitchener.[38]

Callwell's confidence in the feasibility of an expedition to Alexandretta received a further boost by an unusual event which occurred in December 1914. As part of a British squadron in Egyptian waters, the *Doris*, under the command of Captain Frank Larken, had been assigned to watch and harass the movement of Turkish troops along the coast of Syria. Churchill and Kitchener wanted to disrupt any Turkish designs to transfer troops to the Sinai where they could threaten Egypt and the Suez Canal. Late at night on 18 December Larkin landed a party north of Alexandretta, loosened rail lines and cut telegraph cables, before returning to the ship unobserved. An hour later a Turkish train coming from the north was derailed. In the morning a second British landing succeeded in blowing up a bridge and railway station. On the following day Larken sent an ultimatum to the Turkish garrison in Alexandretta demanding the surrender of all engines and military stores. Under the threat of bombardment the Turkish authorities capitulated and agreed to blow up the two locomotives in town providing the British supplied the explosives. Larken agreed and Turkish officials actually supervised their destruction under the beam of the *Doris*' search lights. Once the comic opera ended, the *Doris* sailed away.[39]

Despite the appearance that the Turks were not serious opponents, Kitchener was unwilling to undertake any diversion in the Mediterranean until he was assured that the battle line in France was secure. Thanks to his stewardship the war was going as well as could be expected. He had persuaded the cabinet to prepare for a long war and to discard its policy of limited liability. His objective to build a million-man army was taking shape rapidly and the first divisions would be ready to take the field in the spring of 1915. He extended the means for large-scale armament and munitions production to supply Britain's fast growing army. He impressed

---

37 Sir George MacMunn and Cyril Falls, *Military Operations; Egypt and Palestine*, vol. 1 (London: HMSO, 1928), pp. 20-21; Sir Llewellyn Woodward, *Great Britain and the War of 1914-1918* (London: Methuen, 1967), pp. 95-96; Callwell, *Experiences*, pp. 61-62.
38 Callwell, A written statement submitted to the Dardanelles Commission, CAB 19/28.
39 Julian S. Corbett, *Naval Operations*, vol. 2 (London: Longmans, Green and Co., 1921), pp. 74-76; Callwell, *Experiences*, pp. 62-63.

upon the cabinet the overriding importance of maintaining the alliance especially with France. Thus he did not hesitate to step in when Sir John French intended to beat a retreat to the coast, and not only avoided an Entente defeat, but played an indirect, if vital role, in Joffre's victory at the Marne.

The key to Kitchener's success was the willingness of his colleagues to defer to his judgement. He had been practically faultless in managing the war and had not been compelled to engage in defence of his policies. Unfortunately the period of his quasi-dictatorship would gradually come to an end after the opening months of 1915.

By the end of 1914 the race to the sea was over and the war of movement had given way to siege warfare. The rival armies, facing one another, were dug in along a twisted line that stretched some 400 miles, from the Swiss Alps to the North Sea. Throughout the winter of 1914-1915 the trenches, at first crude and makeshift, were increasingly fortified and protected by barbed wire. What emerged was a different and unprecedented type of warfare. When the armies could not get around one another the generals on both sides tried to break through by frontal assaults. The technological advance in armaments had given the defence a substantial advantage. The attackers, charging out in the open and facing machine guns, breach-loading rifles and quick firing artillery, were usually cut down before they even approached the entanglements protecting the enemy's trenches. Increasing the number of attacks only increased the number of casualties. It was a lesson that the German generals recognized faster than their French and British counterparts and were content to act on the defence.

The British military commander, although technically enjoying an independent command, usually framed his plans to conform with those of his French opposite number General Joffre. Schooled in prewar and outdated tactical concepts, Joffre clung obsessively to the illusion that a breakthrough was attainable after a series of big attacks had worn down the Germans. He lacked vision to carry out a judicious policy or make crucial adjustments in light of the failure of his methods. Sending out battle-worn infantry in broad daylight, with no equipment other than a rifle against a strongly entrenched and well-armed enemy, was not a prescription that was calculated that would lead to victory. On the contrary it should have been evident that his brand of attrition, far from wearing out the enemy, took a greater toll on the attacking forces than on the defenders. It was an illogical strategy to adopt, especially given that France had a significantly smaller population than Germany.

Trench warfare gave rise to many problems that were unprecedented and not easily resolved. Kitchener's difficulties were exacerbated by his increasingly impatient colleagues who were less willing to follow his lead when he could not produce an instant remedy. In fact there was nothing in the study of nineteenth century military doctrine that offered any sure guide on how to deal with trench warfare. In the beginning Kitchener was equally baffled and frustrated by the new conditions of combat. "I don't know what is to be done," he frankly admitted to Grey, "this isn't war."[40] No longer willing to remain on the sidelines, the members of the War Council emerged from Kitchener's shadow to take an active role in trying to find a novel approach to the conflict. Thereafter Kitchener's paramount influenced gradually diminished and the decisions he carried out reflected the general sentiment in the War Council.

---

40 Grey of Fallodon, *Twenty-Five Years*, vol. 2, pp. 71-72.

2

Pulled by the Undertow of the Dardanelles

At the close of 1914 three members of the War Council, each acting independently, submitted proposals calling for a modification of the nation's military policy. All agreed that a deadlock existed on the western front and that the war could not be won unless some new approach was found. Churchill broached the idea of making use of the navy to invade Schleswig-Holstein, pointing out that it would threaten the Kiel Canal and possibly tempt Denmark to join the Entente. If that should follow, control of the Baltic would be opened to the British fleet and under its cover, a Russian army would be able to land within 90 miles of Berlin.[1] An equally impractical plan was advanced by Lloyd George who wanted to transfer the greater part of the British army from France to the Balkans, to attack Austria either from Salonica or the Dalmatian coast, but he made no suggestion as to how such a force could be supplied in view of the mountainous terrain and lack of railways. In advocating a subsidiary operation for a landing on the coast of Syria to sever Turkey's line of communication with Egypt, he was no less derelict in supplying details.[2] Hankey considered that unless armoured mechanical devises were found to force a way through wire entanglements and enemy fire, Germany could be struck most easily through Turkey, the weakest of its allies.[3] Hankey ignored the difficulties of persuading the Balkan states to bury their mutual antagonism long enough to join in a coalition against Turkey.

Although Kitchener never doubted that the war would be decided on the main front, he too was convinced that the German line was currently impregnable. He wanted the Anglo-French armies to refrain from large-scale assaults until the German line had been thinned by diversionary attacks on secondary fronts. The first divisions of the New Armies would be ready to take the field in a few months and he had no wish to concentrate them in France to be frittered away in Joffre's mindless war of attrition. There were several other reasons why Kitchener planned to hold back the New Armies. The first was to maintain a viable force for home defence. The Germans had spread false rumours through their embassies in neutral countries that they intended to launch an attack on the western front to coincide with a military invasion of Britain. The German object of this deception was to cover the transfer of multiple divisions to the eastern front in the fall of 1914 in an attempt to inflict a decisive defeat on the Russians and

---

1   Churchill to Asquith, 29 December 1914, in Gilbert (ed.), *Companion*, part 1, pp. 343-45.
2   David Lloyd George, *War Memoirs* (London: Odhams Press, 1938), vol. 1, pp. 219-226.
3   Hankey, *Supreme Command*, vol. 1, pp. 244-50.

drive them to the negotiating table. Hankey noted that Kitchener had discussed his fears of a German landing on British soil with him on a number of occasions. He wrote: "I had many conversations with Kitchener on the subject and can bear out that he was anxious, not about the immediate present, but about the position if things went seriously wrong in France."[4] There were naval experts, including Fisher, who also believed that a German invasion of Britain was not only possible but imminent. The idea that a German force could somehow evade the Royal Navy and descend on the British coast was unrealistic but it dominated the thinking of Kitchener and others until the opening months of 1915.[5] Secondly Kitchener worried that a prolonged Russian pause might encourage the Germans to launch a massive strike in the west with the object of seizing the channel ports, or worse still, forcing France's surrender. Kitchener wanted the means at hand to deal with a possible emergency on the western front. Finally he thought it important to carry out a limited military diversion that would produce an early victory, both to assist allied diplomatic initiatives and boost the spirit of the nation.

Kitchener was not attracted to the schemes proposed by colleagues, considering them as either too risky or calling for too many men. As we have already seen, he had his sights fixed on a minor landing at Alexandretta in the near future. Only a modest force would be required as the area was only lightly defended by the Turks and intelligence had reported that it was almost certain the invaders would be welcomed and assisted by the local Christian population.

The cabinet at the turn of the year continued to be preoccupied with selecting a theatre outside of France to send the New Armies. While the debates were going on, Kitchener informed Sir John French on 2 January 1915, of the shift of strategic opinion in the War Council:

> The feeling here is gaining ground that although it is essential to defend the line, troops over and above what is necessary for that service could be better employed elsewhere
>
> I suppose we must now recognize that the French Army cannot make a sufficient break through the German lines of defence to cause a complete change of the situation ... If that is so, then the German lines in France may be looked upon as a fortress that cannot be carried by assault, and also cannot be completely invested, with the result that the lines can only be held by an investing force, while operations proceed elsewhere.
>
> The question, *where* anything effective can be accomplished opens a large field and requires a good deal of study.[6]

French was shocked by the note as it had never dawned on him that the British government would ever consider lessening its commitment to offensive operations on the western front. In reply to Kitchener's letter, he was confident that the German line would be unable to withstand frontal assaults if he was provided with sufficient high explosive shells and guns. He urged that no attempt be undertaken elsewhere until it could be proven that the German front was impenetrable. As a related factor, he alleged that it was essential to maintain maximum pressure on the Germans, otherwise they were likely to concentrate more resources on the eastern

---

4   Ibid., p. 216.
5   French, *British Strategy*, p. 64; Brock and Brock (eds.), *Letters to Venetia Stanley*, p. 281; Edward David (ed.), *Inside Asquith's Cabinet: From the Diaries of Charles Hobhouse* (London: John Murray, 1977), pp. 200-1.
6   Kitchener to French, 2 January 1915, Kitchener papers, PRO 30/57/50.

front. He warned that if the Germans defeated the Russians and brought back their forces west, he would not be able to fend off the onslaught without massive reinforcements. Either way he would require every available soldier in Britain. Summing up, French claimed that "there are no theatres, other than those in progress, in which decisive results can be obtained."[7]

French's views were sharply at variance with the mood in the War Council. The battlelines were now drawn for a fight over the future direction of the nation's strategy. The traditional labels "easterners" and "westerners" are somewhat misleading, since both sides recognized the importance of the western front in defeating the Germans. Their differences lay in the way they approached their common objective. Those who favoured an indirect or peripheral strategy were mostly British politicians. They felt it would oblige the Germans to disperse their strength to meet the new threat, opening the way for the Allies to drive them out of France and Belgium. The counterargument, supported by Sir John and his generals, plus the French high command, was that all available soldiers in Britain, save those required to defend imperial interests, should assemble on the western front, either to achieve a breakthrough or to immobilize the greater part of the German army which would permit the Russians to achieve a decisive victory in the east.[8]

About the same time that Kitchener's missive went out to Sir John, he received an unexpected cry for help from Russia. On 30 December 1914 the commander-in-chief of the Russian army, the Grand Duke Nicholas, called in Sir John Hanbury-Williams, head of the British military mission at the Stavka (Russian High Command) and requested a demonstration against Turkey to relieve pressure on his forces on the Caucasus front. A Turkish army of over 100,000 men had invaded the Caucasus in December 1914 and advanced rapidly through difficult country and currently was in the process of attempting a flanking movement. Under the circumstances the Grand Duke explained that he was resisting the urgent plea of his regional commander for reinforcements as he had no wish to weaken the Russian effort against the Germans in the east. Hanbury-Williams was aware that the War Office did not have enough men available for a military expedition but he wondered whether a naval demonstration would be of any use. The Grand Duke, according to Hanbury-Williams, "jumped at it gladly."[9]

Hanbury-Williams had left London in such haste in August 1914 in order to take up his new appointment that the War Office neglected to provide him with a personal cipher which meant that his telegrams or memos went through diplomatic channels and sometimes took several days to reach the War Office. Consequently he immediately contacted Sir George Buchanan, the British Ambassador in Petrograd, who relayed the information to the Foreign Office on New Year's day.[10] Kitchener became aware of Buchanan's telegram the next day.

The plight of the Russians was nowhere as serious as the Grand Duke intimated but initially Kitchener took the appeal for aid at face value. He saw at once that it was essential to keep

---

7   French to Kitchener, 3 January 1915, Kitchener papers, ibid. The letter did not reach the War Office until the next day.
8   David Woodward, *Lloyd George and the Generals* (Newark, DE: University of Delaware Press, 1983), pp. 28-29; Victor Bonham Carter, *Soldier True: The Life and Times of Field Marshal Sir William Robertson* (London: Frederick Muller, 1963), pp. 107-9; Trevor Wilson, *The Myriad Faces of War* (Cambridge: Polity Press, 1986), pp. 104-5.
9   Sir John Hanbury-Williams, *The Emperor Nicholas II: As I Knew Him* (London: Humphreys, 1922), p. 24.
10 Buchanan to Grey, 1 January 1915, in Gilbert (ed.), *Companion*, part 1, pp. 359-60.

the Germans tied down in the east, a design that would be threatened if the Russians suffered a serious reversal against the Turks and were compelled to divert troops to the Caucasus. Nevertheless he could take no action at the moment. There was only one spare regular division at home and he was unwilling to part with it lest the Germans attack in force in the west or make a bid to invade Britain.

Kitchener discussed the Grand Duke's telegram with Churchill on 2 January 1915 during which he inquired if the navy could do anything to relieve Russia's distress as he had no extra troops for a military demonstration. What followed next is not clear. Churchill may have brought up the possibility of limited military assistance to compliment naval action because Kitchener returned to the War Office to consult his advisers. They confirmed that no available forces could be spared for even a limited strike against Turkey as every soldier was required for the western front. Thereupon Kitchener wrote a letter to Churchill on the same day: "I do not see that we can do anything that will very seriously help the Russians in the Caucasus. The Turks are evidently withdrawing most of their troops from Adrianople and using them to reinforce their army against Russia, probably sending them by the Black Sea. We have no troops to land anywhere." Kitchener considered a number of spots where the British could strike and concluded that "the only placed that a demonstration might have some effect in stopping reinforcements going East would be the Dardanelles." He thought it would be especially helpful "if reports could be spread at the same time that Constantinople was threatened." He ended by saying: "We shall not be ready for anything big for some months."[11]

Kitchener wired the Grand Duke on the evening of 2 January, promising to stage a demonstration against the Turks. However, he doubted "that any action we can devise and carry out will be unlikely to affect seriously the numbers of the enemy in the Caucasus or cause their withdrawal."[12] Late on 2 January or early next day, Kitchener received a dispatch from Hanbury-Williams, which amplified the contents in Buchanan's telegram. It must have alleviated a good deal of Kitchener's anxiety as it revealed that the Russians were hardly in dire straits:

> The Turks are pushing the Russians pretty hard in the Caucasus. The Russian commander-in-chief in that region has telegraphed to the Grand Duke asking that he may be reinforced. Though we have a good many troops that properly belong to the Caucasus ... the Grand Duke is determined to stick to his plans and use them against the Germans and do all he can to help the other allies. This being so he wishes Lord Kitchener to be aware of the situation and he also wishes to ask him whether it would be possible to draw off the pressure of Turkish forces by some demonstration on our part against the Turks, either by ship or in such a manner as Lord Kitchener thinks best. In any case the Grand Duke is determined to push on the war against Germany but it would be of great assistance if the Turkish pressure could be somewhat relieved by help from England or France or both.[13]

As it happened, Hanbury-Williams' report reached the War Office just as the fiercely contested battle near Sarikamish in the Caucasus was drawing to an end. By 4 January the Turkish wheeling movement had collapsed, principally because it was carried out in deep snow, in the

---

11 Churchill, *World Crisis*, vol. 2, pp. 86-87.
12 Aspinall-Oglander, *Gallipoli*, vol. 1, pp. 52-53.
13 Hanbury-Williams to Kitchener, 30 December 1914, War Office archives, WO 106/1103.

midst of violent blizzards and in temperature that was 30 degrees below zero. It is estimated that 30,000 Turks froze to death, many thousands surrendered, and only 12,000 returned home.[14] The next day Hanbury-Williams, communicated the Russian victory to Kitchener, stressing that one of the Turkish corps had been practically annihilated and the other badly mauled and in full retreat. Included in the thousands of Turkish prisoners were a corps commander, three generals and 100 officers. "Much rejoicing here in consequence," the note concluded.[15] As the *raison d'être* for a demonstration had disappeared, Kitchener gave the matter no further thought. His attention now passed to overseeing the work of formulating the nation's future war policy.

On 7 January the War Council took up the matter of Sir John's advocacy for an advance along the Belgian coast. A month earlier the Field Marshal had become interested in another one of Churchill's seemingly endless schemes and had contacted the War Office without receiving an encouraging response. Undeterred he broached the idea again at the start of the New Year. The plan called for a combined operation in which the army, with naval support, would advance along the Belgian coast to capture Ostend and Zeebrugge and cut off Germany's access to the North Sea. To carry out the offensive, Sir John explained he would require substantial reinforcements and a large supply of guns and munitions.[16]

The members of the War Council were unimpressed about the proposed operation with only Churchill, as its original author, arguing in its favour but not forcefully. Kitchener was definitely hostile, maintaining unequivocally that he could not supply Sir John with the men and munitions he had requested. In the end the War Council rejected the plan on the ground that the expected heavy losses would outweigh the benefits. There followed a brief discussion on what to expect in the near future from the French and German armies on the western front.[17]

The same subject occupied the early interest of the War Council the next day. Kitchener warned that in his opinion a fresh German offensive was imminent, basing his prediction on the following considerations: German withdrawal of six divisions from the eastern theatre; suspension of its action on that front; calling out the 1916 class of recruits; the interruption of private traffic on its railway system; and the reported movement of the Rhine garrison to the western front. The issue did not gain any traction as the ministers had already determined that the opposing lines were impregnable and virtually everyone favoured finding an alternate theatre to employ the New Armies to strike a decisive blow. Lloyd George was given an opportunity to prove that his Balkan scheme would produce the desired result but his presentation did not arouse any interest. Kitchener read French's memo which he received four days earlier, denying that the western front was impenetrable. Asquith claimed that Sir John had made a very able statement against action outside of France but he was a lone voice in the wilderness. The area that held the most promise, in Kitchener's view, was in the Dardanelles where an attack could be made in cooperation with the fleet. If successful, it would reestablish communications with Russia, settle the Near Eastern question and draw in Greece and perhaps Bulgaria and Romania. He estimated that a force of 150,000 men (according to a prewar Greek military plan)

---

14   There is a good brief description of the battle of Sarikamish in Edward J. Erickson, *Ordered to Die: A History of the Ottoman Army in the First World War* (Westport, CT: Greenwood Press, 2001), pp. 54-60.

15   Hanbury-Williams to Kitchener, 5 January 1915, War Office archives, WO 106/1103.

16   Hankey, *Supreme Command*, vol. 1, pp. 259-60; French to Kitchener, 3 January 1915, Kitchener papers, PRO 30/57/50.

17   Minutes of the War Council, 7 January 1915, CAB 42/1/11.

might be sufficient to capture the Gallipoli Peninsula but he wanted to reserve final judgement until a closer investigation had been conducted. In the interim Kitchener suggested a landing at Alexandretta, as a minor but useful operation, requiring between 30,000 and 50,000 troops, which would have the effect of severing Turkey's link with Syria. He wanted the Admiralty and War Office to study the project further, though he did not deem it practical to take action until after the anticipated German assault in the west had occurred.[18]

On 9 January Kitchener broke the bad news to Sir John that the War Council had rejected his Zeebrugge scheme. He maintained that the abandonment of the project did not prevent French from cooperating, as much as his resources allowed, with any offensive movement Joffre contemplated. He reassured the old soldier that Britain would continue to regard the western front as the decisive theatre and that its forces would fight alongside the French army as long as France was liable to successful invasion and required armed support. On the other hand he warned that if in the next few months it was shown that the western front was firmly deadlocked, with neither side able to break through, it would be desirable to find another theatre where an advance would encounter less obstruction and possibly lead to more productive results.[19]

With the debate heating up as to where Britain might best employ the New Armies (which, in effect, would determine its future strategy), Kitchener found himself caught between the conflicting demands of the War Council and the Anglo-French high command. While he shared his colleagues' conviction that further offensives on the main front would be ineffective and costly, he was equally determined to avoid doing anything that might endanger the survival of the alliance.

An anonymous War Office memorandum written at the time – possibly in reaction to Sir John's note of 4 January – clearly illustrates the dilemma facing Kitchener. The paper underlined the need to maintain the nation's commitment to the western front for to do otherwise would strain relations with France and possibly allow the Germans to reach the channel ports. Its author(s) preferred a passive stance in Flanders, instead of the allied high command's fixation on vigorous offensives, but recognized that the former option posed perhaps insurmountable obstacles. As a compromise, the paper suggested an active defence, that is, local attacks, not so much to gain ground as to inflict damage on the Germans and disrupt their plans.[20] Such a policy appealed to Kitchener, but he held little hope that it would find favour with either the French or hard-pressed Russians.

Kitchener was contemplating his next move when Churchill came forward with a suggestion that seemed to offer him a way out of his predicament. Possessing very lofty ambitions, Churchill felt he needed to engineer a dramatic coup to refurbish his reputation which had been badly damaged by his personal misadventures and the poor showing of the Royal Navy since the start of the war. In fact more than a few newspapers were urging his removal from the Admiralty. In search of a theatre that would produce a cheap victory without the assistance of troops, as none were deemed available, he fastened on the idea of converting a mere demonstration as requested by the Grand Duke, into an all-out attempt to break through the Dardanelles by ships alone.

---

18   Minutes of the War Council, 8 January 1915, CAB 42/1/12.
19   The memorandum is reproduced in its entirety in Arthur, *Lord Kitchener*, vol. 3, pp. 90-94.
20   General Staff, "An Appreciation," nd, but early January 1915, Creedy papers, WO 159/3/2.

The Dardanelles was a long tortuous channel linking the Aegean and the Sea of Marmora. Extending 41 miles in length, from its mouth at Cape Helles to where it reaches the Sea of Marmora, the Dardanelles averages between three and four miles in width and closes to three-quarters of a mile at The Narrows. The currents produced by the tidal action in the Black Sea and Sea of Marmora make the waterway among the most difficult and potentially hazardous in the world. Ships must await the right conditions before entering the Straits. The stretch of water is flanked on the west by the Gallipoli Peninsula and on the east by the coast of Asia. Turkish fortifications, running along both shores, formed three lines of resistance known as "Outer," "Intermediate" and "Inner" defences. A hostile fleet advancing into the Straits would thus be exposed to the enfilading fire from the batteries in Asia and the Gallipoli Peninsula.[21]

Since the days of Nelson a belief persisted that it was counterproductive for ships alone to challenge coastal fortifications. In 1807 Vice Admiral Sir John Duckworth beat the odds and successfully led a squadron through the Dardanelles but eight miles from Constantinople the ships ran into a head wind and stalled. After waiting a week for a favourable wind, Duckworth decided to withdraw. On the return passage he retained all his ships, but enemy batteries along the Straits inflicted 150 casualties among his men.[22] The Duckworth episode showed that ships single-handedly could not force and keep open the Dardanelles. After the Turks multiplied and strengthened the forts on both sides of the waterway in the late 1880s, naval experts considered a purely naval attack not only injudicious but almost certain to fail. As will be seen War Office investigations generally concurred with that assessment during the immediate period before 1914.

In 1906 a dispute with Turkey, which threatened to get out of hand, had led the general staff to investigate the chances of gaining possession of the Straits. The memorandum conceded that, while the successful capture of the Peninsula and the destruction of the forts would pay enormous dividends, it should not be attempted because of the risks involved. The War Office conducted another review of the Dardanelles defences two years later. It claimed that forcing the Dardanelles was feasible if the fleet and invading army arrived on the spot together and unexpectedly. The joint attack would follow with the navy opening fire on the forts while 20,000 troops landed simultaneously at Gaba Tepe with the object of seizing control of Kalid Bahr, opposite The Narrows, which was reportedly undefended. Another study, the last one prior to the outbreak of the war, was undertaken in 1911. This time the general staff echoed the conclusion of the 1906 survey, judging that the element of surprise could not be achieved. That being the case it was too hazardous to recommend that military forces attempt to disembark on the Peninsula.[23] It is interesting to note that none of the surveys had given any consideration to a solo naval assault on the Straits.

Churchill, however, was convinced that advances in technology rendered the old concept of ships versus forts irrelevant. He had been so impressed at the ease with which German heavy howitzers had reduced the powerful fortresses in Belgium in August 1914 that he was led to believe that the antiquated Turkish forts guarding the Dardanelles, with their short-range artillery, would crumble under the salvos of the 12-inch and 15-inch guns on British battleships. It was a misleading analogy. German howitzers on stable positions and firing from moderate

---

21 Aspinall-Oglander, *Gallipoli*, vol. 1, pp. 31-32.
22 Ibid., pp. 25-26.
23 Ibid., pp. 27-29.

range, had a high trajectory and consequently their shells came down vertically on the target. Naval guns with a relatively low trajectory and firing off a moving platform at a range of 8 or 9 miles could not obtain anywhere near the same degree of accuracy. A post-war study of the Dardanelles operation had concluded that even under ideal conditions, the success ratio of naval guns hitting their target, firing from a distance of about 12,000 yards, averaged between 2 and 3 percent.[24]

Before Churchill advanced his plan in the War Council, he made no attempt to consult gunnery experts at the War Office or Admiralty and even failed to solicit the opinion of Rear Admiral Arthur Limpus who had been head of the British naval mission in Turkey until it was withdrawn at the start of the war.[25] A fine officer and currently superintendent of the Malta Dockyard, he would have been familiar with the prewar Turkish defensive arrangements along the Straits and his assessment of the ships' chances to break through was bound to have proven useful.[26] Instead Churchill contacted Vice Admiral Sackville Carden, the commander of the British squadron at the entrance of the Dardanelles, on 3 January 1915 and requested whether in his judgement the forcing of the Dardanelles by ships alone was a practical operation. Carden happened to hold his current position by accident and no one who was familiar with his record had any illusions about the level of his competence. Churchill did not have much use for Carden either, admitting to Fisher that "he has never commanded a cruiser squadron, and I am not aware of anything that he has done which is in any way remarkable."[27] One can only speculate why Churchill would turn to someone he held in low regard for advice. He may have reasoned that he was more likely to receive a reply to his liking than someone well-informed and practical like Limpus. In any case Carden thought that the Dardanelles could not be rushed, but that they might be forced by an extended and methodical operation.[28] Churchill interpreted this guarded appraisal as meaning that the project was feasible.

Churchill claimed in *The World Crisis*, that he read Carden's telegram at the War Council meeting on the afternoon of the 5th when the subject of a possible diversion in the Near East was discussed. It was heard, according to the former First Lord, "with extreme interest." He explained why:

> Its significance lay in the fact that it offered a prospect of influencing the Eastern situation in a decisive manner without opening a new military commitment on a large scale; and further it afforded an effective means of helping the Grand Duke without wasting the Dardanelles possibilities upon nothing more than a demonstration.[29]

From the above declaration, the unsuspecting reader would gain the impression that Churchill, in view of the positive reaction of his colleagues, was encouraged to investigate the matter further. The only problem was that no War Council meeting took place on 5 January. It was

---

24 Christopher M. Bell, *Churchill and the Dardanelles* (Oxford: Oxford University Press, 2017), p. 73.
25 Ibid., pp. 249-50.
26 Arthur J. Marder, *From the Dreadnought to Scapa Flow*, vol. 2 (London: Oxford University Press, 1965), p. 231.
27 Cited in ibid.
28 *First Report of the Dardanelles Commission*, pp. 16-17.
29 Churchill, *World Crisis,* vol. 2, p. 91.

one of many instances in which Churchill's deception was intended to cast a favourable light on whatever activity he was pursuing. Martin Gilbert, Churchill's official biographer, who ought to have known better, carried the charade one step further. Referring to the fictitious gathering of ministers on the 5th, he wrote: "Kitchener pressed his colleagues for action at the Dardanelles. Churchill was able to give some support to Kitchener's appeal by reading out to the War Council the telegram which he had received from Carden an hour before."[30] For the record, the first meeting of the War Council in January was on the 7th and in the ensuing deliberations there was no mention of either the Dardanelles or Carden's telegram.

On 11 January Carden, in response to a request by Churchill, submitted a plan in which he proposed to reduce the forts one by one, beginning at the entrance of the Dardanelles and gradually proceeding to The Narrows where the minefields would be swept, thus opening the way for the fleet to advance into the Sea of Marmara. Fisher and other leading experts in the Admiralty War Staff Group[31] discussed the plan and by all accounts there were no dissenters. It cannot be determined, however, whether Churchill's dominating personality and overwhelming powers of persuasion allowed him to gain the lukewarm support of some and intimidated the others into remaining silent. A senior naval adviser, familiar with Churchill's methods, once complained that it was "no good contradicting or opposing him – it only makes him worse."[32]

The First Lord had one more hurdle to overcome if he hoped to sell his scheme to the War Council: to win over Kitchener who a few days earlier had estimated that 150,000 men would be required to cooperate with the fleet to open the Dardanelles. Lloyd George wrote in hindsight, that whenever Churchill "has a scheme agitating his powerful mind, as everyone who is acquainted with his method knows quite well, he is indefatigable in pressing it upon the acceptance of everyone who matters in the decision."[33] At this time no one carried more weight than Kitchener in the War Council.

Kitchener had read the last two general staff reports but not the one in 1906 as no copy could be found in the War Office safe in 1915 – although a few duplicates did survive and were later located in other departments of the government. Kitchener was at least familiar with the gist of the 1906 memorandum, compiled principally by Callwell who had drawn his attention to it on several occasions. Interestingly enough, the absence of any copies in the War Office of this important investigation can be traced back to the action of Henry Campbell-Bannerman, the previous Prime Minister. In 1906 he had ordered all copies of the document destroyed lest its findings leak out and reach the Turkish authorities. He clearly did not want the British to tip their hand in case they became entangled in a war against Turkey. In such an event, bluffing the Turks into thinking that an attack on the Dardanelles was imminent, would immobilize a major part of their forces on Gallipoli.[34]

30 Gilbert, *Winston S. Churchill*, vol. 3, p. 237.
31 Formed after the outbreak of the war, its purpose was to supervise strategy and the conduct of naval operations. It met every morning under the chairmanship of the First Lord and the other members included the First Sea Lord, the Second Sea Lord (Vice Admiral Frederick Hamilton), the Chief of the Admiralty War Staff (Vice Admiral Henry Oliver), Admiral of the Fleet (Sir Arthur Wilson), and the Naval Secretary (Commodore de Bartolomé).
32 Cited in Bell, *Churchill*, p. 57.
33 Lloyd George, *War Memoirs*, vol. 1, p. 234.
34 Callwell, *Experiences*, p. 88.

In my first two books on Kitchener I introduced and expounded on a theme which I revisited and amplified in the current study, adding to what I had already concluded was compelling evidence that a conference between Churchill and Kitchener had taken place before the War Council made its fateful decision on the 13th.[35] As a start, I maintained that someone as astute as Churchill would not have risked unfurling his highly controversial plan in the War Council without ensuring that Kitchener was on board. Churchill had sent copies of Carden's telegrams over to the War Office but he knew that these alone would not make much of an impression on Kitchener. It was no secret that army leaders continued to cling to the tradition "that any sailor who attacked a fort was a fool." The only way he could overcome the War Office's firmly held belief was in a face-to-face encounter with Kitchener so as to make the case on the viability of a purely naval attack on the Dardanelles and to answer any questions that he might raise. To that end, Churchill arranged a hurried meeting with Kitchener, held presumably at the Admiralty on the 12th or the morning of the 13th before the War Council assembled at noon at 10 Downing Street. In the course of what was likely an animated discussion, Churchill reached an understanding with Kitchener, removing a huge obstacle to the adoption of his naval plan.

Kitchener did not have an opportunity to give his side of the story to the Dardanelles Commission, which was appointed in the summer of 1916, less than two months after his death, but he did tell close aides or members of his inner circle – namely George Arthur (Kitchener's private secretary), Herbert Creedy (Kitchener's departmental secretary), Major General Stanley von Donop (Major General of the Ordnance) and General John Cowans (Quartermaster-General) – of his meeting with Churchill at which time he had agreed to support the purely naval attack on the Straits. Testifying before the Dardanelles Commission, none could remember the exact date of the meeting, although Creedy and Arthur thought it was around the middle of January 1915. All told a similar story of what had taken place, especially the effect the *Queen Elizabeth*, the most powerful battleship afloat, had on their former chief. According to them, Kitchener had strongly opposed the First Lord's idea when it was first broached, fortified by the knowledge that the investigations by the War Office in the decade before 1914 had not even considered unaided naval action and concluded that even a combined operation was unlikely to succeed. Churchill tried to allay Kitchener's misgivings by laying out Carden's methodical plan of attack and insisting that the destructive power of the *Queen Elizabeth* (which he intended to include in the British flotilla) had revised all previous estimates of naval warfare. According to Arthur, the First Lord had painted a graphic picture of the Turkish forts crumbling "like the walls of Jericho," under the blistering fire of the *Queen Elizabeth's* eight 15-inch guns.[36] Cowans gave a similar account to the Dardanelles Commission:

> I have ... a short paper of what Lord Kitchener said to me about the Expedition: he ... gave me to understand that, while impressed by the necessity for action in the Near East to combat Turkish designs, he had doubts about the Dardanelles campaign, but yielded to the

---

35 See Cassar, *Kitchener*, p. 276; and *Kitchener's War*, pp. 125-27.
36 Arthur testimony, 1 December 1916; Creedy testimony; 4 December 1916; von Donop testimony, 4 December 1916; and Cowans testimony, 30 March 1917, all in the Dardanelles Commission Report, CAB 19/33. Arthur also submitted a written statement to the Commission, nd. CAB 19/28.

confident representations of the Admiralty that the "Queen Elizabeth" and naval gunnery generally, had altered the situation, and that the forts would be rapidly demolished."[37]

Callwell independently corroborated the principal charges against Churchill in 1920 in a book about his experience in the Great War:

> The Chief [Kitchener] always claimed to have been led astray by Mr. Churchill concerning the potentialities of the *Queen Elizabeth* ... "They rammed that ship down my throat," said he in effect. "Churchill told me in the first place that she would knock all the Dardanelles batteries into smithereens, firing from goodness knows where.[38]

Although Kitchener appreciated that the guns of the super dreadnoughts could outrange those in the Turkish forts, he had no way of knowing that firing from an unstable platform at a distance of 9 or 10 miles would limit their effectiveness. As he saw it, the planned naval attack was outside the area of his competence and was the responsibility of the Admiralty. Indeed from the moment he entered the War Office, he had never tried to interfere with the war at sea. Since none of the naval experts present ventured to contradict the First Lord, Kitchener assumed they too deemed it feasible. Consequently he did not think it was his place to stand in the way. That was apparent in the evidence given by several of Kitchener's former assistants. Von Donop recalled that he and Kitchener had discussed the naval plan on 17 February 1915: "My impression is that he had been told by the Admiralty that it was a possible thing to do, that he was very doubtful about it, but he was not prepared to give his opinion on a naval matter against the experience at the Admiralty."[39] Creedy gave a similar answer when asked if Kitchener had consulted military experts about the effect of the *Queen Elizabeth's* guns against the Turkish forts: "This is a naval matter," Kitchener told him. "I must take it from the naval experts; and the Admiralty say here is a new and most efficient engine of war."[40] Whatever doubts Kitchener may have entertained were removed by the understanding that if the operation proved too difficult, or too costly, it would be treated as a demonstration and abandoned. Churchill would repeat this reassuring statement each time someone was hesitant or expressed doubts about the naval plan.

The Dardanelles Commission, at one of the numerous sittings with Churchill, asked him about his alleged private talks with Kitchener. Churchill did not want it known that anyone in authority, let alone Kitchener, had reacted disapprovingly to his naval scheme when it was initially proposed. He therefore denied that such a meeting had ever taken place before, on, or after the 13th. Let us test the validity of Churchill's statement. Kitchener always maintained that he initially harbored misgivings about the feasibility of the naval operation but was won over by Churchill's persuasive explanation about the vast potentialities of the *Queen Elizabeth*. Was it possible that the exchange between the two men actually occurred in the War Council on the 13th? The answer is definitely not. In the first place the minutes do not reveal Kitchener expressing any doubts when the idea of a purely naval attack was advanced. In fact Kitchener

---

37 Cowans testimony, 30 March 1917, Dardanelles Commission Report, CAB 19/33.
38 Callwell, *Experiences*, p. 66: Callwell made the same statement when questioned by the Dardanelles Commission, 12 October 1916, CAB 19/33.
39 Von Donop testimony, 4 December 1916, Dardanelles Commission Report, CAB 19/33.
40 Creedy testimony, 4 January 1917, ibid.

who normally dominated the proceedings of the War Council said little. Secondly Churchill did not expound on the merits of the *Queen Elizabeth* to prove that it rendered a task, hitherto impossible, comparatively easy. The *Queen Elizabeth* was mentioned only in passing, as available to conduct its gun trials against the Dardanelles forts instead of a floating target. Finally Churchill would have had no purpose in seeking Kitchener's endorsement after the 13th when he had already given it at the meeting that day. Thus when everything is considered, it is logical to conclude that talks between Churchill and Kitchener must have taken place before the War Council met on the 13th.

Churchill is on even less firm ground when he insisted that it was impossible for him to have met Kitchener before the War Council meeting on 13th because the decision to use the *Queen Elizabeth* had not yet been made. A commissioner reminded him that it "was on the 12th that you sent a wire to Adm. Carden saying you should consider the effect of utilizing the 15-inch guns of the *Queen Elizabeth.*" To which Churchill replied somewhat sheepishly, "I had forgotten about that." Churchill's recollection of events was again wrong when he stated, "I cannot identify any conference of this character nor any protest of this character being made by Lord Kitchener, either when we were alone together, or in the presence of any person at any time. My memory is very strong on this point."[41] Churchill seemed to have conveniently forgotten what happened on 14 May 1915, a day after the Admiralty had decided to recall the *Queen Elizabeth* from the Dardanelles (for reasons which will be discussed in a later chapter). Kitchener, who was upset, read a statement in the War Council at the start of the session. It should be emphasized that Churchill, who was present and in the past had been unafraid to stand up to Kitchener whenever his interests were at stake, *did not challenge any part of it [my italics]*. Kitchener essentially repeated what he had told Arthur and the others in January and February 1915:

> When the Admiralty proposed to force the passage of the Dardanelles by means of the fleet alone, I doubted whether the attempt would succeed, but was led to believe it possible by the First Lord's statements of the power of the *Queen Elizabeth*, and the Admiralty Staff Paper [possibly based on Carden's plan] showing how the operations were to be conducted. The First Sea Lord and Admiral A. Wilson raised no objections at this Council or on the Staff Paper issued by the Admiralty, and apparently agreed in the feasibility of carrying out the projects of the Admiral on the spot. I considered that though there was undoubtedly risk, the political advantages to be gained by forcing the Dardanelles were commensurate with that risk ... I regret I was led to agree in the enterprise by the statements made, particularly as to the power of the *Queen Elizabeth*, of which I had no means of judging.[42]

There is no reason to doubt Kitchener's version of the events. He had discussed it with subordinates before the naval attack on the forts – when he was only peripherally involved in the operation. He repeated it in the presence of Churchill on 14 May in the War Council. Another point to remember was Kitchener's passivity in the War Council on 13 January after Churchill introduced his scheme.

---

41 Churchill testimony, 1 December 1916, ibid.
42 Minutes of the War Council, 14 May 1915, CAB 42/2/19.

Strangely enough, the likelihood of an informal meeting between Churchill and Kitchener on the 12th or early on the 13th after I had alluded to it in earlier works, did not draw any reaction from commentators of the campaign until recently. An Australian writer, Tom Curran, after consulting a wide range of archival sources and private collections came to the same conclusion as I did.[43] By contrast Graham Clews, another Australian, disputed that such a conference had taken place. Before he laid down his case, it is important to remember that no meeting of the War Council occurred on 4 May as he alleges. Presumably he means 14 May as I indicated above. Clews' argument is as follows: "First Kitchener's comments on May 4 might easily have referred to the January 13 War Council meeting itself. The *Queen Elizabeth* was spoken of in that meeting and, as per Kitchener's comments on May 4, both Fisher and Wilson were present and neither spoke out against the plan" To strengthen his case, Clews' maintains that Creedy and Arthur's recollection that the Kitchener-Churchill talks were held on 14 or 15 January approximates the date of the 13th.[44] His assertion that my claim referred to the meeting on the 13th, and not earlier, is contradicted by the documentary evidence. To reiterate there is nothing to suggest in the minutes on the 13th that Kitchener had initially expressed any doubts about the naval plan or that Churchill eventually gained his support by convincing him of the destructive capability of the *Queen Elizabeth*. Interested readers can judge for themselves the details of what occurred at the War Council that day as a published copy of the minutes is available in Gilbert (ed.), *Companion*, vol. 1 (pp. 407-11).

Let us turn next to examine how Churchill gained his colleagues' support for a naval assault to force the Dardanelles on 13 January. The timing for its introduction was brilliant, just as the War Council was about to adjourn. The session had lasted all afternoon and early evening. The air was heavy with smoke and the members were tired of the long, rambling discussions which seemed unable to concentrate on any subject. Hankey recalled the moment that Churchill introduced his naval plan to attack the Dardanelles: "The idea caught on at once. The whole atmosphere changed. Fatigue was forgotten. The War Council turned eagerly from the dreary vista of a 'slogging match' on the Western Front to brighter prospects, as they seemed in the Mediterranean."[45] Churchill started by offering Carden's telegrams of 5 and 11 January to corroborate his assertion that a purely naval attack was feasible and he followed up by building his case clearly and skillfully. The central feature of his presentation was that the powerful guns of the British ships, lying outside the range of old shore batteries, would systematically reduce all the Turkish forts within a few weeks. Once that objective was accomplished, the minefields would be cleared and the fleet would sail into the Sea of Marmara.

Churchill did not elaborate on what would happen after the battered remnant of the fleet entered the Sea of Marmara. He was optimistic that it would overpower the Ottoman navy after which it would threaten Constantinople where ultimately a popular revolution would sweep away the highly unpopular Young Turk regime and bring to power a pro-Entente government eager to reach a peace settlement. All understood that the naval victory, moreover, would

---

43 Tom Curran, *The Grand Deception: Churchill and the Dardanelles* (Newport, NSW: Big Sky Publishing, 2015), pp. 58-59.
44 Graham T. Clews, *Churchill's Dilemma: The Real Story Behind the Origins of the 1915 Dardanelles Campaign* (Santa Barbara, CA: Praeger, 2010), p. 104.
45 Hankey, *Supreme Command*, vol. 1, pp. 265-66.

have electrifying effects: the danger to Egypt would be removed; assistance could reach Russia through the Dardanelles; and the Balkan states would be weaned from their neutrality.

Whatever evidence is available would seem to suggest that, although Kitchener did not express it openly, he retained an element of doubt about the fleet's chances to produce a victory. His lingering uncertainty dissipated after the Turks displayed one form of weakness after another and he became firmly convinced in the success of the projected naval operation. At the War Council meeting on the 13th, Kitchener commented briefly that the operation was worth trying with the proviso that if the bombardment proved ineffective the attack would be called off. Normally Kitchener would not have imposed a precondition on an exclusively naval venture unless an agreement had been reached earlier.

Given that Churchill's scheme was highly popular, it might seem strange to any current scholar or interested reader looking over the minutes on the 13th, why it aroused so little discussion in the War Council. There is a simple explanation, however. Whenever there was virtual unanimity in support of an issue, it was not unusual for Hankey to record the opinion of only a few members, usually the leading lights. Besides Kitchener, only two others were acknowledged in the minutes. Lloyd George admitted that he liked the plan, while Grey, although not opposed, would have preferred a landing at Cattaro as a means to induce Italy to join the Entente. Grey did not pursue the issue after Churchill reminded him that the French were already in the region and it would be awkward for the British fleet to take any action there. Thus without a dissenting voice, the War Council gave its provisional approval that the "Admiralty should prepare for a naval expedition in February to bombard and take the Gallipoli Peninsula, with Constantinople as its objective."[46] The conclusion is absurdly worded. Even if the Turks were not expected to put up much of a struggle, how could the fleet alone seize control of the Gallipoli Peninsula and occupy a city of a million inhabitants? It is strange that no one inquired why a large body of troops, deemed indispensable for the success of an operation against the Dardanelles a few days earlier, was no longer necessary or what had caused Kitchener to change his mind.

Churchill had been told a number of times that surplus troops would not be available for subsidiary operations before the spring of 1915. But patience was not one of his endearing qualities. He suggested to Kitchener on 18 January that a landing should be made at Alexandretta to coincide with the naval attack in the Dardanelles. He explained that "if we are checked in the Dardanelles, we can represent that operation as a mere demonstration to cover the seizure of Alexandretta." He added, "I believe this aspect is important from an oriental point of view." Churchill expected the bombardment to begin around 15 February and he inquired whether the War Office had fixed a date when the landing against Alexandretta could take place.[47] Kitchener replied that currently he did not have the necessary men to carry out the operation. The Anzac troops had not completed their training and, moreover, they might be required to help fend off a likely Turkish assault on the Suez Canal.[48] That being the case, an expedition to seize Alexandretta could not take place concurrently with the naval attack to force the Dardanelles. The British would have to think of an alternative landing to save face in case the ships failed to achieve the expected results and were recalled.

46   Minutes of the War Council, 13 January 1915, CAB 42/1/16.
47   Churchill to Kitchener, 20 January 1915, Kitchener papers, PRO 30/57/72.
48   Aspinall-Oglander, *Gallipoli*, vol. 1, p. 60.

The decision authorizing the navy to prepare for an attack on the Dardanelles defences had not resolved the issue of finding a suitable theatre to deploy the New Armies. The War Council continued to explore a range of possibilities. Fisher was interested in an offensive in the Baltic as well as an attack on the Belgian coast in cooperation with the army. Churchill continued to agitate for the Zeebrugge scheme in addition to calling for a landing at Alexandretta. In discussing the various operations the members dwelled on the perceived benefits, often unrealistic, without sufficiently reflecting on where the troops were to come from, the risks and costs involved, or whether practical. While Asquith considered sending troops to France a criminal waste, he was equally concerned about splitting Britain's limited resources in a number of incoherent subsidiary operations. He was thankful that he could rely on the one man capable of restraining the War Council from steering in different directions. He told his confidante Venetia Stanley, a very attractive young lady with whom he was deeply infatuated, the following:

> There are two fatal things in war – one is to push blindly against a stone wall, the other is to scatter and divide your forces in a number of separate & disconnected operations. We are in great danger of committing both blunders: to neither of which it seems to me is Winston properly alive. Happily K. has good judgement in these matters – never impulsive, sometimes inclined to be over cautious, but with a wide general outlook wh. is of the highest value.[49]

Interest focused on Lloyd George's Balkan option after ominous reports reached London of an imminent Austro-German invasion of Serbia. At a cabinet meeting on 20 January, Asquith agreed with Lloyd George that the fall of Serbia would be a serious military setback as well as inhibit Allied efforts to win over the Balkan states. Sentiment among the ministers favoured helping Serbia. Kitchener took no position, merely saying that he would "examine the situation carefully from a military point of view."[50]

Kitchener might have shown more enthusiasm if he could have been as certain as his colleagues that the Balkan states would rally behind the Entente as soon as British troops assembled in the region. He did not understand the complex nature of Balkan politics but he knew that all the states mistrusted or hated one another. He had to take into account the possibility that even with the presence of an Allied contingent in the region they might refrain from entering the war. Yet he understood that failure to succor Serbia would make it impossible to win over the Balkan states. However, to undertake an eastern expedition would entail major problems, not the least of which was to collect a military force, in his opinion, of at least a corps. Since these would have to be drawn from units destined for, or already in France, he needed to discuss the matter with Alexandre Millerand, the French Minister of War, who was expected in London the next day.[51]

Fluent in French, Kitchener was able to converse with Millerand in his native tongue when he met him on 22 January. He found him congenial, well-spoken and sensible but there were obviously differences between the two men. Millerand, who was a mouthpiece for General Joffre, was chiefly concerned for the security of France and he wanted to be able to count on

---

49 Brock and Brock (eds.), *Letters to Venetia Stanley*, p. 389.
50 Asquith to King George V, 21 January 1915, CAB 41/36/2.
51 Cassar, *Asquith*, p. 64.

maximum British support. Kitchener considered that British contribution to the western front was far greater than had been promised and that the British surely deserved the right to exercise strategic independence elsewhere.

Millerand's specific object was to persuade Kitchener to augment the size of the British army in France so that it could extend its defensive front, freeing French troops for Joffre's projected offensive. He knew perfectly well that any diversion of troops for operations in a secondary theatre would reduce Britain's commitment to France. When sounded out by Kitchener, he answered that the idea of a Balkan expedition should be studied but that no action be taken until after Joffre's offensive had been carried out. Kitchener replied that there was danger in undue delay and that, if the Allies did not move in time, Serbia would be overwhelmed and the chances of uniting the Balkan states would be lost. Millerand was adamant that the chief priority of both France and Britain ought to be to concentrate all available forces on the main front to ensure its inviolability. Kitchener had no wish to provoke a dispute over an issue about which he was somewhat ambivalent. He yielded ground and promised that he "would not press the Serbian scheme just now."[52] Kitchener's arrangement with Millerand placed him somewhat at odds with his colleagues.

The matter was raised again at the War Council which met twice on the 28th. The first session was dominated by a discussion of the Dardanelles. Churchill was in a cheerful mood when given the floor. Two days earlier he had removed a major obstacle to his pet project by working out an agreement with Victor Augagneur, the French Minister of Marine. Under a convention signed on 6 August 1914, the British, in order to concentrate their ships in Home Waters, had left the French to assume general direction of naval operations in the Mediterranean. Now Churchill wanted to alter the accord to permit the British to carry out their assault in the Dardanelles. An avowed colonialist, Augagneur had been suspicious of British designs when initially contacted, thinking that their proposed expedition was in fact a cover to establish themselves in Asia Minor and threaten French cultural and economic primacy in that region. At a meeting held at the Admiralty on 26 January, Augagneur (who had received the cabinet's permission to work out an arrangement) gave up the right to control the operation and consented to French participation in a subsidiary role. In return Churchill promised to abandon the idea of a landing at Alexandretta. Augagneur was not nearly as sanguine as Churchill about the chances of victory but he had been assured that, if the Anglo-French fleet should encounter unforeseen difficulties, it would call off the action.[53]

Churchill opened with preliminary remarks in the War Council before asking whether his colleagues attached importance to the operation which involved some risks. There were optimistic forecasts about the consequences of a naval victory. Leading the discussion, Kitchener stated that the naval initiative was of vital importance and that its success would be equivalent to a successful campaign fought by the New Armies. One merit of the scheme, he again emphasized, was that if the attack proved too costly it could be broken off. Balfour found it difficult to

---

52 Brock and Brock (eds.) *Letters to Venetia Stanley*, p. 391; Oliver Viscount Esher (ed.), *Journals and Letters of Reginald Viscount Esher*, vol. 3, pp. 208-10; David Dutton, *The Politics of Diplomacy: Britain and France in the Balkans in the First World War* (London: I.B. Tauris, 1998), pp. 25-26; Marjorie M. Farrar, *Principled Pragmatist: The Political Career of Alexandre Millerand* (Oxford: Berg, 1991), p. 179.
53 George H. Cassar, *Reluctant Partner: The Complete Story of the French Participation in the Dardanelles Campaign of 1915* (London: Helion Press, 2019), ch. 3.

imagine a more useful operation. Grey was attracted to the idea that it would settle the attitude of Bulgaria and the other Balkan states.[54] All the time that the speakers were indulging in rosy predictions, Fisher sat brooding in silence.

Since the meeting of 13 January, Fisher had developed serious misgivings about the wisdom of attempting to force the Dardanelles by independent naval action. The eccentric First Sea Lord was not subtle about his change of heart which became known to most, if not all, the members of the War Council. During the early deliberations (on the 28th), Fisher rose abruptly from the table and headed towards the door, determined to write out his resignation in the next room. Kitchener had learned through Colonel Oswald FitzGerald, his military secretary, of Fisher's growing hostility to the purely naval operation. Kitchener suspected Fisher was not planning on returning to the meeting and that he might be so dejected as to step down from his post. Consequently Kitchener cut him off, drew him into one of the window recesses and asked him where he was going. Fisher replied that he was leaving the meeting and that he proposed to resign from his post. Kitchener pointed out that he was the only dissident in the room and that it was his duty to abide by the War Council's decision. Fisher admitted in his memoirs that Kitchener's earnest and emotional appeal had an effect on him. He said to himself, "We can withdraw the ships at any moment, so long as the Military don't land" and so he reluctantly returned to his seat.[55] Kitchener had been told that Fisher's objections were based, not on technical grounds, but rather on fears that the naval attack would interfere with his own scheme for a landing in the Baltic as well as weaken the Royal Navy which was the key to the nation's security – a point Churchill had no difficulty in refuting earlier when the issue arose since most of the ships he proposed to use in the Dardanelles were of old vintage and about to be withdrawn from service. What Kitchener and the others did not know was that expert opinion at the Admiralty, for the most part, had also inclined more and more to the belief that no real success could be achieved at the Dardanelles without the aid of troops.

Churchill was under the impression that he had already resolved his differences with Fisher but he was no longer certain after taking notice of the animated discussion between the old Admiral and Kitchener. Anxious to find out what had passed between them, he called Fisher to his room after lunch and learned of his continuing discontent. A long and turbulent conversation followed, at the end of which Fisher, under heavy pressure, withdrew his objections to the naval attack in the Dardanelles.[56]

At 4 pm a subcommittee of the War Council, set up on 7 January to find a new theatre for the New Armies in case the stalemate in the west persisted, assembled at the War Office under the chairmanship of Kitchener. In attendance were the regular members, Lloyd George, Balfour and Churchill, with Hankey, acting as secretary, and two representatives of the War Office, Callwell and Wolfe-Murray. Interest focused on Serbia which was threatened by an Austro-German invasion. Lloyd George again stressed the need to commit troops to rescue Serbia which he envisaged would also sway the other Balkan states to join the war on the side of the Entente. Kitchener, according to Callwell, "was very guarded."[57] He agreed that helping the Serbs was of paramount British interest but he was not sure that the right moment had arrived.

---

54 Minutes of the War Council meeting at 11.30 am on 28 January 1915, CAB 42/1/26.
55 Lord Fisher, *Memories and Records*, vol. 1 (New York: George Doran, 1920), p. 71.
56 Churchill, *World Crisis*, vol. 2, pp. 163-64.
57 Cassar, *Kitchener's War*, p. 132.

The problem was that he had no spare troops unless he was prepared to employ forces earmarked for France, which he considered was not an astute option. The only other place where troops ordinarily could have been released was from Egypt. But that morning Kitchener had received reports that a Turkish army was making its way towards the Suez Canal and so removing troops allotted to the garrison of Egypt was also out of the question.[58] There was always the danger that Serbia might be overcome in the event of undue delay but Kitchener did not believe that it was essential to act immediately. An Austro-German invasion of Serbia could not occur for some time owing to the accumulation of snow in the northern passes.[59]

Discussion on the subject continued when the War Council reassembled at 6.30 in the evening. Kitchener held firm to the view expressed earlier, that sending troops to the Balkans, however important, must wait until it was feasible. He thought that eventually it might be possible to send an army of half a million men to Serbia but as of now he was sending all available troops to France. Balfour suggested that a nominal force, such as a brigade, be despatched to Salonica – the most convenient port in Greece from which to assist Serbia – at once as a sign of Britain's earnest intention to send more men when available. Grey was convinced that the appearance of 5,000 British troops might win over Bulgaria and Greece. Kitchener was less certain. He feared that a brigade, unless followed soon by much larger forces, would become an object of ridicule.

As the meeting wore on, Kitchener felt that a decision regarding a Balkan expedition ought to be postponed, pending consultation with the French. While on a visit to London, Millerand had not welcomed the idea of assisting Serbia and instead pleaded that all available British divisions be sent to France. Moreover, it was certain that Joffre would react badly if the divisions committed to the western front were diverted elsewhere. As a system to work out differences between the two allies had yet to be set up, it was decided that Sir John French ought to be approached before the matter was discussed with Joffre.

As the Zeebrugge scheme had been abandoned, Kitchener asked Churchill to try to persuade his old friend Sir John French to forego three of the four divisions he had been promised. Kitchener was still concerned about the possibility of a German assault in the west and he wanted to keep a reserve in readiness, either to proceed to France if necessary or to deploy in the Balkans. Kitchener wanted Churchill to explain to Sir John the importance of a Balkan expedition and to consult with him on the best way of inducing the French to adopt a similar view.[60]

Before the meeting ended, the War Council returned to the question of the Dardanelles. Churchill, with Fisher at his side, announced enthusiastically that the Admiralty was ready to carry out the task with which it had been charged on 13 January. Vice Admiral Henry Oliver (chief of the naval war staff), followed the First Lord and pointed out that the ships were already on the way and that the first shots would be fired in about a fortnight. He gave a summary of how the operation would proceed after which the War Council gave the First Lord formal approval to go ahead with the naval attack. After listening to Churchill's optimistic scenario, the War Council assumed that the navy's work would end once the ships broke into the Sea of Marmara. No one ventured to ask an obvious question, namely what would happen if the ships

---

58 Hankey, *Supreme Command*, vol. 1, p. 273.
59 Minutes of the subcommittee of the War Council meeting at 4 pm on 28 January 1915, CAB 42/1/27.
60 Minutes of the War Council meeting at 6.30 pm on 28 January 1915, CAB 42/1/33.

appeared before Constantinople and the Turks did not surrender? In such circumstances, the use of force to drive the Turks to submit was out of the question. The indiscriminate bombing of harmless civilians, many of whom were Christians and friendly to the Entente, was not an option that the British government would have entertained. Thus to satisfy perceived political and strategic benefits, the fleet was to attempt to force the Straits, a feat so daunting that during the prewar period experts at both the War Office and Admiralty had concluded was futile without military cooperation. Any potential opposition in the War Council was stilled by the assurance that the ships would be withdrawn in the event of unsatisfactory progress.

3

The Changing Character of the Naval Operation

With the Admiralty left to finalize its plans for the naval attack in the Dardanelles, the War Council shifted its interest towards the Balkan scheme. As requested, Churchill crossed over to France on 29 January to hold talks with Sir John French and on his return two days later submitted a report to Kitchener. Not surprisingly, Sir John was unsympathetic to the idea of a Balkan operation and urged that all four divisions be sent to France. But the British commander, confronted by Churchill's skilful counterarguments, eventually conceded that if no emergency arose, he would place two of the four divisions at the disposal of the government from the middle of March onwards for service elsewhere.[1]

The prospect that two divisions might be available in six weeks' time was not exactly the response the War Council had hoped. Daily reports from the British ambassador in Athens warned that Bulgaria might abandon its neutrality and join Austria in an attack against Serbia. Lloyd George, the most fervent exponent of the Balkan enterprise, found a pretext to hurry over to Paris to seek French cooperation. Once on the scene he discovered that Millerand had not informed the French cabinet of British interest in extending the war to the Balkans. He not only corrected the omission but took it upon himself to lobby the French President Raymond Poincaré as well as several key cabinet ministers and found that they concurred with him on taking immediate action in support of Serbia.[2] After the measure won approval in the French cabinet, Théophile Delcassé, the French Foreign Minister, paid a visit to London on 6 February. He told Kitchener that, if the British decided to send a division to Salonica, his government would do the same.[3] Kitchener favoured the suggestion. The need to help Serbia appeared more urgent than ever. On the previous day the Foreign Office reported that Bulgaria had obtained a loan from Germany and that its adhesion to the Central Powers was imminent. Kitchener thought that the presence of an inter-Allied force might tempt Greece to come to the rescue of Serbia. The Allied divisions could be deployed to protect Greece's flank against any possible Bulgarian attack. He maintained that a Russian contingent should be included in any expedition to the Balkans as he was under the misimpression that the Bulgarians would never fire upon their fellow Slavs. When contacted, the Grand Duke replied that, in view of his own

---

1 Churchill, *World Crisis*, vol. 2, pp. 176-77.
2 Lloyd George, *War Memoirs*, vol. 1, pp. 242-43.
3 Cassar, *Reluctant Partner*, p. 60.

requirements, he could only offer 1000 Cossacks – more trouble than they were worth since they would have to be transported to the Balkans via Archangel.[4]

The pressure on Kitchener to find surplus troops had been somewhat eased by the removal of the immediate threat to Egypt. During the opening days in February 1915 a Turkish force of about 25,000 men reached the eastern bank of the Suez Canal. The Turks had travelled at night, hoping that their imminent assault would be undetected until they had practically arrived on the scene. Maxwell, however, was regularly informed of their movements by aerial reconnaissance and awaited them with confidence. He later explained to Kitchener that he did not think "it was safe to go out and meet them, for it was quite possible they were laying a trap for us, and I felt that anything in the nature of a reverse, or even a check, would have fatal results in Egypt, for there is no doubt that the feeling here is pro-Turk and anti-English.[5]

On 2 February the Turks began bridging operations at night and in the places where they crossed over to the other side they were either killed or wounded and the survivors later rounded up.[6] The number of Turks killed, wounded and missing during the attack and in the ensuing retreat was reported to be slightly below 1300.[7] Maxwell's reports to Kitchener implied that the Turkish soldiers were dismal fighters. He gave further details when the fighting was over, remarking happily that the general public's empathy for the Turks did not extend to the Muslims in the British army, "both Indian and Egyptian," who "showed no disinclination to kill their co-religionists when they had the chance."[8]

Maxwell's appraisal of the substandard quality of the invading force, coming on the heels of the relative ease with which the Indian forces had captured Basra and Qurna in Mesopotamia (as will be explained in the next chapter), the *Doris* experience, and the crushing defeat of the Turks at Sarikamish, suggested to Kitchener that the Ottoman Empire was on its last legs. But Kitchener did not appear to fully appreciate, any more than the British army leaders in the east, that the Ottomans' string of defeats had occurred in large part because they lagged behind the Europeans in technology and modern military organization, not to the perceived inferiority of their troops. For example the Ottoman logistical system was crude with Constantinople and Thrace serving as the hub of the Empire. The farther away from these places, the more difficult the operations became. When the Ottoman divisions were fully mobilized early in August 1914, their rigid training program, under the watchful eyes of German instructors, included progressive changes in their military organization – not the least was the German method of decentralization and control as opposed to the highly top down and centralized system used by the British. The changes introduced provided for a more effective system of command. On Gallipoli the divisions forming the garrison were among the best in the Ottoman army; their needs could easily be met; and they would be fighting to protect their homeland and religion.

Kitchener presented full details of the Turkish defeat at the Suez Canal when the War Council convened on 9 February. Discussion passed quickly to the best means of defending Serbia. Kitchener understood that Serbia's fate rested on gaining the support of Greece. He

---

4   Hankey, *Supreme Command*, vol. 1, p. 277; Brock and Brock (eds.), *Letters to Venetia Stanley*, pp. 418-19.
5   Cited in Arthur, *Lord Kitchener*, vol. 3, p. 107.
6   For the details of the battle see Lieut. Gen. Sir George MacMunn and Capt. Cyril Falls, *Military Operations: Egypt & Palestine*, vol. 1 (London: HMSO, 1928), ch. 3.
7   I am grateful to Dr. Uyar for his research to determine the total number of Turkish casualties.
8   MacMunn and Falls, *Egypt and Palestine*, vol. 1, p. 107.

maintained that only first-rate troops ought to be sent east and for that reason proposed to use the 29th Division which he had originally intended would form part of Sir John French's command. The 29th, the last regular division still available – the 28th had begun to set sail for France in the middle of January and shortly thereafter was followed by the raw 1st Canadians – was composed of experienced army units recently brought home from India and elsewhere. The War Council proceeded to discuss the advantages of the 29th Division going to Salonica: Greece and probably Romania would be drawn into the war; Bulgaria would be neutralized; Serbia would be rescued; and the way would then open for an eventual advance up the Danube. Kitchener felt that the presence of the 29th Division at Salonica might even adversely affect the morale of the Turkish defenders in the Dardanelles. He added that if the navy required troops to follow up its victory in the Dardanelles, the 29th would be near at hand. The War Council concluded its discussion by voting to send the 29th Division to Salonica, contingent on Greece's entry into the conflict.[9]

The offer of two Allied divisions was not enough to provide the Greeks with a margin of safety against Bulgaria, their powerful neighbor and arch-enemy. Indeed the proposal of such limited aid was a confession of weakness and not likely to impress the Greeks. Even though the Greek Prime Minister, Eleutherios Venizelos, was pro-Entente, he required tangible evidence of Allied power in the region if he hoped to shift the attitude of King Constantine from his self-imposed neutrality. Thus he declined to entertain the idea of joining the Entente without the collaboration of Romania which had no interest in entering the war unless there was a good prospect of an Entente victory. Since Russia had been driven back on the east Prussian front as well as forced to withdraw from Bukovina, it seemed pointless to approach the Romanians. Thus on 15 February the Balkan project receded into the background. The sudden disinterest would have an immediate impact on the strategy in the Dardanelles.

While the War Council discussed the benefits of sending troops to Salonica, opinion in the Admiralty War Staff Group, which initially had given perhaps only half-hearted endorsement to Churchill's plan, mounted increasingly towards the belief that no success could be achieved in the Dardanelles without military aid. If troops could be spared for operations in the Balkans why could some not be used in the Dardanelles? Churchill held firm to the notion that the fleet alone could silence the Turkish forts defending the Straits and he saw no reason to exert pressure on Kitchener for military assistance. His only concession was to send two battalions of marines belonging to the Royal Naval Division on 6 February to serve as landing parties to complete the destruction of the guns in the forts. But by mid-February the Admirals were united in deprecating the idea of a purely naval attack and several memoranda were circulated to strengthen their warning.[10] The revolt among the upper echelon of the service shook Churchill and caused him to question whether he had been right to accept Carden's assessment. With the Greeks out of the picture, the 29th Division, earmarked earlier for Salonica, was now free to go elsewhere. There is no evidence that Churchill tried to lobby his colleagues to sanction the employment of the 29th Division in the Dardanelles. It was apparently Asquith, who had been converted by Hankey on the need to support the navy with troops, that was the driving force in altering the whole nature of the operation.[11]

9   Minutes of the War Council, 9 February 1915, CAB 42/1/ 33.
10 Marder, *From the Dreadnought*, vol. 2, pp. 218-28.
11 Hankey, *Supreme Command*, vol. 1, p. 279; Brock and Brock (eds.), *Letters to Venetia Stanley*, pp. 428-29.

On the afternoon of the 16th, Asquith met with one or two of his ministers and as the discussion developed others were called in. Before Kitchener left his office to join the talks, he had summoned Captain Wyndham Deedes, an intelligence officer at the War Office, to seek his views on the prospects of a purely naval attack in the Dardanelles. Deeds had formerly been attached to the Turkish army and knew well the state of its fixed defences. He replied that the operation was fundamentally unsound, that even if the fleet could break through, the Turks could still bottle it up in the Sea of Marmara. As Deedes was developing his arguments, Kitchener cut him off, told him he did not know what he was talking about, and with a wave of his hand signified that the interview was over.[12] Nevertheless in view of Deeds' experience and knowledge, his comments could not be easily dismissed and was bound to have made an impression on Kitchener regardless of his tactless reaction. Incidentally it was characteristic of Kitchener to admit when he had made a mistake – in stark contrast to most politicians. Nine months later while visiting the Dardanelles, he spotted Deedes who was then attached to the 29th Division, drew him aside and personally apologized.[13]

At the informal session only six of the ten War Council members were in attendance – besides Asquith and Kitchener, the others were Churchill, Grey, Fisher and Lloyd George. In the absence of Hankey no minutes of the meeting were taken, a regrettable omission given the sharp turning point in the evolution of the planned operation. At least Asquith recorded the decisions which he later communicated to Hankey. The ministers present agreed to send the 29th Division to the island of Lemnos – made available by an informal arrangement with the Greek government – and it was hoped that it would be able to sail in nine or ten days. Kitchener indicated that the Anzacs stationed in Egypt, would also be available if required. All these forces, together with the Royal Marine battalions already allocated, were to be concentrated in the region to back up the naval assault.[14] The ruling to use troops had been taken informally at a meeting attended by only three-fifths of the War Council ministers. It should be pointed out that the resolution was not confirmed by a regular War Council session. Later in the day Asquith announced to a gathering of all the members at 10 Downing Street that the decisions taken were so important that they had been "recorded as a full meeting of the War Council."[15] There would be other such instances but, as in this case, Asquith would took immediate steps to put the matter into the official channel.

Despite the availability of troops, neither Kitchener nor Churchill expected any major change in the execution of the campaign. Kitchener was ready to employ army units in some capacity – possibly to deal with guns that had escaped the fleet's fire or to occupy Constantinople after the Turks had surrendered – but only after the navy had forced a passage through the Straits. Churchill undoubtedly welcomed the prospect of having troops on hand in case their assistance was required but he did not intend to abandon the original plan, confident that the navy could get through the Straits on its own.

No consideration was given in the War Council to hold up the naval attack until the army arrived to lend a hand. Some writers of the campaign have raised the question of why not. The

---

12 Deeds Diary, entry for 17 February 1915, Deedes papers; John Presland, *Deedes Bey* (London: Macmillan, 1942), pp. 233-34.
13 James, *Gallipoli*, p. 41n.
14 Hankey, *Supreme Command*, vol. 1, p. 281.
15 Minutes of the War Council Meeting, 16 February 1915, CAB 42/135.

answer is not complicated. Kitchener would not have agreed to an amphibious operation for three reasons. One, he had been lead to believe that the army was not needed to assist the fleet gain its objective. Two, he did not have enough men at his disposal to engage in a land campaign to seize control of the Gallipoli Peninsula. Three, in case of failure, a joint operation could not have been presented as merely a feint for a strike elsewhere.

As the naval attack was set to begin in three days, Churchill was worried that the troops, which required to be assembled and transported, would not arrive in time. He implored Kitchener to arrange to have all the troops on the scene during the opening phase of the naval action. He wrote to Kitchener shortly before the start of the naval attack:

> If our operations at the Dardanelles prosper, immense advantages may be offered wh cannot be gathered without military aid ... I think at least 50,000 men shd be within reach at 3 days' notice, either to seize the Gallipoli Peninsula when it has been evacuated, or to occupy C'nople if a revolution takes place. We shd never forgive ourselves if the naval operations succeeded & the fruits were lost through the army being absent.[16]

Since the naval operation was expected to last several weeks, Kitchener could not understand why Churchill insisted on the hurried concentration of so many troops nearby. He had made it clear that the army would not be used in any great numbers until the navy had accomplished its goal of pushing its way into the Sea of Marmora. He assured Churchill: "You get through! I will find the men."[17]

The forces the War Office and Admiralty had earmarked for the Dardanelles were augmented when the French government, which had already sent a naval squadron to join Carden's fleet, resolved on 18 February to commit an infantry division in support of the campaign. France's departure from the rule not to divert military strength from the main front was circumvented only under unusual circumstances. In this case it was to allow the nation to be in a position to take control of certain portions of the sultan's realm in the event that the Ottoman Empire was dismembered at the end of the war. Occupation of the desired territories was the only sure guarantee of their incorporation within France's domain.[18]

At this point the military situation took a sudden turn. News arrived that the Russian front was in danger of collapsing, opening up the possibility that the Germans might rapidly transfer substantial forces to reinforce their main army in the west. Joffre indicated that if the Germans launched a major offensive against the Anglo-French front in the spring, he would need every man, especially every seasoned man, he had been led to expect. The French ambassador in London, Paul Cambon, begged Kitchener not to divert the 29th Division from its previously scheduled berth in France. It was the start of a French drive to induce Kitchener to change his mind. Kitchener told Grey: "The French are splendid – to you they say I have promised the 29th Div. – to me they say you have practically done so. Both statements appear to be equally mendacious."[19]

---

16   Churchill to Kitchener, 18 February 1915, in Gilbert (ed.), *Companion*, vol. 1, pp. 518-19.
17   Esher War Journal, entry for 16 February 1915, Esher papers.
18   Cassar, *Reluctant Partner*, pp. 61-62.
19   Kitchener to Grey, 28 February 1915, Grey papers, FO 800/102.

Kitchener in fact had made no commitment to send the 29th Division to France. He was especially annoyed at Millerand who alleged that, while he was in London, he had received assurances that the 29th Division would soon be placed at the disposal of Sir John French. To Lord Esher, who was used as go-between with the French authorities in Paris, Kitchener wrote:

> Millerand's complaints do not seem to me to be at all well founded. I promised Sir John French to send a certain number of troops, and whether these consist of the 29th Division, or any other division, seems to me a detail that does not come into any agreement as regards troops to be sent to France.[20]

Unknown to Kitchener, the French considered the 29th Division as a symbol of Britain's future attitude towards the western front. If the British allocated their last regular division to the Aegean it would be tantamount to an admission that they held success to be so vital there as to jeopardize the security of the main front. It would also mean that the campaign in the Dardanelles would pass from a sideshow to a major theatre of war. As such there would be no withdrawal in case the naval attack did not prosper, a condition on which the venture had originally been approved.[21]

At the War Council meeting on 19 February, Kitchener announced that he was countermanding his orders to divert the 29th Division to the Dardanelles and would send instead the Australian and New Zealand troops from Egypt. He feared that if the Russians suffered a decisive defeat in Poland where they had lost very heavily in men, the Germans would be in a position to bring back masses of troops to the main front to enable a large-scale attack in France and Belgium. In such an event he wanted to have on hand a mobile reserve to throw in at any threatened point.[22] Kitchener's decision to retain the 29th Division was a prudent measure in view of the potential danger to the western front. In fact it would have been an act of folly to have allowed the last regular division in Britain to proceed to Lemnos when it might have been more urgently needed on the western front.

Churchill, who had not been forewarned of the change of plans until the last moment, protested vigorously that the 29th Division was pivotal to the success of the operation. He had hoped to have 50,000 men available to reach the Dardanelles at three days' notice. He planned to send all ten battalions of the Royal Naval Division but both they and the Anzac units required a stiffening of experienced troops. He maintained that, with the vast forces massed on the western front, the absence of the 29th Division would not be missed, whereas in the Dardanelles it might well make all the difference. Churchill's comments that a division could not possibly have a decisive effect on the western front might be open to question judging by the results of the 2nd Worcesters' action during the First Battle of Ypres (20 October-22 November 1914).[23]

---

20   Kitchener to Esher, 22 February 1915, Kitchener papers, PRO 30/57/59.
21   Aspinall-Oglander, *Gallipoli*, vol. 1, p. 71n1; Corbett, *Naval Operations*, vol. 2, pp. 153-54.
22   Minutes of the War Council, 19 February 1915, CAB 42/1/36.
23   At the height of the fighting, the Germans smashed through the front of the BEF and some in the lead reached the village of Gheluvelt. The regional British commander ordered the last of his reserves, three companies of the 2nd Worcesters, 7 officers and 357 men, to counterattack. The Worcesters lost over 100 men to artillery fire as they crossed an open field but enough survived to fall upon the Germans with the bayonet, sending them fleeing in disorder. Thanks to the fighting spirit of three British companies, the Allied line was restored. John Terraine, *Douglas Haig: The Educated Soldier*

Kitchener was puzzled by Churchill's reaction. It seemed to him unnecessary to have regular troops for mopping up operations or garrison duty. After weeks of self-deception, Churchill at last recognized the limitations of naval power. He admitted for the first time that the navy alone would be unable to keep the Dardanelles open for the unarmoured supply ships. "We should never forgive ourselves," he exclaimed, "if this operation failed owing to insufficient support at the critical moment." The other members of the Council who joined the discussion tended to support the First Lord. Asquith read out some excerpts from the 1906 general staff paper which concluded that military cooperation was essential to success. Lloyd George, in one of his frequent whimsical moments, went so far as to urge Kitchener to send twice as many troops east as Churchill wanted, reasoning that it was "worthwhile to take some risks in order to achieve a decisive operation which might win the war." Kitchener, however, had dug in his heels. His only concession was that he would release the 29th Division if its absence threatened to jeopardize the success of the naval offensive.[24]

While the debate over the fate of the 29th Division was going on, Vice Admiral Carden opened his attack against the forts guarding the entrance to the Dardanelles on 19 February. The next day Kitchener informed General Maxwell that a force was being assembled on Lemnos to cooperate with the naval operation in the Dardanelles and to garrison any forts that fell. He instructed Maxwell to alert the Anzacs under Lieutenant General William Birdwood, to be held in readiness to embark on the arrival of ships sent from Britain. Maxwell was also to communicate with Carden to find out how the army could best fulfil his requirements.[25] Maxwell accordingly contacted Carden who replied on the 23rd, disclosing that he had been informed to prepare to land a force of 10,000 men if needed, but that his instructions went no further. Maxwell who expected more guidance from Carden was understandably startled by the response. He reported back to Kitchener that "Carden's telegram strikes me as being so helpless that I feel unless military authorities take the initiative, no progress is likely to be made."[26]

On receipt of Maxwell's telegram, Kitchener decided to try to gain more precise information on the size of the Turkish contingent on the Gallipoli Peninsula and how Carden intended to exercise control over the forces placed at his disposal. Through Maxwell, he directed Birdwood, his former military secretary and devoted friend, to undertake a special mission:

> Proceed to meet Admiral Carden at the earliest possible opportunity and consult him as to the nature of the combined operations which the forcing of the Dardanelles is to involve. Report the result to me. You should learn from local observation and information the numbers of the Turkish garrison on the peninsula, and whether the admiral thinks it will be necessary to land troops to take the forts in reverse; if so what force will be required, and generally in what manner it is proposed to use the troops. Will the Bulair lines have to be held, and will operations on the Asiatic side be necessary or advisable?[27]

(London: Leo Cooper, 1990), p. 114; David Lomas, *First Ypres 1914* (London: Osprey Publishing, 1999), pp. 73-76.
24 Minutes of the War Council, 19 February 1915, CAB 42/1/36.
25 Kitchener to Maxwell, 20 February 1915, CAB 19/31.
26 Maxwell to Kitchener, 23 February 1915, ibid.
27 Kitchener to Birdwood, 23 February 1915, ibid.

Kitchener wanted to restrict the role of the army to mopping up operations only. He was anxious to avoid a full scale landing on the Peninsula which he regarded as a "hornet's nest." With conditions so uncertain on the eastern front and the country still desperately short of men and munitions, it was not the moment to embark on a new and costly enterprise. Kitchener's views on the operation may be gleaned from a telegram sent to Maxwell the next day (24th):

> The object of forcing the Dardanelles is to gain possession of the Bosporus and overawe Constantinople. The forcing of the Straits is to be effected mainly by naval means, and, when successful it will doubtless be followed by the retirement of the Gallipoli garrison. So far as our information goes, it does not appear a sound military undertaking to attempt a landing in force on the Gallipoli peninsula, the garrison, which is reported to be 40,000, until the passage has been forced. The entry of the fleet into the Marmara would probably make the Turkish position untenable, and enable British troops to occupy the peninsula if considered necessary.

Kitchener told Maxwell that he was relying on Birdwood to provide him with his views as to the number of troops required to secure the forts or positions already gained and to deny their reoccupation by the enemy. Furthermore he requested that, in case more troops could be sent, how Birdwood believed they could best be utilized after the ships had entered the Sea of Marmara. Finally he wanted Birdwood to inform him privately whether, from the result of Carden's bombardment up to date, he considers a large force necessary to take the forts in reverse or whether he thinks that the naval operations will succeed "without having recourse to such a step."[28]

Whatever role Kitchener was prepared to assign to the army rested on the assumption that the navy would get through the Straits. In the event the ships faltered, however, the operation would be cancelled. As it turned out, the original script was not followed. An incident on the home front assured that the campaign would continue, irrespective of the outcome of the naval attack.

On 20 February Churchill, without the approval of either the Prime Minister or War Council, issued a press communiqué announcing the first day's bombardment on the Straits' outer defences and even naming the ships that had been involved.[29] There were a few officials in the Admiralty who questioned the wisdom of releasing too much information to the public lest it make it more difficult to end the operation in case of unforeseen difficulties. One such person who protested vehemently was Vice Admiral Oliver. Captain Herbert Richmond, the Assistant Director of Operations at the Admiralty, recorded the incident:

> Winston had written it [press communiqué] himself, putting in a lot of detail and giving all the names of the ships engaged. He had sent for Oliver & shown it to him, & Oliver had been very indignant and said it was giving much too much information to the enemy to say all that ... He succeeded in making Winston modify his despatch a little, but in the

---

28   Kitchener to Maxwell, 24 February 1915, ibid.
29   The Admiralty released the statement at 2 pm on 20 February 1915, ADM 137/109.

end W. sent it down to the Press room with orders that it was to be published as it was; and there was very little change in it.³⁰

Since the Admiralty press release would have a profound effect in altering the conditions under which the War Council had initially approved of the operation, it is probably best to reproduce it word for word.

> Yesterday, at 8 am, a British fleet of battleships and battle cruisers, accompanied by flotillas, and aided by a strong French squadron, the whole under the command of Vice Admiral Sackville H. Carden, began an attack upon the forts at the entrance of the Dardanelles.
>
> The forts at Cape Helles and Kum Kaleh were bombarded with deliberate long-range fire. Considerable effect was produced on two of the forts. Two others were frequently hit but being open earthworks it was difficult to estimate the damage. The forts, being outranged, were not able to reply to [the] fire.
>
> At 2.45 pm a portion of the battleship force was ordered to close and engage the forts at closer range with secondary armament. The forts on both sides of the entrance then opened fire, and were engaged at moderate ranges by *Vengeance, Cornwallis, Triumph, Suffren, Gaulois, Bouvet*, supported by *Inflexible* and *Agamemnon* at long range. The forts on the European side were apparently silenced. One fort on the Asiatic side was still firing when the operation was suspended owing to failing light.
>
> No ships of the Allied Fleet were hit. The action has been renewed this morning after aerial reconnaissance.³¹

Although the announcement to the newspapers avoided any mention of the purpose of the naval operation, the media in London and Paris took it for granted that the fleet's objective was to force the Straits. *The Times* on 22 February devoted two columns on its front page, providing an elaborate account of the political and military benefits that would flow from a successful attack and urging that, since much was at stake, "having begun it must be ... carried through at all costs."³² In Paris the press expounded along similar lines. The right-wing newspaper *Le Gaulois* explained: "The advantages of an operation which will render us masters of the Dardanelles and the Bosporus are [too] evident not to have been conceived."³³

It had been understood in the War Council from the beginning that no public statement would be released so that if the naval attack proved unsuccessful, it would be treated as a demonstration and abandoned without loss of prestige. However, Churchill took that option out of the hands of the War Council when he drew worldwide attention to what seemed like a major clash in the Dardanelles. James Masterton-Smith, then Churchill's parliamentary secretary, admitted the consequence of his former chief's indiscretion in a conversation with Sir George Riddell (proprietor of the *News of the World* and liaison officer between the government and the press during the war) in July 1916:

---

30 Cited in Bell, *Churchill*, p. 108.
31 A copy can be seen in Hankey, *Supreme Command*, vol. 1, pp. 282-83.
32 *The Times*, 22 February 1915.
33 Cited in the *Manchester Guardian*, 22 February 1915.

The War Council intended that the Fleet should endeavour to force the Dardanelles, but that very little should be said publicly, and that if the operation proved unsuccessful, it should be treated as a feint and the real objective should be described as Alexandretta. Winston's *communiques* to the Press wittingly or unwittingly obscured this programme.[34]

What had prompted Churchill to break his word and deviate from the ground rules he had established to win the War Council's approval of his naval scheme in January? The answer, in my view, was that Churchill, whom Asquith had recently described to his wife as "devoured by vanity," was driven entirely by selfish reasons.[35] He wanted to parade his master plan before the British people and the rest of the world. As he was confident of an eventual victory over the Turks, he was laying the ground work to reap most of the praise and emerge from the war as a great leader and strategist.[36] His brazen action would come back to haunt him, but more importantly it had a devastating impact on the nation and allied cause. It set in motion a tragic train of events that alerted the Turks and accelerated the build-up of their defences; was instrumental in bringing down the Liberal government in May 1915; ultimately destroyed Kitchener's effectiveness in the cabinet and inner councils of war; set back British diplomacy in the Balkans; led to the death of tens of thousands of allied soldiers in the Dardanelles and in other campaigns in the Middle East; reenergized the faltering Turkish Empire; and certainly extended the length of the war.

It should be noted that Churchill made no mention of his statement to the media in his account of the Dardanelles campaign as he was obviously trying to distance himself from the catastrophic damage his blunder had caused. By following Churchill's narrative, Martin Gilbert engaged in a cover up as well.[37] What is unfathomable is the lack of attention scholars have paid to what is undoubtedly the most significant episode of the campaign.

Writers of the operation have ignored, or shrugged off, the effect of the press release for different reasons. Most, if not the vast majority, are unaware that it even happened, presumably because they used Churchill's doctored account as a primary source.[38] Still there is least one author who suggested that, even if Churchill had not issued his press announcement, the moment the fleet began attacking the outer forts, the Turks inevitably would have concluded that its purpose was to force a passage through the Dardanelles.[39] That speculative premise, in my view, is unconvincing. As long as there was no landing on Gallipoli, as Fisher supposed, the Allies could have withdrawn from the Dardanelles at any time and not worried about damaging their prominent standing in the east. The large number of ships did not necessarily mean that they intended to force the Straits. If things went badly, the British could have announce their planned excuse for breaking off the action. It was obvious that a large fleet would have been required to transport 50,000 or 60,000 troops, guns, ammunition, supplies, wagons, horses,

---

34 Riddell War Diary, entry for 21 July 1916, ADD 62975.
35 Brock and Brock (eds.), *Margot Asquith's Great War Diary*, p. 79.
36 Churchill was so certain of an Allied naval victory that in a letter to Grey on 28 February he had already worked out the terms of a Turkish surrender. See Gilbert, *Winston S. Churchill*, vol. 3, p. 315.
37 Ibid., p. 303.
38 See for example Robin Prior, *Gallipoli: The End of the Myth* (New Haven; Yale University Press, 2009), pp. 61-62; James, *Gallipoli*, p. 68. In James' defence his book was published shortly before the minutes of the War Council for 1915 were accessible to researchers.
39 Bell, *Churchill*, p. 109.

etc., to its ultimate destination in the Ottoman Empire, as well as provide cover, if necessary, for the landing. Thus for the feint to be convincing, the large size of the naval task force was actually necessary.

A few other historians, in addition to the Dardanelles Commission Report, have advanced a different reason as to why it was inconceivable that the Turks could have been misled. It is suggested that the presence of a sizeable military force assembled nearby, ruled out any possible deception of the ultimate goal.[40] It is true that the concentration of a large body of troops in the vicinity of the Straits implied that the Allies proposed to use them at some point but there was no clear sign that they intended to commit them to storm the enemy's strongly held positions on the Peninsula. After the naval operation was called off, it would have been a relatively simple matter to load the men on the ships and transport them to occupy a weakly defended area of the Ottoman Empire such as Smyrna, or Haifa or Alexandretta. In short without the effect of Churchill's public statement calling attention to the naval attack, the arrangement established in the beginning could have been carried out without serious repercussions.

No one openly rebuked Churchill for his rashness, but some had grumbled privately about it before the War Council meeting on the 24th got under way.[41] Although most of the outer forts had not been reduced, optimism among the members in the eventual success of the enterprise remained high. No one except Hankey expressed much concern about the press announcement.[42] It was only after disaster struck that the full implications of Churchill's statement became apparent and belatedly he came under sharp criticism. Lloyd George for one blasted Churchill in a letter to his secretary and mistress Frances Stevenson on 15 May 1915, accusing him of making it impossible to call off the operation and ensuring that troops would have to be employed after the failure of the naval attack. He wrote:

> On the very first day that the bombardment commenced, he [Churchill], broke faith with his colleagues & caused the announcement to be made in the Press with great eclat that we had begun the bombardment of the Dardanelles forts & intended to force the Straits. Thenceforth it was, of course, impossible for the Government to withdraw."[43]

To be precise, Lloyd George erred when he claimed that the text of Churchill's declaration to the press included the ultimate aim of the naval attack. Although the First Lord's public announcement made no mention of the allied fleet's intention to force a passage through the Straits, he might just as well have added that information since the media was unrestrained in loudly proclaiming the Admiralty's objective.

With the cat out of the bag, it was felt that the army must help the navy if its advance was halted. "Speaker after speaker reflected this view," Hankey wrote in *The Supreme Command*.[44] Kitchener weighed in as well. He conceded that should the navy prove incapable of forcing the

---

40 See for example, *First Report of the Dardanelles Commission*, pp. 33-34.
41 Lady Violet Bonham Carter, *Winston Churchill: An Intimate Portrait* (New York: Harcourt, Brace and World, 1965), p. 294.
42 Hankey to Esher, in Roskill, *Hankey*, p. 167.
43 A.J.P. Taylor (ed.), *Lloyd George: A Diary by Frances Stevenson* (New York: Harper and Row, 1971), p. 50.
44 Hankey, *Supreme Command*, vol. 1, p. 283.

Straits, the army should see the business through. He went on to say: "The effect of a defeat in the orient would be very serious. There could be no going back. *The publicity of the announcement has committed us.*"[45] Grey followed up by saying that "failure would be morally equivalent to a defeat on land." The only minister who expressed some reservation was Lloyd George who thought that if the naval attack failed, "we were committed ... to some action in the Near East, but not necessarily to a siege of the Dardanelles." Lloyd George's statement was consistent with his preference for a diversion to the Balkans which he had expressed on a number of occasions.

The resolution to send in the army in case the navy ran into trouble passed without dissent. Given the nature of what was at stake, the decision was made quickly and almost casually. Still it is very doubtful that a lengthy debate would have changed the outcome. When the members of the War Council agreed to take a potentially dangerous risk, it was because they felt strongly that they had no other choice. There were nationalist movements in Egypt and India which had been openly active in opposing British rule before the war. After Turkey's entry in the conflict, the sultan had called for a *jihad* and it was feared in London that any loss of face resulting from a British defeat would inspire a revolt, or at the very least, serious trouble in these countries.[46] Kitchener and his colleagues did not want to confront the possibility of having to divert significant forces to deal with major disturbances in some of their territorial possessions and risk jeopardizing the security of the western front.

Churchill engaged in deliberate misrepresentation in *The World Crisis* when he purported to discuss the details of the momentous meeting on the 24th. As a start he omitted the reaction of the civilian ministers in the War Council to his press release. It bears repeating that everyone who spoke out maintained that withdrawal, in the event the fleet could not silence the Turkish forts, was no longer an option. Churchill did refer to most of Kitchener's comments but deliberately left out the crucial last sentence which was, "*The publicity of the announcement has committed us.*" It has been ignored or undetected by virtually all recent writers of the campaign who evidently relied on *The World Crisis* for the facts, instead of choosing to be guided by the minutes of the meeting. Churchill's motives for his deceit are transparent. He desperately wanted to deflect attention from the consequences of his foolhardy action. By distorting the evidence, he inferred it was Kitchener who alone decided, without reference to the War Council, to send in the army to avoid a defeat. He wrote:

> On the 24th Lord Kitchener said that he "felt that if the Fleet could not get through the Straits unaided the Army ought to see the business through. The effect of a defeat in the Orient would be very serious. There could be no going back." Thus, at a stroke, the idea of discarding the naval attack, if it proved too difficult, and turning to some other objective, was abandoned and the possibility of a great military enterprise seemed to be accepted.[47]

Now that Churchill's latest and most serious deception has been exposed, we can continue with the War Council deliberations on the 24th. As the escalation of the operation could no longer be ruled out, Churchill sought as large a force as possible within reach in the event, the navy

---

45 Minutes of the War Council, 24 February 1915, CAB 42/1/42; Hankey, *Supreme Command*, vol. 1, p. 283.
46 Cassar, *Kitchener as Proconsul of Egypt*, pp. 117, 134-38.
47 Churchill, *World Crisis*, vol. 2, p. 183.

required assistance. He pressed Kitchener, not only for the 29th Division but also for a territorial division which according to his calculation would bring the total assembled allied force to over 100,000 men – besides the 29th and a territorial division, the other units would consist of the Anzac corps and Naval Division, plus two Allied contingents, a division from France and a Russian commitment of 40,000 men. The First Lord was calling for large numbers of troops without any clear idea of how, when or where they would be used. It was a strange request from the man whose main selling point in the adoption of his plan in January was that Turkey could be defeated with only the application of naval power.

Kitchener was bewildered by Churchill's rambling state of mind. Would the troops he had already allocated not be sufficient to clear small pockets of resistance and later occupy Constantinople? Churchill was in a dilemma for he held two contradictory positions at the same time. He had come to realize that a sizeable military effort was essential to victory but continued to pretend that the navy alone could get the job done. Kitchener asked the First Lord if he now contemplated a landing on the Gallipoli Peninsula. Placed on the spot, Churchill replied, quite untruthfully, that he did not but that "it was quite conceivable that the naval attack might be temporarily held up by mines, and some local military operation required." Churchill tried to downplay the extent of possible military involvement. If it came to requiring troops to assist the navy to clear the mines, it would have required, not a minor but a major undertaking. Kitchener could not understand the motive for concentrating so many troops in view of their intended use. He expressed the belief that once the fleet had forced its way through the Dardanelle, in fact, as soon as the forts started to fall "the Gallipoli garrison would evacuate the peninsula; the garrison of Constantinople, the Sultan, and not improbably the Turkish army in Thrace, would also decamp to the Asiatic shore." He added that through patience and wise negotiations the Turkish forces on the European side would probably surrender.[48]

Changing the subject, Kitchener asked Churchill what this large force was supposed to do in the Dardanelles while naval operations were in progress. Churchill gave a number of options, several of which must have left Kitchener scratching his head: If the fleet got through they might be used to take possession of Constantinople; another plan was to assemble them in European Turkey near the Bulgarian border; possibly transfer them to Salonica in order to influence the Balkan States; or send them up the Danube in case Romania joined the Entente. Shrugging off Churchill's mostly incoherent ideas, Kitchener remained unwilling to part with the 29th Division, reiterating his concern over the precariousness of the Russian position and the possibility of its requirement on the western front. Since it was understood that there was no going back in case the naval attack broke down, the weight of opinion in the War Council shared Churchill's preference for a large force on the spot. To Churchill's dismay, Asquith was unwilling to overrule Kitchener and so no decision over the 29th Division was reached on the 24th.[49]

Kitchener returned to the War Office to find that a wire from Maxwell had arrived. The Gallipoli Peninsula, Maxwell warned, was heavily fortified everywhere and prepared for a determined resistance.[50] Two days later Maxwell forwarded the gist of a military appreciation by Colonel Maucorps, chief of the French military mission in Egypt. A former military

48 Minutes of the War Council, 24 February 1915, CAB 42/1/42.
49 Ibid.
50 Maxwell to Kitchener, 24 February 1915, CAB 19/31.

attaché in Constantinople, the highly regarded French officer was well acquainted with the nature of the defences in the Dardanelles. He believed that the fleet could not force the Straits unless supported by an army and he advocated a landing in the vicinity of Besika Bay in Asia as presenting the least difficulty. He considered that an attempt to invade the Peninsula, which was heavily fortified, would be extremely hazardous. He pointed out that the Turkish garrison on Gallipoli numbered about 30,000 men and was commanded by Djevad Bey whom he described as energetic and resourceful.[51]

These telegrams stiffened Kitchener's resolve to avoid major military operations on the Peninsula. He signaled Birdwood:

> The forcing of the Dardanelles is being undertaken by the navy and as far as can be foreseen at present the task of your troops until the passage has been actually secured, will be limited to minor operations such as the final destruction of batteries, after they have been silenced, under the covering fire of ships... It is anticipated that when the forcing of the Narrows is practically assured, the Turks will probably evacuate the peninsula, and a small force at Bulair will be able to hold it ... As soon as you can get into touch with local information, send me an appreciation of what is likely to happen at Constantinople, and whether you think that more than 64,000 troops will be required for operations there after the Straits have been forced.[52]

After the War Council convened on the 26th, Churchill steered the discussion on the matter of the 29th Division. He had 48 hours to think of new arguments to bolster his appeal to have the regular division released. The core of his remarks, as recorded in the War Council minutes, were as follows:

> In three weeks' time Constantinople might be at our mercy. We should avoid the risk of finding ourselves with a force inadequate to our requirements and face to face with a disaster. At the previous meeting Lord Kitchener had asked him what was the use to be made of any large number of troops at Constantinople. His reply was that they were required to occupy Constantinople and to compel a surrender of all Turkish forces remaining in Europe after the fleet had obtained command of the Sea of Marmara. With an army at hand this could be accomplished either by fighting, or by negotiations or by bribery ... The actual and definite object of the army would be to reap the fruits of the naval success.[53]

Kitchener refused to alter his position. He indicated that the absence of 33,000 men belonging to the 29th Division and the territorials was unlikely to make a difference between success and failure. He considered that as long as the outlook for the Russians remained critical, it would be a serious risk to part with the only troops he had available as a reserve to send over to France in case of an emergency. He saw no need for serious military operations on the Peninsula and was convinced that once the navy started to demolish the forts, the Ottoman army would evacuate Gallipoli to avoid the risk of being cut off and forced to surrender. He wanted two

---

51 Maxwell to Kitchener, 26 February 1915, ibid.
52 Kitchener to Birdwood, 26 February 1915, ibid.
53 Minutes of the War Council, 26 February 1915, CAB 42/1/47.

events to happen before he sent the 29th Division to the east; one was to wait for the Russian military situation to clear up; and the second for some signs of the enemy's reaction to the naval bombardment.[54]

The War Council appeared to be divided. Balfour and Grey were swayed by Kitchener's arguments. Hankey had doubts that the navy could get through unaided while Lloyd George considered that as many men as possible, including the 29th Division, should be sent east in order to impress and bring in the Balkan states. Asquith was rather ambivalent, hinting that the presence of a first class division like the 29th Division might affect the operation but on the same day telling Venetia Stanley that the "difference between sending to the Dardanelles at once 60,000 troops (which we can certainly do) & say 90,000 cannot, I think, for the moment at any rate be decisive." The discussion became heated during which Churchill, seemingly in a state of desperation, lost his composure and, in the words of Asquith, became "noisy, rhetorical, tactless & temperless [sic]."[55] When Kitchener remained immovable, Churchill wished to place on record that he disclaimed all responsibility if a disaster occurred in the Dardanelles due to insufficient troops. Needless to say, his clumsy attempt at intimidation did not impress Kitchener or anyone else. Before the War Council dispersed, it voted to keep the 29th Division in England.[56] "We accepted K's views as right for the immediate situation to Winston's immense & unconcealed dudgeon," Asquith wrote afterwards.[57]

Churchill's earlier enthusiasm and persuasiveness on the prospects of the naval attack made it difficult for him to convince Kitchener of the importance of having a large army available on the spot. Thus far the record of the Turks in the war was one of unbroken failure. In Kitchener's view, the 64,000 men (which included the Anzac corps, the Royal Naval Division and a French Division) were adequate to deal with minor follow-up operations.

For the next fortnight Kitchener withstood Churchill's onslaught without yielding an inch. It was not until 10 March, when conditions on the eastern front had improved sufficiently, that Kitchener consented to despatch the 29th Division to the Dardanelles. The long period of haggling with Churchill had been an ordeal for Kitchener. It had taken a good deal of his staying power to outlast Churchill who was younger, had a much lighter work load, and considerably more formidable in debate. No less unsettling was the fact that he had been seriously challenged in the War Council on a question of military policy for the first time. Unfortunately it was a harbinger of things to come.

During early March military observers on the spot had watched with alarm at the unrealistic confidence in London of an inevitable naval victory. General Birdwood for one, following his instructions from Kitchener, went to see Carden and submitted the results of his interview on the 4th. He estimated that there were 40,000 Turkish defenders in the vicinity of the Dardanelles with plenty of reinforcements available in Constantinople. Birdwood had made a reconnaissance up the Straits and he had seen enough to conclude that the concealed Turkish batteries presented formidable obstacles. Nevertheless, he pointed out that Carden intended to go ahead with the naval attack and either ignore the damage those guns could inflict on the fleet or wait until the army arrived to cooperate in their destruction. Birdwood reckoned that

54 Ibid.
55 Brock and Brock (eds.), *Letters to Venetia Stanley*, p. 449.
56 Minutes of the War Council, 26 February 1915, CAB 42/1/47.
57 Brock and Brock (eds.), *Letters to Venetia Stanley*, p. 449.

the choice of alternatives would depend on the urgency of an early victory. He claimed that if troops were required to assist the fleet, he thought it would be impossible to confine their movements to minor operations. He and Carden agreed that the best plan would be to make a feint at Bulair, disembark a strong force at Cape Helles, then advance swiftly up the Peninsula as far as the line Gaba Tepe-Kalid Bahr. From there the forts could be taken in reverse and the concealed batteries destroyed.[58] Birdwood's proposed operation went well beyond what Kitchener had in mind.

That same day Kitchener learned from Churchill that Carden expected to break into the Sea of Marmora in about two weeks providing the seas remain calm. The First Lord asked that troops be assembled at Lemnos by the 18th, either to land at Gallipoli or be transported through the Straits to Constantinople.[59]

Kitchener felt it necessary to ensure that under pressure Birdwood did not initiate any unnecessary operations on the Peninsula. To that end he signaled Birdwood shortly before midnight on 4 March, told him of Carden's projection, and forbade him from undertaking large-scale operations without further orders from home. The troops concentrating at Mudros harbour (on the island of Lemnos), he added, were intended for mopping-up action and later for operations in the neighbourhood of Constantinople.[60] Birdwood replied somewhat testily on 6 March that he had already stated that the Admiral's forecast was too sanguine and he doubted the ability of the fleet to force a passage unaided. Still he assured Kitchener that "I have no intention of rushing blindly into the Gallipoli Peninsula and quite realize that my movements must entirely depend on the progress made by the Navy." Birdwood was adamant that even if the fleet managed to break into the Sea of Marmora, the supply ships would be unable to follow as they would be exposed to fire from hidden guns.[61] Birdwood's judgement, together with the ominous warnings by Maxwell and others could not help but make an impression on Kitchener. Still he did not have any serious concern for at the time he had no intentions of assigning the army to invade the Peninsula.

It was desirable, once it was apparent that the French and possibly the Russians would be participating in the campaign, to replace the acting commander, Lieutenant General Birdwood, with an officer of greater seniority and reputation. Birdwood bore the disappointment remarkably well. In replying to Kitchener's telegram notifying him of the reason for a change in the command, he declared: "It would be useless to say it has not come as a bit of disappointment. I know so well, though my dear old chief, no one but you would ever have contemplated my having command at all, in the first instance, of the 60,000 men of the original force."[62]

On 3 March Kitchener informed Churchill that he had chosen General Ian Hamilton to command the growing Allied force – about 70,000 with the arrival of the 29th Division. The news delighted Churchill who replied the next day:

> I heard yesterday with very great pleasure you mentioned the name of Sir Ian Hamilton as the officer you had designated for the main command in this theatre. Certainly no choice

---

58 Birdwood to Kitchener, 4 March 1915, CAB 19/31.
59 Churchill, *World Crisis*, vol. 2, pp. 195-96.
60 Kitchener to Birdwood, 4 March 1915, CAB 19/31.
61 Birdwood to Kitchener, 6 March 1915, ibid.
62 Field Marshal Lord Birdwood, *Khaki and Gown* (London: Ward, Lock and Co., 1941), p. 251.

could be more agreeable to the Admiralty and to the Navy; but I would venture to press upon you the desirability of this officer being on the spot as soon as possible, in order that he may concert with the Admiral on the really critical and decisive operations which may be required at the outset.[63]

Hamilton was witty and charming, combining literary talent with a flair for painting and a keen appreciation for poetry and music. Frail-looking but wiry and full of energy, the 62-year-old Hamilton had seen more active duty than any other serving senior British officer and was twice nominated for the Victoria Cross – denied for odd reasons, once because he was too young and on the other occasion because he was too old. His lengthy military career had included service as Kitchener's chief of staff in the Boer War and a close bond existed between the two men.[64]

Yet Hamilton had not been Kitchener's preferred choice. It was not as if Kitchener had misgivings about Hamilton ability to command an army. In November 1914 he had been ready to replace French with Hamilton but abandoned the idea when Joffre urged that no change in the BEF's leadership take place.[65] It may be that Kitchener thought that Hamilton's talents would be wasted in the Dardanelles where the army's role was expected to be confined to minor operations. There was also the possibility that he wanted to hold back Hamilton for a possible future assignment that he was contemplating. Whatever the reason, Kitchener had initially set his sight on General Leslie Rundle, whose tenure as governor of Malta (1909-1915) had just ended. An old comrade, Rundle had compiled a distinguished military record in colonial warfare and was known to be tough, thorough and resolute without being reckless. What caused Kitchener to change his mind? Kitchener discussed the issue of a commander with both Churchill and Asquith before making the actual selection. Churchill initially tossed out the name of Lieutenant General Aylmer Hunter-Weston but Kitchener never considered his suggestion.[66] It was apparently the Prime Minister who had the final say in the matter. According to his daughter Violet (later Lady Bonham Carter), it was at the insistence of her father that Hamilton was sent to the Dardanelles. Her diary contains the following entry:

> Tuesday I dined with Ava Astor and talked to Ian Hamilton afterwards – I knew he was to be sent in full command (K. had suggested Trundle [the nickname for Rundle] but father was quite firm about I.H.) ... He dined with us a week later when he knew of his appointment – in an ecstasy – I think he probably has just the right dash of irregularity for the situation.[67]

---

63 Churchill to Kitchener, 4 March 1915, Kitchener papers, PRO 30/57/72.
64 For the details on Hamilton's pre 1915 career see Ian Hamilton, *The Happy Warrior: A Life of General Sir Ian Hamilton* (London: Cassell, 1966); John P. Jones, *Johnny: The Legend and Tragedy of General Sir Ian Hamilton* (Barnsley: Pen and Sword, 2012); Evan McGilvray, *Hamilton and Gallipoli* (Barnsley, S. Yorkshire: Pen & Sword, 2015).
65 For the details on this issue see Cassar, *Kitchener*, p. 250.
66 Gilbert, *Winston S. Churchill*, vol. 3, pp. 300-1.
67 Violet Asquith diary, entry during the second week in March 1915. The quote cited in this text is not in the published version of her diary which was edited by Mark Pottle and entitled *Champion Redoubtable: The Diaries and Letters of Violet Bonham Carter 1914-1945* (London: Weidenfeld & Nicolson, 1998).

As was to be expected, Kitchener deferred to the Prime Minister's adamant wish. More puzzling was Asquith's advocacy of Hamilton, a soldier he had described earlier "as having too much feather in his brain."[68] Violet Asquith's last remark may hold the key. Did Asquith think that this was a job which required a unique or non-traditional soldier? To be sure Hamilton did not fit the mold in which career officers were cast. It is also worth remembering that Hamilton was a popular figure in Liberal circles. He had stood by the government during the prewar controversial issues, particularly in 1910 when he had made use of his gifted pen to state the case against conscription. These considerations may have overborne the view that Hamilton had "too much feather in his brain."

Hamilton had been placed in charge of the home army (known as the Central Force) in August 1914 and was working at the Horse Guards when he received word early on 12 March to report to the Secretary of War. Hamilton mistakenly claimed in his book that he had no prior knowledge that he would be sent to the Dardanelles.[69] As we have already seen, he knew about it when he engaged in a discussion with Violet Asquith a week or so earlier, plus he admitted in a letter to Churchill on 10 March that he had just seen Kitchener who "told me he intends me to go to the Dardanelles," lamenting that as yet he had "no instructions" and "no Staff."[70] To be exact all that really remained for him was to receive formal notification of his new appointment.

Hamilton arrived at Kitchener's office around 10 am, opened the door and walked up to his desk and bid him "good morning." Kitchener looked up, dispensed with preliminaries and said tersely: "We are sending a military force to support the Fleet now at the Dardanelles and you are to have Command."[71] Hamilton, referring to their period together in South Africa, answered, "we have run this sort of thing before Lord Kitchener," and he proceeded to thank him warmly for placing faith in his leadership. In the course of the interview, Hamilton recalled that Kitchener repeated on several occasions the nature of his assignment:

> We soldiers are to understand we are string Number 2. The sailors are sure they can force the Dardanelles on their own and the whole enterprise has been framed on that basis: we are to lie low and to bear in mind the Cabinet does not want to hear anything of the Army till it [navy] sails through the Straits. But if the Admiral fails, then we will have to go in.[72]

When Kitchener paused briefly, Hamilton took the opportunity to asked about his staff. He expressed a strong desire to have as his chief of staff Major General Gerald Ellison with whom he had worked hand in glove for the last four years. Without offering an explanation, Kitchener replied that he could not take Ellison with him and substituted instead Major General Walter Braithwaite whom he described as a good officer. Hamilton knew and liked Braithwaite who had once been on his staff. As it turned out, Braithwaite gave Hamilton no reason to complain. Kitchener next identified the units at Hamilton's disposal and made it clear that the 29th Division was only on loan and must be returned as soon as its services could be spared. In

---

68   Brock and Brock (eds.), *Letters to Venetia Stanley*, p. 257.
69   Gen. Sir Ian Hamilton, *Gallipoli Diary*, vol. 1 (New York: George Doran, 1920), p. 2.
70   Hamilton to Churchill, 10 March 1915, Hamilton papers, 7/1/1.
71   Hamilton, *Gallipoli Diary*, vol. 1, p. 1.
72   Ibid., p. 8.

reply to Hamilton's request for an estimate of the enemy's strength on the Peninsula, Kitchener thought it was about 40,000.

At this point Callwell entered the room, spread a map on the table, and gave an outline of a pre-1914 Greek plan to seize the Gallipoli Peninsula. To that end, the Greeks had intended to put 150,000 men in the field but Kitchener interjected (as he had nowhere near that many troops on hand and besides there was as yet no thought of landing on the Peninsula), asserting that half that number would suffice as the Turks were busy elsewhere. Kitchener went on to say: "I hope you will not have to land at all; if you do have to land, why then the powerful fleet at your back will be the prime factor in your choice of time and place."[73] Kitchener brought in Braithwaite who was delighted to again serve under Hamilton. Towards the end of the meeting Braithwaite suggested that it would be helpful if they could have a few planes and pilots to which Kitchener answered rather brusquely that he had none to offer.

As Kitchener had requested, Hamilton returned to the War Office the following day for his final briefing. Kitchener went over much the same ground before handing Hamilton a list of instructions, above which was inscribed "Expeditionary Force to Constantinople." It troubled Hamilton who apparently was superstitious: "I said to Lord Kitchener that being a Scotsman I did not think it was lucky and I asked him if he could not cut out the word "Constantinople" until we got it. He put his pen through it and wrote Mediterranean instead, so that it was a Mediterranean Expeditionary Force."[74]

Hamilton cast a glance at his instructions, some of which were necessarily couched vaguely since the nature of his task was still uncertain: (1) The army was not to engage in land operations until the fleet had exhausted every expedient to get through alone. (2) Before carrying out any serious landing, Hamilton was to await the assembly of all his forces to make certain that their full weight could be thrown into the battle. Kitchener wanted to ensure that the great benefits of tactical surprise would not be discarded by premature use of inadequate forces. (3) Once the army was committed to action, there could be no thought of abandoning the enterprise. It would demand time, patience and close cooperation between army and naval commanders. The essential point was to avoid any check which would jeopardize the chances of strategic and political success. Although there was a lack of reliable information, it was to be presumed that Gallipoli was held in strength and that the Kalid Bahr Plateau had been fortified and armed for a strong-willed resistance. Thus while minor operations might currently become necessary to clear or destroy guns, permanent garrison of the Peninsula was to be avoided. (4) Similarly the military occupation of the Asian shore was "to be strongly deprecated." On this matter Kitchener left no room for discretion. He had no wish to become involved in an extensive campaign in Asia which he felt would place an unjustifiable strain on the country's resources.

The remaining directives referred to events following the fleet's entry into the Sea of Marmora and there were instances in which it would be left up to Hamilton to decide the next move. It was taken for granted that the allied ships would scatter the Turkish navy after which the opening of the Bosporous would allow passage of the Russian corps. Thereupon the Russians would join the Anglo-French force which had been transported close to Constantinople and combined plans of operations against the Turkish army would then be undertaken with the view

---

73 Ibid., p. 6.
74 Hamilton testimony, 13 October 1916, Dardanelles Commission Report, CAB 19/33.

to compel its defeat or surrender. Constantinople was expected to surrender on the approach of the fleet and there were guidelines pertaining to its occupation.[75]

Hamilton knew practically nothing about the Dardanelles. According to his later testimony to the Dardanelles Commission, all that the War Office turned over to him in the way of preparation were a 1912 *Handbook on the Turkish Army*, two guide books of dubious value and an outdated map of Gallipoli. His memory may have failed him when he testified before the Dardanelles Commission and later published his diary, but it is more likely that he deliberately misrepresented the extent of the intelligence he received so as to lessen the damage done to his reputation. Both Callwell who bristled at the inference that his department had been neglectful – and in fact had requested to be interviewed a second time by the Dardanelles Commission to set the record straight – as well as a meticulously researched and fairly recent study entitled *Grasping Gallipoli* have challenged Hamilton's claim.[76] It is apparent that Hamilton received more help than he admitted. At the time of his briefing the material he was provided covered details about the Turkish army as well as the topography and fixed defences of Gallipoli and the Dardanelles. Besides the *Handbook of the Turkish Army*, there were two official handbooks, the 1909 *Report on the Defences of Constantinople* and the 1913 *Manual of Combined Naval and Military Operations*, in addition to an Admiralty report on the defences of the Dardanelles entitled *Turkey Coast Defences May 1908*.

Callwell also gave Hamilton an oral summary of the Greek general staff's plan for an attack on Gallipoli. Similarly he went over the War Office general staff's memorandum of 1906 which, as we examined earlier, concluded that the attempt to land an army on the Gallipoli Peninsula was too hazardous to be recommended.[77] Hamilton was not shown a copy because at the time none could be found in the War Office. Finally Callwell handed over to Hamilton and Braithwaite what maps he found in the War Office, though he later admitted they were inaccurate.

It has been alleged by both James and Hickey, among others, that Lieutenant Colonel Frederick Cunliffe-Owen, the military attaché in Constantinople from the end of 1913 until the outbreak of war, had sent to the War Office detailed and accurate reports on the Dardanelles defences. Cunliffe-Owen on his own initiative had sailed up and down the Dardanelles several times and also surveyed much of the ground of Gallipoli in the spring of 1914, providing data regarding possible landing places, sites of fixed batteries, topography of the Peninsula, minefields and the arrival of new armaments. A number of writers of the campaign could not understand why the results of Cunliffe-Owen's research were not turned over to Hamilton.[78] The answer is simple. In the first place much of the information submitted by the former military attaché was known to the War Office – such as the fixed guns along the Straits – and turned over to Hamilton. On the other hand the reports affecting the Ottoman army and defensive arrangements on Gallipoli would have been irrelevant after November 1914. They would not have included the build-up of fortifications in the interior of Gallipoli; obstacles on the beaches which began after November 1914; and the tactical deployment of Turkish regiments, most of which did not arrive on the Peninsula until mid-autumn.

75 Ibid. See also Hamilton, *Happy Warrior*, pp. 279-81.
76 Callwell, *Experiences*, pp. 94-96; Peter Chasseaud and Peter Doyle, *Grasping Gallipoli: Terrain, Maps and Failure at the Dardanelles 1915* (Staplehurst: Spellmont, 2005), pp. 102-5.
77 Chasseaud and Doyle, ibid., p. 104.
78 James, *Gallipoli*, pp. 53-54; Michael Hickey, *Gallipoli* (London: John Murray, 1995), pp. 28-30.

By the time Hamilton completed his military plan early in April he had received much inside information about the Turks. From constant aerial observation and patrolling ships he had formed a good picture of Ottoman beach defences; as well as the nature of the terrain, location of Turkish front-line units and reserve camps on the Peninsula. In short there was nothing in Cunliffe-Owen's observations before the war that would have assisted Hamilton at the operational or tactical level.[79]

Kitchener left it up to Hamilton to work out a plan for a military landing if necessary, instead of turning to the general staff which normally attended to such tasks. The Dardanelles Commission was anxious to know the reason Kitchener had failed to direct the general staff to supply Hamilton with a preliminary plan of operation as mandated under *Field Service Regulations*. Questioned by the commissioners in the fall of 1916 to justify the omission, Callwell maintained that it would have served no purpose. He pointed out that the general staff did not know the location of the Turks forces on the Peninsula or the nature and site of their defensive works. Such indispensable information, he insisted, could only be gleaned by the commander on the spot.[80] Callwell offered another interesting reason in his postwar volume:

> A single "preliminary scheme of operations" would have been of little service to the C-in-C of "Medforce"– it must have been based on the mistaken assumption (which held good when he started) that the fleet would force the Straits, and it would consequently have concerned itself with undertakings totally different from those which, in the event, Sir Ian had to carry out. If the army was to derive any benefit from projects elaborated in the War Office, there must have been a second "preliminary scheme of operations" based on the assumption that the fleet was going to fail. What profit is there in a plan of campaign that dictates procedure to be followed after the first great clash of arms?[81]

There was a vital issue that Kitchener did not cover because it also involved the Admiralty over which he had no jurisdiction. Left undefined was the relationship between Hamilton and the person with whom he was expected to work closely, the naval commander. There existed no central mechanism in Whitehall to coordinate the activities of the two services. Thus the army and navy operated as separate entities, often without reference to one another. The question of who should command a combined operation in case one become necessary was never addressed.

The interview lasted until late in the afternoon and as it was about to end Kitchener stressed that if large-scale operations were unavoidable, Hamilton was not to press forward until the arrival of the 29th Division and he was to exercise caution and restrain at every stage. This meant that Hamilton, other than engage in minor action, would be unable to support the fleet in any major fighting for about a month. Kitchener's parting words to Hamilton, as he picked up his cap and turned to leave, were: "If the Fleet gets through, Constantinople will fall of itself and you will have won, not a battle, but the war."[82]

79 The information was supplied to me by Lieut. Col. Erickson and confirmed by Dr. Mesut Uyar, also an expert on the Ottoman army.
80 Callwell testimony, 12 October 1916, Dardanelles Commission Report, CAB 19/33.
81 Callwell, *Experiences*, p. 95n.
82 Hamilton, *Gallipoli Diary*, vol. 1, p. 16.

Churchill, however, was unwilling to wait until Hamilton's forces were ready for action. His mood swings at this time suggested that he nursed doubts that the fleet alone could get past the defences at The Narrows without military assistance. Before Hamilton left for the Dardanelles, Churchill tried to persuade him to ignore Kitchener's instructions and to employ the 40,000 troops that would soon be at his disposal for a landing to coincide with the impending naval attack. Churchill in effect was applying pressure on Hamilton to effect a landing before he would have been ready. No less serious he was asking Hamilton to commit an act of insubordination, which was outrageous by any measure, not to mention that it was the sort of behavior that he would never have tolerated from any of his senior Admirals. But Hamilton was understandably cool to the proposal, saying that he was bound to follow Kitchener's instructions. Churchill conveniently omits the incident from his book, but Hamilton revealed it to Hankey who noted in his diary: "Sir Ian told me he is in an embarrassing position as Churchill wants him to try to rush Straits by a *coup de main* with such troops as are available in the Levant (30,000 Australasians and 10,000 Naval Division)."[83]

Kitchener had made his position clear from the outset. He wanted to avoid confronting the estimated 40,000 Turks occupying strong defensive positions on the Peninsula and assumed they would retreat after the navy had blasted a way through the Straits. Given that he was responsible for overseeing the war as a whole, not just a campaign, he could not overlook the possibility that once the army landed on Gallipoli it might become bogged down which would necessitate sending reinforcements at the expense of fronts either in Egypt or in France. Churchill's attention focused only on the Dardanelles and he kept changing the conditions under which the operation should be carried out, from an attack by the navy alone to one calling for troops, first to reap the fruits of victory, then possibly to assist the fleet get through The Narrows. The War Office and Admiralty were following different paths. The fog that was rapidly enveloping the naval-led undertaking should have raised a red flag.

Of all the members of the War Council, only Hankey was concerned about the nature of the ongoing enterprise which had started out as a strictly naval concern and was now on the verge of morphing into a combined operation. As a former marine and intelligence officer, he worried about the possibility of a military landing when the chance of surprise had been lost and the Turks afforded several extra months to strengthen their defensive works on the Peninsula. He urged that before the War Council embarked on a new commitment, it ought to ensure that preparations had been thoroughly worked out.[84] His warning failed to excite Asquith and the other members of the War Council who looked to Kitchener to deal with whatever arrangements were necessary before any major military action commenced. At the time the members of the War Council seemed more interested in working out a formula with their Entente partners to partition the Ottoman Empire.

The Russian government had initially approached its western allies to formally acknowledge the nation's right to annex Constantinople and the Straits, an age-long dream, at the end of the war. Of course Petrograd would not have needed to force the issue if it had fulfill its pledge to send troops to the scene. The British had a long tradition of opposing the incorporation of the Dardanelles into Russia's Empire as presenting a threatening naval base, but attitudes do

---

83   Hankey also included Hamilton's disclosure in his book, *Supreme Command*, vol. 1, p. 290.
84   Ibid., pp. 291-95.

not always remain constant. Hankey discovered an investigation conducted by the Admiralty in 1903 which concluded that Russia's possession of Constantinople and the Straits would not fundamentally alter the strategic position in the Mediterranean.[85]

The Russian note laying down its territorial claims was circulated to the cabinet ministers on the 8th and discussed at their meeting the following day and again in the War Council on the 10th. Kitchener and Churchill stated that it was not in Britain's interest, either on military or naval grounds, to resist Russia's ambitions. The sentiment among the other ministers was no different and the decision was taken to accept Russia's proposals, providing Britain and France received similar assurances with regard to their own territorial aspirations.

Attention was next directed at considering Britain's share of the Ottoman spoils. The matter gave rise to much rambling speculation at the meeting of the War Council on the 10th and the next one nine days later. Kitchener pressed for the annexation of Mesopotamia with Alexandretta as its corridor to the Mediterranean in order to counter any postwar threat Russia and France might pose to British interests in the Mediterranean. Lloyd George thought that the expediency of occupying Alexandretta could lead to friction with the French and suggested Palestine as an alternative. Kitchener considered Palestine to be of no value whatsoever and saw no reason why the French should object to Britain's occupation of Alexandretta if it was put to them in the right way. After all, he insisted, the port was beyond the French sphere of interest in Syria. Support for Kitchener came from both Churchill and Fisher. The Admiralty was interested in building a naval base at Alexandretta and exploiting the rich oil fields of Mesopotamia. The India Office was opposed to the possession of Alexandretta but took a different view in regard to Mesopotamia on account of its vast agricultural and large unsettled areas which could serve as an outlet for the surplus population of India. Given the wide differences among the cabinet ministers, it was decided to postpone further discussions to determine the country's territorial aspirations in Asiatic Turkey.[86]

It is strange that no one in the Asquith administration, in particular Churchill and Kitchener, saw the contradiction between the postwar division of Ottoman lands and the expected submissive attitude of the new regime in Constantinople following the overthrow of the previous one. If a revolution had occurred, it is difficult to see how any incoming government, no matter how much it desired peace, could have acquiesce in the surrender of most of Turkey's Empire and survived. It is obvious that that the members of the Asquith government wore blinkers as they were so dazzled by prospect of acquiring Ottoman territory that they could not see the wider picture. There was another indispensable matter they apparently overlooked. They first had to defeat Turkey.

---

85 Ibid., pp. 289-90; Asquith to George V, 9 March 1915, CAB 41/36/9.
86 Minutes of the War Council, 10 and 19 March 1915, CAB 42/2/5 and CAB 42/2/14; Cassar, *Kitchener's War*, pp. 147-50; and *Asquith*, pp. 74-76.

4

From the Navy to the Army

By the second week in March, naval progress in the Dardanelles had stalled. During the opening stages the battleships, lying stationary in the open sea and firing beyond the effective range of land defences, had been able to overcome the outer forts with comparative ease. It was a different matter when they turned their attention to the intermediate forts and were compelled to operate inside the reduced width of the channel. As they came within the reach of the enemy's guns they were forced to keep moving which substantially reduced their chances of silencing the forts. Even more disconcerting was the inability of the ships to locate the mobile howitzers protecting the vital minefields. Trawlers sent to clear a path through the minefields were exposed to deadly fire, not only during the daylight hours but also at night under the glaring rays of searchlights. The minesweepers had no armour and were manned by civilian crews who would turn back each time the enemy's fire became too intense. As long as the minefields remained intact, passage through the Straits was effectively blocked.

By now Churchill had become convinced that military cooperation was essential to ensure that the fleet successfully achieved its objective. Since Churchill had failed to win over Hamilton to his idea of an immediate *coup de main*, he approached Kitchener directly, requesting a landing on the Peninsula with what troops were available as soon as possible. Kitchener gave Churchill no reason to think that he would change his mind when he replied on 13 March:

> In answer to your question, unless it is found that our estimate of the Ottoman strength on the Gallipoli Peninsula is exaggerated and the position on the Kilid Bahr Plateau less strong than anticipated, no operations on a large scale should be attempted until the 29th Division has arrived and is ready to take part in what is likely to prove a difficult undertaking, in which severe fighting must be anticipated.[1]

The issue of securing troops to assist the fleet was momentarily pushed into the background by a strange episode that was unfolding simultaneously. It all started in January 1915 when the Director of Naval Intelligence, Captain William Reginald Hall, alerted that a powerful section of Turkish opinion was anxious to break with Germany, sent two agents, to the Greek town of

---

1   Kitchener to Churchill, 13 March 1915, Churchill papers, CHAR 13/54/85.

Dedeagach to negotiate a peace treaty with a representative of Talaat Bey, the Minister of the Interior in the Young Turk government. Hall requested that his agents offer the Turks the sum of £3,000,000, an additional million if deemed necessary, in exchange for withdrawing from the war, observing strict neutrality and opening the Dardanelles to Allied shipping. Hall had acted entirely on his own initiative without informing anyone in the War Council, not even Churchill or Fisher. While the negotiations were going on, civilian codebreakers in Room 40, the Admiralty's cryptanalytic bureau, deciphered a message from Berlin to a German officer overseeing Ottoman defences on the evening of the 13th, implying that the Turkish supply of ammunition was running low. Given the importance of the telegram, Hall took it at once to Fisher and found him in Churchill's office. Both men were naturally very excited over the communication from which they surmised that the Turks were experiencing a serious shortage of ammunition.[2] Churchill asked Hall whether as part of his activities he had people in touch with authorities in Constantinople. Thereupon Hall broke his silence and remarked that he had authorized payment of as high as £4,000,000 to the Turks in exchange for a peaceful settlement. Fisher and Churchill were incredulous when Hall explained that he had acted on his own without informing anyone. With both Fisher and Churchill captivated by the prospect of an immediate and decisive naval victory, Hall was ordered to break off the negotiations. Hall did what he was told, deeply regretting that all the intelligence work had been in vain.[3]

Besides Churchill and Fisher at least two other members of the War Council were aware of the negotiations before they were terminated. One was Hankey and in his diary entry on 4 March indicated that he had been tipped off by Hall who was a close friend.[4] The other was Kitchener and the source of his information is a mystery. Kitchener evidently told Callwell who did not elaborate when he appeared before the Dardanelles Commission. It seems that Kitchener thought there was a good chance the war with Turkey would be over before serious fighting occurred on the Peninsula. Unfortunately the Dardanelles Commission did not follow up with an inquest after Callwell declared: "There was a certain amount of negotiations going on with certain Turks whom Lord Kitchener knew personally and knew about."[5]

At the Admiralty, Churchill and Fisher, declining to wait any longer to try to convince Kitchener to provide large scale military help, insisted that Carden immediately adopt more vigorous sustained action.[6] Under pressure, Carden went along and decided to shift his step-by-step approach to an all-out assault which he speculated would be carried out around 17 March. A day later (16 March) Carden, who was becoming increasingly pessimistic about the ability of the fleet to penetrate into the Sea of Marmara, suffered a nervous breakdown and resigned his post. By all accounts he had, to quote A.J. Marder, "imparted no vigour to the operations and

---

2   Gilbert's account in *Winston S. Churchill*, vol. 3, pp. 357-58, is confusing as it claims that the three way discussion occurred on 19 March, contradicting Hall who listed 13 March as the date of the meeting. I am at a loss to understand this vital discrepancy, not to mention that the naval attack had taken place a day earlier.
3   For details of the incident see Hall's unpublished memoirs, Hall papers, 3/5; Admiral Sir William James, *The Eyes of the Navy: A Biographical Study of Admiral Sir Reginald Hall* (London: Methuen, 1955), pp. 62-64; Patrick Beesly, *Room 40: British Naval Intelligence 1914-1918* (New York: Harcourt Brace Jovanovich, 1982), pp. 80-82.
4   Roskill, *Hankey*, vol. 1, p. 159.
5   Callwell testimony, 12 October 1916, Dardanelles Commission Report, CAB 19/33.
6   Bell, *Churchill*, pp. 129-30.

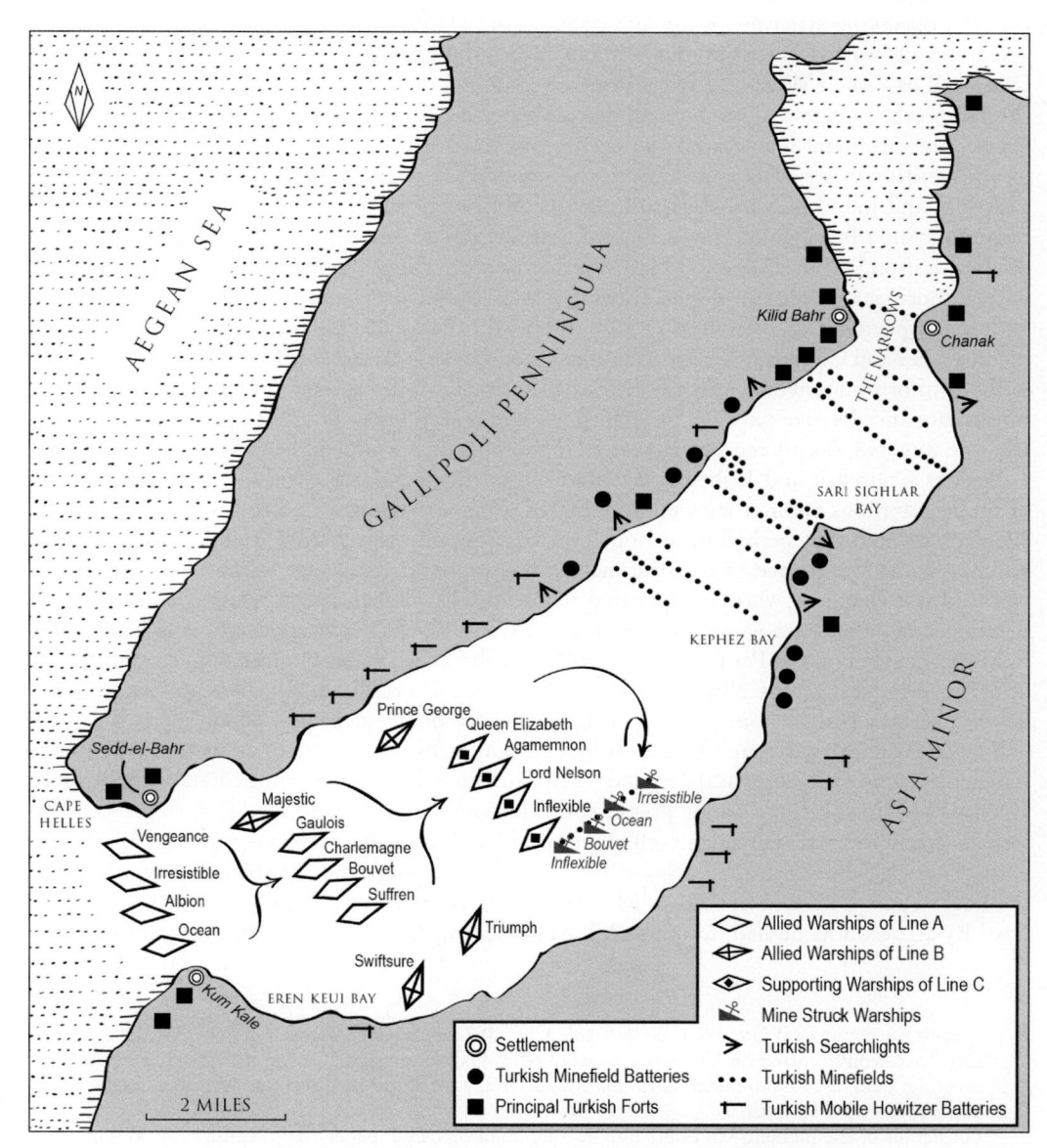

Map 3 The Allied Naval Attack at the Dardanelles, 18 March 1915.

a change was overdue."[7] Churchill at once appointed Vice Admiral John de Robeck, Carden's second-in-command, to take charge after receiving assurances that he approved of the existing naval plan. The change in command had minimal impact, pushing the start of the naval attack back by only one day. De Robeck was confident that he could take out the forts but he was worried about the mobile howitzers which would make clearing the minefield an exacting task. Still he thought that he could force a passage through the Straits without the army's help. Thus on 18 March he deployed his fleet and around 11.30 am gave the signal to start the action.

As the fleet moved steadily up the Straits, enemy batteries responded with a heavy and relatively accurate fire but without causing serious damage. The ships on the other hand made good progress and at 1.45 pm, when most of the enemy's guns fell silent, de Robeck called for the sweepers to begin their approach to the Kepez minefield. Although protected by two warships they were greeted by such murderous fire from the concealed guns that they turned and fled. More bad luck followed. As the French squadron had finished its run and turned into Eren Keui Bay to exit the Straits, the *Bouvet* was rocked by a violent explosion a little before 2 pm. Inside of two minutes the old French warship heeled over, capsized and vanished with almost all of its 600-man crew. Action was momentarily renewed with both battleships and forts intensifying their fire. Near the spot where the Bouvet had gone down, the *Inflexible* reported that it had hit a mine and, while remaining afloat, limped out of the Straits towards Tenedos. Several minutes later the *Irresistible* suffered a similar fate and drifted in the direction of the Asiatic shore. In each case the cause of the disaster was not known for sure. The sea had been checked by both minesweepers and sea planes and the only explanation was that the Turks had fired torpedoes from undetected tubes across the Straits, or released floating mines down the rapid current. It was not revealed until after the war that during the night of 7/8 March a small Turkish steamer had laid a fresh row of mines, not across the Straits as was customary, but parallel to the shore in Eren Keui Bay. The line remained undetected because earlier the area had been thoroughly swept.[8]

The unexpectedly high cost incurred and the uncertainty of what had caused the damage, induced de Robeck to break off the engagement. Now the *Ocean*, in an attempt to assist the *Irresistible* also struck a mine and both ships foundered in the night. Out of 18 battleships, three had been sunk and three disabled.

The naval offensive had been an unmitigated disaster as the navy's heavy losses had not been counterbalanced by any serious damage to Turkish defences. Only a handful of the guns in the forts had been put out of commission and neither the mobile howitzers nor the Kepez minefield had been touched. In the War Council on the 19th, Churchill read out the telegrams from de Robeck but thought it was impossible to form an opinion until he had received more reports. There was no panic as it was assumed that during the attack a few ships would be lost. The War Council agreed with Churchill's suggestion that he instruct the Admiral to use his discretion on whether to continue the naval operation.

Given the floor, Kitchener gave a brief survey of the army's ongoing preparations, in addition to revealing, on the basis of the available evidence, the disposition of Turkish defences which

---

7   Marder, *From the Dreadnought*, vol. 2, p. 244.
8   A fuller account of the naval attack from the British side is available in such works as Julian S. Corbett, *Naval Operations*, vol. 2, pp. 216-23; Victor Rudenno, *Gallipoli: Attack from the Sea* (New Haven: Yale University Press, 2008), pp. 49-52; and Marder, *From the Dreadnought*, vol. 2, pp. 245-49.

"appeared to have been made with German thoroughness." Asquith inquired if a general plan and a scheme for disembarkation had been worked out. Kitchener replied that the War Office had considered the question but lacked the information to devise a detailed invasion scheme. He added that this would have to be done by Ian Hamilton and his staff in concert with the naval commander.[9] According to Hankey, there was not a single dissenting voice against employing the army if it became a matter of upholding the nation's honour.[10] Sir Lewis Harcourt, the Colonial Secretary, and a new member of the War Council, wrote in his notes: "We shall push on with the Dardanelles operation at almost any cost."[11]

With his career on the line, Churchill was understandably despondent after the momentary suspension of the naval assault. Esher who spoke with the First Lord on 20 March has the following passage in his War Journals: "Winston is very excited and 'jumpy' about the Dardanelles; he says he will be ruined if the attack fails."[12] For the next few days Churchill focused on encouraging de Robeck to resume the naval attack at his discretion. De Robeck signaled the Admiralty that he was prepared to go forward as soon as he had made arrangements to deal with the mines.[13]

Kitchener, like Churchill, expected a fresh attack by the fleet with as little delay as possible. He was not discouraged by the result of the first day's battle which he regarded only as a temporary check. He remained reasonably confident that the forcing of the Straits by ship alone was practical and anticipated that the outcome would be different the next time an attempt was made. Still his optimism ran counter to the impression formed by Hamilton who had arrived at Lemnos with his staff on the 17th.

The next morning Hamilton boarded a naval vessel to catch a glimpse of the Gallipoli landscape, travelling up the west coast where he halted briefly to survey the Bulair position before heading back south to Cape Helles. Although Hamilton's reconnaissance was cursory, in extended low lying stretches between hilly terrain, he was struck by the plethora of freshly dug trenches, redoubts and entanglements, in addition to rows of barbed wire strung up on the beaches. When he rounded Cape Helles, he witnessed part of the navy's unsuccessful attack on the Straits. Returning to Lemnos, the initial impression of his investigation, as he would convey to Kitchener, was that the Gallipoli Peninsula would be a "much tougher nut to crack than it did over the map."[14] Hamilton was more specific in his next cable to the War Office on the 19th. In his prelude he maintained that his views were shaped by what he had seen personally, not on any official report. He opened by saying that he was most reluctantly driven to the conclusion that the Straits were not likely to be forced by battleships as at one time seemed probable. If the Army was to cooperate, he continued, it must take the form of a deliberate and progressive advance by his whole force rather than mere landings of small parties to destroy forts as previously envisaged.[15]

9 Minutes of the War Council, 19 March 1915, CAB 42/2/14.
10 Hankey, *Supreme Command*, vol. 1, p. 293.
11 Harcourt notes, entry for 19 March 1915, Harcourt papers, AS. Eng. c. 8270.
12 Esher War Journals, entry for 20 March 1915, Esher papers.
13 Churchill, *World Crisis*, vol. 2, pp. 235-36.
14 Hamilton, *Gallipoli Diary*, vol. 1, p. 27.
15 Hamilton to Kitchener, 19 March 1915, CAB 19/31.

Kitchener replied on the same day: "You know my views that the Dardanelles passage must be forced, and if large military operations on the Gallipoli Peninsula by your troops are necessary to clear the way, these operations must be undertaken after careful consideration of the local defences and must be carried through."[16] The telegram was worded carelessly and could not have reflected his accurate thinking at the time. Kitchener's often-repeated condition for a landing in force (that is until the fleet had exhausted every effort to get through) was inconsistent with his cable in which he gave Hamilton the discretion to undertake extensive operations on the Peninsula. Bearing in mind that there was as yet no thought at the Admiralty of abandoning the naval attack on the Straits. That said, it is difficult to see how Hamilton could have interpreted Kitchener's order any other way than he did. Hamilton answered on the 20th that he understood Kitchener's "views completely."[17] Notwithstanding that Hamilton was convinced that a change in strategy was essential, he claimed that the initiative should come from the sailors.

De Robeck had been shaken by the losses on 18 March, but as we have noted, he gave every indication that he was ready to renew the naval offensive at the earliest opportunity. Nevertheless that mood of resolution disappeared within forty-eight hours. He began to have second thoughts after a meeting with Rear Admiral R. E. Wemyss (commandant of the base at Lemnos) who had come to accept that some form of military intervention was necessary to deal with the mobile howitzers.[18] Probably the most compelling factor was de Robeck's discovery on the evening of the 21st that Hamilton's new instructions no longer confined him simply to mopping-up action after the fleet had forced a passage but authorized him to descend with his full force upon the Peninsula. De Robeck had the option of taking the easy way out and abdicating responsibility to the army or staking his career on a high risk gamble. De Robeck had no difficulty reaching a decision, announcing at a conference held with Hamilton and Birdwood on board the *Queen Elizabeth* on the 22nd that he could not get through without the support of the army.[19] Of course Hamilton and Birdwood were of the same mind and there was no further discussion on the subject.[20]

Hamilton told both Birdwood and de Robeck that he would not be able to act earlier than 14 April, which meant a delay of three weeks. Hamilton considered postponement of the combined operations unfortunate but unavoidable. It must be remembered that when the troops left England and Egypt their role was still undefined. Consequently the ships were loaded without due regard to the army's tactical requirements on arrival. Units were split up; wagons were separated from their horses; guns were in one ship, ammunition in another and fuses at the bottom

16 Kitchener to Hamilton, 19 March 1915, ibid.
17 Hamilton to Kitchener, 20 March 1915, ibid.
18 James, *Gallipoli*, p. 66.
19 Marder, *From the Dreadnought*, vol. 2, pp. 251-52; Bell, *Churchill*, pp. 143-44; Aspinall-Oglander, *Gallipoli*, vol. 1, p. 99.
20 What occurred during the brief discussion on the subject is not clear. Hamilton insisted that he and his staff had agreed before the meeting that "whatever we landsman might think, we must leave the seamen to settle their own job," but the moment they sat down de Robeck announced that he could not get through without the support of the army. De Robeck, however, claimed in an appreciation sent to the Admiralty that Hamilton's reasoned argument in favour of a joint operation had caused him to change his mind. The slight variation in the two accounts is inconsequential. De Robeck was already aware of Hamilton's views. Hamilton, *Gallipoli Diary*, vol. 1, p. 41; Churchill, *World Crisis*, vol. 2, pp. 249-52.

of the hold of a third. All the vessels had to be emptied and reloaded before the troops landed under fire. As it was impossible to do the reshuffling at Mudros owing to inadequate facilities and heavy gales, Hamilton decided to transfer the base of the expedition to the Egyptian port of Alexandria.[21]

On 23 March Hamilton telegraphed the War Office that both he and de Robeck were convinced that it would be necessary to use his whole force to enable the fleet to force the Dardanelles. The success of his scheme would depend on the thoroughness of his preparations and for that reason he desired to organize the expedition at a convenient base like Alexandria.[22]

While this was going on, de Robeck wired Churchill of his change of plans and added that the army would not be ready to land before the middle of April. Churchill read the dispatch with stunned disbelief. The Admiral's decision ran counter to all his conviction and hopes. He immediately drew up a reply, in which he pointed out that a delay would attract German submarines to the area; impose a heavy cost on army operations which, even if effective, would not resolve the danger from mines. That being the case, he ordered de Robeck to make the necessary preparations to resume the naval attack at the earliest favourable hour.[23] The telegram was never sent. Fisher, backed by the Admiralty War Group, argued vehemently that the final decision must rest with the commander on the spot. As we have already seen none of the senior admirals had shown much enthusiasm for the naval operation and de Robeck's position gave them the excuse they needed to stand up to Churchill. The First Lord argued with all his passion to convince them of the merits of his case but to no avail. "For the first time since the war began," he admitted, "high words were used around the octagonal table." Churchill did not give up easily and once rebuffed, he appealed to Asquith and Kitchener, hoping that their support might be enough to induce Fisher and the other admirals to reconsider.[24]

Churchill was encouraged by the response from both men. The Prime Minister told Venetia Stanley he was convinced that "the Navy ought to make another big push so soon as the weather clears." He reasoned that if "they wait & wait, until the army is fully prepared, they may fall into a spell of bad weather, & (what is worse) find that submarines, Austrian or German, have arrived on the scene."[25] Asquith had not altered his opinion when he wrote his memoirs more than a decade later: "Personally I was anxious, as I believe was Mr. Churchill, that the naval attack should be pushed. I thought at the time, and am still disposed to think, that it offered the best prospect for the prompt success of the expedition."[26]

Kitchener agreed with Churchill and Asquith that another attack, pressed with determination, would have a good chance of getting through the heavily defended Straits. He assumed that the army would be ready for action in about a week and that in the interim de Robeck should keep up naval pressure to deny the Turks a respite and to identify any weakness in their defences. To his dismay, however, he learned from the Admiralty that Hamilton would not be ready to undertake military operations any sooner than 14 April. After attending a cabinet

21 Aspinall-Oglander, *Gallipoli*, vol. 1, pp. 116-17.
22 Hamilton to Kitchener, 23 March 1915, CAB 19/31.
23 Churchill, *World Crisis*, vol. 2, pp. 237-39.
24 Bell, *Churchill*, p. 147; Marder, *From the Dreadnought*, vol. 2, pp. 254-55.
25 Brock and Brock (eds.), *Letters to Venetia Stanley*, p. 501. Asquith expressed similar sentiments in a letter to his confidante two days later, p. 506.
26 Asquith, *Memories*, vol. 2, p. 90.

meeting on the 23rd, he sent Hamilton the following telegram: "I am informed you consider the 14th April as about date for commencing military operations if fleet have not forced the Dardanelles by then. I think you had better know at once that I consider any such postponement as far too long, and should like to know how soon you will act on shore."[27] Hamilton replied immediately, reminding Kitchener that among his instructions was an entry prohibiting him from carrying out any major operation until his army was fully assembled.[28] Kitchener countered with another telegram suggesting to Hamilton that he no longer had to wait for the arrival of the 29th Division before landing on Gallipoli with the men he already had on hand. He considered it important for the ships in the interim to continue to both bombard enemy defences and try to rush through the Straits. He remained confident that once the ships broke into the Sea of Marmara, "the Gallipoli military position ceases to be of importance."[29] Kitchener was worried about allowing the Turks a breathing space and two days later (25 March) drafted a telegram impressing upon Hamilton to avoid undue delays:

> I have not changed my original view, but your fixing a date rather upsets me. I can, I know, implicitly trust you not to waste time, and I have no wish in any way to rush the situation so long as it is being pushed by you and the Admiral with all dispatch as to a final successful conclusion.[30]

Kitchener's telegrams during this period show that he persisted in clinging to the hope that sustained naval pressure might yet yield the benefits initially anticipated and spare the army the ordeal of storming the Peninsula. Hamilton telegraphed de Robeck on 30 March to tell him that Kitchener had not abandoned thoughts of a naval victory and encouraged him to continue to bombard the forts:

> War Office still seems to cherish the hope that you may break through without landing troops. Therefore as regards yourself I think wisest procedure will be to push on systematically though not recklessly in attack on Forts. It is always possible that opposition may suddenly crumble up.[31]

De Robeck had assured Churchill on 25 March that even within prescribed limits he would resume a "vigorous offensive" until the army was ready for a combined assault. The means he propose to adopt included sustained and determined sweeping operations, extensive reconnaissance flights to help naval gunfire locate and destroy mobile howitzers and also other guns so as to permit the *Queen Elizabeth* to carry out an indirect attack on the Chanak forts.[32] However, de Robeck, contrary to his pledge, was determined to hold his ships back until after the army had captured the Peninsula. He was convinced that naval gunfire alone was incapable of dominating the forts or knocking out the hidden guns which inhibited trawlers from clearing the minefield.

27 Kitchener to Hamilton, 23 March 1915, CAB 19/31.
28 Hamilton to Kitchener, 23 March 1915, ibid.
29 Kitchener to Hamilton (copy of draft), 23 March 1915, Churchill papers, CHAR 36/3.
30 Kitchener to Hamilton, 25 March 1915, CAB 19/31.
31 Cited in Churchill, *World Crisis*, vol. 2, pp. 252-53.
32 Gilbert, *Winston S. Churchill*, vol. 3, p. 369.

After 23 March both de Robeck and the Admiralty War Group held out against the intense pressure exerted by the First Lord. Churchill did not possess the authority to overrule the Admirals, sack de Robeck and appoint a new commander who would do his bidding. In the face of the senior sailors' unwavering defiance, the devastated First Lord was ultimately compelled to accept that the navy's lead in attacking the Dardanelles defences was over.[33] It has become the trend among the campaign writers in recent years to hold the two commanders on the spot, de Robeck and Hamilton, as primarily responsible for converting the naval initiative into essentially an army operation.[34] The only thing that can be attributed to Hamilton and de Robeck is that their action ended the naval operation. It was the War Council which on two occasions, 24 February and 19 March, declared its willingness to escalate the operation if the navy was unable to get through the Straits.

Churchill was never reconciled to the decision to call off the naval offensive as he deluded himself into thinking that the fleet had given up when it was on the verge of achieving a breakthrough. He was bitter that his career and reputation had been badly damaged but seemed unconcerned at the lives that would have been lost if the navy had persisted in trying to silence the Ottoman forts. Several months later Churchill spent an evening discussing the campaign with Ellis Ashmead-Bartlett, a British war correspondent who had recently returned from Gallipoli. In the course of explaining why the naval attack "ought to have gone on" at all costs, he uttered a crass comment, one that Ashmead-Bartlett (to his credit) never revealed in print: "What does it matter if more ships were lost with their crews? The ships were old and useless and the crews mostly old reservists. They were sent out there to die, it was their duty. That is what they were mobilized for."[35]

Thus the first phase of the great adventure was over. Looking back there is no doubt that the attack on the Dardanelles by ships alone was terribly ill-conceived. The first major miscalculation was that the navy lacked the means to silence the enemy's land defences. Firing from a range of 7000 or 8000 yards, the fleet might cause structural damage on the Turkish forts but it was of little value unless the guns were put out of commission. The only way to silence individual guns was to score direct hits and that rarely happened even when naval fire was directed by seaplanes. An even greater challenge for the navy was to deal with the hidden guns. Churchill always maintained that if the naval attack had been renewed it would have succeeded because the Turkish forts had fired off most of their ammunition.[36] His case does not stand up to scrutiny. The Turkish forts appear to have had enough heavy and lighter calibre shells to hold off at least another attack on the scale of 18 March. In the final analysis the issue is irrelevant. The main barrier to the ships' entry into the Sea of Marmara was the minefield and it was not only intact but defended by hidden howitzers for which there were an ample supply of ammunition.[37]

Another serious flaw in Churchill's plan was that it ended with the ships getting through The Narrows as if it automatically followed that Ottoman resistance would collapse. Actually even if by some miracle part of the Anglo-French fleet had broken into the Sea of Marmara it

---

33 Bell, *Churchill*, pp. 148-50.
34 See for example, James, *Gallipoli*, p. 69.
35 Cited in Bell, *Churchill*, p. 191.
36 Churchill, *World Crisis*, vol. 2, ch.13.
37 Edward J. Erickson, *Gallipoli: Command Under Fire* (Oxford: Osprey, 2015), pp. 73-74; Prior, *Gallipoli*, pp. 57-58; Marder, *From the Dreadnought*, vol. 2, p. 263.

is probable that nothing dramatic would have occurred. Presumably battered, short of ammunition and fuel, the surviving ships would have had to dispose of the Turkish navy – by no means certain as it included the heavily armoured German battleship *Goeben* and its consort the light cruiser *Breslau*. It is useful to recall that Churchill's scenario envisaged a revolution occurring in the Ottoman capital and on the establishment of a friendly government. To be sure there was plenty of unrest in the city but no credible evidence exists that the Young Turk regime was in danger of being overthrown. In fact the Turkish authorities were unconcerned about a possible internal outbreak and their attention centred on making plans to defend the city at all costs. There was an exodus of women and children; trenches were dug and additional artillery moved forward for additional protection, and the state archives and gold bullion were moved to the safety of Asia Minor.[38] The statement of Liman von Sanders, the German General who commanded the Turkish army on Gallipoli, added weight to the evidence that the Turks would not have collapsed in the event the fleet had forced its way through the Dardanelles. He wrote to Churchill after the publication of *The World Crisis*, contesting some of the former First Lord's key predictions. He maintained with absolute confidence that Constantinople was thoroughly prepared to resist a possible breakthrough "as I had arranged everything myself." Nor did the General envisage an internal challenge to the regime. He wrote: "There could be no danger of a revolution… The strong bodies of troops [defending the capital] were quite reliable and in safe hands."[39] Thus if we assume that the expected surrender or overthrow of the Young Turk regime would not have occurred, Allied ships in front of Constantinople, unable to be supplied by vessels lacking armour, would have had no choice after about a fortnight but to turn back and again endure the fire from the plethora of Turkish batteries along the Straits.

A strategic plan must be evaluated on the strength of its achievement, or at least on meticulous preparation, including responses to all possible contingencies, and not on a rosy speculative premise. The objective of the naval operation was to drive Turkey to the negotiating table, weaken Germany and shorted the war. In this sense it was an utter failure. To quote Lieutenant General Ellison, "the underling idea of the whole plan was Utopian in the extreme."[40]

As the next phase of the operation unfolded, Kitchener worked closely with Hamilton to finalize plans for the impending landing on Gallipoli. While Kitchener wanted to be kept informed of what was happening and occasionally offered suggestions, at no time did he interfere with Hamilton's discretion. As he had charged Hamilton with preparing a scheme, he was anxious to know at which places he intended to disembark the main body of troops. Pouring over a report by Vice Admiral Limpus, Kitchener thought that Hamilton might benefit by his local knowledge. Accordingly he sent Hamilton a wire on 2 April:

> Limpus's report, which I have been reading … seems to point to the advisability of effecting the main landing in the neighbourhood of Cape Helles and Morto Bay, while making a feint in considerable force south of Gaba Tepe. With the possibility of landing and of commanding the ground of Sari Bair, so that the enemy, on its southern slopes, may be

---

38 Prior, *Gallipoli*, p. 250; Henry Morgenthau, *Ambassador Morgenthau's Story* (Garden City: Doubleday, Page & Co., 1919), pp. 199-200; Harry Stuermer, *Two Years in Constantinople* (London: Hodder & Stoughton, 1917), p. 85.
39 Bell, *Churchill*, p. 319.
40 Sir Gerald Ellison, *The Perils of Amateur Strategy* (London: Longmans, Green and Co., 1923), p. 66.

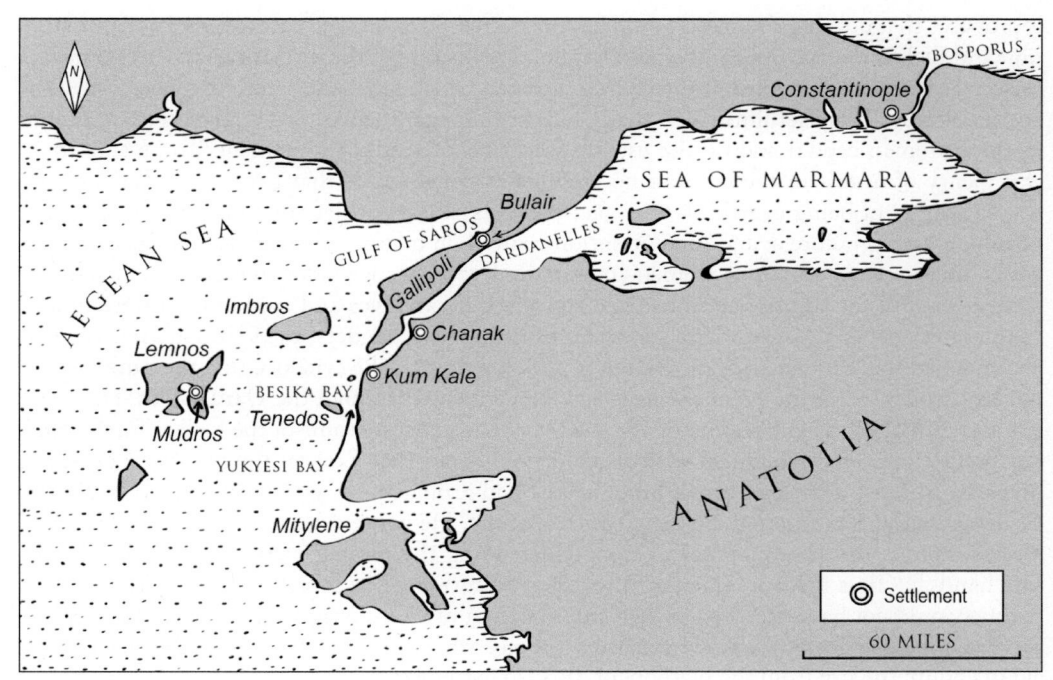

Map 4 Theatre of Operations.

prevented from supporting those on the Kalid Bahr Plateau. I assume that preparatory to destroying the forts at the Narrows, you will attack in force to occupy this plateau … I do not in the least wish to influence your judgement, formed locally, on the situation to be dealt with in the Gallipoli Peninsula, but only give you all this for what it is worth… When you have decided on your plans, I shall be glad to have a general idea of them.[41]

By the time the cable arrived, Hamilton was already in Alexandria where the cargos of all the supply ships were in the process of being unloaded, sorted out on the quays, and then reloaded, while he attended to the administrative work associated with the enterprise, including preparing a plan for a landing. Hamilton replied to Kitchener's two days later: "Reference concluding sentence there is no need to send you my general idea as you have already got it in one, even down to the details."[42]

Meanwhile on 30 March Asquith summoned Kitchener, Churchill and Hankey to 10 Downing Street for an informal meeting of the War Council. The purpose, according to Asquith, was "to go over carefully & quickly the situation, actual & prospective, at the Dardanelles." No record of the discussion exists, but Asquith in a letter to his beloved – presumably summing up Kitchener's expectations about the approaching assault on Gallipoli

---

41 Kitchener to Hamilton, 2 April 1915, CAB 19/31.
42 Hamilton to Kitchener, 4 April 1915, ibid.

– wrote: "There are risks, & it will in any event be an expensive operation, but I am sure we are right to go through with it."[43] A second such conclave occurred on 6 April for which this time Hankey took brief notes. Kitchener read out excerpts of Hamilton's telegrams, adding that he had not yet received the final plan of attack. Churchill urged that the assault be pressed home vigorously. Kitchener was presumably thinking along the same lines but he is recorded merely as saying that a landing would have to take place – which given the purpose of the meeting does not make much sense. Hankey would have preferred that the army strike elsewhere than in the Dardanelles. He observed that a landing would be extremely hazardous because of the howitzers in the ravines which intersected the Peninsula. Churchill thought otherwise and did not envisage any great difficulty.[44] All except Hankey favoured the landing to occur as soon as Hamilton was ready.

Although Kitchener was cautiously optimistic of a victory, he realized that much would depend on the result of the first attack which he wanted Hamilton to carry out with all possible strength. There is little doubt that his estimate about the quality of the Turkish soldier had evolved. Initially uncertain he had in a matter of weeks formed a dim view of the fighting attributes of the Ottoman army as a result of its series of defeats. Thereafter contrary evidence slowly accumulated which must have given him pause for concern. Kitchener's first warning came from the reports of Maxwell and Birdwood, both of whom intimated that the capture of Gallipoli, with its estimated 30,000-man garrison, supplemented by formidable defences, was far from a foregone conclusion. Kitchener had a good deal of confidence in the judgement of these former subordinates and furthermore they were backed by Colonel Maucorps, the former French military attaché in Constantinople, who warned against trying to land on the Peninsula. Then too the efficiency of the Ottoman army on Gallipoli, under the rigorous training and discipline of German officers was bound to have improved. Such thoughts may explain why he wired Maxwell on 6 April: "You should supply any troops in Egypt that can be spared, or even selected officers or men that Sir Ian Hamilton may want for Gallipoli … This telegram should be communicated by you to Sir Ian Hamilton."[45]

Kitchener's concern was confirmed when he received reports of the fighting near Basra in Mesopotamia where the British and mainly Indian forces had occupied Abadan Island, at the head of the Persian Gulf, in the opening days of the war so as to safeguard the oil works and pipeline. From there they moved inland and seized the port of Basra and by early December 1914 advanced as far north as Qurna, situated at the confluence of the Tigris and Euphrates. There was no further action in the region until the start of April 1915 when the Turks made a serious bid to recapture Basra. Strengthened in the nick of time, the British and Indian forces held off a fierce Turkish onslaught during two days of almost continuous fighting before routing them on the third day in a counterattack.[46] By all accounts the Turks had shown unexpected discipline and courage and only skilful leadership and indomitable spirit had gained the day for the British led forces. On 19 April Kitchener gave Hamilton a brief account of the fighting:

---

43   Brock and Brock (eds.), *Letters to Venetia Stanley*, p. 520.
44   Minutes of the informal War Council, 6 April 1915, CAB 42/2/17.
45   Kitchener to Maxwell, 6 April 1915, CAB 19/31.
46   A.J. Barker, *The Bastard War: The Mesopotamian Campaign of 1914-1918* (New York: Dial Press, 1967), chs. 1-2.

> The Turks are brave, well trained, and well disciplined. Their trenches were well sited [and] at the foot of a slope leading from us down to them. Their machine-guns were effectively concealed and well used. They had no idea of being shot out of their trenches, and had to be turned out by a charge of the whole line with the bayonet. If our force had not been handled with initiative and decision, and if the pluck of our troops, British and Indian, had not been of the sternest, the battle would not have been won.[47]

By now Kitchener realized that the Turks were not likely to fold unless hammered into submission and he could not even be certain in the ultimate outcome. Still he remained fairly confident that after the fighting was over, Hamilton's men would be in possession of Gallipoli. In discussing the imminent invasion with close associates he estimated that the number of casualties in the army would amount to about 5,000 or 10 percent of the fighting force.

By the 20th Hamilton's preparations were complete and the troops were back, assembled on their transports off Mudros and ready to move out. The landing was scheduled for the 23rd but delayed forty-eight hours on account of the bad weather. On the day that the operation was supposed to start, Kitchener sent Hamilton a telegram to wish him and his troops good luck.

> My best wishes to you and all your troops in carrying to a successful conclusion the operations you have before you, which will undoubtedly have a momentous effect on the war. The task they have to perform will need all the grit Britishers [sic] have never failed to show, and I am confident that your troops will victoriously clear the way for the Fleet to advance on Constantinople. When operations commence all my thoughts will be with you.[48]

Hamilton elected to strike in the southern half of Gallipoli. Under cover of a feint at Bulair, troops would disembark at five points on Cape Helles, designated as S, V, W, X, and Y beaches, while further north another force landing above Gaba Tepe fought its way across to Maidos, compelling the defenders in the south to surrender or be taken in the rear. In the meantime the French under General Albert d'Amade, were also to undertake a diversionary landing at Kum Kale on the Asiatic side to achieve a double purpose: to distract Turkish artillery in the region from firing on S beach; and to deceive Turkish leadership long enough to delay sending its Asiatic troops to reinforce their comrades on the Peninsula until after the initial clash of battle. As soon as the beachheads were secured, the French would withdraw from Kum Kale and be transported to Cape Helles where they would take up a position on the right of the British.

A division of strength in battle is seldom justifiable, but in this case it was not possible to concentrate all the troops on a single beachhead for a decisive thrust. Hamilton's tactical plan was expected to confuse the enemy and on the whole was bold and intelligent. The Turks would be forced to hold back their reserves not knowing where the main landing would take place until it was too late and the British forces had secured a firm foothold on the Peninsula.

The military attack commenced on the early morning of 25 April and in the course of the day nearly 30,000 men, including those belonging to the 29th Division, succeeded in landing at various sites on Cape Helles and north of Gaba Tepe. On the separate battlefields they struggled

---

47 Kitchener to Hamilton, 19 April 1915, ibid.
48 Kitchener to Hamilton, 23 April 1915, ibid.

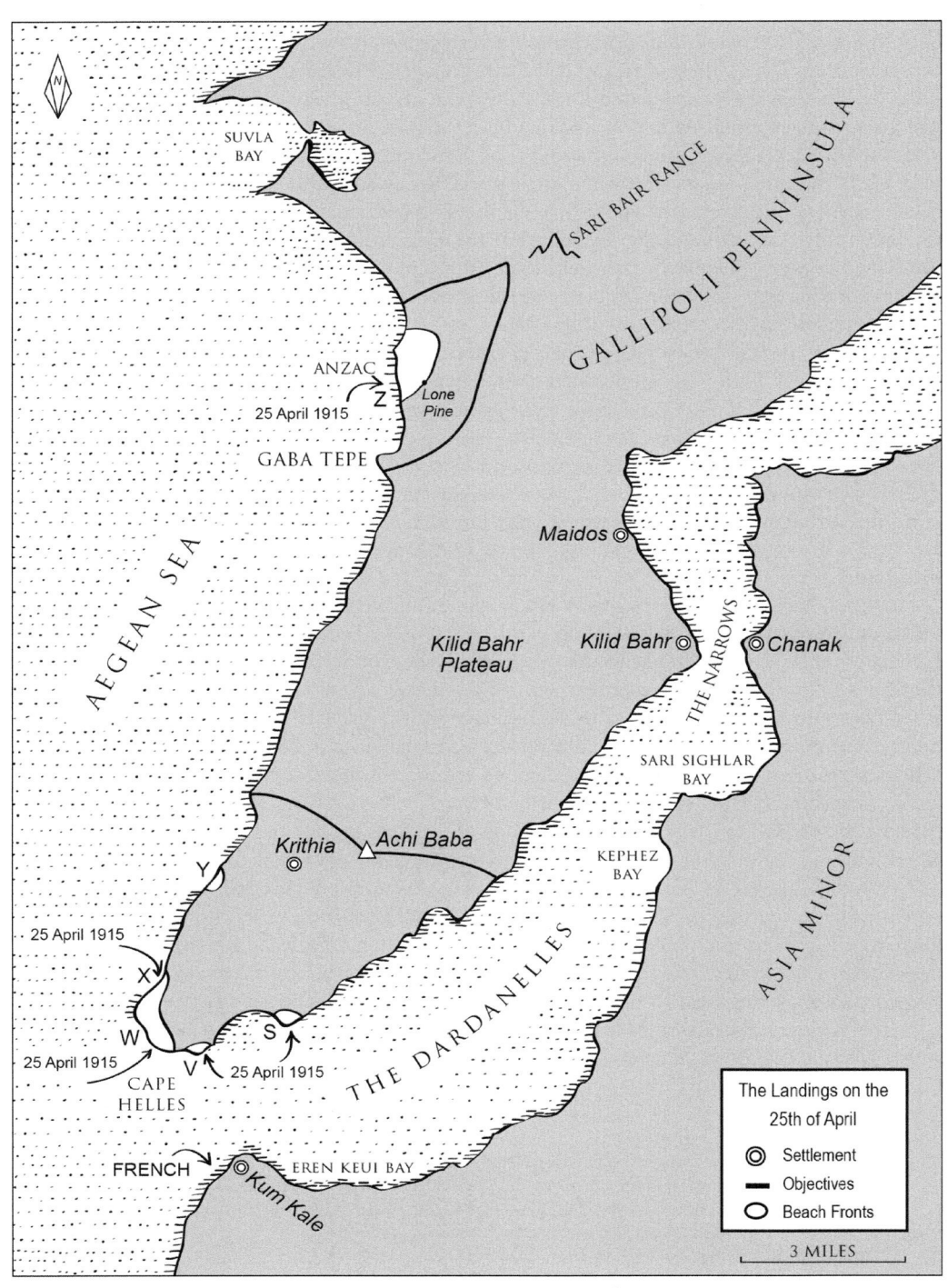

Map 5 The British Landing on 25 April.

to push forward a few hundred yards from the beaches and none of the objectives were attained, except at Kum Kale. There were many factors that contributed to the slower than expected progress. The Turks were prepared for the invasion, almost always occupied the high ground, and many were experienced as they had fought in the Balkan wars. On the British side, communication between Hamilton's commanders and their men was not always reliable; the attacks were uncoordinated; orders were often unclear; the fleet was unable to provide effective cover as it had insufficient information about how far the men advanced inland; and there was a failure to exploit uncontested landings. By nightfall the British had taken staggering casualties and the survivors were exhausted, short of food and ammunition and badly shaken. Some of the commanders judged conditions to be so hopeless that they advocated that the troops withdraw. Hamilton dismissed such talk and ordered them to dig in, pending a resumption of the advance as soon as the men had consolidated their position.[49]

Hamilton was under the impression that Kitchener could spare no more troops for the Dardanelles and that he would have to make do with what he had. He knew nothing of Kitchener's telegram to Maxwell on 6 April which permitted him to draw forces from Egypt. Maxwell disliked the Gallipoli campaign and since he worried that the Turks would repeat their earlier assault against the Canal, resented releasing any part of his army. Kitchener's telegram did not mandate him to follow a script but was simply a request that he make available any troops he could spare. Consequently he said nothing about it to his British counterpart in the Dardanelles.

Hamilton had always been in awe of Kitchener and his first reports of the battle tended to be overly optimistic and gave no indication of the extent of his difficulties. For example he signaled Kitchener on the 27th: "Thanks to the weather and the wonderfully fine spirit of our troops all continues to go well."[50] Kitchener learned of Hamilton's urgent need for more men, indirectly from Rear Admiral E. P. Guépratte, commander of the French naval squadron. During the night of the 26th, the French Rear Admiral alerted his superior in Malta that "in order to ensure continued success it is of utmost importance to reinforce immediately the Expeditionary Force which is insufficient for such extensive operations."[51] The message was transmitted the next day to London and caught the Secretary for War by surprise. Kitchener could not understand why Hamilton had failed to make a request for reinforcements in view of the offer stated in his telegram to Maxwell on the 6th of the month. He was unaware that Maxwell had not passed on his cable to Hamilton. Kitchener at once contacted Hamilton to tell him that he was free to turn to Egypt to draw more troops if needed. Hamilton confirmed his need for additional men and in a subsequent telegram, based on information supplied by d'Amade, told of a second French division being held in reserve for the Dardanelles and requested that it be despatched as well.[52] Kitchener arranged to send the 42nd Division (East Lancashire) from Egypt, overruling Maxwell's protest, and simultaneously contacting the French War Minister to solicit the

---

49 The detailed accounts of the two British landings can be followed in such works as Aspinall-Oglander, *Gallipoli;* James; *Gallipoli;* Prior, *Gallipoli*, Hickey, *Gallipoli*; Nigel Steel and Peter Hart, *Defeat at Gallipoli* (London: Macmillan, 1994); and C.E.W. Bean, *Official History of Australia in the War of 1914-18* (Sydney: Angus & Robertson Ltd., 1938), vols. 1-2.
50 Hamilton to Kitchener, 27 April 1915, CAB 19/31.
51 Cited in Aspinall-Oglander, *Gallipoli*, vol. 1, p. 304.
52 Hamilton, *Gallipoli Diary*, vol. 1, p. 174.

dispatch of the reserve division to reinforce d'Amade's contingent. Millerand raised no objections but added it would take several weeks before the French troops arrived on the Peninsula.

Hamilton had drawn plans to seize control of Krithia which he proposed to use as a launching point against Achi Baba, a ridge about 700 feet high serving as the enemy's main observation station to the south. Hamilton assumed that the capture of Achi Baba would allow him to turn his heavy guns against the forts at The Narrows which the navy had been unable to destroy. Actually this was a misconception as the ridge did not provide a direct view of The Narrows defences owing to the intervening high ground and the Kilid Bahr Plateau. Before the Narrows could be seen it was necessary to move east about a mile or so to a lesser summit.[53]

The action commenced at 8 am on the 28th with a desultory bombardment, followed by the infantry's advance along the Cape Helles front. Good progress was made in the early stages but on reaching the main Turkish position, the attack lost momentum and ground to a halt. The British had gained a mile or so of ground and the French about half that distance. Out of the 14,000 men engaged, the Anglo-French force had suffered 3000 casualties. A far greater effort, involving 25,000 men, got under way on 6 May and lasted three days. When it was over the Allies had acquired 600 yards of worthless ground at a cost of 6500 casualties and were still half a mile from the objective initially set. If the Allies learned anything from the two battles of Krithia, it was that the Turks, far from being mediocre fighters as had been supposed, showed that they were tough, well-led and prepared to die in defence of their homeland.

Yet in the best of circumstances, it is difficult to see how the outcome of the landings on Gallipoli could have been significantly different. The naval operation had compromised the vital element of surprise. The damage could not be repaired. On top of this, the army was handicapped again by factors beyond its control. It was poorly prepared for the nature of its new task, a condition that stemmed from the expectation that its role would be subservient to the navy. Consequently Hamilton was often compelled to make decisions based on faulty assumptions and misinformation. Then too Hamilton's army required at least a two to one advantage to overcome a well-fortified enemy holding the high ground. As it happened he did not even have access to as many troops as his German counterpart, General Liman von Sanders.

When the Allied fleet began to concentrate in the Mediterranean early in February 1915, there were two Turkish divisions (about 36,000 men) on Gallipoli with nine more available within a two day's march; the following month the number of Turkish divisions rose to four; early in April the number of divisions stood at five; and on 25 April, a total of six Turkish divisions garrisoned the Peninsula, in addition to six concentrated in areas within a two days' march and six more available inside a week.[54] During the five weeks that elapsed between the naval attack and the military landing, the Turks on the Peninsula not only increased their presence but their defensive system was upgraded and placed on a thoroughly sound footing. Hamilton did not know it but his army was doomed before it hit the beaches. Hamilton was in low spirits when he broke the unhappy news to Kitchener on 8 May:

> The result of the operation has been a failure, as my object remains unachieved. The fortifications and their machine-guns were too scientific and too strongly held to be rushed,

---

53 Aspinall-Oglander, *Gallipoli*, vol. 1, p. 156n1; James, *Gallipoli*, p. 2.
54 Information about the growing number of Ottoman divisions between February and April was kindly supplied to me by Lieut. Col. Erickson.

although I had every available man in today. Our troops have done all that flesh and blood can do against semi-permanent works and they are not able to carry them. More and more munitions will be needed to do so.[55]

The operation had not followed the course that Kitchener had expected and he was naturally disappointed. Thankful that the landing had succeeded, he assumed that resistance would lessen, enabling Hamilton's men to advance in good order and ultimately occupy the heights dominating the defences at The Narrows. Instead the army had failed to carry key positions such as Achi Baba in the first rush with the result that further progress would be slow, difficult and entail deliberate methods. Hamilton had not given any indication that the forces under his command were inadequate to gain control of the Peninsula. On the contrary he was euphorically confident before the main battle started. Kitchener kept his feelings to himself when he replied to Hamilton the following day:

> I had hoped the naval artillery would be more effective than it is apparently on the enemy's fixed positions. The whole situation naturally gives me some anxiety, particularly as our transport service is much hampered by want of ships. More ammunition is being pushed to you via Marseilles. I hope you and the admiral will be able to devise some means of clearing the way through.[56]

As a field commander Kitchener rarely tolerated excuses from subordinates as a justification for failure but he had mellowed in later life. Hamilton, who could hardly forget the unforgiving nature of his old chief when orders were not carried out to his satisfaction, had to be buoyed up by his reaction. He wrote back giving his impression of the recent action. He attributed the repulse of his men to the quality and numerical superiority of the Turks, protected by machine guns and wire entanglements – obstacles he termed "inventions of the devil" which in his view produced a ten to one ratio in favour of the defence. He thought that on occasions it might be worth sacrificing ten Englishmen or Frenchmen for one German, but he resented "such high rates of payment where our enemy is the Turk."[57] After a fortnight of fighting, conditions on the Peninsula resembled those on the western front with the combatants facing one another in two lines of trenches stretching from the Aegean to the Straits and supported by a lavish supply of machine guns. In a subsequent telegram, Hamilton acknowledged that a stalemate had begun to set in:

> The only procedure is to hammer away until the enemy gets demoralised. Meanwhile, grand advances are impractical and we must make short advances during the night and dig in for the day until we get to Achi Baba. I then hope we will be able to make progress without this trench method, but Achi Baba is really a fortress. If two fresh divisions organized as a corps could be spared me I could push on from this end [Cape Helles] and from

---

55 Hamilton to Kitchener, 8 May 1915, CAB 19/31.
56 Kitchener to Hamilton, 9 May 1915, ibid.
57 Hamilton to Kitchener, 11 May 1915, ibid.

Gaba Tepe with good prospects of success, otherwise it will generate into trench warfare with its resultant slowness.[58]

Hamilton was aware that surplus troops were in short supply at home and for that reason was always uneasy about approaching Kitchener for reinforcements. Consequently his requests were quite modest and in his view no more than was necessary to achieve what he considered his goal. Even then Kitchener's reaction was to tell Hamilton to manage with what he had or meet his requests partially. When Hamilton indicated that he would need two divisions for the next phase of his operations, Kitchener replied that he could only offer him the Lowland Division, a territorial unit which was still in England.

The breezy optimism in London at the outset of the campaign that the navy would, at best, require only the assistance of a small force to breach The Narrows had disappeared. The War Office had strained its resources to meet the expectations of Turkish resistance at the first military landing and it went without saying that even greater means would be required if a second one were to follow. But the country did not have the capacity to sustain two major fronts. The War Council would have to decide whether it lay in the Dardanelles or in France.

---

58 Hamilton to Kitchener, 10 May 1915, ibid.

5

The Last Throw of the Dice

In April and May events appear to conspire to frustrate British and Entente efforts everywhere. As already noted, Hamilton, in spite of his men's courage and will to win, had been unable to overcome Turkish resistance on the Gallipoli Peninsula. The Russians were in difficulty again, forced to retire from Galicia under the hammering blows of an Austro-German offensive. In Belgium the Germans had released poison gas in violation of the Geneva Convention, initiating a long drawn-out battle around Ypres that was causing a good deal of anxiety as to its outcome. Sir John French's assault at Aubers Ridge on 9 May, designed to ease pressure on the Russians, had been beaten back with such ease that the Germans had not found it necessary to call on any reserves. Rome's pledge to join the Entente became uncertain when the Italian prime minister, confronted by a parliament hostile to his policy, resigned on 13 May.

Kitchener was further troubled by several issues that affected him personally. On 12 May the old battleship *Goliath* was torpedoed off Sedd-el-Bahr with the loss of 570 men by a Turkish destroyer manned by a German crew. The incident, fortified by reports of impending U-boat activity in the area, prompted Fisher to insist unequivocally that the *Queen Elizabeth* be recalled from the Dardanelles. To avoid Fisher's resignation, Churchill was compelled to acquiesce. In the evening he invited Kitchener to a meeting at the Admiralty and broke the news.[1] Kitchener became extremely angry on hearing of the Admiralty's decision to withdraw the *Queen Elizabeth*. "His habitual composure in trying ordeals left him," Churchill later wrote. "He protested vehemently against what he considered the desertion of the Army at its most critical moment." Fisher flew into a rage over Kitchener's remark that virtually accused the Admiralty of treachery and was emphatic that he would leave his office if the *Queen Elizabeth* were not ordered home at once. Churchill tried to allay Kitchener's concerns by explaining that he proposed to replace the *Queen Elizabeth* with two 14-inch gun monitors and that the navy would do its utmost to sustain the army. Churchill thought that Kitchener was "to some extent reassured before he left."[2] Churchill did not read Kitchener correctly. As it was, Kitchener saw no point in prolonging the debate in which he was overmatched. All the same it is difficult to understand why the warlord attached so much importance to the retention of the *Queen*

---

1   Churchill erred in citing 13 May as the date of the conference. It actually took place on the previous day.
2   Churchill, *World Crisis*, vol. 2, pp. 360-61.

Elizabeth which had not only failed miserably to live up to its advanced billing but for all practical purposes was no longer required.

Early next morning Kitchener called Callwell to his office and informed him of what the Admiralty intended to do. He proceeded to excoriate Churchill and others at the Admiralty for deceiving him by painting a glowing picture of how the *Queen Elizabeth*, with its vastly superior firepower, would settle the matter of the Dardanelles practically on its own. At the end of the tirade he asked Callwell's opinion on the effect the loss of the *Queen Elizabeth* would have on the operations. Callwell observed that no battleship however formidable, given the flat trajectory of its guns, could render much help to the army. He implied that by remaining in the Dardanelles the battleship would be running a considerable risk and thought it would be a mistake to contest the matter. Kitchener conceded that, while the power of the *Queen Elizabeth* had been greatly exaggerated, he believed that its presence in the vicinity provided moral support for the troops fighting on shore. It seemed to Callwell that Kitchener resented being duped by Churchill more than the departure of the battleship.[3]

Kitchener had arranged a second meeting at the Admiralty to try to persuade Churchill to reconsider his decision as he seemed reluctant during the previous session to send the *Queen Elizabeth* back home. The Field Marshall was accompanied by Callwell, and the two went over to the Admiralty where they found Churchill and Fisher waiting in the First Lord's room. Churchill had barely begun to speak when an excited Fisher bounced up from his chair and repeated his outburst of the previous day. Consequently Churchill determined that, in view of the unbending attitude of his principal naval adviser, he had no choice but to let the decision to recall the *Queen Elizabeth* stand. Kitchener made no fuss and protested only mildly.[4]

After Kitchener returned to the War Office he lodged a formal protest in a letter to the Prime Minister, expressing his concern about the consequences of the *Queen Elizabeth's* departure as well as his anger at the Admiralty which had laid its self-made troubles at his feet. He pointed out that the departure of the principal naval unit from the Dardanelles would have a serious and depressing effect on the army. He was appalled that, while Fisher talked of the risks of keeping the *Queen Elizabeth* in unsafe waters, he had to face the loss of 15,000 men in a campaign that had been initiated to bail out the navy. He ended by accusing the Admiralty of deserting the army when it was struggling for its life.[5]

Asquith empathized with Kitchener but, like Churchill, did not want to risk Fisher's resignation. He was unsure of how to frame a reply to Kitchener, given that the issue lay well outside the area of his competence. He solicited advice from Hankey who suggested the following explanation:

1   The Queen Elizabeth was sent out to the Dardanelles when an attack by the Navy alone was contemplated, and she had the specific functions of smashing the forts at the Narrows by indirect fire over the Gallipoli Peninsula. Now that the army is cooperating with the Navy this necessity no longer exists, since the Fleet will not attempt to effect a passage of the Narrows until the Army has occupied, or dominated, the forts on either side.

3   Callwell, *Experiences*, pp. 66-67.
4   Ibid., pp. 67-68.
5   Kitchener to Asquith, 13 May 1915, Kitchener papers, PRO 30/57/72.

2   The Army can equally well be supported by the Monitors which have guns of equal caliber with the Queen Elizabeth and were built for the specific purpose of operations against shore batteries and have no value for purely naval operations.[6]

Asquith's reply to Kitchener repeated Hankey's arguments. The explanation did not satisfy Kitchener but both he and the government were about to face a far more serious crisis. On the morning of the 14th, *The Times* featured a highly provocative item about the recent abortive offensive against Aubers Ridge under the headline: NEED FOR SHELLS. BRITISH ATTACKS CHECKED. LIMITED SUPPLY THE CAUSE. According to its military correspondent Charles à Court Repington, British soldiers died in droves because the field guns were desperately short of high explosive shells. He went on to say: "The Government who have so seriously failed to organize adequately our national resources must bear their share of the grave responsibility." The story, which was a direct challenge to Asquith and meant to undermine confidence in Kitchener, sent shock waves throughout the country.

The article contained facts and figures that only General Headquarters could have supplied. French's relations with Kitchener had worsened in recent months. Kitchener considered French's field generalship at best mediocre and had warned him in March that he was essentially on trial and needed to make more of an impression on the Germans.[7] Treading on dangerously thin ice, French tried to deflect attention from the disaster at Aubers Ridge by claiming that it was due to a shortage of high explosive shells. By shifting the responsibility onto Kitchener's shoulders, he believed he would be preempting any possibility of being recalled. French used the military correspondent of *The Times*, who was staying with him at General Headquarters, to make the case that Kitchener, not he, was responsible for the unsuccessful attack.

What made French's behavior unpardonable was that on two separate occasions before the impending battle he had assured Kitchener that he had enough ammunition on hand.[8] Although Kitchener was furious at French's treachery, he behaved with dignity and restraint, adamant that in wartime personal animosities should be laid aside. Close associates at the War Office wanted to reply to the charges, but he prohibited them from doing so, telling them that he was out to fight the Germans, not Sir John. Asquith refused to believe that French, who always wrote to him in "affectionate and almost fulsome terms" had inspired the story in *The Times* and, actually was more upset with Kitchener.[9] On 20 April Asquith had given a speech at Newcastle aimed at impressing upon employers and workers engaged in the production of munitions of the need to increase their output.[10] In the course of his address he categorically denied statements in the press that the army's operations in France were being hampered by insufficient ammunition. Before travelling to Newcastle, Asquith had asked Kitchener to obtain from French a concise report on the state of his ammunition. Kitchener replied on 14 April: "I have had a talk with

---

6   Hankey to Asquith, 13 May 1915, CAB 63/5.
7   Cassar, *Kitchener's War*, p. 167.
8   Ibid., pp. 177-78; Arthur, *Lord Kitchener*, vol. 3, pp. 235-36.
9   Asquith clung to that illusion until 1919 when French admitted his part in the shell crisis in his book *1914*. See Spender and Asquith, *Life of Herbert Henry Asquith*, vol. 2, p. 142. At the time of the shell crisis, French wrote to the prime minister and again thanked him for his kindness, stressing that he had been strengthened by his unfailing sympathy and encouragement. Cassar, *Kitchener*, p. 355.
10 Cassar, *Asquith as War Leader*, p. 87.

French. He told me I could let you know that with the present supply of ammunition he will have as much as his troops will be able to use on the next forward movement."[11] Kitchener was referring to the amount of munitions for French's impending regional attack, not on the army's overall needs since the start of the war. Asquith had overstated Kitchener's assurance. The press was aware that ammunition was in short supply from earlier comments made by Kitchener and army leaders and naturally blasted Asquith for trying to deceive the country. As a result the Prime Minister was made to look like a liar or woefully out of touch with conditions on the front and he wrongly blamed Kitchener for his gaffe.[12]

Asquith knew as much about the effort involved in the manufacture of munitions as the other members of the cabinet. He had concluded as early as March 1915 that Kitchener was negligent in attending to the army's munitions requirements. Violet Asquith overheard a discussion between her father and Edwin Montague, then Chancellor of the Duchy of Lancaster, in which they attributed the munitions shortages to Kitchener's apathy.[13] There were others in the Liberal party, especially Lloyd George, who felt the same way. Let us briefly examine the facts.

Prior to 1914 Britain's small munitions industry was accountable mostly to supply the country's scattered forces in the colonies and territorial possessions with the means to carry on their police activities. It did not even have the capacity to meet the normal requirements of the mere six regular divisions that left the shores of Britain after August 1914 to fight on the Continent. One of the greatest obstacles to increase home production were the trade unions which refused to suspend, even temporarily, the privileges won after many years of hard bargaining. Kitchener's challenge became many times more daunting with the advent of trench warfare on the western front and the rapidly expanding army projected to be ten times larger than the old one, imposing a demand for munitions on a scale that was unprecedented. The hurried increase in the output of munitions in Britain required the building or expansion of factories, the purchase and installation of machinery, the acquisition of chemicals, and the training of workers. The War Office also vastly supplemented home production by turning to foreign manufacturers which too frequently accepted larger orders than they could deliver. It was thus ludicrous for the Liberal politicians to think that a crisis, which was of their own making, could be resolved overnight by waving a magic wand. They were either ignorant or refused to acknowledge that the real responsibility lay with the pre-war Liberal administration. The general staff of the army must also take a share of the blame because during the immediate period before the war they wanted the army supplied with shrapnel, instead of high explosive shells. A shrapnel shell containing several hundred lead pellets was deadly against unprotected troops in the open but trench warfare reduced its effectiveness. Under the new conditions it was seen that high explosive shells produced better results in chewing up barbed wire and battering down field fortifications. The switch from shrapnel to high explosive shells could not be accomplished, in the words of noted historian

---

11 Kitchener to Asquith, 15 April 1915, Asquith papers, vol. 14; Jenkins, *Asquith*, p. 357; Stephen Koss, *Asquith* (London: Allen Lane, 1976), p. 181.
12 Cassar, *Asquith*, pp. 87-88.
13 Mark Pottle (ed.), *Champion Redoubtable*, p. 33. It was not until Asquith wrote his memoirs in 1928, by which time he had seen enough contemporary evidence, that he belatedly acknowledged publicly the work of the War Office in vastly expanding the supply of munitions. It was done to answer French's charge in his book *1914* that the government and Kitchener in particular had been guilty of criminal apathy in attending to the munitions requirements of his army. *Memoirs*, pp. 76-78.

Trevor Wilson, "just by altering a requisition order."[14] New machinery had to be purchased and installed and workers given additional training.[15] Too often the politicians wore blinkers and measured success only by instant results, no matter how back breaking the challenge.

The relationship between Kitchener and the other members of the cabinet, never close, began to fray in the spring of 1915. The war was not going well for Britain in France or in the Dardanelles and consequently his colleagues were less willing to tolerate his methods. From the very beginning, Kitchener found it difficult to conform to cabinet procedure in which members pool their talents and work together as equals. He had lived in isolation throughout most of his professional career and the responsibilities that he had borne were individual, not collective. He never had to explain or apologize, adopt decisions based on discussion or debate, receive or act upon advice from any but those from whom he chose to request it. Because of his autocratic temperament and long experience in the east he did not always square his opinion and actions as Secretary of War with his cabinet colleagues. While he did not carry out policies inconsistent with the wishes of the War Council, he sometimes withheld information from its members and refused to admit them freely to his confidence. When confronted he would try to evade or parry their questions and if this failed he would give them false information. "K. can tell nothing to anybody," Lord Emmott, First Commission of Works, wrote in his diary. "He is never frank and tells lies if he does not want to tell at all."[16] An astute politician would not tell a direct lie or break a promise unless he had expressed it in language so ambiguous that he could not be charged with breach of faith. Kitchener lacked such cleverness in expression.

Kitchener's natural secretiveness was reinforced by a distrust of his colleagues' indiscretion. He found that classified information which he had revealed to ministers in confidence had leaked out. Actually the problem had become more widespread than he suspected. The most egregious offender among the politicians was the love-smitten Prime Minister who often sought Venetia Stanley's company – for lunch or dinner, for accompanying him on motor drives, or visits to her home – and wrote to her once, sometimes twice, a day, revealing decisions taken or principal issues under discussion in the War Council or cabinet. [17] A case in point was a letter he sent on 9 February 1915: "The only exciting thing in prospect ... is what will happen in the Dardanelles next week. This as I said is supposed to be a secret ... [but] naturally I shall tell you *everything*."[18] On top of this, in what can only be described as inexcusable conduct, he sometimes asked for her opinion on complex problems.[19] Lloyd George was almost as guilty as his chief for there was little that he kept from Frances Stevenson as her diary reveals. Other ministers had no qualms about passing state secrets to newspaper proprietors or friends. Churchill, for one, told Violet Asquith, with whom he was on close terms, that the naval division was earmarked

---

14 Trevor Wilson, *The Myriad Faces of War* (Cambridge: Polity Press, 1968), p. 218.
15 For a detailed account of the munitions issue see ch. 15 of my study *Kitchener*.
16 Lord Emmott diary, entry for 13 June 1915, Emmott papers.
17 Jenkins, *Asquith*, pp. 258-59.
18 Brock and Brock (eds.), *Letters to Venetia Stanley*, p. 423.
19 See for example in ibid., pp. 434-35, 494-95. In 1973 or 1974 I had a long discussion over the telephone with Mrs. Judith Gendel, Venetia's daughter, about the Asquith letters then in her possession. I remember she told me that Asquith's habit of asking for her mother's opinion on issues about which she knew little or nothing terrified her, and was a compelling factor in her acceptance of a marriage proposal from Edwin Montague, a man she did not love.

for the Dardanelles and allowed her to convey the information only to her brother "Oc" and a good friend (Rupert Brooke).[20] Another dangerous source open to the enemy was the gossip at social functions. Anyone sensitive to the need for tight security arrangements in war cannot but sympathize with Kitchener's reluctance to reveal military secrets to twenty-three men, some to assist their intrigues or from a desire to seem important, did not hesitate to violate their oath of office.

The only person that Kitchener put his faith in, outside a few close aides, was Hankey. The two men frequently discussed military problems and possible solutions. Hankey respected Kitchener and, while not oblivious to his faults, recognized his immense contribution to the nation's war effort. He tried whenever possible to smooth the difficult relationship between Kitchener and his colleagues. As he was concerned over the strength of ill-feeling in the cabinet against Kitchener for imparting so little vital information, he let him know that his policy was creating discontent. To which Kitchener replied: "I cannot tell them everything because they are so leaky … If they will only all divorce their wives I will tell them everything!"[21]

Returning to the munitions controversy, its fallout was already being felt when the War Council assembled later in the morning on 14 May (after an interval of eight weeks), adding to the recent spate of bad news. It was held, according to Hankey, in an atmosphere of "almost unrelieved gloom."[22] Asquith was hard pressed at times to keep bitterness and recriminations from getting out of hand. The recent events had subjected Kitchener to immense strain and he was tired and depressed. Shortly after the meeting got under way, the Prime Minister turned to Churchill for an update on the navy in the Dardanelles. The First Lord proceeded to explain that the reported arrival of German submarines in the eastern Mediterranean, together with the conversion of the operation from naval to military, had led the Admiralty to recall the *Queen Elizabeth*. In its place he intended to send two monitors with 14-inch guns and two light cruisers to de Robeck. He had notified de Robeck of the new arrangements and to impress on him that the "moment for a renewal of a naval attempt to force the Dardanelles had passed and was not likely to arise." He advised that the next step was to prepare plans that would ensure the success of the enterprise within three months. In attempting to minimize his culpability as the architect of the disastrous naval attack he said: "If we had known three months ago that an army of from 80,000 to 100,000 men would now be available for the attack on the Dardanelles, the naval attack would never have been undertaken. Three months ago, however, it was impossible to foresee this."[23] Churchill's statement was unquestionably contrary to the facts and he was guilty, not merely of stretching the truth, but of a blatant lie. The remark was so ridiculous that in the War Council no one bothered to challenge it, but everybody knew that, in addition to a number of territorial units, the first installment of the New Armies would be ready to take the field in the spring and the discussions during the opening weeks of the year were to determine where they should be sent.

When the floor was turned over to Kitchener, he began by reading a statement in which he raised the issue of the *Queen Elizabeth*'s withdrawal and practically accused the navy of

---

20 Violet Bonham Carter, *Winston Churchill*, pp. 295-96.
21 Hankey, *Supreme Command*, vol. 1, p. 221.
22 Ibid., p. 303.
23 Minutes of the War Council, 14 May 1915, CAB 42/2/19.

treachery. It will not be repeated here as it has already been cited in an earlier chapter.[24] Briefly put, Kitchener claimed the revelation that the *Queen Elizabeth* with its matchless firepower would be on the scene had been a major factor in his decision to support the naval campaign in the Dardanelles. Churchill tried to strike an optimistic note by saying there was no cause for alarm, the fleet, with the new additions, would be larger than ever and that it was essential to press on. Kitchener maintained that the loss of the *Queen Elizabeth* would have very harmful consequences. It would be taken as the first sign of the abandonment of the enterprise and might spark an uprising in Egypt where a large part of the garrison had been diverted to the Dardanelles. With demand for troops from other quarters, he was finding it difficult to meet Hamilton's call for reinforcements. He would like to withdraw from the Dardanelles but such a move was not practical.

Grey asked Kitchener what Hamilton's prospects were of forcing a way through the Turkish lines to seize the heavily defended Kilid Bahr Plateau? Could the task be accomplished with the new reinforcements that would be dispatched? Kitchener's reply was an emphatic no. Lloyd George observed the Turks could always bring up additional men to meet allied reinforcements sent to the Peninsula. He inquired if it was possible to send a force large enough to eject the estimated 150,000 Turks from their position? Once again Kitchener expressed a negative opinion. He maintained that the allied army in the Dardanelles was held up, as in France, by barbed wire and machine guns. He observed that Sir John French had a dense concentration of forces at his command but was still unable to advance. He did not see how Kilid Bahr could be captured with such reinforcements as he was able to send. Churchill interjected to say that in determining the future course in the Dardanelles he hoped that Kitchener would not be unduly influenced by the withdrawal of the *Queen Elizabeth*. Arguing vigorously against hints of withdrawal, Churchill pointed out that the sacrifice of 28,000 men from the Empire and France should not be in vain. He stressed that if the operation was not carried through, "it could be said that a disaster had happened to this country." Kitchener claimed that the manpower and the amount of ammunition necessary to achieve a victory were unavailable and the only option, in his opinion, was to carry on as best they could. To do otherwise was to risk a rising in the Muslim world. Lloyd George felt that, as the strength of the Turks had been underestimated, it was essential not to repeat the same mistake. He felt that before a decision was made, the general on the spot should be contacted to give an estimate of the force required to ensure success.

Kitchener asserted that if such a question was put to Hamilton he was bound to give an impossibly high number. Thus far he had promised Hamilton only one division as reinforcements. Kitchener was desperate to avoid a heavy drain on the nation's limited forces and supply of ammunition. In his estimation, the best recourse would be to keep the troops up to strength in the Dardanelles and allow Hamilton to make slow progress, avoiding any operations that might entail heavy casualties. He left no doubt that he opposed abandoning the enterprise which he feared might cause serious trouble in Muslim states. Crewe, Haldane and Balfour acknowledged that Kitchener's solution seemed to provide the only viable option. Churchill chimed in, saying he could not understand Kitchener's grounds for pessimism over the current state of the nation's military resources. He observed that the total number of British forces amounted to 644,000 men out of which some 80,000 were assigned to the Dardanelles. Churchill's claim

---

24 See pp. 55.

that there were well over half a million men in England, besides the 80,000 in the Dardanelles, was misleading as he included the men in training. He went on to say that every month the training of New Armies was nearing completion – flagrantly contradicting his earlier statement – and the stock of ammunition was improving rapidly. The Dardanelles enterprise was a very small affair compared to the nation's total resources. He saw no reason to believe that the allied line in France could be pierced. Churchill seemed to imply that, as the Germans posed no threat on the western front, all available reinforcements and such ammunition as was necessary, be sent to the Dardanelles to reach a decision there at the earliest possible moment. By contrast Kitchener, unwilling to risk weakening the western front, preferred to continue the stalemate in the Dardanelles to tie down large Ottoman forces and avoid trouble in the Near East.

There was broad sentiment among members that there was no harm in asking Hamilton what additional forces he would require to ensure success.[25] Conforming to the wishes of the War Council, Kitchener cabled Hamilton in the evening: "The War Council would like to know what force you consider would be necessary to carry through the operations upon which you are engaged. You should base this estimate on the supposition that I have adequate forces to be placed at your disposal."[26] Hamilton had earlier requested two divisions (on 10 May) after his offensive was held up and Kitchener was only able to offer him one, the Lowland Division.

Since Hamilton complained from time to time (in his diary) that his army was starved of replacements, he was naturally excited at the possibility of an imminent windfall. He replied on 17 May that if a Balkan ally, Greece or Bulgaria, could be enlisted to distract elements of the Turkish army, an additional two division would suffice to complete his task. Otherwise he would require three more divisions, in addition to the one already promised, or a total of four.

He explained that lack of space would make it impossible to land the reinforcements until he had advanced 1000 yards at Cape Helles. In the interim he suggested that the extra divisions be transported to nearby islands under British control – Tenedos, Lemnos and Imbros – where they would be used for later fighting on the Peninsula. Hamilton underlined that if he had a liberal supply of guns and ammunition he believed he could advance with half the loss of life than had been anticipated.[27]

Kitchener replied to Hamilton the next day, expressing disappointment over the unsuccessful effort to take control of the vital high ground which he erroneously believed would have exposed the enemy's defences in The Narrows. He added:

> A serious situation is created by the present check, and by call of men and munitions that we can ill spare from France. From the standpoint of an early solution of our difficulties your views are not encouraging. The question whether we can long support two fields of operations draining our resources requires grave consideration. I can rely on you to do your utmost to bring the present state of affairs in the Dardanelles to as early a conclusion as possible, so that any consideration of withdrawal with all its dangers in the East, may not enter the field of possible solutions.[28]

---

25 Minutes of the War Council, 14 May 1915, CAB 42/2/19.
26 Kitchener to Hamilton, 14 May 1915, CAB 19/31.
27 Hamilton to Kitchener, 17 May 1915, ibid.
28 Kitchener to Hamilton, 18 May 1915, ibid.

Hamilton's telegram on the 17th provided the War Council with the information it had called for and normally would have been considered at once. As it happened no action was taken until 7 June. What caused the three-week delay was a political crisis which would spell the end of the Liberal government.

The Asquith government had been badly bruised by the army's unsuccessful attack in the Dardanelles and the shells controversy. What brought matters to a head, however, was the resignation of Fisher as First Sea Lord on 15 May in protest against Churchill's methods of conducting Admiralty business and the constant additions to the fleet in the Dardanelles at the expense of naval resources from Home waters.[29] The political background to the ministerial crisis, about which much has been written, merits only a brief description here. When the Conservatives learned that Fisher, the man they admired and trusted, would be leaving the Admiralty and that Churchill, whom they considered unstable and a menace to the nation, would be staying, they warned of an imminent eruption on the floor of the House. On 17 May Asquith bowed to the Opposition's demand and agreed to form a coalition government. Asquith's motives for capitulating are uncertain as he enjoyed a comfortable majority in parliament and could easily have beaten back a vote of no confidence. The most plausible explanation is that Asquith wanted to avoid all-out party warfare, which would have damaged the nation's morale, and possibly deter Italy from fulfilling its commitment to join the Entente.[30]

The composition of the new cabinet was announced on 25 May and included 12 Liberals, 8 Conservatives, 1 Labour and 1 non-party. Asquith kept most of the higher offices in Liberal hands. Grey remained at the Foreign Office; Lloyd George left the Treasury to head the new Ministry of Munitions; and Reginald McKenna became Chancellor of the Exchequer. Kitchener, who did not belong to any party but was regarded as a virtual Tory, was kept as Secretary for War; and Tory statesman Arthur Balfour was appointed First Lord of the Admiralty with Admiral Henry Jackson as his First Sea Lord. The Conservative leader Andrew Bonar Law, viewed as less than brilliant, accepted his relegation to the Colonial Office. The most notable casualty in the reshuffle was Churchill whose removal from the Admiralty was a condition laid down by the Conservatives for their participation in the government. In truth Churchill had few influential friends and his dismissal from the Admiralty was applauded, not only by the Conservatives, but by every major group – the navy, the press and even his own party.[31] While Churchill's fate hung in the balance he had desperately pleaded to remain at the Admiralty but he had only succeeded in annoying Asquith. Lloyd George was as close to a friend as Churchill had in the cabinet but he was, if anything, even more trenchant in his criticism. To Frances Stevenson, he expressed his sentiments about Churchill during the political crisis: "When the war came he saw in it the chance of glory for himself & has accordingly entered on a risky campaign without caring a straw for the misery and hardship it would bring to thousands, in

---

29 The tense relationship between Churchill and Fisher can be followed in Marder, *From the Dreadnought*, vol. 2, ch. 11; and Bell, *Churchill*, ch. 7, among other works.

30 For detailed information on the political crisis see Lord Beaverbrook, *Politicians and the War*, bk. 1, ch.8; Trevor Wilson, *The Downfall of the Liberal Party 1914-1945* (London: Collins, 1966), pp. 53-64; R.J.Q. Adams, *Bonar Law* (Stanford: Stanford University Press, 1999), pp. 181-88; Jenkins, *Asquith*, pp. 355-62; Cameron Hazlehurst, *Politicians at War, July 1914–May 1915* (London: Jonathan Cape, 1971), part. 3; Cassar, *Asquith*, ch. 6.

31 Bell, *Churchill*, pp. 181-85.

the hope that he would prove to be the outstanding man in this war."[32] Given the long list of enemies and critics Churchill had accumulated during the last nine months, he was fortunate to be given the sinecure post of Chancellor of the Duchy of Lancaster and to retain a seat in the committee controlling the direction of the war. As Churchill was preparing to leave the Admiralty, Kitchener was practically alone in paying him a courtesy call. Churchill acknowledged with gratitude that the "overburdened Titan" was the "first, and with one exception the only one of my colleagues who paid me a visit of ceremony."[33] It was a noble gesture on the part of Kitchener, given that Churchill's misjudgements had added immensely to his troubles.

After the formation of the coalition government, Asquith set up a new body formally known as the Dardanelles Committee to replace the War Council. The work of the Committee, initially restricted to the Dardanelles operation, soon extended to include all aspects of war policy. Serving under the chairmanship of Asquith, its original members consisted of Kitchener, Grey, and Churchill, plus five conservatives, Bonar Law, Balfour, Lord Curzon, Lord Selborne, and Lord Lansdowne.[34] Within a few months Lloyd George, Lord Crewe and Edward Carson were added, bringing the total to 12. The perceptive and indispensable Hankey acted as secretary and informal adviser. The Dardanelles Committee, like the War Council, lacked executive authority. Its conclusions had to be ratified by the full cabinet where arguments on both sides were often restated before a final decision was taken.

The First Coalition was national only in name and would turn out to be more cumbersome as an instrument of war than its predecessor. It never worked together as a team. Asquith had reached an accommodation with his opponents not because he expected them to contribute anything meaningful but to defuse political tension and to avoid criticism by involving them in the process of framing policy. The Conservatives for their part deeply distrusted Asquith and within the cabinet assumed the role of hostile critics rather than cordial and constructive colleagues. On top of this the diverse opinions of strong personalities inhibited bold and decisive action. While in the previous government vital issues were handled by three or four ministers there were now twice that many who insisted on asserting themselves. The result was that decisions were obtained only after prolonged, heated and exhausting discussions which often led to unsatisfactory compromises.

Kitchener's control of strategy, once rarely challenged, had begun to break down during the last months of the Liberal administration. After the creation of the coalition government his remaining authority eroded rapidly under the hammering blows administered mostly by Conservative ministers, until it was all but gone. The Tories identified him with the fiasco in the Dardanelles and generally believed that he had mishandled the production of munitions. Their distrust of his judgement was reinforced by a dislike of his style, his secretiveness and complaints lodged against him by their military friends like Sir John French. They made no attempt to act as genial and helpful colleagues or to make allowances for his political inexperience and peculiar habits. Instead they badgered him for classified information and on other occasions compelled him, in the manner of a barrister interrogating a hostile witness in court, to explain and defend his policies. It is impossible to exaggerate how seriously handicapped

---

32　Taylor (ed.), *A Diary by Frances Stevenson*, p. 50.
33　Churchill discusses Kitchener's courtesy visit in *World Crisis*, vol. 2, p. 391, but the quote is in the revised and abridged edition (1931), p. 140.
34　Jenkins, *Asquith*, 367-70.

he was by his ineffectiveness as a speaker. Had Kitchener been able to hold his own in debate and expose the flawed thinking of his tormentors, his influence in the War Council would have remained practically intact. For many politicians who equated a person's intelligence with clarity of expression, Kitchener's incoherent explanations drew increasing challenges in which his every move was scrutinized and questioned. No person could operate effectively under such circumstances.

The first major task after the formation of the new government was to propose a course of action in the Dardanelles. It was no secret that Kitchener was disappointed with the progress of the operation thus far. In gaining a tenuous hold on the Peninsula, Hamilton lost 14,000 men, nearly three times higher than Kitchener had anticipated. For the heavy cost, Hamilton was currently cramped into two widely separated fronts and confronted by lines of entrenchments and entanglements, possession of which could be gained only by the deliberate methods of trench warfare. Thus it meant that the number of drafts and reinforcements to achieve a victory would need to be raised to an unexpectedly high level.

For Kitchener no decision on the future of the Gallipoli campaign could be taken without reference to events on the other fronts. Although Kitchener shared the general perception that the engagement in the Dardanelles, if successful, would yield important results, he was nevertheless adamant that it was and would continue to be subsidiary to the operations in France and Belgium. On no account could the main front be neglected. The recent disappointing results at Aubers Ridge made it apparent that the demands of the British army in the west were likely to increase rather than to diminish. There were also requirements in Egypt and elsewhere which had to be met.

Kitchener sat in his office carefully weighing the pros and cons before he drew up his appreciation on the Dardanelles campaign on 28 May. In deciding the next step, Kitchener laid down three options. The first was to withdraw, putting an end to an operation whose difficulties were underestimated, made considerable inroads into the nation's resources and would continue to absorb both military and naval forces before it could be brought to a successful conclusion. On the other hand the evacuation of the Peninsula would result in heavy casualties and loss of huge quantities of stores and ammunition; the abandonment of all hope of drawing in the Balkan states; surrendering to Germany Constantinople and opening the way for it to dominate the east as well as giving up territory won by great gallantry and huge cost; and damaging Britain's prestige and creating for it serious difficulties and dangers in Muslim countries. As far as Kitchener was concerned, the disadvantages of withdrawal were so acute that such a step could only be justified to avoid an even greater disaster.

The second consideration was to send Hamilton large-scale reinforcements to permit him to resume the offensive. It was not a course that Kitchener favoured. He claimed that he could spare neither the troops nor, more importantly, the supply of ammunition to bring the affair to a rapid conclusion. He added that from the experience of trench warfare in Flanders, he doubted that, even with the requested reinforcements, Hamilton would be able to make the kind of progress that he imagined. Kitchener pointed out that "Sir John French's forces have been increased very greatly, but no such advance as he anticipated has occurred."

The only feasible solution, as Kitchener had argued a fortnight earlier, was to replace Hamilton's losses, leaving him to make such progress as was possible. He went on to expound the advantages of following such a course: it would avoid embarrassment in the Muslim world; keep the door open to Balkan intervention; and in all probability limit or eliminate the threat of Turkish operations against Egypt, Mesopotamia and the Caucasus. Although Kitchener favoured the third option, he conceded that it carried certain risks. In the first place it was conceivable that German submarines might be able to impose an effective blockade which would compel the Anglo-French forces to surrender. Secondly with German assistance, the Turks might succeed in concentrating sufficient heavy artillery to render the Allied position untenable.[35] Kitchener assumed that the new cabinet committee (Dardanelles Committee) would select one of the two latter electives. Until that occurred he could not address Hamilton's request for reinforcements contained in his telegram on 17 May.

There was a sense of urgency on the part of Hamilton in view of the recent news about the debilitating state of the Russian army. On 2 June Hamilton cabled that as a result of the Russian reverses in Galicia he anticipated that 100,000 Turks would be set free and that ultimately 250,000 men might be brought against his forces. He observed that unless a Balkan ally could be found, he would require all the divisions he had asked for earlier.[36]

Although at the time Kitchener remained unconvinced that the Turkish front could be broken, he was willing to allow Hamilton to prove him wrong. He wrote to Hamilton the next day:

> Owning to the restricted nature of the ground you occupy and the experience we have had in Flanders of increased forces acting in trench positions, I own I have some doubts of an early decisive result being obtained by at once increasing the forces at your disposal, but I should like your views as soon as you can ... Are you convinced that with immediate reinforcements to the extent you mention [you]could force the Kilid Bahr position and thus finish the Dardanelles operations?[37]

Back came Hamilton's reply:

> I believe the reinforcements asked for ... will eventually enable me to take Kalid Bahr and will assuredly expedite the decision. I entirely agree that the restricted nature of the ground I occupy, militates against me in success, however much I am reinforced; that was why ... I emphasized the desirability of securing co-operation of new Allied Forces acting on a second line of operations.[38]

Hamilton's inability to explain how he would capture the hill when previous attempts had failed did not inspire confidence in Kitchener or alter his thinking. When Kitchener attended the meeting of the Dardanelles Committee on 7 June, the members were already in possession of two other memoranda on the subject of the Dardanelles campaign, one by Churchill and the other by Selborne. Both men pleaded for a vigorous conduct of the operation.[39]

---

35 Kitchener, "The Dardanelles," 28 May 1915, CAB 37/128/ 27.
36 Hamilton, *Gallipoli Diary*, vol. 1, pp. 263-65.
37 Ibid., p. 266.
38 Ibid., pp. 276-77.
39 Churchill, "A Note on the General Situation," 1 June 1915, CAB 37/129/1; Selborne,"The Dardanelles," 4 June 1915, CAB 37/129/10.

The deliberations got under way at 5 pm at 10 Downing Street. The members were chiefly concerned with addressing Hamilton's request for reinforcements in his telegram on 17 May. As Hankey was absent, no minutes of the meeting were taken. Kitchener pronounced himself opposed to evacuation but doubted that, even if Hamilton was supplied with the reinforcements he had requested, he would succeed in putting an end to the operation. The solution he recommended was to supply Hamilton with just enough reinforcements to allow him to carry on and make such progress as was possible. It apparently aroused little interest compared to the powerful arguments Churchill and Selborne advanced in favour of a decisive push in the Dardanelles. Selborne noted that "the decision of the Committee contemplated a more vigorous continuation of the operations than the course proposed by Lord Kitchener."[40] Thereafter Kitchener took a back seat and ultimately bowed to the will of the majority which voted overwhelming to provide Hamilton with the three remaining divisions of the First Army (in addition to the territorial unit already sent) to allow him to launch an assault in the second week of July.[41] In *The World Crisis* Churchill minimized his role in the debate, but if the past and immediate future are any indication, it can be taken for granted that he was relentless in urging that Hamilton be given the necessary forces to finish off the Turks.[42] A few of the Tories, notably Bonar Law, had never been keen about the Dardanelles operation but gave their reluctant consent when Selbourne, one of their own, pleaded for a big effort. Kitchener broke the news to Hamilton the next day:

> Your difficulties are recognized by the Cabinet who are determined to support you. We are sending you three divisions of the New Army. The first of these will leave about the end of this week, and the other two will be sent as transport is available.
>
> The last of the three divisions ought to reach you not later than the first fortnight in July. By that time the Fleet will have been reinforced by a good many units which are much less vulnerable to submarine attack than those now at the Dardanelles, and you can then count on the Fleet to give you continuous support.
>
> While steadily pressing the enemy, there seems no reason for running any premature risks in the meantime.[43]

Kitchener had been a bit hasty in making the announcement for the last word on the matter of reinforcements rested with the cabinet, which assembled on the 9th. Asquith's remarks on the subject were simply confined to disclosing the decision of the Dardanelles Committee and the approximate date the reinforcements were expected to arrive in the Dardanelles.[44] It was not until 18 June that he sought confirmation from the cabinet which normally rubber stamped the conclusions of the Dardanelles Committee. But the discussion on this occasion revealed there was a sharp divergence of opinion. A handful of ministers led by Carson were bitterly opposed

---

40 *Final Report of the Dardanelles Committee*, pp. 25-26; Aspinall-Oglander, *Gallipoli*, vol. 2, p. 59. The official historian erroneously maintained that Kitchener had been persuaded by Hamilton's last missive and, as a result, took the lead in pressing for a vigorous offensive. If that had been the case, Kitchener would not have argued in favour of the course he had recommended in his memorandum.
41 Minutes of the Dardanelles Committee, 7 June 1915, CAB 42/3/1.
42 Churchill, *World Crisis*, vol. 2, pp. 410-12.
43 Kitchener to Hamilton, 8 June 1915, CAB 19/31.
44 Asquith to George V, 9 June 1915, CAB 41/36/25.

to the dispatch of large reinforcements, viewing such a move as preparatory to "an offensive strategy on a large & increasing scale." Eventually the impasse was broken when the cabinet agreed by a wide margin that, with the additional forces, the aim ought to be at a "starving rather than a storming operation."[45]

Several members of the Dardanelles Committee had floated the idea at their earlier meeting on 12 June while searching for the best landing site on the Peninsula. It was hoped that Hamilton would consider their recommendation before drawing up his plan for the second landing. Asquith got the discussion under way when he circulated copies of a memorandum by the war correspondent Ellis Ashmead-Bartlett based on his observations while he was in the Dardanelles. In his paper the journalist was critical of Hamilton's strategy and suggested that rather than advance from Anzac or Cape Helles, neither of which offered any prospect of success, the army should land at Bulair in order to sever the land communications of the Turkish forces in the Peninsula with Constantinople and Thrace.[46] Kitchener remarked that the possibility of a movement along the Bulair lines had been examined on several occasions in the past. Hamilton's chief objections were first that the few landing beaches in the vicinity of Bulair lacked space and the actual disembarkation would have to take place on the other side of the Gulf of Saros. This would entail a line of communications 30 miles long from the landing site to Bulair; furthermore, after the position had been occupied, the force holding it would be exposed to attack from two sides. Asquith then read an extract from a general staff report in 1909 on the "Defence of Constantinople" which recommended an attack at Bulair as offering the best strategic advantages and indicating that landings were possible at two points in the area. Rather than attacking the Turks, the prospect that deprived of food, munitions and reinforcements they might be forced into surrendering, appealed to some members who thought that the issue should be explored again. Kitchener agreed to sound out Hamilton.[47]

After the arrival of Kitchener's telegram, Hamilton did not waste any time in returning an unfavourable reply. Besides repeating the old arguments he advanced another one: that in de Robeck's view the arrival of German submarines would make it impossible to render sufficient naval protection to the supply ships as far north as Bulair.[48] Given the attitude of both the army and naval commanders, there was no further consideration of the Bulair plan.

The ministers in the inner war council had barely voted to reinforce Hamilton with three divisions when Churchill, emboldened by their earlier favourable disposition, advanced another proposal. With the demands of administrating the Admiralty no longer occupying most of his attention, he had plenty of free time to attend to his pet project. Aware that a victory in the Dardanelles was the surest means to rehabilitate his sagging reputation, he lobbied tirelessly to send out more divisions to Hamilton.[49] Moreover he drew up a memorandum which he circulated to the cabinet on 11 June and further pleaded his case in a personal letter to Kitchener four days later.[50]

---

45   Asquith to George V, 19 June 1915, CAB 41/36/27; Hankey, *Supreme Command*, vol. 1, pp. 340-41.
46   The memorandum can be found in Gilbert (ed.), *Companion*, vol. 2, pp. 1004-8.
47   Minutes of the Dardanelles Committee, 12 June 1915, CAB 43/3/2.
48   Hamilton, *Gallipoli Diary*, vol. 1, pp. 290-93; Churchill, *World Crisis*, vol. 2, p. 417.
49   Hankey, *Supreme Command*, vol. 1, p. 342.
50   Churchill, *World Crisis*, vol. 2, pp. 415-16, 418-19.

The possibility of sending Hamilton further reinforcements was raised at the Dardanelles Committee on 17 June. Churchill took the lead to urge that, as a matter of prudence, two territorial divisions should be added to the four already assigned to Hamilton. Balfour explained that it would be difficult to find sufficient escort ships and he doubted that the troops would reach the Dardanelles before 20 August. The second wave of the New Armies had finished their training and their transport to France would take up the entire month of July. With two divisions of the Third Army ready to take the field and the remaining four soon to follow, Kitchener could afford to spare the additional territorial units to Hamilton. He claimed he would be willing to provide an additional division if the transport arrangements could be expedited. Balfour conceded that he would further press his experts to determine whether the Admiralty could arrange to hasten the transportation of the troops. Kitchener thought that it would be better to postpone the decision, pending assurances that the additional units would arrive in time to be included in Hamilton's next offensive.[51]

On 21 June Balfour informed Kitchener that by using fast liners the three divisions could reach the Dardanelles by 28 July. Thereupon Kitchener contacted Hamilton and asked if he needed a fourth division. Hamilton answered that he did not feel justified in refusing the offer. Admiralty notification that the fourth division would arrive on the spot by the start of August opened the possibility of sending the fifth one to Hamilton.[52] The matter was discussed at the Dardanelles Committee on the 25th and there was much support in favour of sending the two extra divisions. Kitchener, on the instructions of the Committee, asked Hamilton whether he would consider a fifth division necessary or desirable. Hamilton replied in the affirmative, although it was apparent that, since the fourth and fifth divisions could not arrive simultaneously with the first three, he proposed to adhere to his original plan. Hamilton ended by stating:

> To summarize, I think I have reasonable prospects of eventual success with three divisions, with four the risk of miscalculation would be minimized, and with five, even if the fifth division had little or no gun ammunition, I think it would be a much simpler matter to clear the Asiatic shore subsequently of big guns, i.e., Kilid Bahr would be captured at an earlier date, and success would be generally assured.[53]

Kitchener continued to nurse misgivings that even with the promised reinforcements, all of which were untested, Hamilton could defeat the Turkish army and capture Constantinople. The vital element of surprise had been forfeited long before the military operation got underway. The Turks occupied the high ground, had shown themselves to be good fighters and their numbers on the Peninsula had increased in recent weeks to an estimated 80,000. Kitchener knew he could not match the number of divisions the Ottomans were capable of sending to the battle scene. Turkey reportedly could count on 200,000 men under arms, many of whom were stationed in nearby Thrace as a precaution against the Russians or possibly Bulgarians – should they enter the war on the side of the Entente. A movement against the Ottoman capital was certain to attract the bulk of the Turkish army and was an undertaking that called for more forces than were available.

---

51   Minutes of the Dardanelles Committee, 17 June 1915, CAB 42/3/4.
52   Aspinall-Oglander, *Gallipoli*, vol. 2, pp. 61-63.
53   Hamilton, *Gallipoli Diary*, vol. 1, pp. 348-51.

1 H.H. Asquith. A brilliant parliamentarian and orator possessing exceptional intellectual qualities, he was more of a conciliator than a war leader. (Library of Congress)

2 David Lloyd George. An opportunist with no fixed principles, he had no compunction about resorting to gutter tactics against anyone who opposed him or stood in his way. (Open source)

3 (Far left) Winston Churchill. Intelligent, energetic, resolute but impulsive, opinionated and self-absorbed, his personal concern in 1915 overrode national interests. (Open source)

4 (Left)Edward Grey. If the quality of his work sometimes drew criticism, no one had reason to question his sense of duty, personal conduct and integrity. (Open Source)

5 Kitchener clad in civilian clothes, leaves the War Office to attend his first cabinet meeting where his unexpected disclosures startled his colleagues. (*Illustrated London News*)

6 Maurice Hankey. The brilliant ex-Royal Marine provided sound advice as well as indispensable service as secretary to the inner councils of war. (Library of Congress)

7 The most iconic recruiting poster, contrary to long held common belief, was not a vital factor in rousing young men to enlist. (Open source)

ii

8 In a typical scene throughout Britain on Parliament's declaration of war against Imperial Germany, crowds of young men from all social classes form long queues outside Whitehall recruiting station to join the colours. (IWM)

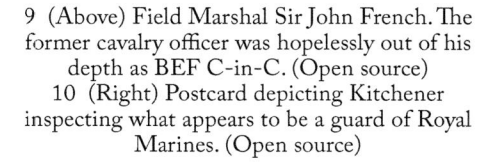

9 (Above) Field Marshal Sir John French. The former cavalry officer was hopelessly out of his depth as BEF C-in-C. (Open source)
10 (Right) Postcard depicting Kitchener inspecting what appears to be a guard of Royal Marines. (Open source)

11 Kitchener and Hankey after attending a conference, Paris September 1914. (Open source)

12 Kitchener arriving at the War Office during the political crisis of May 1915. (*Manchester Guardian History of the War*, vol. 2)

13 General Joffre acknowledges the cheers of the crowds on leaving the War Office with Lord Kitchener during his visit to London at the end of October 1915. (*Illustrated London News*)

14 Hamilton is chatting with General Henri Gouraud, the fearless and talented French commander he much admired and respected. Several days after this picture was taken, Gouraud was critically wounded by a shell fired from a gun on the Asiatic shore and was transported back to France. (*Illustrated London News*)

15 Kitchener (with a walking stick) following an inspection at Mudros on 11 November 1915. Monro is speaking to him. Immediately behind is Maxwell. (Australian War Memorial)

16 Kitchener walking through the ruins of Sedd-el-Bahr fortress on Cape Helles. To his right are abandoned Turkish shells. (Australian War Memorial)

17 Lieutenant General Francis Davies, VIII Corps commander, leading his small party to survey enemy positions at Cape Helles. At the moment he is pointing towards Achi Baba. Next to Kitchener are Generals Birdwood and Maxwell. (Picryl)

18 Kitchener shaking hands with General Maurice Bailloud who had succeeded Gouraud. Hamilton's relations with Bailloud were strained as he was not nearly as competent as his predecessor. (Australian War Memorial)

19 Australians watching the arrival of Kitchener at Anzac. (Australian War Memorial).

20 Birdwood introduces Kitchener to Australian officers. (Australian War Memorial)

21 Kitchener chatting with a group of Australian soldiers. (Australian War Memorial)

22 Kitchener and Birdwood observing the Turkish position from Russel's Top at Anzac. (Australian War Memorial)

23 Kitchener was at the time this photograph was taken, actually within 30 yards of an enemy trench manned by hundreds of Turks who were unaware of his presence. Maxwell is on the right of Kitchener and nearest to the camera. (Australian War Memorial)

24 Kitchener's farewell salute after visiting Anzac. (Australian War Memorial)

25 Kitchener in late 1915. His worn out appearance was caused by an enormous workload, constant stress imposed by the war and sharp differences with his colleagues, mainly over strategic policies. (Library of Congress)

Kitchener's most fervent desire in light of his gloomy outlook was for Hamilton's second landing to make enough progress to allow the fleet to get through The Narrows. The army's work would then be done and the initiative would pass back to the navy. Thus Kitchener no longer held expectation that the army could take control of the Peninsula and push on to Constantinople. Scaling down the objectives to opening a sea route to Russia seemed the only way to wind up the enterprise and leave in safety and honour. Kitchener hinted of a change in policy in a discussion with George Riddell. When the influential newspaper proprietor asked Kitchener if the campaign had become exclusively a military one, he was told: "Oh no! We shall not allow the Navy to escape in that way. They started the campaign, and now it has proven troublesome they will have to continue to bear their share of the blame and trouble."[54] Kitchener was more forthcoming with Major General Henry Wilson (liaison officer at GQG), who was in London on another matter. Kitchener spoke of his difficulties and how he had been pushed into the Dardanelles adventure. He admitted that the expedition had been mishandled but added that he could not clear out under the existing circumstances. He indicated that once the army had completed its assignment, he would transfer most of it to the western theatre.[55]

Kitchener directed Major General Ellison who was on his way to the Dardanelles (where he would serve as Deputy Quartermaster-General to the MEF) to verbally inform Hamilton to consider a drive towards Maidos as soon as the three new divisions arrived; and that he did not intend for the army to go to Constantinople.[56] Kitchener did not trust his political colleagues to keep classified information to themselves and only told Hankey of the army's future restricted role.[57]

Up until the latter part of June, the Committee had made no attempt to decide whether the Dardanelles campaign should be given priority over the western theatre. The want of men and munitions meant that the British could not pursue major assaults on more than one front at a time. For Kitchener the choice was simple. He wanted to pursue an active defence in the west and concentrate on wrapping up the army's end in the Dardanelles. Kitchener produced a long memorandum on 26 June in which he urged that the Allies refrain from any large-scale operations until the spring of 1916 because the New Armies were not fully trained and large supplies of guns and ammunition needed to be accumulated. He was convinced that the Allies would be forfeiting the chances of victory if a combined attack on the western front could not be coordinated with an advance from the east which was impossible until the Russian armies had recovered from their successive defeats and were equipped with enough munitions.[58] Before distributing the paper to the cabinet, Kitchener forwarded a copy to Asquith who wrote back, "in the main I heartily agree"[59] The only question was whether the policy Kitchener recommended would be acceptable to the French.

---

54 Lord Riddell, *War Diary* (London: Nicholson & Watson, 1933), p. 105.
55 Wilson diary, entry for 30 June 1915, Wilson papers.
56 Ellison testimony, 23 January 1917, Dardanelles Commission Report, CAB 19/33; and Ellison's written statement to the Dardanelles Commission, nd, CAB 19/29.
57 Hankey diary, entry for 19 July 1915, Hankey papers.
58 Kitchener, "An Appreciation of the Military Situation in the Future," 26 June 1915, CAB 37/130/27.
59 Asquith to Kitchener, 26 June 1915, Kitchener papers, PRO 30/57/76.

The British cabinet held sessions on the 2 and 3 July to formulate a strategic policy to lay down at a conference with the French.[60] The result essentially amounted to support for Kitchener's military outlook. While the government would not renounce Britain's freedom of action, it acknowledged the western front as the primary theatre of war. Moreover it authorized Kitchener to give Joffre a timetable, showing when the New Armies would be preceding to France but at the same time to emphasize that they were to be used to take over additional lengths of the line, not for offensive purposes. Finally it should be strongly represented to the French that they ought to defer major operations until 1916.[61] Thus the British position was firmly set when Asquith, Kitchener and the other members of the British delegation – Balfour, Crewe and Hankey – crossed over to Calais on the evening of the 5th and stayed at the Hotel Terminus. A few days earlier Wilson had arranged a private meeting between Kitchener and Joffre to be held before the start of the conference. At 7.45 on the morning of the 6th, Kitchener left the hotel and reached the town's railway station slightly after Joffre and the key French ministers had arrived by special train. Once the usual pleasantries were exchanged, Kitchener and Joffre broke away and held private talks in the train's saloon. The two soldiers settled their differences in an amicable fashion. Kitchener turned over a schedule of the times of the arrival of the New Armies and Joffre agreed that an all-out offensive, if considered necessary, would be undertaken by French forces alone.

Kitchener tried hard to persuade Joffre to abandon his proposed offensive in favour of a policy of limited attrition. Kitchener's concept of attrition differed from that of Joffre who endorsed mass attacks aimed at a rapid breakthrough. Setting distant objectives, as proven repeatedly, was unrealistic and had only resulted in unnecessary loss of life. Kitchener was an early advocate of the "bite and hold" strategy. What he and a few other like-minded soldiers were espousing was a step-by-step advance that focused on killing Germans rather than gaining territory. The approach called for a series of surprise attacks, each of which was intended to seize a narrow and lightly defended area of the enemy's front. Once the Allies had attained their objective, they were to fortify their new position and inflict heavy casualties on the Germans when they counterattacked. By the time the British army reached its maximum strength in 1917, the Germans would be so weakened by losses that they would be unable to hold back a large-scale offensive.[62] Kitchener had caught up to the learning curve a few months earlier but Joffre throughout 1915 had yet to move from the starting line.

Joffre had heard Kitchener's strategic arguments before and the prospect of a war lasting an additional two or possibly three years did not resonate with him or Sir John for that matter. The French general was undeniably a mediocre field commander but he was, in contrast, a first rate politician. Kitchener was under the impression that he was on the verge of convincing Joffre to limit the scope of future operations on the western front when they ended their discussion to attend the conference which was set to begin at 9 am.

The English delegates rose late from bed and the start of the first Anglo-French conference was pushed back an hour. It was badly organized. There was no agenda, no notes were taken and no conclusions officially recorded. Kitchener was the only member of the British delegation who spoke French fluently – Hankey could make himself understood in French but he was

---

60   Asquith to George V, 3 July 1915, CAB 41/36/31.
61   Cassar, *Asquith*, pp. 116-17.
62   Cassar, *Kitchener's War*, pp. 163-64.

not present at the conference as only the principals were allowed to attend. "I have never heard so much bad French spoken in my life (I think – deserved the prize)," Asquith subsequently wrote.[63] Except whenever Kitchener spoke, the French had to rely on translators since none of them could put a sentence together in English.

Kitchener was in fine form and dominated the proceedings to the delight of his colleagues. He was calm, deliberate, and consistent in his arguments and made an immense impression on the French political delegates. He spoke frankly about the shortage of munitions and the purpose for sending reinforcements to Hamilton. He deprecated the idea of a too vigorous offensive in the west and stressed the need to economize men and munitions for the time being. The French ministers were won over, despite their earlier inclination to follow Joffre's lead. There was wide agreement that the Dardanelles campaign should be pushed to a successful conclusion and that a policy of limited attrition be adopted on the western front. There would be small local attacks aimed at demoralizing and wearing down the enemy but no full-scale offensive unless the Russian army was on the point of defeat.[64] Joffre made a brief defence of his strategy and thereafter said little. Kitchener assumed that he had been swayed by the general tenor of the discussions.[65] As it turned out, he was wrong.

Now that a joint policy with the French had finally been settled, Kitchener threw himself into playing a more active role in the preparations for another landing in the Dardanelles. He carefully studied and occasionally questioned some of Hamilton's proposals. If he perceived possible flaws he had no qualms about making suggestions, but at no time did he try to impose his views on Hamilton. To cite an example he gave Lieutenant General Frederick Stopford, just before he left for the Dardanelles early in July to take charge of the three new divisions – which were organized as a corps – a message to deliver to Hamilton. The first part, as Stopford later conveyed to Hamilton, read as follows:

> Lord Kitchener told me to tell you he had no wish to interfere with the man on the spot, but from closely watching our actions here, as well as those of General French in Flanders, he is certain that the only way to make a real success of an attack is by surprise. Also, that when the surprise ceases to be operative, in so far that the advance is checked and the enemy begin to collect from all sides to oppose the attackers, then, perseverance becomes merely a useless waste of life. In every attack there seems to be a moment when success is in the assailant's grasp. Both the French and ourselves at Arras and Neuve Chapelle lost the opportunity.

The next points that Stopford covered merely repeated the advice Kitchener had imparted in a telegram to Hamilton a month earlier.

> It is not the wish of the Cabinet that Sir Ian Hamilton should make partial attacks. They consider it preferable that he should await the arrival of his reinforcements to make one

---

63 Asquith, *Memories*, vol. 2, pp. 106-7.
64 Crewe to Bertie, 8 July 1915, Bertie papers, FO 800/161; Hankey, *Supreme Command*, vol. 1, pp. 348-49; Cassar for both *Kitchener*, pp. 381-82, and *Kitchener's War*, pp. 210-11; Reginald Viscount Esher, *The Tragedy of Lord Kitchener* (London: John Murray, 1921), pp. 140-41.
65 Callwell to Wilson, 9 July 1915, Wison papers, HHW 2/75/51.

great effort, which, if successful, will give them the ridge commanding the Narrows. It is not intended, however, that Sir Ian should do nothing in the meantime and if he gets a really good opportunity he is to seize it.[66]

Perhaps because Kitchener was under greater pressure than usual at the time, he longed for a respite from Churchill, who owing to his obsession over the Dardanelles, badgered him constantly for information or to offer him unwanted counsel. During the second week in July the War Secretary suggested to Asquith and Balfour that it would be helpful to send Churchill to collect firsthand information from the scene of the fighting. Both gave their approval and, when contacted, Churchill welcomed the opportunity to undertake the mission. On further reflection Kitchener doubted the wisdom of sending Churchill alone and reached out to Asquith to tell him that he wanted Hankey to go along to bring back an independent report.[67] Asquith thought it was a good idea and sent for Hankey to request that he accompany Churchill to the Dardanelles. Hankey was reluctant to accept, suspecting that the real purpose of the assignment was to act as a check on Churchill. However Churchill, far from raising objections, replied that he would be delighted to have Hankey's company on the trip. Hankey accordingly gave his consent and his status was officially confirmed by the Prime Minister.[68]

The fact-finding mission had been made without the agreement or knowledge of the Conservatives and when they found out that Churchill was one of the delegates, they protested heatedly against his selection. Asquith notified Churchill that a serious crisis might develop if he went ahead with the trip. In these circumstances, Churchill felt he had no alternative but to withdraw from his proposed visit and so Hankey went on alone.[69] Kitchener saw Esher on the 21st and commented on the effect of the Conservative veto. Esher recorded the following: "He laughed a good deal about it and admitted that he would not have been sorry to get rid of Winston for a while."[70]

During the latter part of July, the French government called upon Kitchener to resolve a dispute between its successive commanding officers in the Dardanelles and Hamilton. The French divisions held the eastern end of the line on Cape Helles and each day were subjected to heavy shelling from the batteries in Asia. When d'Amade was recalled to France in May, he was replaced by General Henri Gouraud who was badly wounded six weeks later and thereupon the command devolved upon General Maurice Bailloud. Both Gouraud and Bailloud favoured landing a modest force in Asia to silence the batteries but their pleas to Hamilton had fallen on deaf ears. Hamilton never took into account the toll the constant shelling was having on the French troops, regarding it as mere inconvenience. After numerous complaints from the last two commanders, Millerand finally decided to take the matter in hand. On 20 July he wrote to Kitchener, claiming that the appalling situation called for the destruction of the Turkish batteries in Asia without delay. He observed that the daily shelling was eroding the strength and undermining the morale of the French corps and he urged Kitchener to instruct Hamilton

---

66 Hamilton, *Gallipoli Diary*, vol. 2, pp. 1-4.
67 Gilbert, *Winston S. Churchill*, vol. 3, pp. 510-12.
68 Hankey, *Supreme Command*, vol. 1, p. 376.
69 Gilbert, *Winston S. Churchill*, vol. 3, p. 513.
70 Esher War Journal, entry for 21 July 1915, Esher papers.

to take immediate measures consistent with the recommendations of Gouraud and Bailloud.[71] Kitchener, in turn, signaled Hamilton almost immediately:

> The French state that the fire from the Asiatic side allow them no rest... They propose secondary operations on the Asiatic side to deal with enemy artillery, and suggest employment of 20,000 British assisted by French 75 monitors. Would the main scheme of our operation be jeopardised by thus detaching a considerable force, which may find itself employed with hostile forces of undetermined strength. What do you and De Robeck think? Could the guns near Kum Kale be silenced by monitor?[72]

Hamilton replied two days later. He was sure that Kitchener would agree that a diversion, if and when it became necessary, must be made at his own time and without prejudicing his main operation.[73] Kitchener was satisfied with Hamilton's decision. He had from the very beginning opposed involvement in Asia, not to mention that he had no wish to interfere in Hamilton's plans. On 28 July he wrote back to Millerand: "You will understand how difficult it is to impose upon a commander-in-chief an operation which does not fit in with his own carefully prepared plan."[74] To allow a military chief freedom of action in the field was a principal from which Millerand himself never deviated and he could hardly fault Kitchener for adopting the same course. Still there was nothing to prevent Millerand from conducting an inquiry as to whether it would be feasible for the French alone to undertake an operation in Asia at a future date. Everything would hinge on Hamilton's impending attack.

To deceive the Turks into thinking that the next major effort would again take place on Cape Helles, Hamilton conducted operations from that front in June and July. It will be remembered that Kitchener had impressed upon Hamilton on 8 June that he was to avoid major attacks until the arrival of his reinforcements. A few days earlier the Third Battle of Krithia (4 June) had taken place and the results were no better than in the two previous engagements. If the latest reverse at Krithia had a sobering effect on Hamilton, it lasted only briefly. In reacting to Kitchener's recommendation, he purported to be in full agreement, saying that he would confine his activities to keeping pressure on the enemy here and there "to maintain ourselves." He added: "But to expect us to attack without giving us our fair share – on Western standards – of high explosives and howitzers shows lack of military imagination."[75] Several weeks later, Hamilton had a change of heart. Kitchener received no hint from Hamilton that he was pursuing the very course he had condemned earlier. Why Hamilton persisted in launching attacks in Cape Helles between 28 June and 13 July is difficult to comprehend. Although they advanced the Anglo-French line slightly and eased pressure on the Anzac front, the main objective, the capture of Achi Baba, was not achieved and in the process the casualties had totaled 12,300 – 7,700 British and 4,600 French.[76]

---

71 Millerand to Kitchener, 20 July 1915, Millerand papers, 470 AP/1.
72 Kitchener to Hamilton, 21 July 1915, CAB 19/31.
73 Hamilton to Kitchener, 23 July 1915, ibid.
74 Kitchener to Millerand, 28 July 1915, *Archives du Ministère de la Guerre*, 5N 132.
75 Cited in James, *Gallipoli*, pp. 217-18.
76 Prior, *Gallipoli*, pp. 152-58; Hickey, *Gallipoli*, pp. 216-34; Aspinall-Oglander, *Gallipoli*, vol. 2, chs. 7-8; James, *Gallipoli*, pp. 229-34.

While this was going on, Hamilton was accelerating his preparations to avoid the autumn winds and waves which would make a landing more difficult. Kitchener would have preferred that Hamilton delay his attack until after the arrival of the last two divisions but avoided imposing his opinion. Hamilton was not only given a free hand to plan and direct the operation, but provided with greater resources than he had requested to ensure success. After receiving notice that the ammunition which he had requisitioned was en route, Hamilton acknowledged the extent of Kitchener's support with gratitude: "You have done everything for us that man can do."[77]

The plan that Hamilton worked out was similar to the one he had adopted on 25 April, except that the focal point of the attack was at Anzac rather than at Cape Helles. The idea was to break out from the Anzac beachhead after a feint at Lone Pine and converge on the dominating Sari Bair ridge. At the same time a complimentary assault would be mounted at Suvla Bay to the north to protect the Anzac flank and establish a base. As the area was not heavily defefended the army was expected to advance rapidly, size control of the Anafarta ridge and join hands with the Anzac attack on Sari Bahr. There would also be a diversionary attack at Cape Helles to hold the Turks there as well as attract some of their reinforcements from the Anzac front. The scheme was overly complicated and its success was contingent on the proper execution of all the entities that were often interrelated. Then too the objective had been reduced as the advance was no longer intended to push across the Peninsula but end with the capture of Sari Bair. Another operation requiring more troops would have to follow to sweep down from the north to overwhelm the defences on Kilid Bahr.

The second landing was launched on 6 August and Hamilton's early reports were encouraging, naturally delighting Kitchener who sent him the following telegram: "Glad to hear that your operations have started so well. I am sure you will push all you can to obtain command of the Marmara shore without being held up by the trenches. Your forces have all our best wishes."[78] But the forward movement stalled without reaching any of its objectives. On the 17th Hamilton delivered the bad news to Kitchener, followed by a chilling request for 95,000 additional troops – a huge number for a sideshow.

The politicians in London were exasperated and bitter over Hamilton's failure. They had built up high hopes on the outcome of the operation because Hamilton, who received considerably more troops than he had requested, led them to believe that success was all but certain. It was on the basis of that assurance, they had gone along with the idea of a storming, rather than a starving, operation against the Turks.

The Dardanelles Committee gathered at 10 Downing Street on the 17th. Kitchener was absent as he was in France. With the inclusion of Carson, opposition against the Dardanelles campaign had begun to harden. All the speakers, except Churchill, blamed Hamilton for the abortive offensive. Asquith observed that Hamilton had lost 23,000 men but still remained confident that he could accomplish his goal, adding that the "reason was not easy to see." Both Bonar Law and Carson considered that a new attack would be a useless sacrifice of life. The members had an opportunity to air their views but it was clear that no decision on the future of the operation could be taken until after Kitchener returned to London.[79]

---

77   Hamilton, *Gallipoli Diary*, vol. 2, p. 43.
78   Kitchener to Hamilton, 9 August 1915, CAB 19/31.
79   Minutes of the Dardanelles Committee, 19 August 1915, CAB 42/3/15.

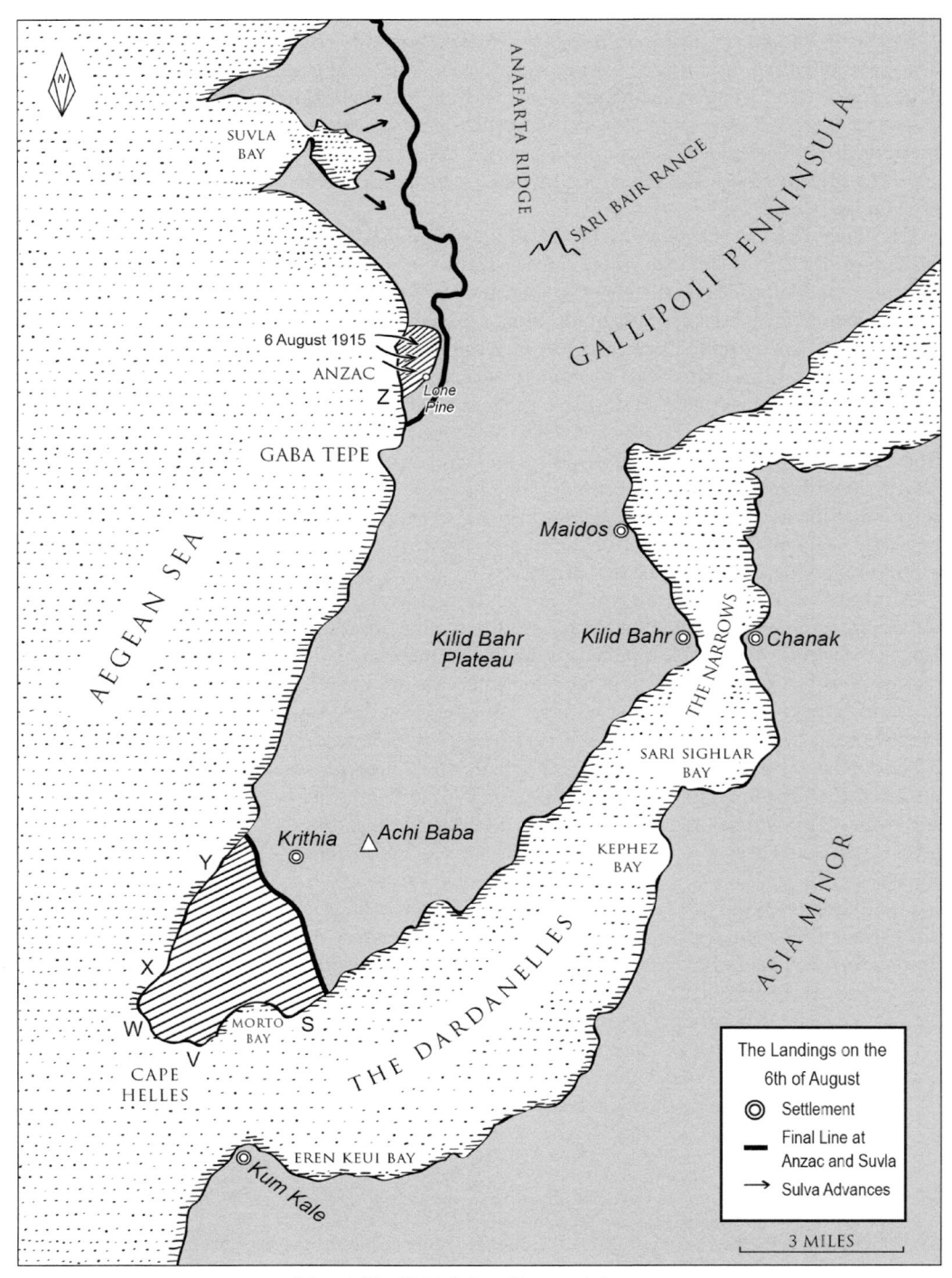

Map 6 The British Landing on 6 August.

Kitchener had been called to France by Joffre who hoped to enlist British participation in his next great offensive. Ignoring the decision at Calais, Joffre had gone ahead and laid plans for a large offensive in Champagne in September. Sir John had turned down Joffre's request to cooperate as the ground over which the British attack had been assigned was a mining area, interspersed with villages, mine heads and slag heaps, practically nullifying any chance of achieving anything meaningful. Joffre thereupon invited Kitchener to Chantilly to persuade him to intervene on his behalf.

Kitchener crossed the channel on 15 August and held prolonged talks with Joffre and Millerand. By then there were ample signs that the German drive eastwards was meeting with great success. Warsaw had fallen on 4 August and the Russian army, which had lost nearly half a million men in recent battles, was in full retreat. Joffre maintained that if vigorous action in the west were not taken immediately, the Russians might be defeated and forced to make a separate peace. He even hinted that with so much of France under the heels of the German invaders, the appearance of inactivity might drive the war weary public into demanding a release from the war. Henry Wilson, who was at GQG, confirmed the danger of inactivity on the western front. Possessing unbounded faith in Joffre and his strategy, Wilson argued that the failure to attack would bring in a new government, one likely bent on making peace with the enemy. It is true that the idea of a negotiated peace had begun to spread among the parties of the left but he vastly exaggerated the extent of the movement. Unfortunately Kitchener trusted Wilson's information which proved to be inaccurate.[80]

After the bitter results of the Anglo-French armies in the field in April and May, Kitchener did not for a moment believe that Joffre's proposed offensive would lead to appreciable gains, let alone be decisive. Nevertheless he felt compelled to enter into a disastrous commitment because he saw no other way of avoiding a fatal rupture with the French. Consequently he instructed the British high command to "act with all our energy, and do our utmost to help the French, even though, by doing so, we suffered very heavy losses indeed."[81] Kitchener certainly would have adopted a different line had he known that Joffre's intentions were contrary to the declared policy of the French government. Actually Joffre used Kitchener's assent to persuade the civil authorities to sanction his offensive. It was well known in Paris that the British warlord had hitherto favoured acting on the defence in the west and so his change of heart was all the more significant.[82]

Hamilton's telegram of 17 August was forwarded to Kitchener while he was still in France. A disheartened Kitchener no longer held any hope that the army could reach the forts protecting The Narrows. He conveyed his feelings to Asquith in a correspondence:

> To send such reinforcements as those asked for would be a very serious step to take at the present moment when an offensive in France is necessary to relieve pressure on Russia and keep the French Army and people steady… I personally feel that it is not certain that even if they were sent the result would be decisive and relieve us of the Dardanelles incubus.[83]

---

80 Cassar, *Reluctant Partner*, p. 174; Llewellyn Woodward, *Great Britain and the War*, pp. 135-36; Wilson diary, entry for 16 August, Wilson papers.
81 Haig diary, entry for 19 August 1915. The diary is also available at the National Archives.
82 Cassar, *Reluctant Partner*, p. 175.
83 Kitchener to Asquith, 17 August 1915, Creedy papers, WO 159/7.

Kitchener returned to London on the evening of the 19th and the next day attended a meeting of the Dardanelles Committee. He explained to his colleagues that to ensure that Russia and France remained in the war he had been compelled to support Joffre's late summer offensive. Churchill reacted angrily to the announcement that the Calais agreement had been overturned. He protested that the offensive would not alter the line but lead to a vast expenditure of lives and ammunition and do little to relieve pressure on the Russians. He pointed out that a superiority of two to one was laid down as necessary to make gains in an attack and the Allies simply did not possess that advantage in the west. Kitchener admitted there was a good deal of truth in what Churchill said "but unfortunately we had to make war as we must, and not as we should like to." He offered no expectations of military success but stressed that if the British remained inactive there was "some chance of the Russians and the French making separate terms of peace in October."[84] There were others who may have felt like Churchill but the possible political fallout muted their open opposition to Kitchener's agreement with Joffre. The general sentiment was that it was preferable to honour Britain's commitment than to risk shattering the alliance with France.

The decision to cooperate with Joffre's forthcoming operation in France meant the immediate starvation, or at best malnutrition, of the army on the Peninsula. Kitchener would have been happy to cut his losses and abandon the Dardanelles operation but, in his view, that was not a practical option. He continued to maintain that withdrawal would seriously damage Britain's reputation in Egypt and India and could not be carried our without appalling losses. On the other hand if the decision favoured remaining on the Peninsula, it was unthinkable to ask Hamilton to fight on without drafts to replace his losses and an adequate supply of ammunition. Kitchener's anxieties were further increased during this period by rumours of Bulgaria's imminent entry into the war as an ally of Germany. In such an event Germany, with the advantage of a direct route once Serbia was overwhelmed, would be able to pour guns and ammunition into Turkey. Kitchener recognized that backed by heavy artillery support, the Turks could blast the allies off the Peninsula.

Kitchener announced to the ministerial gathering on the 20th that he proposed to send enough men to Hamilton to enable him to hold on until he was able to do more. Kitchener made it clear that he would not consider retirement. He implied that once Joffe's offensive was over he would take the necessary steps to try to finish off the Turks. This prompted Carson to ask Kitchener "if it was the intention in case of success at the Dardanelles to press on to Constantinople." Bearing in mind that Kitchener no longer had any intentions of doing so, he chose his words carefully, answering "that the object was for the fleet to force and clear the Dardanelles."[85] It was evident that Kitchener did not want to engage in a debate with colleagues to justify reducing the army's task.

Kitchener returned to the War Office after the meeting and sent Hamilton a telegram, the essential part of which ran as follows:

> A serious offensive in the Western theatre is being organized in co-operation with the French. When your troops have been pulled together and you have been joined by any

---

84 Minutes of the Dardanelles Committee, 20 August, CAB 42/3/16.
85 Ibid.

reinforcements you can obtain from Egypt we greatly hope that you will find it in your power to carry out effectively the operations you have in hand. You must understand that under the circumstances no large divisional units can be diverted from the main theatre of operations in France. We feel confident that you will do your utmost, as we are doing ours to support you. In case of failure you will have to remain for some considerable time on the defensive.[86]

Hamilton's response painted a gloomy picture of his predicament. With normal wastage and the incoming drafts at the current level, he calculated that by mid-December his total fighting strength, including the French corps, would be about 60,000. Of these a percentage would be given time off to rest away from the Peninsula. The remainder would only suffice to hold Cape Helles and Anzac Cove. In default of reinforcements, he might have to relinquish the newly acquired Suvla Bay front.[87]

Kitchener expressed his disappointment, not only that the army had failed to achieve better results but the 47,000 men (drafts and reinforcements) he had sent since 6 August was deemed insufficient to enable Hamilton to hold his positions.[88] Hamilton was puzzled by Kitchener's reference to so large a number of troops and according to his calculation the figure was actually 29,000 – which had not yet been dispatched. The misunderstanding was corrected in Hamilton's favour but it did not resolve his current dilemma.

Discussion in the Dardanelles Committee on 27 August centred on trying to fix a policy for the campaign. The Committee was divided and unable to reach a consensus. Asquith interjected at a certain point, to say that Hankey was due back from his mission in the Dardanelles in two days and his report, based on an unbiased opinion, would be useful in reaching a decision. The Dardanelles Committee concluded that in the meantime Hamilton should hold his ground and draw up an appreciation containing his future prospects and the requirements to carry them out.[89]

On the same day Kitchener wired Hamilton, soliciting his opinion on several issues. From the military and strategic viewpoint, what were the prospects on the Peninsula? Drawing on his earlier experience, how did he propose to drive out the Turks? What force did he consider would be required to achieve the main objective?[90] Hamilton replied on 2 September, recommending that a fresh effort be made at the narrow neck of the Peninsula (Bulair) – which he had steadfastly opposed earlier. He noted that the imminent arrival of 29,000 fresh troops of whom 12,000 were drafts, would not reduce his present deficit and only bring his total force up to 63,000. He added: "The launching of a grand new attack would need new formations up to 50,000, besides sufficient drafts to bring my divisions up to establishment."[91]

The main barrier to supplying the quantity of reinforcements Hamilton requested was that it could only have been obtained from the western front. Before Kitchener was driven to his wits' end trying to find a resolution, there came an offer of assistance from an unexpected quarter.

86   Kitchener to Hamilton, 20 August 1915, CAB 19/31.
87   Hamilton to Kitchener, 23 August 1915, ibid.
88   Kitchener to Hamilton, 25 August 1915, ibid.
89   Minutes of the Dardanelles Committee, 27 August 1915, CAB 42/3/17.
90   Kitchener to Hamilton, 27 August 1915, CAB 19/31.
91   Hamilton to Kitchener, 2 September 1915, ibid.

On 1 September the French government expressed a willingness to add four divisions to the two already in the Dardanelles subject to four conditions: that the expeditionary force led by a French general be allowed to operate in a new theatre, independent of, but in close liaison with the British on Gallipoli; that the Royal Navy assist in transporting the new divisions; that the allied fleet together cover the disembarkation of the French forces; and that the French be permitted to establish a separate base at Mudros or Mitylene. A subsequent message from Paris requested that the British replace the two French divisions on Cape Helles with units of their own.[92] The arrival in the Dardanelles of large scale French reinforcements to compliment Hamilton's army was expected to breathe new life into the flagging operation. As little in war is predictable, it remained to be seen whether any impediments would emerge to delay or cancel the proposed expedition.

92   Cassar, *Reluctant Partner*, p. 178.

6

The Darkening Scene

The French announcement, arriving at a critical juncture, immediately lifted a huge weight off Kitchener's shoulders. It came as no surprise when the French military attaché in London paid him a visit and explained that his government wanted to open a new theatre in Asia but offered no further details. Kitchener subsequently contacted Millerand to lend his support for the proposed French landing, though in truth he could hardly have done otherwise. In a rare mood of optimism, especially astonishing in light of his warning to Hamilton to avoid operations in Asia, Kitchener maintained that an expedition made up of at least four divisions would be required to take the forts commanding The Narrows and open the way for the fleet. He urged haste in getting the operation under way before the onset of bad weather and that preparations for it be kept absolutely secret in order to deny the Turks time to concentrate more divisions in Asia. He pointed out that the two divisions intended to relieve the French contingent on Gallipoli would be withdrawn from the western front but that these would be replaced by fresh divisions from England. Kitchener added that he would be happy to meet with Millerand, if that was his wish, to discuss details of the plan.[1]

The strength of the Turkish garrison on the Asiatic shore was estimated to be no more than two divisions or around 20,000 men. If Hamilton was reinforced and allowed to make another major assault simultaneously with the French advance on Chanak, Kitchener was reasonably confident that the way would be cleared for the fleet to enter the Sea of Marmara. As soon as Kitchener sent off his reply to Millerand, he cabled Hamilton:

> The sending of a force of three or four Divisions to operate on the Asiatic mainland, independent as regards command, but in close relation with the British forces on the Peninsula is being considered by the French government … So far I have not discussed any details with the French, and have simply told them we shall be delighted to have the help which would be given by such an expedition … Wire me any points that you think I had better settle with the French authorities.[2]

---

1 Kitchener to Millerand, 2 September 1915, Millerand papers, 470 AP/15.
2 Kitchener to Hamilton, 2 September 1915, CAB 19/31.

Kitchener also shared the news with his colleagues in the Dardanelles Committee who were naturally as pleased as he was.[3] Many saw that opening a new front, from which to press forward with a large army, might be the remedy to turn the tide in the Dardanelles. Spirits were lightened and there was no longer any talk of evacuating the Peninsula. In fact Bonar Law, the most persistent critic of the Dardanelles campaign, joined Churchill in urging the dispatch of still more British forces "to make a good job of it."[4] Churchill begged Kitchener to send him as a major-general to command a corps in the Dardanelles. Churchill felt frustrated at the Duchy where he spent much of his time writing memos, frequently on the Dardanelles, and letters to Asquith providing him with advice on a wide variety of subjects. He no longer had any influence or friends in the cabinet. The trenches seemed to him the only escape. Still Kitchener objected to giving Churchill a senior command in the British army. Much as he wanted to get rid of Churchill, who had become an incessant gadfly since compelled to leave the Admiralty, he had no wish to offend the army.[5]

As the first flurry of excitement began to recede, the Asquith government could not help but wonder what was at the bottom of the French offer to play a more significant role in the campaign. It was well known that their ally had always opposed diverting large formations from the principal scene of action. Kitchener admitted on 3 September at the Dardanelles Committee that he was uncertain as to why the French had changed their attitude. He imagined that perhaps they were prepared to make a big effort to put an end to the enterprise so that British troops in the eastern Mediterranean could be transferred to the main front. This would serve the dual purpose of bringing relief to Russia and strengthening the French line. Whatever the French motive, Kitchener welcomed their new-found resolve which was bound to help Hamilton's operations. Actually Carson came closest to hitting the mark by warning that they needed to ensure that they "were not being led into a disastrous adventure from political motives on the part of the French."[6] The real reason for the new French outlook was somewhat more complicated and forms an interesting case study.

Throughout the first half of 1915 the French political authorities showed little disposition to look beyond the security of France. They responded to the needs of the Dardanelles campaign as though it were an illegitimate child, providing only such troops as were available without weakening the front in France or arousing the ire of GQG. Joffre's attacks in the spring and summer had started with high hopes and ended the same way, with casualties out of all proportion to the gain of a mile or two of worthless ground. With no signs of an imminent breakthrough, gloom and frustration settled over the country. Naturally the government was frequently berated by the press and parliament for the costly and disappointing failure of Joffre's offensives. Looking for a new theatre which might produce benefits at a lower cost, the French ministers were drawn to the Dardanelles campaign where they already had a modest investment. Near the end of July, the French authorities concluded that if Hamilton's forthcoming attack should miscarry, they would send substantial troops to finish the job. What galvanized them into action was the controversy over the removal of a prominent general from his command.

---

3   Hankey, *Supreme Command*, vol. 1, p. 410.
4   Churchill, *World Crisis*, vol. 2, p. 492.
5   Asquith to Kitchener, 9 September 1915, Kitchener papers, PRO 30/57/76; Hankey diary, entry for 10 September 1915, Hankey papers.
6   Minutes of the Dardanelles Committee, 3 September 1915, CAB 42/3/23.

Joffre's victory at the Battle of the Marne in September 1914 had elevated him to near demigod status in the eyes of the French people but in the months that followed he would experience plenty of setbacks but no major success. As his fame dimmed with each inconclusive bloody battle and there was talk of replacing him, the name of General Maurice Sarrail invariably surfaced. Joffre, ever-alert to any threat to his authority, struck when a favourable opportunity presented itself and dismissed Sarrail from command of the Third Army, citing incompetence as the reason. In an army whose high-level officer corps was dominated by Catholics and royalists, Sarrail, who was an anticlerical republican and a member of the Masons, was wildly popular with political parties on the left. His supporters claimed that he had been the victim of a witch hunt and insisted that he be given a new important assignment. With the Viviani ministry in danger of collapsing, Sarrail was offered command of the French contingent in the Dardanelles. Sarrail reluctantly accepted the proffered post but only on condition that the French contingent be adequately increased and that he be allowed to exercise an independent command. It so happened that the government was considering adding four divisions to the two currently in the Dardanelles and an arrangement satisfactory to Sarrail was reached. Nevertheless, Sarrail was initially adamant that he would not leave the country without the promised reinforcements.[7]

Joffre was no longer strong enough to block Sarrail's new appointment but he succeeded in making it a condition that no troops would leave France until after his autumn offensive had taken place. As already noted, the French government had grudgingly yielded to Joffre's wishes for an offensive after learning of Kitchener's endorsement. If as Joffre expected, his attack fared well, he was sure that the idea of an Asiatic expedition would be cancelled to permit him to follow up his victory.

Kitchener and his colleagues were under the impression that with the imminent dispatch of large French forces to the eastern Mediterranean, the forward movement on the main front would be postponed. However, Sir John arrived in London on 6 September and in talks with Kitchener disclosed that Joffre intended to carry on with his operation as planned. If this was true, Kitchener wondered, what was the status of the proposed French expedition to the Dardanelles? Neither he nor the other members of the Dardanelles Committee would contemplate the proposition of attacking simultaneously in France and in the Dardanelles. It was evident that, if the Allies divided their strength between the two theatres, they ran a good risk of meeting with failure in both places. The cabinet concluded that Kitchener should proceed to France to find out precisely the intentions of the Viviani government.[8]

On 11 September an Anglo-French conference was held at Calais. Besides Kitchener, the British were represented by Hankey (back from his inspection tour of the Dardanelles), Sir John French and Wilson; the French by Millerand, Joffre and Sarrail. Kitchener took the chair at the request of Millerand and Joffre. He opened the proceedings by formally thanking, on behalf of the British government, the French decision to send four divisions to the Dardanelles. He inquired if Joffre now proposed to modify his plan for an autumn attack. Joffre replied that he did not. Kitchener impressed upon Joffre the desirability of ending the operation in the Dardanelles as soon as possible as it would set free a considerable allied force which could be used elsewhere. As the allies could not simply abandon the project, the only option was to

---

7   Cassar, *Reluctant Partner*, ch. 10.
8   Asquith to George V, 10 September 1915, CAB 41/36/43.

see the business through. Joffre countered by making a plea against removing any troops from his front. He was deeply apprehensive that, if the expedition to Asia was held up, it would necessitate more troops and ammunition which he could not spare without endangering the safety of France. He maintained that even if the allies achieved their objective and opened the Dardanelles they might find themselves committed to a second major campaign in the neighbourhood of Constantinople.

Kitchener indicated that he had no intentions of embarking upon further operations in the east. The army's role was only limited to help the fleet get through the Dardanelles after which its work would be completed. Instead of opening a new dialogue his remarks failed to elicit any reaction from the French. It is evident that they did not fully comprehend the implications of Kitchener's statement which aimed to abandon any plan to further involve the army once it had silenced the forts at The Narrows. Wilson left an account of his private talks with Kitchener at Calais: "Kitchener's one idea is to get out of the mess he is in, and he said so specifically, and that there was now no intention of going to Constantinople."[9] Kitchener confided to Wilson that he would be thankful if the British army could gain possession of the high ground west of Maidos from where it would be possible to dominate the principal defences of The Narrows.[10] Once in control of the waterway, his intention apparently was to leave the navy, which was responsible for his nightmare, to its own devices.

Kitchener must have known by now that, even if a segment of the fleet managed to break into the Sea of Marmara, it stood no chance of inducing Constantinople to surrender. Kitchener held his cards close to his vest so his long range objectives in that part of the world are unknown. Was he willing to allow Constantinople to remain in Turkish hands and settle instead to opening a southern sea route to Russia which would have mitigated the admission of failure and facilitated evacuation of the Anglo-French troops when the time came? One can only speculate what Kitchener had in mind.

Throughout the deliberations Joffre made no secret of his dislike of the whole Dardanelles affair and he refused to set a precise date when it would be possible to remove the four divisions from his front. It was hoped that the troops would be ready to leave by 10 October and that operations could begin around the middle of November, but nothing was definite. If the offensive drive in the west succeeded, the decision to send the four divisions to the Dardanelles would be cancelled to permit Joffre to use them to exploit initial gains.

Millerand wanted Sarrail appointed supreme commander of the Allied force in the Dardanelles but Kitchener strongly objected on the grounds that Hamilton had more troops at his disposal, possessed greater experience and was senior in rank. A compromise was reached under which Sarrail could operate independently in Asia but in close liaison with Hamilton on the Peninsula. Any differences that might arise between the generals would be referred to the two governments to resolve.[11]

After the conference was over, Joffre told Kitchener in private that the Asiatic scheme was ill-advised and that it would require more than six divisions. He lashed out at Sarrail, accusing him of intriguing with politicians and questioning his fitness to command. Kitchener learned that the French offer to send an expedition to the Dardanelles had been motivated as much by

---

9   Wilson diary, entry for 11 September 1915, Wilson papers.
10 Ibid.
11 Anglo-French and Allied Conferences, 11 September 1915, CAB 28/1.

political consideration as by military necessity. The French government had tried to kill two birds with one stone – send a large force to finish the job in the Dardanelles and find a berth for Sarrail who had been sacked by Joffre, an incident that outraged left-wing parties and threatened the survival of the Viviani government. Kitchener had occasion to chat with Sarrail but was unimpressed by his attitude. At Hankey's suggestion he tried to persuade Sarrail to visit the Dardanelles in order to make a personal inspection. The French general politely declined, saying he could not absent himself from the country.[12]

Kitchener was not pleased with the results of the conference but had avoided taking a firmer line on some issues lest he strain the alliance, or cause it to fracture. In fact he was not certain that the French scheme would ever materialize. He reasoned that even if the French divisions embarked on the fixed date, they could not arrive on the scene before the fierce winter storms made a landing impossible. As it happened the whole French plan collapsed under the pressure of events in the Balkans.

In the late summer of 1915 the chief of the German general staff, General Erich von Falkenhayn, decided that in order to keep Turkey in the war he must dispose of Serbia and open a direct route to the Ottoman capital so that heavy artillery, supplies and reinforcements could move freely. To achieve that objective he required to coax Bulgaria to join the Central Powers. Since the start of the war Bulgaria had wavered back and forth in tantalizing fashion, weighing competing offers of territory from the two coalitions, before signing a secret military convention with Germany and Austria on 6 September.

It could not have happened at a worst time as it was during this period that Kitchener's isolation from his colleagues became complete. His aloofness, secretiveness, unwillingness to impart classified information and autocratic disposition often exasperated them. Yet they were unrealistic in thinking that a soldier who was 65 years old, had spent his professional life abroad and left undisturbed in executing government policy, could adjust easily in a system of collective responsibility. Put simply they needed to accept him the way he was. It is to their eternal discredit that they were unwilling to cut him some slack after he had rescued the nation from a sure catastrophe. When he was left in charge during the early months in office he had, thanks to his creative talent, courage in accepting daunting challenges, and understanding of the nature of modern warfare, produced miraculous results. Yet the politicians, notwithstanding their sorry record on defence prior to 1914, deluded themselves into thinking that they could devise a strategy that would win the war. The upshot was that under their management the tide of war took a sharp turn for the worse. Kitchener's policy differences with some of his colleagues fueled rising tensions in the cabinet. An influential section of the cabinet, which included Lloyd George, Bonar Law and Carson, blamed Kitchener's methods, rather than their own interference, as the principal cause of the military reverses and their remaining faith in his judgement vanished altogether.

Kitchener was as sick of his cabinet colleagues as they were of him. He often felt that he was waging a war on two fronts, one against the Germans and the other against the politicians. He resented spending long hours at meetings and preparing for them, which diminished the time he could devote to urgent work at the War Office. He despaired at the backbiting, the rambling deliberations that led nowhere, and the confusion that reigned in the inner councils

---

12 Hankey, *Supreme Command*, vol. 1, p. 411.

of war. He could not understand how his political associates could be so adamant about issues in which they knew precious little. Their attention shifted back and forth, often influenced by daily impressions, and their decisions were neither far-sighted nor took into consideration the larger aspects of the war. Feeling helpless and frustrated, more so than usual one day, Kitchener poured his heart out to Hankey, who recorded the following in his diary:

> For three-quarters of an hour he rampaged against the Cabinet, whence he had just returned, declaiming particularly against the irresponsible members – Churchill in particular, also Lord Curzon, Lord Selborne and Lloyd George. Also against the Dardanelles Ctee. He said so much time was wasted in arguing with these people that he simply couldn't get time to do his work at the War Office. He was almost in a hysterical condition; he even talked seriously of resigning.[13]

Much of the ills in the conduct of cabinet business can be attributed to Asquith and to the absence of collegiality on the part of Lloyd George and the Conservatives in the coalition. Before 1914 Asquith had shown great skill in handling his able, though willful, cabinet ministers and in delaying decisions on contentious issues until compromises had been reached. However, his wait and see approach was more of a liability in war when events sometimes required instant decisions. What was needed was a forceful political figure in command. Asquith failed miserably to pull the cabinet together, as Churchill would do in his coalition during the Second World War. In particular the Prime Minister made no effort to rein in Lloyd George whose mischievous conduct sowed dissention and confusion; and his constant criticism of the War Office did much to undermine Kitchener's handling of the war effort. In the previous Liberal government, Asquith had frequently come to Kitchener's rescue by cutting off questions or rephrasing in a more cogent way ideas that were awkwardly expressed. But Asquith found himself under attack by Conservatives in the current administration and, with his natural instinct for self-preservation, left Kitchener to fend for himself. For Kitchener, interaction with politicians, never a pleasant task in the best of circumstances, became an ordeal in the face of antagonistic confrontations by some of his influential colleagues. The harassment, cross-examinations, and demands for lengthy explanations, even on trivial matters, in the cabinet and Dardanelles Committee robbed him of his vigour and inhibited his capacity for bold, firm and clear-headed action which had characterized his earlier conduct of the war. He became indecisive, frequently changed his mind and lost touch with his war aims.

Kitchener was partially at fault for his own predicament. Forced to engage in lengthy debates with colleagues and grappling with an inhuman work load, he lacked the time and energy to focus on the broad strategic view of the war. Kitchener's failure to infuse the general staff at the War Office with new blood and consult with it regularly, left him, as Churchill pointed out, "to face the rushing, swirling torrent of events with no rock of clear, well-thought-out doctrine and calculation at his back."[14] On more than one occasion, he was compelled to reverse a decision because of an unforeseen development which a trained general staff might have anticipated and provided for.

13 Hankey diary, entry for 30 September 1915, Hankey papers.
14 Churchill, *World Crisis*, vol. 2, p. 171.

By September nearly all the members of the cabinet had lost confidence in Kitchener's strategic vision. Taking advantage of Kitchener's absence while he was in France, they passed a resolution on the 22 September instructing him to reconstitute the general staff. Asquith realized that things would remain the same unless he replaced the incompetent Wolfe-Murray. The man he chose as the new CIGS was Archibald Murray, Wolfe-Murray's deputy. Murray was only slightly better than Wolfe-Murray in dealing with authority but he was a competent administrator and, more important, he was available when a change was deemed essential. The next day Asquith in a delicately worded letter formally notified Kitchener of the cabinet's decision.[15] Kitchener, on his return, implemented the changes without comment. Under Murray the general staff finally began to play a more active role in the decisions affecting the nation's policies.

While this was going on, significant developments had occurred in the Balkans. On the 22nd Bulgaria began to mobilize and it was evident that in a week or two it would march with Germany and Austria against Serbia. About to be attacked simultaneously from the north and east, Serbia looked to Greece for immediate assistance. Greece was directly affected by what happened to Serbia as a defensive alliance existed between the two countries in the event either was attacked by Bulgaria. By the terms of the treaty, Serbia had to provide 150,000 men to defend its eastern frontier. However since the Serbs would have their hands full protecting their northern front against an Austro-German onslaught, they could not supply the 150,000 men needed to fight the Bulgarians. The Greek Prime Minister, E. Venizelos, back in power after an electoral victory in June, was willing to honour his country's treaty obligations to its northern neighbour, providing London and Paris agreed to deploy 150,000 men on the Bulgarian frontier.[16] For the Entente partners, it seemed at first glance well worth the cost to save an ally and enlist a new one.

In Paris the prospect of a Balkan campaign, which the cabinet had briefly entertained earlier in 1915, was revived with Aristide Briand, Minister of Justice, taking the lead. Disparaging a fresh attack in the Dardanelles as likely to end in heavy losses with nothing achieved, he was wildly optimistic in calculating the benefits of a Balkan enterprise. Here were the surest means to keep Serbia afloat, frustrate Germany's dream of establishing a *Mitteleuropa* and uniting the Balkans states in a common front against Turkey and Austria. Briand dropped hints which did not require further explanation. Grasped at once by President Poincaré and the cabinet ministers was the opportunity to further France's imperialistic ambition in the eastern Mediterranean. With the British in Egypt and Russia's eventual occupation of Constantinople and the Straits, a foothold in the Balkans would better ensure France's control of Syria and other areas of economic interest in the region. Incredibly in one sitting on 23 September the French cabinet decided to divert the troops earmarked for the Dardanelles to the Balkans without consulting either the general staff at its Ministry of War or the Asquith government which was expected to furnish half of the 150,000 troops.[17]

The sudden shift of attitude was striking evidence of how completely the French had withdrawn their confidence in the successful conclusion of the Dardanelles adventure. Yet to drift into a new campaign without definite objectives, adequate preparation and a precise plan of

---

15 Asquith to Kitchener, 22 September 1915, PRO 30/57/76, Kitchener papers.
16 Dutton, *The Politics of Diplomacy*, pp. 44-46.
17 Cassar, *Reluctant Partner*, pp. 187-88.

Map 7 The Balkan States in 1915.

action after the lamentable Dardanelles experience, revealed a shocking lapse of judgement. The proposed drive in the Balkans was another example of politicians determining the benefits to be derived from a successful enterprise before considering the means to achieve that victory.

The British remained unaware of the French change of plans when the Dardanelles Committee assembled for the first time in nearly three weeks on 23 September to consider Venizelos' appeal for 150,000 men from the Allies to enable Greece to go to the assistance of Serbia if Bulgaria should attack. The challenge for the Asquith government was to determine if it could spare its quota of 75,000 men. Joffre's large-scale attack on the German line was pending and until its result were known it was difficult to determine if the requisite British force from the western front would be available. Troops could always be withdrawn from the Dardanelles but it was assumed only at the expense of abandoning Suvla Bay.

Kitchener opened the meeting by giving a report on his recent visit to Chantilly where his discussion with Joffre centred mainly on the approaching offensive on the western front. Curzon asked Kitchener if Joffre had expressed his views on the proposed French action on the Asiatic side of the operation. Kitchener said that Joffre had discussed the matter briefly and he appeared opposed to sending the French detachments to the Dardanelles. Since Kitchener did not expect Joffre's assault to make significant gains, he saw no reason to suppose that the French divisions would not be sent. Kitchener fielded several questions regarding Joffre's coming offensive in the west before discussion turned to determine the best action the British should take to thwart the designs of the Central Powers against Serbia. Virtually all the members had an opportunity to express their views but the issue boiled down to whether they were prepared to assemble a contingent for the Balkans to the detriment of Hamilton's army. Lloyd George and Bonar Law were the most vocal proponents in favour of opening the new front, arguing that drawing four divisions from Suvla was a small price to pay for saving Serbia and obtaining two new allies, Greece and (supposedly) Romania. Churchill was strongly opposed to the move, suspecting that the real aim of the two men was to bring about the evacuation of the Dardanelles. Kitchener did not say much but tipped his hand when he warned that the operation "might really be jumping from the frying pan into the fire." The discussion seemed to be going nowhere when the Prime Minister requested that the general staff produce a memorandum on the subject before the meeting of the Committee next day.[18]

Hankey came over to the War Office to help Kitchener and the general staff to investigate the feasibility of the proposed expedition. Hankey commented that "Kitchener's dictatorial methods caused me some amusement but they were effective."[19] The Field Marshal estimated that the Austro-Germans could, without diminishing their effort against the Russians, detach 450,000 men for operations in the Balkans. To rescue Serbia, Kitchener felt that the allies would require no fewer than 300,00 men, in addition to Greece's 180,000-man army.

The next day the general staff memorandum, which in the main reflected Kitchener's views, was laid before the Dardanelles Committee. It weakened the case for involvement by implying that even with the assistance of Greece there was little chance of rescuing Serbia.[20] During the night, however, a good deal of fresh information had arrived in London: The Bulgarian

---

18 Minutes of the Dardanelles Committee, 23 September 1915, CAB 42/3/28.
19 Hankey, *Supreme Command*, vol. 1, p. 417.
20 "Appreciation of the Situation in Balkans by the General Staff," 24 September 1915, CAB 42/3/29; Roskill, *Hankey*, vol. 1, pp. 219-20.

mobilization was confirmed; the Russians were urging that strong measures be adopted against Bulgaria; and the French had accepted Venizelos' condition and were ready to send their share of the 150,000 men. In view of the changed conditions, the general staff memo was laid aside without discussion and the Dardanelles Committee unanimously agreed to join the French in sending an expedition to the Balkans.[21] Asquith summed up the attitude of his colleagues when he later wrote to the King that once the French agreed to comply, it "was impossible for us in the circumstances to hold back."[22]

With the cupboard nearly bare at home and Joffre's offensive about to be launched, Kitchener had no option but to draw the first consignment of British troops from the Dardanelles. Accordingly, the War Secretary telegraphed Hamilton on 25 September, directing him to release two divisions for Salonica and at the same time assuring him "that there is no intention of withdrawing from the Peninsula or of giving up the Dardanelles operations until the Turks are defeated." Still to compensate for the loss of manpower, Kitchener suggested to Hamilton that he might consider pulling out of Suvla.[23] Hamilton strongly objected to the idea, replying that he could hold the line with fewer troops as the northern zone had recently been strengthened by reinforcements and supplies in anticipation of a local advance. He insisted that a withdrawal would be seen as a great moral victory for the Turks.[24]

In addition to finding the necessary men, the current political uncertainty in Greece was also a barrier for the British authorities to formulate a Balkan policy. Without Greek intervention, there was no chance that an Anglo-French force could arrive in time to save Serbia from being overrun. It soon transpired that Venizelos had made overtures to the Allies without consulting Constantine. The Greek King, anticipating the abandonment of the Dardanelles, believed that a substantial part of the Ottoman army would then be free to reinforce the Bulgarians. He was convinced that the only safe course was to preserve strict neutrality. The internal struggle between Constantine and Venizelos was reflected in the confusing messages reaching London. On one occasion the Greek government wanted troops sent as quickly as possible to Salonica; on another it thought that the troops should go to Mudros to be transferred later to Salonica; and still again it threatened to register a formal protest if foreign troops disembarked on its soil. In view of the equivocal attitude of Athens, the Asquith administration hesitated to give final approval to the dispatch of its troops to Salonica.

On 3 October the outlook in Greece took a turn for the better. Venizelos called the British and French ambassadors in Athens to his office and requested that the Allied troops be transported at once to Salonica where he gave his word that all the facilities of the port would be placed at their disposal. Somewhat reassured the French and British authorities decided to go ahead with the landings.[25]

The next day the Dardanelles Committee met to discuss specific issues associated with the Balkan expedition. Kitchener suspected that neither Joffre nor the French general staff knew about the Viviani government's promise to send its half of the 150,000 troops requested by the

---

21 Minutes of the Dardanelles Committee, 24 September 1915, CAB 42/3/30; Hankey, *Supreme Command*, vol. 1, pp. 419-20.
22 Asquith to George V, 2 October 1915, CAB 41/36/46.
23 Kitchener to Hamilton, 25 September 1915, CAB 19/31.
24 Hamilton, *Gallipoli Diary*, vol. 2, p. 206.
25 Hankey, *Supreme Command*, vol. 1, pp. 419-22; Palmer, *Gardeners of Salonika*, pp. 33-34.

Greeks. He thought that it was essential to obtain a definite commitment from Joffre, otherwise he might later say that he could not spare the men. Kitchener, moreover, observed that such details as to how the force would be completed and transported and what role it would play upon arrival had yet to be resolved.[26] These were issues that could be settled at the Anglo-French conference which had already been arranged to take place at Calais on the 5th.

Kitchener and Balfour crossed the channel on the 4th and the next day held talks with two members of the French cabinet, Millerand and Augagneur.[27] Seated at a table facing the two French service ministers, they were told that Joffre was not only cognizant of, but agreed to provide a sizeable number of the troops for the expedition. Millerand turned next to list the formations that were either on their way to, or would be leaving for Salonica. Kitchener did the same from his end. Each side roughly committed 64,000 troops to the Balkans, thus falling short of some 20,000 of the number the Greeks had requested. The balance was to be made good at a later date. As regards the supreme command, it was decided that each commander would act independently and in concert with the Greek and Serbian armies. Balfour indicated that he would provide transportation for the French as well as the British divisions.

The only discordant note was over a plan after the disembarkation of the Anglo-French troops at Salonica. Kitchener pointed out that there was a difference of opinion between the French and the British as to the purpose of the operation. The British were under the impression that the Allies were sending troops to the Balkans to help Greece fulfil its obligations. On arriving at Calais he and his colleague discovered that the French aim was to try to save Serbia. Kitchener insisted that 150,000 men were insufficient to complete the task and he was troubled that Millerand had directed French forces to move swiftly north into Serbia. He adamantly refused to allow British troops to follow suit unless he was certain that the Greeks were irrevocably committed to the Entente and the lines of communication were secured.[28] This is how matters stood when the meeting came to a close.

Before Kitchener returned to London, the future of the Salonica scheme was again placed into jeopardy, this time more seriously by events that were taking place concurrently in Athens. On 5 October Constantine repudiated the invitation issued to the Allies and dismissed Venizelos. As the motive for the Allied expedition to Salonica had entirely disappeared, Kitchener hastily countermanded the orders of the 10th Division and directed its commander, Lieutenant General Sir Bryan Mahon, to return to Mudros if he had already left. He also sent a message to Maxwell to hold back the Yeomany regiment until further instructions. The next day the Dardanelles Committee overruled Kitchener's decision but agreed that the remaining formations should not proceed to Salonica until the Greek political picture was in sharper focus.[29]

The Dardanelles Committee's response did not necessarily imply commitment to a campaign in the Balkans, even though it was apparent that the collapse of Serbia would allow the Central

---

26   Minutes of the Dardanelles Committee, 4 October 1915, CAB 42/4/2.
27   Hankey rarely made mistakes but he committed one when he wrote in *The Supreme Command*, vol. 1, p. 422, that Joffre was part of the French delegation. The French minutes of the meeting, which are quite detailed, make that abundantly clear. I hate to admit that in my two previous books on Kitchener I erroneously included Joffre as a member of the French delegation.
28   Falls, *Military Operations: Macedonia*, vol. 1, p. 42; "Compte rendu de la conférence tenu à Calais 5/10/15," in France, *Les armées françaises*, tome 8, vol. 2, annexe no. 108.
29   Falls, *Macedonia*, vol. 1 (London: HMSO, 1933), pp. 42-33; Minutes of the Dardanelles Committee, 6 October 1915, CAB 42/4/3; Kitchener to Hamilton, 6 October 1915, WO 33/747.

Powers to open a direct route to Constantinople. Benefitting from the flow of supplies, heavy artillery and reinforcements, the Turks would make Hamilton's position on Gallipoli untenable and later conceivably reactivate the front along the Suez Canal. The members were equally aware that the nation's resources, which had been unable to attend to the needs of two theatres of war, could not support three. They were therefore confronted with three possible courses of action: (1) the sideshows in the Near East could be liquidated in favour of exclusive concentration in the west; (2) Gallipoli could be evacuated and the troops transferred to Salonica; (3) if the Balkan scheme were abandoned, reinforcements could be sent to Gallipoli for one final desperate effort to achieve decisive results.

In France Joffre's offensive, launched on 25 September, was effectively over by the early days of October. For slight advances of no strategic significance, 250,000 men were added to the already heavy toll suffered by British and French armies in the west. As no further frontal attacks were likely to occur in the west for some months, the next logical question was to determine whether the concentration of troops ought to take place in Salonica or Gallipoli. The Dardanelles Committee met on 6 and 7 October and because it could not reach a decision, Asquith set up a committee of military and naval experts to prepare a memorandum either to recommend the merits of restricting Britain's obligations only to the western front or extending its commitment to the Near East.[30]

On the afternoon of the 7th, Kitchener joined Asquith, Grey and Balfour at 10 Downing Street to confer with Viviani and Augagneur whose objective in coming to London was to wrest concessions from the British government. The French Prime Minister stressed the political and strategic importance of preventing Serbia from falling into the hands of the Central Powers and denied that the agreement to provide military assistance had been made solely to allow Greece to fulfil its treaty obligations to Serbia. Viviani acknowledged that 150,000 men would be insufficient to save Serbia. He now suggested that the Allies send an army of 400,000 with the French, owing to the imperative need to defend their own soil, contributing 67,000 and the British the remainder.[31] The position of most of the British ministers had hardened after the resignation of Venizelos. As they had already repudiated the agreement at Calais on the 5th, they were in no mood to entertain Viviani's unrealistic suggestion.

As it happened the French ministers, in advancing their government's agenda, revealed that Joffre had not been consulted before they left. It was well known that the Generalissimo had always resisted efforts to deploy large numbers of troops outside of France. Consequently it was decided to send Kitchener to sound out Joffre on the matter.

Kitchener left for Chantilly on the 8th and the face-to-face encounter with Joffre occurred the next day. By then the dam in the Balkans had broken. The impending Austro-German offensive had finally gotten under way on the 7th and fallen on Serbia like an avalanche. Kitchener maintained that an army of 250,000 was needed to save Serbia and that an additional 150,000 would be required if the Allies planned to initiate a major drive in the Balkans. Joffre knew that the Allies could not afford to wage great campaigns simultaneously in the west and in the Balkans. He admitted that Serbia was beyond help, but that it was still possible to save the Serbian army. In his opinion, the Anglo-French force should confine its activities to securing Salonica as a

---

30 Minutes of the Dardanelles Committee, 6 and 7 October 1915, CAB 42/4/3 and 42/4/4.
31 Hankey, *Supreme Command*, vol. 1, p. 428.

base, holding the railway between Salonica and Uskub and covering the right of the Serbian army against Bulgaria. For such a defensive role, he thought 150,000 men would suffice. Still he warned that should a more substantial effort be required at a later date, the responsibility for sending more men must be borne by the British government alone.[32] As Kitchener saw it, the French were prepared to throw caution to the wind and embark on an extremely hazardous expedition but if things should go awry, they expected the British to allocate more resources to avert a disaster. No wonder he opposed Joffre's plan but nevertheless promised to submit it to the Dardanelles Committee and did so when it met on 11 October.

Set against Joffre's views at the meeting was the report of the combined military and naval staffs, which slammed the door on Allied involvement in the Balkans on the grounds that it was too late to save Serbia or prevent supplies and reinforcements from reaching the Turks. Instead they recommended a continuance of steady pressure on the main front as the only place where decisive results could be obtained. They urged, however, that no attack in the west take place for three months and, if Joffre should refuse to acquiesce, Britain would be justified in sending some of its troops elsewhere. They considered a renewed attack in the Dardanelles as the only practical secondary operation, laying down that eight more divisions from France would suffice to capture the Peninsula. Attached to the report was a memorandum by Sir Henry Jackson which indicated that the navy would be prepared to join the army's assault and accept heavy losses.[33]

The combined staff appreciation had no effect in uniting the divergent views in the Dardanelles Committee. As there was no interest in another offensive in the west for the remainder of the year, the choice boiled down to either Salonica or the Dardanelles. The case in support of Serbia had continued to deteriorate. Serbia fought as best it could but its gallant effort was hopeless. Belgrade fell on the 9th and two days later Bulgaria abandoned its wobbly neutrality and struck from the east.

Kitchener left no doubt as to which of the two options he favoured. Although he understood the strategic ramifications of a Serbian defeat, quite apart from the political and human costs, he had good reason to oppose opening a new front at a time when his resources were barely meeting the nation's current commitments. Understandably, he did not want to be dragged by politicians into another Gallipoli, with an inferior force that would ultimately be thrown back and bottled up against the coast. All along he had known that Britain, which would have to bear most of the burden, would be unable to stop a determined Austro-German bid to break through to Constantinople. Resources determine policy and Kitchener had none to spare. He had initially hoped that any major military effort to counteract enemy designs in the Balkans would be undertaken mainly by Bulgaria or Romania. When Foreign Office initiatives failed to entice either state and the Greeks went back on their latest offer, Kitchener realized, with such troops as the Allies could muster, an expedition to save Serbia was destined to fail before it began.

On the other hand Kitchener was adamantly opposed to the withdrawal from Gallipoli. He stated in the Dardanelles Committee on 11 October that its "abandonment would be the most disastrous event in the history of the Empire", placing losses at about 25,000 men as well as a

---

32 "Summary of General Joffre's Note to the Secretary of State for War," 9 October 1915, annexed to the Minutes of the Dardanelles Committee for 11 October 1915, CAB 42/4/6.
33 Aspinall-Oglander, *Gallipoli*, vol. 2, pp. 381-82.

countless number of guns. To make matters worse he expressed the belief that the fall of Egypt and the Suez Canal would follow. In short he considered the dangers of withdrawal to be very grave but he hoped eventually to be able "to liquidate the situation."[34]

Asquith and a majority of members in the Committee agreed with Kitchener in favouring a renewed attempt in Gallipoli before German supplies and reinforcements could reach Constantinople. By contrast, Lloyd George, Bonar Law and Carson, thought it was inexcuseable to send reinfocements to support a lost cause when Serbia was desperately in need of help. Basing his case strictly on hypothetical political considerations, Lloyd George argued vigorously that deserting Serbia would be sending a signal to the entire east that Britain could not be counted on to protect its friends and "that Germany was the country to be followed."[35] As the meeting dragged on, the debates heated up but no resolution appeared to be in sight. The Prime Minister eventually stepped in to break the impasse and restore a semblance of civility. The majority of the members accepted his recommendations that 150,000 men should be drawn from France and sent to Egypt to be assigned to the place that offered the best results; and that a specially selected general be dispatched to the Near East to study and determine whether the troops should be used in the Dardanelles or the Balkans.[36] The pro Salonica group was furious at the decision which they maintained virtually left Serbia in the lurch. Carson was so upset that he resigned from the cabinet, citing as his reason the governmen's refusal to rescue the Serbs.[37]

Lloyd George saw Kitchener as the main obstacle to his Balkan plan to rescue Serbia and the dispute between the two became acrimonious. Lloyd George gave his side of the story in his *War Memoirs* in which he sought to use Kitchener, whom he hated, as a scapegoat for the unfolding tragedy in the Balkans. Prior to 1914 Lloyd George had not involved himself, any more than his political colleagues, in the study of warfare and yet he suddenly advanced himself as a military expert – in contrast to Bonar Law who frankly admitted to Hankey in seeking his advice that he "felt very ignorant of military affairs, especially in the east."[38] In his book he thundered in an I-told-you-so vein that some months earlier he had warned against the very disaster that was now occurring in the Balkans and held that it was Kitchener's irresolution and want of foresight that had prevented timely action.

A brief digression is justified here to examine Lloyd George's charges which too many historians have continued to accept uncritically. As we have already seen, Lloyd George had urged the dispatch of an expedition to the Balkans when the cabinet looked for a new theatre to send the New Armies at the turn of 1915. After a shift in the tide of war later in January, the Asquith government grasped the Balkan option as offering the best means to send direct help to Serbia and possibly encourage Greece to join the Entente. To the Welshman's dismay, interest in the Balkan expedition lost its appeal several weeks later when the Greek Prime Minister refused to abandon his country's neutral status. Lloyd George tried to rekindle interest in his project by drafting a second memorandum, which was circulated to members of the War Council on 22 February, three days after the start of the naval bombardment on the Turkish forts in the

---

34 Minutes of the Dardanelles Committee, 11 October 1915, CAB 42/4/6.
35 Ibid.
36 Ibid.
37 John Grigg, *Lloyd George: From Peace to War 1912-1916*, pp. 316-17.
38 Roskill, *Hankey*, vol. 1, p. 229.

Dardanelles.[39] In it he painted a gloomy picture of the Allied war record and believed one way to reverse the downward trend was to draw the neutral Balkan states into the allied camp. His solution as to how this could be achieved is either confusing or borders on the absurd.

Lloyd George maintained that a show of force in the region would likely have the effect of inducing Greece, Romania and Bulgaria in declaring for the Entente. Together with Serbia, an aggregate army of 1,500,000 could be hurled against the Austrian flank to relieve pressure on the Russians. On the other hand if the allied fleet was repulsed in the Dardanelles, the chances of forming a coalition of Balkan states would be lost unless countered by an immediate expedition to that quarter. Thus it was important to have a military force ready to be transported overseas at a moment's notice. As part of the enterprise, transport ships would be needed to carry troops to their destination and so preparations to assemble them should start immediately.

There is often value in material readiness depending on the circumstances. When it involves something as imprecise as possibly sending a force to the Balkans in the future, it is counterproductive if the resources are not readily available. It made no sense to keep transport ships lying idle in ports at home when they would be badly needed to carry rations, war material and reinforcements to sustain operations in the Dardanelles and on the westen front. As for the other half of Lloyd George's proposal, it is difficult to understand how anyone in government could advocate holding back a sizeable military force, with its necessary supply of munitions and guns, on the assumption that an expedition might materialize at some future date when the nation was incapable of meeting all of the army's requirements on the western front. Besides the Welshman had an oversimplified view of Balkan politics – caused at least in part by his lack of a traditional education – which gave him a false sence of confidence that a regional coalition could be formed. He never understood, among other things, that the fierce animosities among the states in the area posed an insuperable obstacle to uniting them as one.

For obvious reasons the memorandum aroused no interest among Lloyd George's colleagues and was not even discussed in the War Council, either on the 23 February – when it was circulated – or at subsequent meetings. Still Lloyd George did not abandon the idea of an expedition to the Balkans and on occasions when he mentioned it in the inner councils of war there was no reaction from his colleagues until after the Cenral Powers attacked Serbia in the fall of 1915.

Lloyd George was naturally within his rights to advocate a different course of action, no matter how impractical, but what was inexcusable was his propensity to forge evidence to support his claims. In his campaign to denigrate Kitchener as responsible for the fall of Serbia he concocted a fictitious scenario in his *War Memoirs*. He maintained that shortly after the decision had been taken to force the Dardanelles, he laid down the case on the advantages of sending an expedition to the Balkans in the event allied ships met unexpected difficulties and had to be recalled. He insisted that his arguments were persuasive and gained the unanimous approval of the War Committee which impressed upon Kitchener to take steps immediately to expand the transport facilities from Salonica to Nish in Serbia. Specifically, we are told, Kitchener was charged with increasing the carrying capacity between the two places by doubling the rail line where feasible and by augmenting locomotives, sidings and carriage wagons; as well as widening and

---

39   The lengthy paper is reproduced in its entirety in Lloyd George's *War Memoirs*, vol. 1, pp. 250-254.

mending the roads along the way. According to Loyd George, Kitchener took no notice of the War Committee's directive. As a consequence, when the Central Powers attacked Serbia, the lack of transport accommodation precluded the timely arrival of the expeditionary force to the battle scene.[40]

Before proceeding it should be pointed out that Lloyd George's reference to the War Committee as the governing body on policy at the time his story played out, is inaccurate. The War Committee held its first meeting early in November 1915 by which time it would have been far too late to attempt to succor Serbia. The only conclusion that can be drawn from his timeline was that British strategy was controlled by the War Council. If so, the official records do not substantiate Lloyd George's assertion that this body, or for that matter the Dardanelles Committee that succeeded it in May, had entrusted Kitchener to take steps to improve the transport arrangements between Salonica and the interior of Serbia. In fact I closely examined the minutes of the inner councils of war from February to October at least half a dozen times and I have no hesitation in accusing Lloyd George of fabricating the story to prove his point, namely that but for Kitchener's inaction, his proposal to extricate Serbia would have succeeded. As someone who has researched and written a book about Lloyd George as war leader (between 1916 and 1918), I concluded a long time ago that he was narcissistic and a habitual liar. When there were no facts to bolster his argument, he had no quams about inventing them, as he often did in his *War Memoirs*.

Out of curiosity if Lloyd George's plan to rescue Serbia had not been a hoax but actually devised during the early months of 1915 and closely followed as he suggested, would it have succeeded? In my opinion the plot that he sketched bore no semblance to reality. To begin with the requisite engineers, supervisors and building materials to increase and improve the transport facilities between Salonica and Nish could only be drawn from the western front where they were already at a premium. He disregarded or was unaware of the distance between the two locations (195 miles by rail or 245 miles by road) and the difficulty posed by the rugged terrain that had to be traversed.[41] Thus to assemble a work force, conduct surveys, double the line where possible, construct sidings, and increase the rolling stock would have taken years, not months. Although Lloyd George did not think that it mattered, it would have been illegal to occupy Greece, then a neutral country. Finally the rail project would have been vulnerable to damage or destruction by enemy raids, unless it was protected by a fairly considerable force. In short even with the advantage of hindsight, Lloyd George could not advance a credible case to justify a leap into the Balkan quagmire. So much for his judgement, foresight and strategic acumen.

To continue with our story. After the Dardanelles Committee accepted Asquith's recommendation to send substantial forces to Egypt to await their ultimate destination, Kitchener returned to the War Office and wired Hamilton, asking for an estimate of the losses if it became necessary to withdraw from Gallipoli.[42] Hamilton's reply the next day was framed to discourage any idea of evacuation. While he claimed that much would depend on the elements and reaction of the Turks, he predicted that departure from the Peninsula might lead to the loss of half his

---

40   Ibid, p. 235.
41   Geography was not exactly Lloyd George's forte. Asquith once found him looking for the Dardanelles on a map of Spain.
42   Hamilton, *Gallipoli Diary*, vol. 2, p. 249.

force.⁴³ The estimate greatly exceeded the most pessimistic calculations at home. The members of the Dardanelles Committee determined that he was too deeply committed to the operation to give an unbiased evaluation and consequently it hardened their mood to have him replaced.

Hamilton's recall had been in the air for some time. General Stopford who had been justifiably relieved of command for gross incompetence, submitted a lengthy statement to the War Office on his return home, defending his action at Suvla and levelling serious charges against Hamilton's handling of the battle.⁴⁴ While in the Dardanelles, Hankey sent long letters to Asquith and in the final one on 12 August described in detail the military landings, during which he levelled a number of veiled charges against Hamilton's military judgement.⁴⁵ Even some of Hamilton's own staff officers were convinced that he had mismanaged the operation and they feared an imminent disaster unless he was superceded. On 10 September Major Guy Dawnay arrived in London from the Dardanelles, ostensibly to lay out the case for reinforcements but his real purpose was to alert the authorities of Hamilton's shortcomings. He reported directly to Kitchener and subsequently saw Asquith, nearly all the cabinet ministers and the King who, alarmed over the lengthy casualty list, was furious with Hamilton. Dawnay's visit to London had a significant impact on the Dardanelles Committee.⁴⁶ With rising uneasiness among the ministers, Kitchener appointed four senior generals to review Hamilton's conduct of the recent battle.⁴⁷ Although the committee of inquiry refused to come to any definite conclusion without information from those on the spot, it did feel that Hamilton had given insufficient consideration to both the difficult terrain over which the British had to cross and the strength of the enemy's defences.⁴⁸ Kitchener informed the Dardanelles Committee on 6 October that the investigation had resulted in "considerable criticism of Hamilton's leadership."⁴⁹

It was an Australian journalist named Keith Murdoch, who drove the last nail in Hamilton's coffin. Murdock had spent four days at Anzac and Suvla on his way to London to take up a post as the representative of various Australian newspapers. On reaching London, he wrote a dispatch to his own prime minister, in which he castigated in lurid detail Hamilton, his staff and every section of the army except the Anzacs whom he praised lavishly. He showed the explosive document to a number of politicians, including Lloyd George, who, for reasons of his own, suggested he send a copy to Asquith. The Prime Minister did not forward a duplicate of Murdoch's report to Hamilton for his comments, as presumably he should have, or wait until Kitchener had studied it. He took the unusual step of printing it as a state paper and circulating it to the members of the Dardanelles Committee on 30 September. Hankey who had an

---

43   Ibid., p. 253.
44   Aspinall-Oglander, vol. 2, *Gallipoli*, p. 383. Stopford's report, written less than a fortnight after the landing, contained many errors as an investigation of his conduct would later show.
45   Hankey, *Supreme Command*, vol. 1, pp. 390-402.
46   James, *Gallipoli*, pp. 315-16.
47   The four generals involved were Leslie Rundle (who had replaced Hamilton in March 1915 as chief of the Central Force), James Wolfe-Murray, Archibald Murray and Henry Sclater (Adjutant General of the Forces).
48   The generals had initially recommended that Hamilton should be relieved of his command. At the suggestion of Sclater that judgement was omitted in the second draft sent to Kitchener. Since they were all junior to Hamilton, they did not think it was proper for them to advise his removal. Wolfe-Murray testimony, 23 May 1917, Dardanelles Commission Report, CAB 19/33.
49   Minutes of the Dardanelles Committee, 6 October 1915, CAB 42/4/2.

opportunity to coss-examine Murdock reported to Asquith that he was unable to corroborate some of his statements. Although Asquith was aware that there were numerous inaccuracies in Murdock's graphic account, he gave it more credence than he should have.[50] The only explanation for his action was that having lost all confidence in Hamilton, desired his immediate removal – Asquith could not help but have been influenced to some extent by his son Arthur (known a "Oc"), one of many servicemen who wrote back home pouring scorn on Hamilton's leadership. The Murdock document was discussed in the Dardanelles Committee on 6 October and at least heightened the effect of other Hamilton detractors.[51]

The decision on whether or not to supersede Hamilton dragged on until Asquith finally brought matters to a head in the Dardanelles Committee on 14 October. The Prime Minister introduced the issue at the start of the meeting and said that it was necessary to reach a decision without further delay. The minutes of the meeting leave no doubt as to how he stood:

> That officer [Hamilton] had had very great chances, but had been uniformly unsuccessful, and had lost the confidence of the troops under him. There was corroboration on all sides of their dejection. He was of the opinion that Sir I. Hamilton should be recalled and should hand over his command to General Birdwood.[52]

Kitchener could not help but be troubled by the cascade of criticism emanating from different quarters. He knew that the cabinet no longer held any faith in Hamilton's leadership and he had good grounds to suspect that the army on Gallipoli felt the same way. Leaving aside personal feelings, Kitchener concluded that he could not defend Hamilton's serious lapses in judgement. "The general effect produced upon Lord Kitchener's mind and upon my mind," Asquith later told the Dardanelles Commission, "was that it was in the interest of everybody that Sir Ian Hamilton be removed."[53]

Churchill was astute enough to see the handwriting on the wall and confined his remarks to dwelling on the appalling difficulties confronting his old friend as justification for his failure. He observed that Hamilton, notwithstanding his serious challenge, had "made most strenuous efforts" and he "trusted that his recall would be effected without casting a slur on him." Kitchener followed and agreed with Churchill "as to the great difficulties under which Sir I. Hamilton had been place, but the necessity for replacing him existed, and he would do it with the greatest consideration." Among the other ministers who expressed an opinion none objected to Hamilton's removal.[54]

Kitchener notified Hamilton the next day that, while the government fully appreciated his work, it considered it advisable to make a change in the command.[55] The announcement shook Hamilton to his core but he maintained a brave front. "He is, I must say, most wonderfully good about it," Birdwood wrote to his wife. "No ranting and raving that it is someone else's fault,

---

50 James, *Gallipoli*, pp. 312-15; Aspinall-Oglander, *Gallipoli*, vol. 2, p. 384; Evan McGilvray, *Hamilton and Gallipoli*, passim; Hamilton, *Happy Warrior*, pp. 396-97.
51 Minutes of the Dardanelles Committee, 6 October 1915, CAB 42/4/2.
52 Ibid., 14 October 1915, CAB 42/4/9.
53 Ibid.
54 Ibid.
55 Hamilton, *Gallipoli*, vol. 2, p. 272.

etc., but just saying that he has not been fortunate enough to succeed and that there is an end to it."[56] After his commanders and staff had gathered to bid him goodbye, Hamilton set sail for England on the 17th. His dismissal effectively ended his military career. Birdwood was left in charge pending the arrival of Hamilton's successor.

It is hard to imagine Hamilton as anything but a tragic figure, given his unequalled military experience and many fine qualities – such as thorough knowledge of his profession, courageous, imaginative and self-confident – demanded of a successful field general. No one attempting to measure Hamilton's skill as a commander in the Dardanelles can deny that he had been given an almost impossible assignment. A landing on a hostile beach can hope to succeed only without advanced warning or possessing overwhelming numerical superiority. Hamilton had been denied the advantage of strategical surprise owing to the naval attack and he had been sent to capture a Peninsula with a force inferior to that of the defending garrison. Yet some of his troubles were of his own making. He had failed to take advantage of several excellent opportunities offered by the tide of battle which would have allowed him to achieve better results. His breezy optimism, frequently crossing into the realm of wishful thinking, induced him to make light of obstacles. Moreover he lacked strength of character to assert his authority and to obtain sufficient drive from less competent subordinates. In later life Hamilton admitted that he lacked a vital quality in a gifted field general. In reliving his experience in the Dardanelles he often asked himself what Lord Roberts, with whom he had a long personal and professional experience, would have done in similar circumstances and sadly concluded that "Lord Roberts had not succeeded in grafting on to me his gift for taking the bull by the horns."[57]

On 19 October Kitchener telegraphed Birdwood, who had been left temporarily in charge, to request his views on the future prospects in the Dardanelles.[58] Birdwood replied that rapid progress on the Peninsula was out of the question but thought it was possible to make some headway on the northern front at Suvla, if units were brought up to strength, plus the addition of two divisions sent out from England with plenty of ammunition. In his opinion the best means to end the campaign would be to hold the Turks on the Peninsula while a large force landed in Asia and marched on Chanak.[59] Kitchener wired back, saying that Birdwood had considered only offensive action. He wanted to know whether the army could withstand repeated attacks by the Turks, supported by German heavy artillery and munitions.[60] Birdwood's answer was not encouraging. He maintained that the frontline trenches could be made secure but that the beaches and the resting areas could not be protected against the enemy's shell fire; and with the approach of winter he doubted that the men would be able to withstand a prolonged strain. As far as he could see, the only solution was to increase the depth of the British position by driving the Turks back further inland. Such a move, however, would require a huge outlay in manpower, artillery and ammunition.[61]

While this was going on, Kitchener selected General Charles Monro, commander of the Third Army in France, to replace Hamilton. An expert on infantry-fire tactics, Monro was talented,

---

56 Cited in James, *Gallipoli*, p. 320.
57 Cited in ibid.
58 Kitchener to Birdwood, 19 October 1915, WO 33/747.
59 Birdwood to Kitchener, 21 October 1915, ibid.
60 Kitchener to Birdwood, 23 October 1915, ibid.
61 Birdwood to Kitchener, 26 October 1915, ibid.

dispassionate and orthodox – that is he opposed sideshows and believed that the Germans could only be beaten on the western front. Churchill questioned Monro's qualifications when his selection was announced, but Kitchener defended him, saying that he was a man of ability whose judgement could be trusted.[62] Notwithstanding Kitchener's comments, the choice of Monro is difficult to rationalize in view of his known attitude towards operations outside of France. Kitchener dreaded the thought of withdrawal with so much invested in the operation and the estimated high army losses that would occur. He may have felt that Monro would approach his task with an open mind but that was expecting a lot from a confirmed westerner. Callwell has written that, Monro "in so far as he understood the situation before satisfying himself of the various factors on the spot, leaned towards complete and prompt evacuation."[63]

Monro insisted on a thorough briefing before leaving and held four private meetings with Kitchener who made it clear that considerable forces would be available should he recommend a renewed effort on the Peninsula. Monro's instructions were quite precise: he was to report "fully and frankly" on the best means to break the deadlock on Gallipoli and an estimate of the number of men necessary to carry it out; or whether it was preferable on military grounds to abandon the Peninsula in which case he was to express an opinion on the probable losses that might be incurred in such an operation. He was to base his appraisal on the assumption that the Germans had not established direct communications with Constantinople.[64]

Kitchener's dilemma in trying to determine whether it was feasible to try again in the Dardanelles was exacerbated by events in France. The Viviani government had packed off Sarrail to the Balkans but, owing to Joffre's resistance, was unable to provide him with adequate forces.[65] The plight of Serbia was becoming more desperate with each passing day and Sarrail could do little on his own, as the British troops, instead of advancing northwards, showed every intention of staying at Salonica during the coming winter months. The socialists in the French parliament, worried that Sarrail's campaign would end in disaster, threatened to bring down the Viviani ministry unless more Allied divisions were committed to the Balkans. Although the administration easily beat back a vote of no confidence in the chamber of deputies on 13 October, the appearance of faith in its conduct of the war was deceptive as over 100 left wing deputies refrained from voting.[66]

In London, the number of abstentions in the French parliament was interpreted as a growing sign of war weariness, renewing fears that the collapse of the Viviani cabinet might propel the peace-minded (Radical Socialist) Joseph Caillaux to power. The British embassy in Paris confirmed that political chaos might ensue if the British wavered in support of Serbia.[67] Millerand arrived in London on the 15th to urge that the British send several additional divisions to the Balkans. His most compelling argument was that unless left-wing radicals in the chamber were placated, Viviani would be forced to resign and the alliance itself might be endangered. Still he had to fight an uphill battle to overcome the general sentiment in London that

---

62 Minutes of the Dardanelles Committee, 14 October 1915, CAB 42/4/9.
63 Callwell, *Experiences*, p. 103.
64 Aspinall-Oglander, *Gallipoli*, vol. 2, pp. 399-400.
65 Sarrail agreed to leave for Salonica without the promised number of divisions because he wearied of enforced inactivity and concluded that he could not advance his career by remaining at home.
66 Dutton, *Politics of Diplomacy*, p. 53.
67 Bertie to Grey, 23 October 1915, FO 371/2270.

there was no military rationale for sending more troops to the Balkans as it was too late to save Serbia. His despair was partially relieved by Lloyd George who indicated that a few like him in the cabinet saw merit in a Balkan expedition. Kitchener was reluctant to commit more than the division already at Salonica but would not exclude sending additional troops destined for Egypt if circumstances so warranted.[68]

The British government's attitude became even more rigid after Bulgaria took possession of Uskub on 22 October, cutting the Salonica-Nish railway and isolating the Serbian army.[69] Given the military reality there was no longer any point in maintaining a presence in Greece, galling as it may have been to abandon Serbia to its fate. On 24 October Kitchener received an emotional plea from the French military attaché in London to the effect that British troops withdrawn from the western front be sent, not to Egypt, but directly to Salonica, since any delay would ensure the destruction of the Serbian army.

The following day Kitchener brought the note to the attention of the Dardanelles Committee, explaining that it was couched in such a way as to suggest that the French position was based less on strategic grounds than on political considerations. In these circumstances, Kitchener wondered if Britain's refusal to comply with France's urgent request would spell the collapse of the Viviani government. Selborne and Chamberlain pointed out that, as Serbia was done for, it seemed senseless to risk the lives of British troops in a hopeless campaign just to save the Viviani ministry. For Kitchener, domestic issues could not be divorced from strategy. There was more at stake, he replied, than to preserve a tottering government. He added: "It was to save the alliance; that if we were to break with France the war would be over."[70] Despite the sense of urgency a decision was postponed, pending the results of Archibald Murray's consultation with Joffre and representatives of the French general staff.

The British authorities were unaware that Joffre, who for months had resisted all attempts to divert forces from the western front, had become a late convert to the Balkan enterprise. Joffre was astute enough to understand that, if Sarrail's political supporters were not pacified, the government would fall, placing his own position in peril. Since his resources in men and munitions were required to fight for the survival of France where the Germans were installed barely 50 miles from Paris, he expected the British to supply the bulk of the forces for the Balkans. That was his mindset when he met Murray at Chantilly on 27 October and proposed that the British send four divisions to Salonica. Murray rejected the idea and remained immovable, despite the immense pressure. He later reported:

> Questions such as limitations of port accommodation and landing facilities, Railway capacity, the transport arrangements for and the equipment of the troops, etc., left the French General Staff quite unmoved. It was clear that their only intention was to support the French divisions already landed at Salonica without regard to the difficulties involved.[71]

---

68 Cassar, *Reluctant Partner*, pp. 198-99.
69 Jan K. Tanenbaum, *General Maurice Sarrail, 1856-1929* (Chapel Hill: University of North Carolina Press, 1974), p. 72.
70 Minutes of the Dardanelles Committee, 25 October 1915, CAB 42/4/17.
71 Ibid., 30 October 1915, CAB 42/4/20.

Joffre was so upset at Murray's unwillingness to be more accommodating that he hurried across the channel to personally plead his case to the British authorities. Once in London, Joffre was invited to an informal conference held at 10 Downing Street. Asquith, Kitchener and Balfour were present, in addition to Lieutenant General William Robertson (representing Sir John French) and Admiral Jackson. Joffre argued that a major effort was required in the Balkans to save the Serbian army, observing that if the Central Powers could be held up, the Greeks might still come in on the side of the Allies. He claimed that the Bulgarian force, which had cut the railway in the vicinity of Uskub was small and it could be driven away with a modest force. Although he wanted the British contingent augmented by four divisions, he was not asking it to play more than a defensive role. While Sarrail's three divisions moved northwards in an attempt to reestablish communications with the Serbian army, the five British divisions would simply be guarding Salonica and the railway up to the Serbian border. Joffre was a good speaker with a well-organized presentation, but the good impression he created did not rise to the extent of overriding the British general staff's contradictory analysis.

Kitchener was at a loss to understand how plans could be based on the entry of Greece which so far had rejected every offer made by the Entente. He went on to say that according to the British general staff, Serbian communications were cut beyond any hope of repair. Joffre made a greater impact after the meeting when, during an informal conversation, he indicated that his own position as commander-in-chief as well as the alliance itself would be endangered by a British refusal to cooperate.[72]

The issue was debated in the Dardanelles Committee on the morning of the 30th and, while only a few ministers shared Joffre's views, no one wanted to risk a quarrel with the French government which was deeply committed to the enterprise. Later in the day Joffre was given a written promise that the British government would send reinforcements to Salonica on the understanding that, if communications with the Serbian army could not be reestablished, the entire Allied force would withdraw.[73] The four divisions on their way to Egypt would be diverted to Salonica, making five British divisions in all. At the time the British did not understand the implication of their commitment to Paris. A precedent had been established that maintaining the existing pro alliance regime in France overrode all other considerations. This meant that the British would be abdicating their right to an equal voice in determining Allied strategy whenever their proposed action threatened to add to the instability of French domestic policy.

Ironically Joffre's successful mission came too late to save the Viviani administration. By the time he returned to Paris, Aristide Briand was the new prime minister and in the process of forming his cabinet. Briand had long championed a front in the Balkans, less on military grounds than as a base to expand French interests in the Middle East. His political survival depended on continued allied presence in the Balkans. Britain was now trapped in a morass mainly to ensure French postwar preponderance in the eastern Mediterranean.[74]

---

72 "Notes of a Conference Held at 10 Downing Street," 29 October 1915 in Anglo-French and Allied Conferences, CAB 28/1; Memoranda by Joffre on 29 October and Kitchener the next day can be found in CAB 42/4/20. See also Hankey's version of the discussions in *Supreme Command*, vol. 1, pp. 433-34.
73 Minutes of the Dardanelles Committee, 30 October 1915, CAB 42/4/20.
74 Cassar, *Reluctant Partner*, pp. 198-99.

Britain's pledge to assist France in the Balkans practically predetermined the fate of the Dardanelles operation before Monro's report was even received. It is useful to remember that Britain simply did not possess the resources to sustain two sideshows. As Kitchener sat in the War Office, he searched in vain for a formula which would stave off the army's withdrawal from the Dardanelles. Perhaps Monro might provide it. All he could do was hope.

7

The End of the Ill-Fated Expedition

Monro arrived at Imbros on 27 October and next day visited Gallipoli. He toured the fronts and spoke to the corps commanders and sent a report back of his first impressions on the afternoon of the 28th. He found the divisions were less than half their regular strength and that disease and sickness were widespread among the men but that their morale was good and the officers he had had seen were generally optimistic. He gave no hint that he was considering evacuation. Instead he requested building materials to provide winter shelter and the dispatch of experienced company commanders.[1]

Kitchener was encouraged by the preliminary report. As he was feeling the heat in the Dardanelles Committee where more members had joined Lloyd George and Bonar Law in pressing to liquidate the enterprise, he replied impatiently: "Please send me as soon as possible your report on the main issue at the Dardanelles, namely, leaving or staying."[2] Kitchener unwittingly forced Monro to reach a rapid conclusion, though in truth, even if he had been given more time, it is highly unlikely that it would have made a difference.

Monro submitted a lengthy appreciation to Kitchener on the last day of October. After inspecting the Peninsula, he had reached a conclusion based on the following factors: that the troops, with the exception of the Anzacs, were incapable of sustained effort owing to the inexperience of their officers, lack of training and poor condition; that only frontal attacks could be carried out which held no prospect of success as the Turks occupied the high ground and were numerically superior; that the beachheads were exposed to observation, ruling out tactical surprise and offered insufficient room to mass troops; and intelligence reports pointed to the impending arrival of the Germans with heavy artillery and reinforcements, rendering the British position on the Peninsula untenable. On purely military grounds, Monro was convinced that evacuation was the only feasible course open.[3] Monro might not have been totally objective when he arrived on the scene, but it is difficult to argue with the reasons on which he based his decision.

Kitchener reacted to Monro's recommendation with dismay. He had just learned that Commodore Roger Keyes, de Robeck's chief of staff, was back in England trying to persuade

---

1 James, *Gallipoli*, p. 323.
2 Aspinall-Oglander, *Gallipoli*, vol. 2, p. 401.
3 The telegram is quoted in its entirety in Aspinall-Oglander, *Gallipoli*, vol. 2, pp. 402-4.

the Admiralty to sanction another naval attack to force the Straits.[4] While waiting for the outcome, he telegraphed Monro on 1 November asking for the opinion of his corps commanders on the issue of evacuation. He also wanted Monro to consider a message he had received from Maxwell who maintained that the effect of evacuation would be disastrous unless the Turks could be struck elsewhere. Finally Monro was to send him as quickly as possible an estimate of probable losses in the event of a withdrawal.

As directed, Monro conducted a survey of the corps commanders and found that Lieutenant General Sir Julian Byng and Lieutenant General Sir Francis Davies agreed with his assessment; but Birdwood, while acknowledging that the chances of progress were remote, was opposed to evacuation, partly because of the deplorable effect it would have on the Muslim population in India and Egypt, and partly because of the many difficulties which would necessarily attend its execution. The next day Monro transmitted the views of his corps commanders, added that his own opinion remained unaltered and estimated that losses would run between 30 and 40 percent in men and material.[5]

Kitchener had a hard time reconciling Monro's recommendation with his prediction that losses might reach as high as 40 percent. He now clutched Keyes' naval scheme with all his might as possibly the last hope of sustaining the campaign. The War Committee, which replaced the Dardanelles Committee, held its first meeting on 3 November and considered Keyes' project and Monro's recommendation. The new Committee initially consisted of Asquith, Kitchener and Balfour; but given the usual process of growth, Grey and Lloyd George were added before the second meeting on the 5th and ten days later Bonar Law and Reginald McKenna also became regular members. The most notable omission in the new body was Churchill. Without a voice in the conduct of the war, he resigned his sinecure office (although he retained his seat in the Commons) and as he had requested to serve in the field, arrangements were made to place him in command of a battalion on the western front with the rank of lieutenant colonel.[6] Before leaving Churchill told Keyes that "he admired Lord K.'s action more than he could say – they had had many rows, but tho' he knew he had let Lord K. in for all this he (Lord K.) never reproached him – and when he said good-bye he [Kitchener] wrung his hand and wished him luck."[7] In the interest of self-preservation, Churchill's good will toward Kitchener faded when it came time to testify before the Dardanelles Commission and write his account of the campaign in *The World Crisis* – as we shall see.

There was no secretary to take notes in the War Committee on the 3rd but Hankey was present at the subsequent meetings. Monro's estimate of the heavy losses was a barrier for some members of the War Committee to accept evacuation. The only decision taken was that Kitchener should hurry out to the Dardanelles and report on the situation there. Kitchener's stock had fallen so low in the cabinet that his mission to the Dardanelles was intended more to get rid of him than to obtain another opinion on the next step in the Dardanelles.[8] Asquith

---

4   Although de Robeck remained unalterably opposed to another naval attack he had generously allowed Keyes to travel to London to state his case personally to the authorities at the Admiralty.
5   Aspinall-Oglander, *Gallipoli*, vol. 2, pp. 405-7; Gen. Sir George Barrow, *The Life of General Sir Charles Carmichael Monro* (London: Hutchinson & Co., 1931), pp. 73-74.
6   Grigg, *Lloyd George*, pp. 318-21; Jenkins, *Asquith*, p. 382; Cassar, *Asquith*, p. 134.
7   Paul Halpern (ed.), *The Keyes Papers*, vol. 1 (London: William Clowes & Sons, 1972), p. 228.
8   Cassar, *Asquith*, pp. 132-33.

knew that his government would never survive if he bowed to the wishes of Lloyd George and Bonar Law to dismiss Kitchener who was still revered by the masses. His solution was to send Kitchener on a fact-finding mission to the Dardanelles and at the end to persuade him to remain in the east. Both Lloyd George and Bonar Law tried to force a decision about the Dardanelles before Kitchener submitted his report. They insisted on the immediate evacuation on the grounds that the Germans had reportedly opened a direct route to Constantinople and it was only a matter of time before the Anglo-French force on the Peninsula was overwhelmed. They wanted the Gallipoli garrison transferred to Salonica even though there was no chance, and never had been, of reaching the Serbian army. To avoid Bonar Law's resignation, Asquith promised that he would back a resolution for the withdrawal of the BMF, irrespective of Kitchener's recommendation.[9]

Before Kitchener left for the Dardanelles, he continued to look for an arrangement that would allow British forces to remain on the Peninsula. On the afternoon of the 3rd, Keyes called on him at the War Office and the two men conferred for about half an hour. Kitchener revealed the contents of Monro's report and said that he had refused to sign the order of evacuation despite pressure from the cabinet to do so. He could not understand how any responsible officer could advocate a course of action in which he expected to lose as much as 40 percent of his army. Kitchener went on to say that he was departing for the Dardanelles the following evening and if the government was bent on withdrawal, he would carry it out in person and be the last one to leave the shore. Kitchener found a sympathetic listener in Keyes who was asked for his thoughts on what needed to be done. Keyes was convinced that the only solution lay with the fleet and he proceeded to lay out his plan of attack which thus far had not aroused the interest of Jackson and the Sea Lords.[10]

Kitchener was very much attracted to Keyes' proposal which seemed to him the only way to avoid a disaster in the Dardanelles. He urged Keyes to try to get a definite commitment from the Admiralty. He indicated that he was ready to cooperate in a joint operation by supplying the ships with coal, ammunition and food after they had broken into the Sea of Marmara. His idea was to land 40,000 men to seize and hold the Isthmus of Bulair, transporting the necessary stores from the Gulf of Saros to the Sea of Marmara. Thus even if the Turkish authorities held out after the Straits had been breached, all the ships' needs would be moved overland. Kitchener thought he would probably need to evacuate Suvla to find the requisite troops. Keyes disagreed with Kitchener's recommended course of action. He observed that it would open Anzac to bombardment from the north and meant giving up newly won valuable beaches. He thought that it would entail less risk if the army attacked from Suvla. Furthermore he did not think that anyone with local knowledge would support a landing at Bulair at this time of the year or the feasibility of hauling goods across the rugged Peninsula. Besides, he added, it would not assist the naval attack. Keyes was certain that Birdwood and Byng would agree with his assessment.[11] On that note the interview ended. Any decision regarding a military plan naturally rested on

---

9 Robert Blake, *The Unknown Prime Minister: The Life and Times of Andrew Bonar Law 1958-1923* (London: Eyre & Spottiswoode, 1955), p. 271.
10 Sir Roger Keyes, *The Naval Memoirs of Admiral of the Fleet*, vol. 1 (London: Thornton, Butterworth, Ltd., 1934), pp. 449-50.
11 Keyes testimony, 16 May 1917, Dardanelles Commission Report, CAB 19/33; Halpern (ed.), *Keyes Papers*, vol. 1, p. 222; Keyes, *Naval Memoirs*, vol. 1, p. 450.

a favourable signal from the Admiralty. As Kitchener requested, Keyes made an appointment to see Jackson that afternoon and found him non-committal, saying that he could not risk adding a naval disaster to a military one. The First Sea Lord considered the idea of a landing at Bulair simply fantastic but Keyes was certain that Kitchener could be persuaded to drop it at once. As soon as Kitchener had consulted Birdwood, he would recognize that the next attack should take place in the Suvla region. Eventually Jackson softened his attitude and thought that, if Kitchener "meant business," there was a good chance that the Admiralty would sanction another attempt to force the Straits. Keyed telephoned Colonel Oswald FitzGerald (Kitchener's military secretary) to break the good news. As a consequence, Fitzgerald invited him to see Kitchener after dinner at his temporary London residence (York House).[12]

With the Admiralty seemingly on board, Kitchener sent a personal communication to Birdwood beginning with the words "Most secret. Decipher yourself. Tell no one." Kitchener went on to say that he was leaving for the Dardanelles the next day to see the state of affairs for himself. If as expected the navy rushed the Straits, it followed that the army must do what it can to assist. Kitchener asked Birdwood to examine the ground near Bulair for a new landing so that a line could be drawn across the Peninsula to supply the ships as soon as they passed into the Sea of Marmara. To pick a force, the garrison on the Peninsula would have to be pared to the bone and it might even be necessary to evacuate Suvla. Kitchener realized that he would need to replace Monro who could not be expected to agree to a new offensive. The Secretary for War informed Birdwood that he was to take permanent control of the Mediterranean Expeditionary Force and that Monro would be appointed to command the British contingent at Salonica. Birdwood was instructed to carefully select the commanders and troops and work out a plan for the Bulair landing or any alternative one "as you may think best" to ensure that everything was done "right this time." Kitchener was adamant that he would refuse to sign an order for evacuation which he felt would be a catastrophe and condemn a large percentage of the garrison to death or imprisonment.[13] A second War Office telegram on the heels of the first confirmed Birdwood's elevated status and the transfer of Monro to Salonica.[14] Birdwood was upset by what Kitchener had in mind. He wrote in hindsight:

> I knew the country and the local conditions, which my old Chief did not; and I knew him well enough to realize that once he had set his mind on a scheme it was terribly hard to deflect him from it. Yet I knew that his proposals would be utterly impractical, especially at that late season of the year: that it would be all but impossible to extricate the troops necessary for a new landing without leaving our Peninsula garrison – even if Suvla were given up – so weak that they would be at the mercy of the Turks.[15]

Birdwood replied at once to Kitchener. Enjoying the latitude of an established favourite, he bluntly told Kitchener that any attempt to cut across the Peninsula from Bulair would end in disaster. He also questioned Kitchener's action in dismissing Monro for merely giving a

---

12   Halpern (ed.), *Keyes Papers*, vol. 1, pp. 223-24; Keyes, *Naval Memoirs*, vol. 1, p. 452.
13   Aspinall-Oglander, *Gallipoli*, vol. 2, p. 409.
14   Ibid., p. 409.
15   Field Marshal Lord Birdwood, *Khaki and Gown: An Autobiography* (London: Ward & Locke, 1932), p. 279.

military opinion. He urged Kitchener to refrain from make a change in the command. "Monro, he wrote, "has already established confidence in those who have seen him, and his experience in France, which I lack will be absolutely invaluable. He will, I know, carry out any orders of the Government better than I can." Because of Birdwood's respect and affection for Monro, he withheld the announcement of his supersession as he hoped to persuade Kitchener to reverse the decision after his arrival.[16]

Before Birdwood's telegram reached the War Office, the Admiralty had ruled out the Bulair landing. Balfour contacted Kitchener to explain the Admiralty's reasons:

> The scheme which you suggested this morning … seems impractical. I do not speak of the military difficulties (which it is not our business in this Office to consider) … To land thousands of tons of coal in the Gulf of Xeros [Saros]; to transport it, probably under shell fire, over the rough and roadless peninsula, is, we believe, impossible. But were this accomplished, our difficulties would be only beginning. The ships could only coal with the help of lighters[17] … we could not take them up the Dardanelles … If we had them, it would not be easy to load them with coal, and during the operation they would always be open to submarine attack.

In the final analysis the Admiralty would agree to implement Keyes' plan for a surprise rush only on condition that the army simultaneously advance to seize the forts at The Narrows.[18] To Kitchener the land operation called for by the Admiralty was much more difficult to execute than the one at Bulair and certainly would require several fresh divisions, a requirement that could not be met owing to Britain's commitment to help sustain the front in the Balkans.

When Keyes returned to see Kitchener late in the evening he found him in an angry mood. Kitchener showed him Balfour's letter and claimed that the "Navy was afraid to wet its feet." Keyes tried to assuage Kitchener by placing a more hopeful interpretation on its contents:

> I pointed out that the letter … merely concentrated on Lord K's claim that he could supply the ships in the Marmara across the Peninsula. This was of course impossible, and he had unfortunately given them [Admiralty] something to write him off on. I suggested that what we wanted was that the Admiralty should accept in principle the absolute necessity for a naval attack on the Straits. Sir Henry Jackson had already practically agreed to that, and I was sure that if the Admiralty knew that Lord Kitchener would be prepared to take advantage of the Navy's action by launching a new attack they would agree.[19]

Kitchener remarked that the navy had no reason to make a big fuss over the Bulair plan, that it was only a suggestion and if deemed unworkable, "the attack would be made elsewhere." Keyes thought that Kitchener ought to emphasize the point that "the Navy had started the campaign, and it was up to the Admiralty to make a great naval effort to retrieve the situation." Kitchener

---

16 Aspinall-Oglander, *Gallipoli*, vol. 2, pp. 409-10.
17 A large, open, flat-bottomed barge, used in loading or unloading of ships and in transporting goods a short distance. Lighters were also used to land troops on hostile beaches.
18 Balfour to Kitchener, 3 November 1915, Asquith papers (copy), vol. 15.
19 Keyes, *Naval Memoirs*, vol. 1, p. 452.

seized on the suggestion and he immediately sat down to reply to Balfour's letter. Kitchener had good reason to feel bitter but he needed to be more tactful in addressing his dilemma. It did not advance his cause when he practically accused the Admiralty of deserting the army after it had gone to the assistance of the navy. Keyes thought that the tone of the note was acerbic and rather unfair and told Kitchener that he was sure "the Admiralty would order the attack if he was ready to make a vigorous offensive."[20]

Balfour later told Keyes that he considered Kitchener's missive "intemperate and impossible."[21] Kitchener and Balfour had settled their differences, at least they were civil to each other, when Keyes joined them at the Admiralty to discuss the naval project on the afternoon of the 4th. After the conference broke up, Kitchener and Keyes were optimistic that the naval attempt to rush the Straits would be carried out. An hour later there was an informal gathering of ministers and regrettably, in the absence of records, the details of what occurred are unknown. What can be established is that they decided not to sanction the naval attack unless the army made a determined bid to seize the forts at The Narrows. Given that the necessary number of fresh troops were unavailable to stage such a forward movement, Kitchener lost heart and after the meeting telegraphed Birdwood to cancel his previous message. "I fear," he said, "the navy may not play up... The more I look at the problem the less I see my way through, so you had better very quietly and very secretly work out any scheme for getting the troops off."[22]

When Kitchener left London on the evening of the 4th, his spirits could not have been much lower. It had been arranged that he would stop in Paris for two days, after which he would travel overland to Marseilles where the *Dartmouth* was waiting to convey him to the Dardanelles.

Once in Paris Kitchener was surprised and delighted to discover that the new French ministry was opposed to the evacuation of the Dardanelles. There were two factors that had influenced its change of attitude. First, General Hubert Lyautey, the brilliant Resident General of Morocco, had warned his civilian chief that an admission of defeat in the Dardanelles would be a signal for the Turkish government to encourage its co-religionists to rise against the French in North Africa. In these circumstances he believed that, if reinforced, he could probably defend Morocco but he doubted that Algeria could be held.[23] Second the French did not have extra resources to foster the various Arab nationalist movements designed to throw off Turkish rule. They held little hope that these movements would be able to prosper in the event that the Dardanelles were abandoned.[24]

Kitchener engaged in lengthy conversations with Briand and General Joseph Galliéni, Millerand's replacement at the War Ministry, in the afternoon on the 5th. All three agreed that it was essential to cling to Gallipoli but there were sharp differences over the merits of the Balkan enterprise. Briand in particular insisted on sending massive reinforcements to Salonica with the object of rescuing the remnant of the Serbian army and possibly tempting Greece and Romania to forsake their neutral status. Galliéni was too good a soldier to think that an Allied force, consisting of about one-third of the numbers deemed essential, could accomplish anything significant in the Balkans but supported his political chief out of loyalty. Kitchener

---

20 Halpern (ed.), *Keyes Papers*, vol. 1, p. 225.
21 Keyes, *Naval Memoirs*, vol. 1, p. 454.
22 Aspinall-Oglander, *Gallipoli*, vol. 2, p. 410.
23 Kitchener to Balfour, 6 November 1915, Balfour papers, vol. 44.
24 Kitchener to Asquith, 5 November 1915, Kitchener papers, PRO 30/57/66.

was frustrated with the French government's tendency to base its plans on imaginary results and believed it had lost its bearings. His disappointment was reflected in a letter he sent to Asquith on the evening of the 5th: "They simply sweep all military dangers and difficulties aside and go on political lines... I could get no idea when the troops could come out [of Salonica]: they only said they must watch events."[25]

In conversation with Galliéni, Kitchener asked him if he could borrow the services of Colonel Pierre Girodon, a young officer who had served on Gallipoli and was reputed to possess outstanding qualities as a soldier. Invalided home after a severe lung injury, Girodon was currently attached to Galliéni's staff. Kitchener explained that it would be valuable to have Girodon during the voyage so that he could supply him with first-hand information. Galliéni was surprised by the unusual appeal and indicated that he would give him an answer the next day. If Galliéni was reluctant to heed to Kitchener's request it was because he had an assignment in mind for Girodon; and additionally he was aware that his young subordinate had not fully recovered from his wound.

When Kitchener returned to the British Embassy, he expressed a wish to see Girodon. The French Colonel was located and on arrival at the embassy late at night was escorted to a room Kitchener occupied on the upper level. Kitchener liked him immediately. Girodon spoke English as though it were his native tongue and he shared Kitchener's fears about the adverse consequences of withdrawing from the Dardanelles. When the discussion ended and Girodon rose from his chair to leave, Kitchener asked him if he would accompany him on his journey as a member of his staff. Caught off guard, Girodon hesitated before replying that it would be up to his superior. Kitchener chuckled and said "I shall see you at the station tomorrow evening."[26]

The next day Kitchener lunched with Galliéni who, as promised, gave his answer, consenting to temporarily releasing Girodon. He was sympathetic to Kitchener's predicament and proved generous in other ways as well. He indicated that, if Girodon considered it necessary after he arrived on the spot, he would divert two French brigades destined for Salonica to the Dardanelles. No less important, he was willing to send French troops from France to the eastern Mediterranean provided an equal number of battle-weary soldiers from Cape Helles or Suvla went to Salonica. These arrangements revived Kitchener's hope of staving off evacuation. With fresh troops on hand it would be possible, not only to dig in for the winter but even take the initiative in the spring if the British navy agreed to cooperate by rushing the Straits.[27] Consequently Kitchener sent two telegrams. The first was to the Admiralty asking that Keyes, meet him at Marseilles so that they could discuss the plan for a naval attack on their way to the Dardanelles. The other one to Birdwood ran as follows:

> I mean to do my very utmost to enable you to hold and improve your position, as I regard evacuation as a frightful disaster which should be avoided at all costs. Think over any plan which would enable us to improve our positions so as to render them ... secure ... against

---

25 Ibid.
26 Esher, *Tragedy of Lord Kitchener*, pp. 171-72.
27 "Lord Kitchener's report to the Cabinet on his East Mediterranean Mission in November 1915," 2 December 1915, Kitchener papers, PRO 30/57/66; Bertie to Grey, 6 November 1915, Bertie papers, FO 800/172.

increasing artillery fire. I cannot say what troops I can now gather for this, but I much hope to assemble two divisions of regular tried troops.[28]

On the final leg of his stay in Paris, Kitchener motored to Chantilly where he was cordially greeted by Joffre. The two men engaged in private conversation for several hours. Surprisingly, Joffre did not deviate from his government's announced policy. He seemed as set on the campaign in the Balkans as he was on the need to hang on to Gallipoli and had no objections to the exchange of troops as long as the numbers were kept up at Salonica. In truth the French General disliked both enterprises. He had fought too long and too hard to keep the focus on the western front to suddenly reverse his purpose. But as a practical politician he towed the government line and paid lip service to the Dardanelles operation lest he irritate Kitchener on whom he depended to keep sending newly trained British divisions to France. Kitchener had stressed the absolute necessity to remain in the Dardanelles especially to discourage a Turkish attack on Egypt. He was reported to have said: "If we stay at the Dardanelles an attack on Egypt is always possible; if we withdraw, it is certain."[29] Joffre tried to persuade Kitchener to send 90,000 of the 150,000 men to Salonica without delay but to no avail.[30]

Kitchener left for Marseilles on the 7th, expecting to see Keyes on arrival. As it happened Keyes never received Kitchener's telegram. The secretary to the First Lord did not bother to forward the message in the mistaken belief that he could not reach Marseilles in time. When Keyes failed to show up at Marseilles, Kitchener concluded that the Admiralty had definitely closed the door on the naval scheme and so left without him.[31] It would be erroneous to attach much significance to this episode. Once Monro's report had been submitted, Bonar Law and Lloyd George would have brought down the government, rather than allow a joint military and naval action in the Dardanelles.

During the voyage, Kitchener had plenty of time to discuss with Girodon the two theatres that were foremost on his mind. With regard to the Balkans, he indicated that at the very beginning of the crisis, an army of 400,000 men would have been required to save Serbia. He thought that it was now fruitless to send a 150,000-man force to Salonica which was too small to make much of a difference and would arrive too late. He resented the French government's decision to embark on such a risky enterprise without consulting London and he only half-heartedly went along in the interest of the alliance. He considered it vital to keep an eye on developments in the Balkans and be ready to pull the troops out the moment they ceased to be of help to Serbia, lest their rear communications be severed.

As for the Dardanelles, Kitchener firmly believed that it was necessary to hold on to the Peninsula as long as possible to avoid forfeiting Allied prestige in the Muslim world and to prevent the Turks from attacking Egypt and the Suez Canal. He admitted that evacuation was unavoidable as soon as the Germans crushed Serbia and began pouring heavy guns and reinforcements into Turkey. Nevertheless before the withdrawal process got under way, it was necessary to take measures to ensure the safety of Egypt.[32]

---

28 Cited in Aspinall-Oglander, *Gallipoli*, vol. 2, p. 411.
29 Joffre, *Personal Memoirs*, vol. 2, pp. 423-24; Arthur, *Lord Kitchener*, vol. 3, p. 186.
30 Raymond Poincaré, *Au service de la France*, vol. 7 (Paris: Plon, 1931), pp. 225-26.
31 Keyes, *Naval Memoirs*, vol. 1, p. 458.
32 Cassar, *Reluctant Partner*, pp. 202-3; Girondon to Galliéni, 11 November 1915, in France, *Les armées françaises*, tome 8, vol. 1, annexe no. 282.

Kitchener reached Mudros on the evening of 9 November and on hand to greet him were Birdwood and de Robeck. Kitchener's first words to Birdwood were, "I can't tell you how glad I am to have you with me again Birdie and to be away from all those bloody politicians." Birdwood also recalled : "I always remember how he squeezed my arm and pressed it. He was normally so very undemonstrative."[33] Kitchener was transported to the flagship *Lord Nelson* the following day and waiting for him were Monro, Maxwell and Sir Henry McMahon, the High Commissioner of Egypt.

Prior to Kitchener's arrival, Monro had visited Cairo to discuss with Maxwell and McMahon on how best to counter a Turkish advance against Egypt in case disengagement from Gallipoli became inevitable. Maxwell had given the matter plenty of thought in recent weeks and concluded that a landing at Ayas Bay, which would threaten the flank of any Turkish force moving south to attack the Suez Canal, was the surest means to ensure the safety of Egypt. A secondary benefit, in his view, was that it would reduce the effect of defeat if the operation preceded the evacuation of the Peninsula. Interestingly, Maxwell had not initially favoured disembarking in Ayas Bay. At the start of November he suggested to Kitchener that, if it became necessary to leave Gallipoli, the ideal solution to protect Egypt would be to sever the Turkish main line of communications in the vicinity of Alexandretta. Kitchener replied that Ayas Bay, on the opposite side, would be a better choice.[34] His preference for the Ayas Bay landing was based on three considerations. The port of Ayas was sheltered and would offer protection against submarine attacks; was well beyond the French sphere of interest in Syria; and the main Turkish rail communications could be severed at nearby Adana, thus preventing the flow of Ottoman troops east and south. Very few westerners knew more about the Middle East than Kitchener and so Maxwell willingly accepted his reasoning. Ayas Bay, however, was nearly 700 miles by sea from Gallipoli and the proposed move would have presented considerable challenges for both the army and navy.

Maxwell, Monro and McMahon had met several times to exchange ideas on the subject of a diversion when they were urged to leave for Mudros at once to meet Kitchener. On the northern journey, Maxwell and McMahon indicated they would raise no objections to a withdrawal from Gallipoli on condition Monro agreed to a landing at Ayas Bay. Monro agreed to the proposal, convinced that it would strengthen the case for evacuation. Still he felt a little guilty and ill at ease for going along as he saw no practical purpose in the Ayas Bay scheme.[35]

The three men arrived at Mudros on the 9th and a day later Kitchener joined them aboard the *Lord Nelson*. Kitchener was invited to use the Admiral's drawing room as his headquarters and he spent the remainder of the 10th and most of the next day holding a series of conferences. Kitchener was anxious to know whether Birdwood, with his present force, could still bring off a victory. Birdwood was adamant that he could not do so without significant reinforcements. If given several fresh divisions he could maintain his position throughout the winter, and with additional troops in the spring, he was confident that he could break through the Turkish defences. The main obstacle was that the number of troops Birdwood was calling for were unavailable. Moreover, de Robeck was opposed to another attempt to rush the Straits on the grounds that it would entail heavy sacrifice without advancing the army's ultimate objective

33 Cited in Magnus, *Kitchener*, p. 363.
34 Aspinall-Oglander, *Gallipoli*, vol. 2, pp. 413-14.
35 James, *Gallipoli*, pp. 329-31.

even if a few ships managed to reach the Sea of Marmara. No one spoke in favour of a naval attack, with or without military support. Everyone was ready to leave Gallipoli and, save for Birdwood, favoured striking the Turks elsewhere. Kitchener, seeing no prospect of another offensive, was slowly becoming reconciled to the notion of withdrawal.

To avoid a blow to the nation's military standing and to ensure the safety of Egypt, Kitchener clasped tightly the Ayas Bay project which he had discussed with Maxwell only a week or so earlier.[36] Kitchener underestimated the difficulties that had to be overcome but his adhesion to the Ayas Bay plan placated the fears of Maxwell and McMahon. By contrast Birdwood, though moving reluctantly into the evacuationists' camp, argued unsuccessfully against undertaking a new landing which he considered futile and a waste of manpower.

On the evening of 10 November, Kitchener cabled his preliminary report to the Prime Minister. He observed that he could not make a definite recommendation regarding evacuation until he had an opportunity to personally inspect the Peninsula. Nevertheless with Monro, Maxwell and McMahon advising withdrawal, he was inclined to accept their judgement. Along with all three men, he recommended that retirement should be preceded by a landing in Ayas Bay. After explaining the political and military reasons for suggesting the move, he thought that the operation could be carried out by four divisions from Egypt and France and later reinforced by the Gallipoli garrison after the evacuation was over.[37]

Asquith was startled by the proposal and hurriedly consulted the general staff at the War Office. Freed from the dominating presence of Kitchener, the general staff strongly advised against the Ayas Bay scheme. It argued that because the landing would occur near the nodal point in the Turkish railway system, the neighbourhood was certain to be defended by large enemy forces. That being the case, between 10 and 12 British divisions would be required to hold the area for the duration of the war. If the Turks intended to mount an attack on Egypt, it would be easier to meet them at the line of the Canal, that is at the end of their long advance rather than at the outset. Finally the general staff's most compelling objection was its insistence that Britain must retain the freedom to concentrate its utmost strength on the main front.[38]

The memorandum was telegraphed to Kitchener but a decision in the cabinet was postponed pending his response. Kitchener was frustrated by the rebuff. A report that the Germans were making plans to attack the Suez Canal had fueled his fears about the safety of Egypt and he saw a landing in Ayas Bay as the only way to prevent an absolute disaster. In reply, Kitchener seized on the obvious flaw in the general staff's appreciation, observing that to defend the Canal at the perimeter of Egypt was unsound politically and strategically. He reminded the Prime Minister that the proponents of the Ayas scheme were experts on Egypt and that there was nothing in the general staff's objections they had not foreseen and discussed. Kitchener maintained that retirement from Gallipoli without delivering a countervailing blow, would have the effect of driving the Arabs into the hands of the Germans and endanger British and French possessions in the Muslim world.[39]

---

36 Aspinall-Oglander, *Gallipoli*, vol. 2, pp. 415-16.
37 Kitchener to Asquith, 10 November 1915, Asquith papers, vol. 121.
38 Aspinall-Oglander, *Gallipoli*, vol. 2, p. 415; Alan Moorehead, *Gallipoli* (New York: Harper & Brothers, 1956), pp. 323-24; Lieut. Gen. Sir George MacMunn and Capt. Cyril Falls, *Military Operations: Egypt & Palestine*, vol.1 (London: HMSO, 1928), pp. 80-83.
39 Arthur, *General Sir John Maxwell*, pp. 197-98.

A copy of Kitchener's plan advocating a landing in Ayas Bay had been sent to Paris which responded at once, firmly opposing its execution on both military and political grounds – GQG hated the idea of opening another sideshow and the government would not hear of British troops occupying an area close to Syria.[40] The French, moreover, were worried about the ramifications of the British proposal to add a new military commitment while confusion reigned in the Balkans and the fate of the Dardanelles operation remained so uncertain. Consequently they requested a conference to review and coordinate Allied strategy in the eastern Mediterranean.

The British and French delegates assembled at the Quai d'Orsay (French Foreign Affairs Office) on 17 November. The Ayas Bay project was discarded almost immediately and the two sides agree to await Lord Kitchener's recommendation before ruling on the future of the Gallipoli campaign. The greater part of the discussion centred on the Balkan operation. The British representatives – Asquith, Balfour, Grey and Lloyd George – fared poorly as none of them could speak French with any semblance of clarity. The upshot was that the French pressured the British into sending two more divisions than had been previously promised. To mollify the British, Briand pledged that if juncture with the Serbian army proved impossible, the French government would consider withdrawing from the Balkans.[41]

In the meantime, Kitchener spent three days (12th, 13th and 14th) on the Peninsula, consulting with the corps commanders and examining the battle fronts. He was disheartened by the precarious hold of the army on the beaches and the seemingly impregnable nature of the Turkish defences. After glancing at the countryside from a high post at Anzac, he put his hand on Birdwood's arm and said: "Thank God, Birdie, I came to see this for myself... I had no idea of the difficulties you were up against. I think you have all done wonders."[42]

Kitchener telegraphed his overall impressions to Asquith on the 15th: "The country is much more difficult than I imagined and the Turkish positions ... are natural fortresses ... which if not taken by surprise at first could be held against very serious attack by larger forces than have been engaged." He was certain that the Allied fronts on the Peninsula could not be retained if the Turks received outside help and he again urged a landing in Ayas Bay as the best antidote to frustrate Germany's designs on Egypt and in the east. While he made no definite recommendation, it was evident from his comments that he was leaning towards evacuation, acknowledging that it would be difficult and dangerous but believed that it could be accomplished with far less loss of life than had been previously feared.[43]

Kitchener's final report was delayed when his attention was diverted by new developments in the Balkans. Yielding to French pleas, the British cabinet had given the 10th Division permission to act in support of Sarrail's push up-country. After crossing into Serbia the Anglo-French advance had been effectively blocked by the Bulgarians, foreclosing any possibility of linking up with the Serbian army, and leaving them with no option but to fall back into Greece. Under German pressure, the Greek government hinted that it would disarm the Allied troops if they retired into Greek territory.

Kitchener wanted to see what could be done and set off for Salonica in the *Dartmouth* on the 16th. On arrival, Sarrail came on board to urge Kitchener of the need to take strong measures

40 Cassar, *Reluctant Partner*, pp. 204-5.
41 Anglo-French and Allied Conferences, 17 November 1915, CAB 28/1.
42 Birdwood, *Khaki and Gown*, p. 280.
43 *Final Report of the Dardanelles Commission*, p. 56.

to bring the Greeks back in line. He explained that there were 60,000 Allied forces at the front and between them and Salonica lay an army of 150,000 Greeks. He held that the retreating Anglo-French troops as well as those in Salonica would be at the mercy of the Greeks if they should become actively hostile. In such circumstances the only way to redress the imbalance was to raise his force up to 300,000 men.[44]

It was in the Greek port on the 18th that Keyes, on his way back to the Dardanelles to resume his duties, caught up with Kitchener. The interview occurred on the *Dartmouth* and started with Kitchener saying: "Well I have seen the place. It is an awful place and you will never get through." Keyes replied that an inspection of several hours at Helles, Anzac and Suvla was hardly enough time to properly assess the nature of the defences in the Dardanelles. By contrast he had studied the Straits for nine months and he was convinced that the navy could get through. What, he inquired, had induced Lord Kitchener to change his mind? While in England he had given every indication that the army would mount an attack on the Peninsula if the navy agreed to rush the Straits simultaneously. Kitchener declared that he had sounded out the Admiralty on several occasions but received no definite assurances that the navy would be ready to take part in a joint operation. Keyes maintained that, although the Admiralty had thrown cold water on the Bulair scheme, he was confident that it would allow the navy to cooperate in a major army offensive. With unwavering obstinacy, Keyes kept insisting that the navy could break into the Sea of Marmora if given the opportunity. Kitchener shook his head and remarked that he only wished it could happen. He rose to his feet, walked out of the room into his sleeping cabinet and shut the door. "So I was dismissed," Keyes wrote in his diary that night, "feeling very sick but I could not help feeling sorry for him, he looked so terribly weary and harassed."[45]

Returning to Mudros on the 19th, Kitchener received instructions from home to proceed to Athens to arrange to see Constantine. He was to tell the Greek King that the Allies had no wish to pressure Greece into taking up arms against Germany, but if their troops were interned and disarmed it would be regarded as an act of war. As a neutral nation, Greece was within its legal rights to carry out its threat. Nevertheless the Greek government was hardly likely to invoke international law when the survival of the country depended upon Allied control of the seas. Before leaving for Athens, Kitchener received word that the Anglo-French Conference had vetoed the Ayas Bay scheme and he was now asked to give his considered opinion on the question of the "evacuation of the Peninsula in whole or in part."[46]

Kitchener reached the King's palace shortly before noon on 20 November and was received in audience at once. The details of the verbal exchanges between the two men do not concern us here. It is sufficient to say that Constantine made light of the incident and claimed it was a misunderstanding and gave his word that Allied troops would not be ill-treated or harassed if they crossed back into Greece.[47] As tension with the Greek government subsided, Kitchener was once again able to concentrate on reaching a final decision about the Dardanelles.

---

44   Arthur, *Lord Kitchener*, vol. 3, pp. 197-99.
45   Keyes, *Naval Memoirs*, vol. 1, pp. 460-61; Halpern, (ed.), *Keyes Papers*, vol. 1, pp. 243-44.
46   Asquith to Kitchener, 19 November 1915, WO 33/747.
47   The details of the interview are available in Cassar, *Kitchener*, pp. 424-25. One of my principal sources was a full record of the exchange between Kitchener and Constantine, kindly made available to me by Mrs Dondas, then archivist at the Greek Foreign Ministry. My student assistant at the time George

While Kitchener's attention had been diverted by the developments in Greece, Keyes worked tirelessly trying to enlist the support of the main players in the Dardanelles drama.[43] He argued that it made no sense to evacuate a hard won position and risk losing 25,000 men without taking advantage of proffered naval cooperation which he was certain could turn defeat into victory. Keyes got nowhere with Monro, as was to be expected, but he won over Major General Henry Horne, the most influential member on Kitchener's staff. He was equally successful with Birdwood who had been a late, if unenthusiastic, convert to evacuation. Both Maxwell and McMahon wavered after Keyes stressed that, with the Ayas Bay landing off the table, the most effective way to protect Egypt was to defeat the Turks on the Peninsula. Keyes was indefatigable in pursuit of his objective, but he must have known that he stood little chance of reversing the tide.

Back at Mudros, Kitchener called de Robeck and the generals for a final conference on the evening of 21 November. At the end of the discussion, Kitchener had made up his mind to advocate the evacuation of the Peninsula. He based his decision on a combination of factors: the uncertain attitude of the Admiralty towards another naval attack; the requirements of Salonica; and the impression caused by Monro's firm and constant position – in contrast to some of the other generals who changed their minds so often that it diminished the value of their judgements.

The next morning Kitchener cabled home his long expected report. He observed that as soon as German assistance arrived on the scene, Allied positions would become untenable and therefore retirement was inevitable. He therefore recommended the evacuation of Suvla and Anzac, retaining Cape Helles for the time being in order to facilitate the withdrawal of the two northern beaches as well as deny the Turks an opportunity to establish a submarine base in the Straits. Kitchener went on to say that he deeply regretted that he and the government had prevented a resumption of the offensive at Suvla by denying Hamilton's request for reinforcements in August. Another forward thrust from that point might have turned the Kilid Bahr position and enabled the fleet to pass through the Straits, thus changing entirely the situation in the east. No such operation took place because of "a mistaken policy we have followed" in the Balkans at the dictation of France and now it was too late to attempt it.[49]

The War Committee met on the 23rd to considered Kitchener's report in addition to a general staff memorandum which maintained that the Straits could no longer be opened. The general staff agreed with Kitchener's recommendation on the retention of Cape Helles (as did the Admiralty so that its ships could block the entrance of the Straits), but the War Committee favoured total evacuation. Asquith conveyed the War Committee's decision to Kitchener on the 23rd, adding that its conclusion had been referred to the cabinet for confirmation. Kitchener thereupon appointed Monro to command all British forces in the eastern Mediterranean outside of Egypt, while Birdwood was left in charge at Gallipoli with the responsibility to carry out the forthcoming evacuation.

Before Kitchener departed for England on the 24th he rejected Asquith's request – in what was a clumsy attempt to induce him to leave the War Office on his own – that he return to

---

Contis, a native of Greece, took the time from his own studies to translate the material into English. Kitchener's account of his discussion with Constantine is in Arthur, *Lord Kitchener*, vol. 3, pp. 202-4.
48   Keyes, *Naval Memoirs*, vol. 1, pp. 463-69; Paul G. Halpern (ed.), *The Keyes Papers*, vol. 1, pp. 247-51.
49   Kitchener to Asquith, 22 November 1915, Asquith papers, vol. 121.

Egypt "where his presence would be valuable when the moral effect of the evacuation was being felt." Kitchener refused to play into the hands of the politicians, believing that he would be of greater service to the nation by remaining where he was. His reply to Asquith was prompt and firm: "I feel very strongly that I should be back in England, as time is passing and I can do no good here. I have arranged with McMahon to quiet the effect in Egypt as far as possible. If necessary, I could go out again. My attention here calls attention to what is going on."[50]

Kitchener reached Paris on 29 November and spent the remainder of the day in private meetings with several key French politicians, explaining his reasons for recommending the abandonment of Gallipoli and adding, to their dismay, that he had reached a similar conclusion with regard to Salonica.[51] Kitchener left on the 30th and upon arriving at the War Office learned that important developments had occurred at home and abroad during his absence, adding to the confusion and deepening the divisions in the Asquith ministry. The cabinet led by Curzon had refused to ratify the War Committee's ruling that Gallipoli should be evacuated. In two powerful memoranda listing the reasons against withdrawal, Curzon alluded to the prestige factor, painted a lurid picture of the horrendous losses that were predicted to occur during the evacuation and claimed that transportation difficulties would prevent the Germans from bringing up enough heavy guns to endanger the British positions. He urged that the Peninsula be held throughout the winter and that a new attack, bolstered by fresh reinforcements, be launched in the spring. Hankey followed with a paper that further strengthened anti-evacuation sentiment in the cabinet.[52] He repeated some of Curzon's observations but his main point was that pulling out of Gallipoli would allow Turkey to concentrate all of its forces against Russia and Britain's possessions in the Near East. In all this there was even a danger that Russia might be driven to sign a separate peace. He pleaded that (in view of the failure to reach the agreed objective to link up with the Serbian army) the four divisions about to be removed from Salonica should be used "to save the position on the Gallipoli Peninsula and, if possible, to take the offensive."[53]

From the Dardanelles, Rear-Admiral Rosslyn Wemyss, who succeeded de Robeck in command of the fleet, made a last-ditch effort, with the close collaboration of Keyes, to renew the naval assault. Both men approached Monro together to beg him to reconsider but he was non-committal, promising to reply by letter. Wemyss subsequently telegraphed Balfour on 28 November to win his endorsement for a combined military and naval operation. A violent thunderstorm on the 26th, followed by two days of heavy snow and an exceptionally bitter frost, which dropped the temperature below zero, created appalling conditions for men in the open trenches. There were thousands of cases of frostbite and trench foot and hundreds died through exposure and drownings in flooded trenches.[54] Wemyss used the abnormal severe weather, together with the losses estimated at 30 percent by Monro, to stress the extreme danger of evacuation. On the other hand he insisted that a combined attack had every prospect of achieving decisive results.[55]

50 Both excepts are cited in Cassar, *Kitchener*, pp. 426-27.
51 For more information on Kitchener's activities in Paris see Cassar, *Reluctant Partner*, p. 207.
52 Marquess of Zetland, *The Life of Lord Curzon*, vol. 3 (London: Benn, 1928), pp. 130-32.
53 Hankey, *Supreme Command*, vol. 1, pp. 461-62.
54 James, *Gallipoli*, pp. 334-36.
55 Keyes, *Naval Memoirs*, vol. 1, pp. 472-76; Lord Wester-Wemyss, *The Navy in the Dardanelles Campaign* (London: Hodder and Stoughton, 1924), pp. 216-23; James, *Gallipoli*, pp. 334-36.

Complicating matters was the arrival of news that the British-led Indian army in Mesopotamia had encountered unexpected trouble and was in grave peril. As we already noted the Indian army, after landing at Abadan Island, had moved inland and advanced as far north as Qurna. Kitchener saw no reason to extend the operation given that the oil instillations on Abadan Island were safe and no worthwhile objectives lay ahead. Nevertheless it was the Indian government, which supplied most of the troops, that dictated policy, subject as always to London's approval. Kitchener, except offering advice when requested, made no effort to intervene. The Anglo-Indian army had covered the 55-mile route with such ease that to those in charge of the operation a further advance towards Baghdad became irresistible. Pushing into the interior of Mesopotamia, the expeditionary force under the command of General John Nixon made phenomenal progress, overcoming heat, disease and imperfect lines of communications. By the end of September a division led by Major General Charles Townshend captured Kut-al-Amara on the Tigris after a three-day battle.

Nixon next cast his eye on Baghdad, some 90 miles further up the Tigris, confident that Turkish resistance was on the verge of collapsing. In contrast, the general staff at the War Office produced two memoranda during the first half of October, warning that any attempt to capture and hold the Mesopotamian capital with the forces presently available was to court disaster. Kitchener echoed similar sentiments. Still the last word rested with the cabinet which disregarded the advice of both the general staff and Kitchener. Although Baghdad was of negligible military value, a majority of the ministers believed that its capture would bolster the prestige of the government and help offset the misfortunes in the Dardanelles and the Central Powers' invasion of Serbia. They were concerned less with the long-range prospects of the expedition than the lure of several days of sensational newspapers headlines. The thinking of the majority of ministers was best expressed by Bonar Law who wanted a "victory now, badly and as cheaply as possible, but that we should have to take some risks to achieve success."[56]

Thus the cabinet, influenced by an overly optimistic Nixon, sanctioned an advance on Baghdad. Townshend met little resistance until he ran into a superior Turkish force near Ctesiphon, about 16 miles south of Baghdad, on 22 November. When his attack broke down after suffering heavy losses, he fell back on Kut with the Turks in pursuit. On reaching the town Townshend, convinced that his weary men could march no further, prepare to withstand a siege.[57]

The sudden downturn in Britain's fortunes in Mesopotamia dominated much of the proceedings of the cabinet ministers during the closing days of November and the start of the following month. At the War Committee meeting on 1 December the Secretary for India opened the discussion by informing his colleagues that he had tried to obtain a commitment from the Viceroy (Charles Hardinge) to provide Nixon with reinforcements but thus far had received no answer. Asquith asked Kitchener to give his views on the issue. The War Secretary was not one to dwell on the mistakes of others. He refrained from saying "I told you so" or chastise his colleagues for embarking on an ill-advised forward policy. His first words were that he regretted the army's forced withdrawal from the recent action in Mesopotamia and the losses incurred.

---

56 Minutes of the Dardanelles Committee, 21 October 1915, CAB 42/4/15.
57 Barker, *Bastard War*, chs. 4 and 5; The debate over whether or not to press forward all the way to Baghdad can be followed in Paul K. Davis, *Ends and Means: The British Mesopotamian Campaign and Commission* (Cranbury: Associated University Presses, 1994), ch. 6; and Great Britain, *Report of the Mesopotamian Commission* (London: HMSO, 1917), pp. 20-28.

As for the question of reinforcements, they were required from practically every quarter and he doubted that he could supply the men in every instance. He thought of asking the general staff to make a general survey of the theatres of war to determine where surplus troops could be released.

Balfour interjected to say that troops could be withdrawn from Salonica where they were no longer needed. Kitchener agreed that it would be an ideal solution. He went on to say that while he was in Paris the French government had resisted his call for a withdrawal from Salonica. Balfour and Chamberlain pointed out that it had been explicitly laid down that the force was intended, not for the defence of Salonica, but to save Serbia. Grey believed the Allied force would be destroyed if it remained in Salonica. On the other hand both Lloyd George and Bonar Law argued in favour of retaining Salonica but they were lone voices. It was apparent that the matter could not be resolved unless an understanding was reached with the French.

A brief discussion followed over the interpretation of Kitchener's telegram sent from the Dardanelles in which he recommended the evacuation of Suvla and Anzac but the retention of Cape Helles. The powerful memoranda by Curzon had made such an impression that opposition to evacuation had mounted. Kitchener fielded a number of questions about the condition of the various Allied fronts before the War Committee turned to other issues.[58]

The next day the dialogue over the fate of the Gallipoli expedition continued and went on for hours in both the cabinet and War Committee. The Admiralty, skeptical about Wemyss' naval scheme from the start, vetoed it after de Robeck arrived in London and argued persuasively that nothing would be accomplished by the navy's attempt to rush the Straits. Even with the navy bowing out, sentiment, especially in the cabinet, remained high in favour of another military assault on the Peninsula. Surprisingly, Kitchener had climbed aboard as well. In a memorandum dated 2 December and distributed to the cabinet, Kitchener explained that since his report on 22 November two emerging factors had caused him to reverse his position: first, four divisions would soon be brought back from Salonica; and second that Townshend's abortive advance on Baghdad had made it imperative to deny the Turks a victory at Gallipoli.[59] Kitchener's proposed attack was intended to increase the depth at Suvla. He hoped that the navy would play a major role, such as advocated by Wemyss, but thus far the Admiralty's willingness to cooperate was confined to only providing artillery support.

It is difficult to rationalize the strategic value of the nature of the operation that Kitchener had in mind. His strategic grasp during his past experiences in war and at the start of the current one had been excellent. By his own admission another offensive to drive the Turks from the high ground in the region was at best a long shot. The proper course to have taken after he had personally inspected the fronts and consulted with the generals on the spot, would have been to remain unwavering in his recommendation to withdraw from the Peninsula. It is unfortunate that he allowed political considerations to override military logic. As Philip Magnus correctly observed, it was "the act of a passenger in a feeble team, rather than that of a leader of men in a critical situation."[60] The only explanation for his waffling was his exhaustion caused by his heavy work load and the constant harassment by colleagues like Lloyd George and Bonar Law. On top

---

58 Minutes of the War Committee, 1 December 1915, CAB 42/6/1.
59 Aspinall-Oglander, *Gallipoli*, vol. 2, p. 436n1; Minutes of the War Committee, 2 December 1915, CAB 42/6/2.; and Asquith to George V, 3 December 1915, CAB 41/36/53.
60 Magnus, *Kitchener*, p. 369.

of this, his inability to solve the Dardanelles puzzle, had taken a huge toll, robbing him of his confidence and steadiness. Encouraged by the level of support in the cabinet, Kitchener wired Monro on the 2nd:

> The Cabinet has been considering the Gallipoli situation all day. Owing to political consequences, there is a strong feeling against evacuation, even of a partial character. It is the general opinion that we should retain Cape Helles. If the Salonica troops are placed at your disposal for an offensive operation to improve the position at Suvla, could such operations be carried out in time, with a view to making Suvla retainable by obtaining higher positions and greater depth? The Navy will also take the offensive in co-operation.[61]

Monro, to his credit, refused to buckle under the pressure. He replied to Kitchener the following day:

> I fully recognize the complexity of the situation which has arisen. I do not, however, think that the proposal to employ four fresh divisions in order to gain a more secure position at Suvla can be regarded as an operation offering a reasonable chance of success... In respect of naval co-operation, the character of the terrain on the Peninsula is such that naval guns cannot search the Turkish positions... The many deep ravines and gullies are very favourable for the concealment and protection of the Turkish reserves and for their rapid transference in case of bombardment.[62]

Kitchener was unwilling to rely only on Monro's judgement and requested that he solicit the opinions of Birdwood and Julian Byng. Before the two commander's views were returned, Kitchener crossed the channel, along with Asquith, Balfour and Murray, to hold talks at Calais with key members of the Briand cabinet. Aware of the British hardline position over Salonica, the French had requested a meeting which was arranged for the 5th. Lloyd George had not been included in the British delegation, presumably to avoid giving the impression of a division within the ranks of the administration

The meeting opened with Kitchener invited to take the chair. He was in good form, demonstrating a sense of resolution that had been missing in recent weeks. His message was to the point. The conditions of British participation had not been fulfilled. Serbia was beyond saving and communications with its army could not be reestablished. The Anglo-French force was in great danger and the only sensible course was to withdraw immediately. Briand was the most vocal among the French representatives and used familiar arguments to urge the British on the necessity to remain at Salonica: A disengagement would mean that Greece and Romania would be lost to the Entente; Salonica would become a base for enemy submarines; Russia would lose faith in its allies; and the Serbian army would be destroyed.

As the clash of wills persisted, Kitchener suddenly announced that he would resign as Secretary for War if it was decided to keep the Anglo-French force in Salonica as he had no wish to shoulder the responsibility for a military catastrophe. Kitchener's threat took the wind

---

61 Cited in Keyes, *Naval Memoirs*, vol. 1, p. 481.
62 Ibid., pp. 481-82.

out of the French sails and during a brief recess they almost certainly discussed the effect that Kitchener's departure from the War Office would have on France's security. It was no secret that the British authorities relied on Kitchener's name to bring in the unending flood of recruits for the New Armies and that without him no one could remotely match the high level of popular enthusiasm that he inspired. It was also well known that Kitchener was an exponent of the western school of thought and that he would never abandon the struggle until Germany was defeated. Their inevitable conclusion was that it would be contrary to the interests of their country if they forced Kitchener's resignation. After the assembly reconvened Asquith read a formal statement, declaring that to keep 150,000 men at Salonica was certain to invite a disaster and he insisted that preparations for withdrawal should take place immediately. The French by then had probably made up their mind. Exasperated but with little room to manoeuvre, Briand saw no purpose in prolonging the discussion and conceded.[63]

For the British it turned out to be a hollow victory. The conference had barely ended when a report arrived that the Bulgarians had attacked Sarrail's forces. When Briand returned to Paris he faced a political crisis. The socialists were up in arms claiming that their hero had been left in the lurch. There was an impasse in the cabinet between those who were opposed to evacuating Salonica and those who felt that it was impossible to remain there without British support. The most uncompromising objection came from key socialist ministers. Briand realized that his government would not survive if they left the cabinet. As an act of desperation Albert Thomas, the minister of munitions and a good friend of Lloyd George, was hurriedly sent to London at his request to try to convince the Asquith government to reverse the decision at Calais.

In London Thomas, accompanied by Lloyd George, visited many members of the Asquith cabinet and his set-piece message was effective. He explained that the Briand ministry was deeply committed to the Balkan expedition and would collapse if it became known that it had consented to pull out. If that should occur, there was a chance that the crisis could thrust to power an anti-hawkish administration that would seek a way out of the war.[64] Both Bonar Law and Lloyd George did their part in the cabinet and War Committee to reinforce Thomas' arguments. Lloyd George justified the retention of Salonica, not on military grounds which was past resonating with any of his colleagues, but on the need to preserve the alliance – cleverly echoing a line Kitchener had often used, most recently to gain support for Joffre's disastrous fall offensive.[65] On 6 December, Sir Francis Bertie, British Ambassador in Paris, confirmed the threat of political instability in France, warning the Foreign Office that a British withdrawal from Salonica would be badly received by the public and probably result in the fall of Briand's ministry.[66] The resolve of the British cabinet began to weaken.

Another significant blow was administered by a conference, currently taking place at Chantilly between Joffre and chiefs of staff from Entente nations, to define a concerted policy for all theatres of war. Joffre's guided resolutions to liquidate the Dardanelles campaign passed

---

63   Anglo-French and Allied Conferences, 5 December 1915, CAB 28/1.
64   Cassar, *Reluctant Partner*, pp. 211-12.
65   Dutton, *Politics of Diplomacy*, pp. 72-74; Minutes of the War Committee, 6 December 1915, CAB 42/6/4.
66   Bertie to Grey, 7 December 1915, Foreign Office Archives, FO 371/2278.

unanimously, while everyone, except the British delegate, voted to retain a presence in Salonica.[67] The news from Chantilly, save for the pro Salonica clique, disturbed the remaining members of the Asquith regime which had expected a different outcome. Given Joffre's avowed support of the Briand government's Balkan policy and his dislike of the Dardanelles campaign, it should not have come as a surprise. In any case it was left up to Petrograd to seal the matter. At the instigation of the French, the Russians became actively involved in the dispute. They contacted the Foreign Office and Tsar Nicholas II sent a personal letter to King George V and in each case the contents urged that the Allied force at Salonica be retained.[68] Actually the Russians did not need much persuasion to lend the French a hand. It was evident that the Balkans would tie down a significant number of enemy divisions and lessen pressure on their fronts.

In the final analysis the British were unwilling to risk alienating their allies on an issue in which the cabinet itself was divided, though not evenly. Kitchener accepted that the effort to pull out of Salonica had failed and raised no objections. Among most of the members it caused hard feelings against the French. "You can guess (& share) my feelings for the Frogs at this moment," Asquith disclosed to his new confidante, Sylvia Henley (sister of Venetia Stanley). He added that the "damn Alliance is costing us a heavy price."[69] It is interesting to speculate whether the War Committee would have stuck to its guns on the matter of Salonica if it had known that on 7 December Sarrail had informed his government "that with the forces currently at his disposal, no meaningful result was possible and that, diplomatic and political considerations aside, evacuation seemed the logical conclusion."[70] Be that as it may, the die had been cast. The next day the War Committee decided to send Kitchener and Grey to Paris with plenary powers to settle the Balkan matter as best they could.[71]

Once it was evident that troops would not be released from Salonica, the cabinet gave up the idea to reinforce Suvla. Instead it made a decision on 7 December to evacuate Suvla and Anzac but to retain Cape Helles for the present. There was no reaction from Paris on receiving the news. With its obsession on Salonica, the French government had accepted the recommendation of the Allied military conference – or that of Joffre to put it bluntly – to evacuate the Dardanelles.

Under Monro's leadership, plans for the evacuation of two of the three fronts were prepared with thoroughness and care in sharp contrast to the sloppy manner in which the campaign had unfolded. A withdrawal on such a large scale was unprecedented in the annals of warfare. With the prospect of heavy, possibly horrendous, casualties, the tension in London was immense. "I pace my room at night," Kitchener told Asquith, "and see the boats fired at and capsizing, and the drowning men."[72] The operation was to be carried out at night, secretly and in stages, with

---

67 "Report of a Military Conference of Allies Held at the French Headquarters," 6 December 1915, CAB 28/1.
68 Nicholas II to George V, 7 December 1915, Royal Archives, GV Q838/53; Poincaré, *Au Service*, vol. 7, p. 312.
69 Asquith to Sylvia Henley, 8 December 1915, Asquith/Henley papers, C 542/2. Asquith's correspondence with Venetia Stanley ceased after she announced at the time of the political crisis in May 1915 that she planned to marry Edwin Montague.
70 Dutton, *Politics of Diplomacy*, p. 75.
71 Minutes of the War Committee, 8 December, 1915, CAB 42/6/6.
72 Arthur, *Lord Kitchener*, vol. 3, p. 185; Asquith testimony, 29 March 1917, Dardanelles Commission Report, CAB 19/33.

the removal of the sick and wounded, equipment, artillery, stores and finally the infantry. All this activity was to take place during the worst season of the year and under the eyes of the unsuspecting Turks. Means to deceive the Turks included using timing devices to fire off rifles after the men had slipped down to the boats. The weather was fine and the Turks never suspected what was going on. The withdrawal process began during the second week in December and, when it was over on the 20th, not a single man had been lost.[73]

Attention now focused on Cape Helles which had been retained, partly on naval grounds and partly because it immobilized a significant part of the Turkish army. The new CIGS, Lieutenant General Sir William Robertson, who was a hardcore westerner and much more forceful than his predecessor, maintained that the number of Turks tied down on Gallipoli was a secondary consideration. The main issue was that the British troops were cooped up in a precarious position and to continue to hang on to the place was not only a waste of men but a constant source of anxiety. Balfour challenged Robertson's arguments and pressed to retain Cape Helles, but he found little support in the War Committee. Kitchener had come around to share the view of the majority that the campaign had already been lost and that no useful purpose would be served by keeping a force on the Helles front. The cabinet confirmed the War Committee's action on 27 December and orders for evacuation were issued the same day. Thanks again to faultless staff work, good luck and fine weather, the last men were all safely removed on the night of 8th/9th January 1916.

The evacuation was far more competently conducted than any other phase of the operation. It came at a time when saving a sizeable part of the army had almost disappeared. For Kitchener and his colleagues, the news caused such relief and joy that it was acclaimed as a sort of victory. But campaigns are not won by retreats, no matter how well executed. The removal of troops from Gallipoli, like at Dunkirk a quarter of a century later, was the last stage in a defeat.

---

73 The execution of the stages of withdrawal are covered in depth in Aspinall-Oglander, *Gallipoli*, vol. 2, chs. 31-32; but good brief accounts are available in James, *Gallipoli*, pp. 339-47; Prior, *Gallipoli*, pp. 226-35; and Hickey, *Gallipoli*, pp. 329-334.

Conclusion: General Review and Reflections on the Dardanelles Campaign

The eight-month military campaign in the Dardanelles had consumed huge Allied resources, involving 410,000 troops from the British Empire, and a further 79,000 from France and its North African colonies. Estimates of the total killed and wounded on both sides are difficult to determine as the belligerent countries were apt to apply different criteria to account for their losses. British Empire casualties (including those evacuated for sickness and accidents) are placed at 205,000, while the French, using the same standard, sustained about 47,000 casualties.[1] Of the sick and wounded, a significant number (90,000 for the British Empire alone) were invalided out of the army and many of these would never be the same again. Western writers are apt to speculate that the Turkish government's official statement of 251,000 casualties is probably an underestimate of the actual figure because its records were haphazardly kept.[2] Lieutenant Colonel Erickson has refuted that conjecture, observing that Turkish authorities in fact maintained detailed and complete data.[3] Thus the losses among the opposing combatants were approximately equal.

The Anglo-French retirement from Gallipoli had ominous and extensive repercussions. Russia remained blockaded and isolated from its western allies. It hardened the determination of Greece and Romania to remain neutral. It damaged the prestige of the Allies in the east and Asia, though in Muslim states under their control there were no serious disturbances as had been feared. The historic victory over two European powers boosted the confidence of the Young Turks, lifting the stigma of inferiority which had marked their armies in light of stinging defeats in the Balkan Wars and in the early battles of the Great War. Entertaining visions of rejuvenating the Empire, the Ottomans became a more confident opponent in the eastern Mediterranean. In Mesopotamia they compelled the Anglo-Indian force locked up in Kut to surrender in April 1916.[4] From southern Palestine Turkish forces drove into the Sinai with the object of capturing the Suez Canal and expelling the British from Egypt. The British eventually turned the tide but the war in the Middle East consumed substantial manpower and related

---

1 Aspinall-Oglander, *Gallipoli*, vol. 2, p. 484; Moorehead, *Gallipoli*, p. 361.
2 James, *Gallipoli*, p. 348; Aspinall-Oglander, *Gallipoli*, vol. 2, p. 484.
3 Erickson, *Gallipoli*, p. 198.
4 The details of the siege can be followed in Nicholas Gardner, *The Siege of Kut-al-Amara* (Bloomington: Indiana University Press, 2014); and Russell Braddon, *The Siege* (New York: Viking Press, 1970).

resources that could have been employed more productively elsewhere. Instead of shortening the war, the Gallipoli campaign extended it, possibly by as much as a year.

Churchill had set everything in motion as the driving force of a plan to force the Dardanelles by ships alone. He had obtained the endorsement of the War Council for his half-baked scheme on condition that the naval attack be conducted devoid of publicity so that it could be broken off if necessary without loss of face. Had he kept his word, the political consequences of the naval defeat on 18 March would have been insignificant and the allies would have been spared a military campaign that was extremely costly and ended in failure with unimaginable consequences. Unfortunately Churchill gave priority to embellishing his reputation over doing what was in the best interest of the nation's war effort. To gain popular and media recognition as the prime mover in the campaign to defeat the Turks, he violated his colleagues' trust by issuing a press release at the outset of the naval bombardment. Newspapers in the west concluded at once that a major battle was developing in the Dardanelles, a revelation that drew much of the world's attention. On the other hand if Churchill had remained silent, the naval shelling against the Turkish defences, far removed from the life and death struggles on the main fronts, would have been seen as a mere demonstration. Unfortunately Churchill's folly meant that the War Council would have no option but to turn to the army to assist the navy if its ships were held up in the impending attack. The general perception in the War Council was that Britain could not afford to be defeated by a third rate power like Turkey as any serious loss of prestige would hinder diplomatic efforts to win over the Balkan states, and more importantly, was likely to spark serious nationalist disturbances in Muslim countries under Britain's control. When the naval attack was turned back, Kitchener and his colleagues felt it was vital to send in the army to take control of the Gallipoli Peninsula which would then allow the fleet to pass into the Sea of Marmora. In short if Churchill had adhered to the terms he had established at the outset, the land operation would have been avoided altogether.

Kitchener never anticipated after he agreed to dispatch troops to the Dardanelles that they would be called upon to pull the navy's "chestnuts out of the fire". Initially it was understood that the army's role would be confined to assist the navy in clearing pockets of resistance. That condition changed in light of Churchill's costly indiscretion. Kitchener and his colleagues did not have the advantage of hindsight and their decision to use the army to redress the naval defeat on 18 March is understandable, although requiring a miracle to succeed. Simply put, the invading force was doomed from the start. It lacked the resources, as there was no thought initially of effecting a major landing on the Peninsula and, to make matters worse, the element of surprise had been lost. Badly handicapped, the army faced an enemy which had been well trained, occupied the high ground, had been reinforced, fought well behind strong fortifications and was prepared to die in defence of its homeland and religion. Kitchener had initially formed a dim view of the fighting capability of the Ottoman army based on its series of defeats. But evidence gradually accumulated which gave Kitchener pause for concern and led him to revise his evaluation of the quality of the Ottoman army. The reports of his trusted subordinates, Maxwell and Birdwood, warned him that the Turkish garrison was well prepared to resist an invasion of Gallipoli, an assessment confirmed by Colonel Maucorps. The event that probably had the most impact on Kitchener's thinking was the receipt of a note describing a recent battle fought in close proximately to Basra in April. It was pointed out that the Turks had shown unexpected resilience and tenacity and it was only the extraordinary effort of British-led forces that had driven them back. While Kitchener understood that with less than half the troops called for by a Greek prewar plan to take control of the Peninsula, there were obviously risks and he anticipated that the fighting would be severe with casualties amounting to about 5,000 men. Still he remained confident that the forces under Hamilton's command were superior fighters and in the end would scale the vital heights from where British artillery would be able to reduce the forts protecting The Narrows. Hamilton had not given him any reason to think otherwise. At no time did he hint that overcoming Turkish resistance might prove insurmountable. On the contrary he gave every indication that the campaign would ultimately succeed. But without the advantage of surprise, outnumbered and forced to slog across rugged terrain after the landings, Hamilton's men advanced only a short distance before they were halted.

Kitchener was upset when informed of the bad news, although he retained a stoic demeanor as he normally did in such circumstances. He realized that he had underestimated the tenacity of the Turks, and with the limited reinforcements he could provide Hamilton, he doubted that the tide of battle could be reversed. Hamilton casualties totaling 14,000 were nearly three times higher than he had estimated, the army had fallen well short of its objectives and the prospect of trench warfare was equally disheartening. Kitchener found himself in a quagmire for which there was no easy way out. Judging victory no longer within reach, at least for the time being, Kitchener proposed replacing Hamilton's losses and leaving him to make such progress as was possible. Prolonging the stalemate, however, was rejected by the new coalition government which wanted enough reinforcements sent to Hamilton to allow him to finish the job. With the Conservatives acting more as hostile critics, rather than helpful partners, Kitchener's authority vanished rapidly as he was often overruled and no longer exercised much influence in the Dardanelles Committee. His prestige almost gone, his role was confined to supplying Hamilton with the assigned troops for his impending offensive in August. Kitchener would have preferred that Hamilton wait until all the forces had arrived before launching his assault but as was his habit, avoided interfering with the process of military planning. It would have made more sense for Hamilton to use all the forces placed at his disposal but it is doubtful that even such a course would have allowed his second landing to fare any better than the first one. Thereafter Kitchener tried desperately to find a formula that would avoid withdrawing from Gallipoli. His efforts were hindered by the French who urged that the British join them to sustain the new theatre in the Balkans. The British calculated that the diversion was a waste of manpower as it was too late to save Serbia and argued long and hard against it. Yet rather than risk fracturing the alliance, they ultimately yielded to French pleas. Lacking resources to maintain three fronts, British commitment to reinforce the Balkan front brought the curtain down on the Dardanelles campaign.

One final issue needs to be addressed. As it is the judgement of most current studies that the plan to force the Dardanelles by ships alone was a dreadful mistake, how should the western Allies have reacted when Turkey entered the war on the side of the Central Powers? There are some writers – presumably following the unfounded claims in Churchill's account and the Dardanelles Commission Report – who believe that at the outset a surprise attack by both the army and navy in February 1915, while Gallipoli was lightly defended, probably would have succeeded. The disposal of this canard is long overdue. What made such an idea implausible was the absence of available troops to take part in an amphibious operation. The only regular division left in Britain in February – after the 28th left for France and the raw 1st Canadian followed suit about ten days later – was the 29th and Kitchener, whose authority then was unchallenged, wanted to retain it for home defence or in case of a crisis on the western front. At any rate the enterprise surely would have required more than one division. Although the Turks had only two divisions spread over the Peninsula in February, there were plenty of others nearby, and in the likely scenario that the invading troops would have bogged down after landing, the only place from which to draw reinforcements would have been the western front.

A more practical policy for the allies would have been to avoid tipping their hand and allow the Turks to make the first move. The Turks were hardly a dangerous foe and the options opened to them almost certainly would have ended in their defeat. They could have mounted attacks against the Russians through the Caucasus or the British in Egypt, as they had done earlier in the war, but the results would have been the same. If they had tried a different strategy, as seems likely, they would not have fared any better. All the allies had to do was to lay back and allow the Turks to take the initiative until they had revealed their intention before striking back – like a skilled boxer counterpunching to wear down a slow-moving and awkward opponent. Ultimately the Turkish leaders would have wearied and recognized that their army was overmatched. Their only hope to remain in power in view of deepening discontent at home and rising Arab nationalism would have been to seek a release from the war. With the Turks no longer a factor, the Allies would have avoided the bloody campaigns in the Dardanelles, Mesopotamia and Palestine, concentrating their resources instead on defeating the Germans on the Western Front and accelerating an end to the war.

Appendix: Assessing the Charges Against Kitchener

As Churchill was the mastermind of the attack on the Dardanelles, the costly failure of the campaign, which the press linked directly to his leadership as a dangerous amateur strategist, discredited him in the eyes of the British public. Mindful that the legacy of the Dardanelles stood in the way of reviving his political career, he lied and distorted facts to cover up his mistakes and worked unceasingly to portray himself in heroic terms by blaming others, mostly Kitchener, in his speeches, articles for newspapers, testimony before the Dardanelles Commission and *The World Crisis*. In an early complaint he maintained that contrary to Kitchener's frequent declaration, there were plenty of troops ready for combat in England in January/February 1915 and he proceeded to name the available divisions. In the absence of serious enemy pressure on the western front, there was nothing to prevent the War Office from sending some of these elsewhere. He added that if he had access to eight or nine divisions, he would never have considered the idea of a purely naval assault. It was an assertion that he made in *The World Crisis* and in his testimony to the Dardanelles Commission.[1] He was wrong in both instances. In the first place Hankey had investigated the number of trained troops in Britain at the start of 1915 and his findings only identified one experienced division (the 29th) from among those Churchill had cited. An excerpt from Hankey's memorandum, which he submitted to the Dardanelles Commission in 1916, summed up the results of his research:

> In the UK apart from [Territorial troops] allotted for Home Defence the only complete divisions were the 28th, which embarked for France between 15 & 28 January & the 1st Canadian [Division] which embarked [for France] on 8 February. The 29th Division had not all arrived in the country, and was earmarked for service in France. The 1st North Midland Territorial Division did not leave for France until end of February [1915], and other Territorial Divisions followed in April and May [1915], *but none of these were armed or fully trained trained by the middle of January.*[2]

Brigadier General C. F. Aspinall-Oglander confirmed Hankey's data in the first volume of his official history of the Gallipoli campaign published in 1929. He stated that at the close of December 1914, apart from the 300,000 British and Indian troops in France, there were in the country two complete divisions, the 28th and the 1st Canadian. The 29th Division, or most of

---

1   See for example Churchill testimony, 28 September 1916, Dardanelles Commission Report, CAB 19/33; Churchill, *World Crisis*, vol. 2, pp. 170-71.
2   Cited in Curran, *Grand Deception*, p. 175.

its units, had not yet arrived in England from overseas garrisons. The 28th and 1st Canadian divisions, which had been promised to France, would soon be fully prepared to take the field. Behind them stood 11 first-line territorial units, some of which were employed in home duties, as well as all the divisions of the New Armies, but none would be battle-ready for several months.[3]

Moving on to Churchill's other charge that he would have preferred an amphibious operation at the outset, that too, is inaccurate, if not an outright lie. Bearing in mind that when troops became available after Greece had been ruled out in the middle of February, Churchill did not suggest that they be sent to the Dardanelles. Ultimately it appears to have been Hankey who saw the advantages of using troops to support the naval attack. At the outset, however, everyone was in agreement about confining the Dardanelles enterprise to a purely naval attack so that it would be easy to call off if it met unexpected resistance. Sir Edward Grey, who among politicians exhibited the rare qualities of modesty and integrity, confirmed in his memoirs that the use of troops was never proposed and, if it had been, "the operation would never have been agreed to." He provided further details:

> My recollection is very clear that the attack on the Dardanelles was agreed to on the express condition that it should be a naval operation only; it was under no circumstances to involve the use of troops. The British and French armies were at death's grip with the Germans on the Western Front, the situation was critical for the Allies, and it was important that there should be no diversion of force to other parts of the world, except under the pressure of absolute necessity. If the attack on the Dardanelles did not succeed, it was to be treated as a naval demonstration and abandoned. It was on this condition only that Kitchener agreed to it.[4]

Churchill made a big issue of Kitchener's delay in releasing the promised 29th Division, insisting that the loss of valuable time retarded Hamilton's landing by three weeks and fatally compromised the operation. Churchill argued that if the 29th Division had sailed in February, as originally scheduled, it would "have been put on board ship in a condition to disembark for fighting, without the need of going to Alexandria to repack."[5] As the former First Lord, Churchill had to know that he was making a disingenuous statement. There was as yet no plan to use troops in heavy fighting when Kitchener cancelled the departure of the 29th Division on 19 February. The troops had been expected to start boarding the ships on the 22nd. That being the case, the loading process, like on the other ships that left England for the Dardanelles at roughly the same time, would have been chaotic, necessitating that the mess be straightened out on arrival of the troops. In fact when the 29th Division reached Lemnos at the start of April it was, according to several credible sources, rerouted directly to Alexandria because its equipment – that is heavy guns, shells, machine guns, entrenching tools, etc., – had been loaded so badly that it required

---

3 Aspinall-Oglander, *Gallipoli*, vol. 1, p. 25.
4 Grey, *Twenty-Five Years*, vol. 2, p. 78.
5 Churchill testimony, 28 September 1916, Dardanelles Commission Report, CAB 19/33; Churchill, *World Crisis*, vol. 2, p. 216.

Appendix: Assessing the Charges Against Kitchener

to be sorted out in a harbor where proper facilities existed.[6] Moreover, landing on a hostile beach when the element of surprise had been forfeited was a risky and complicated process and could not have taken place without careful preparations beforehand. This meant a battle plan, lighters to carry the men to landing sites, a medical staff, and arrangements to deal with the sick and wounded – none of these essentials elements was available until well into April. Thus when everything is considered, it was absurd for Churchill to claim that, if the 29th Division had left as originally scheduled, it would have been ready to fight on reaching the Dardanelles.

In any case, the attack could not have taken place during the period Churchill asserted. Whether he knew it or not, the turbulent weather in the Dardanelles in April 1915 ruled out disembarking on the Peninsula. It would be difficult to find an authority with more credibility than Aspinall-Oglander, who, as a colonel, had been on Hamilton's staff and believed that the concept of attacking the Dardanelles was sound but, once put into effect, was ruined by a succession of errors. He dealt with the weather issue in succinct terms:

> Had combined operations been able to begin three weeks earlier the chances of success would undoubtedly have been better. But in point of fact the weather was so unsettled throughout this period that 25th April – the eventual day of the landings – was actually the first day in April on which the disembarkation of a large force on exposed beaches could have been safely undertaken. Regrettable, and infinitely serious, though the delay might have proved, it is not historically accurate to attribute to it any of the subsequent lack of success.[7]

Churchill's indictment of Kitchener continued, this time over an incident that occurred after the army had landed on the beaches of Gallipoli. At the height of the fighting on 28 April Churchill and Fisher visited Kitchener to urge that he send Hamilton reinforcements from the troops in Egypt. Churchill described what happened:

> Fisher pleaded eloquently and fiercely and I did my best. Lord Kitchener was at first incredulous that more troops could be needed, but our evident anxiety and alarm shook him. That evening he telegraphed to Sir John Maxwell and to Sir Ian Hamilton assigning an Indian Brigade and the 42nd Territorial Division then in Egypt to the Dardanelles. There was no reason whatever why these forces and others should not have been made available as a reserve to Sir Ian Hamilton before his attack was launched ... These reinforcements aggregating 12,000 or 13,000 rifles could have fought in the battle of the 28th or enable it to be renewed at dawn on the 29th.[8]

Churchill hinted that the presence of additional troops from Egypt might have given Hamilton's attack enough weight to break through. It is difficult to know how much faith to place in

---

6   Tim Coates (ed.), *Defeat at Gallipoli: The Dardanelles Commission,* Part II (London: HMSO, 2000), pp. 41-45; Robert Rhodes James, *Churchill: A Study in Failure 1900-1939* (London: Weidenfeld and Nicolson, 1990), p. 73n2.
7   Aspinall-Oglander, *Gallipoli,* vol. 1, p. 72n. The landing was originally set for 23 April, but owing to stormy conditions, was postponed for 48 hours.
8   Churchill, *World Crisis,* vol. 2, pp. 338-39.

Churchill's recollection or description of events when he was personally involved. After all it was not as if he was the epitome of integrity. As already mentioned, the French had notified London a day earlier that Hamilton needed to be reinforced so that the duo from the Admiralty did not catch Kitchener by surprise.[9] Besides it is improbable to say the least, that the meagre addition of 12,000 or so troops would have tipped the scales in Hamilton's favour when the defenders had access to ample reserves. In the final analysis Kitchener was not responsible for depriving Hamilton of reinforcements. We saw that he had contacted Maxwell during the first week in April, instructing him to supply Hamilton with any troops that he could spare. Maxwell was directed to forward the telegram to Hamilton but he never did for reasons of his own. Churchill alluded to the episode in which he and Fisher had allegedly pressured the War Office to reinforce Hamilton at one of his numerous sittings before the Dardanelles Commission. One of the commissioners interrupted him and referred to Kitchener's telegram to Maxwell sent three weeks before Hamilton's landing on Gallipoli. Without missing a beat, Churchill adeptly changed the subject.[10] When he recalled the incident in his book, which included his fraudulent claims, he conveniently omitted any mention of the telegram Kitchener had sent to Maxwell.[11]

Churchill, moreover, filtered the proceedings and twisted the facts horribly in his version of what had occurred at the crucial meeting of the War Council on 24 February when the decision was made to employ the army if the fleet was unable to overcome the Dardanelles defences. As we have already examined and commented extensively on his falsified account in *The World Crisis*, it is sufficient to say that he made no reference to his press release and its consequences. By omitting the key part of Kitchener's comments, Churchill implied that it was his colleague who had first raised the idea of using troops in case the navy required assistance.[12] Churchill expanded the same theme when he held that after the failure of the naval attack, Kitchener was responsible for sending the army to storm the Gallipoli Peninsula without receiving formal ministerial approval. He wrote:

> It was with grief that I announced to the Cabinet on the 23rd [of March] the refusal of the Admiral and the Admiralty to continue the naval attack … It was now open … to the Prime Minister, Lord Kitchener, to the Cabinet if they wished to withdraw from the whole enterprise and to cover the failure by the seizure of Alexandretta… Lord Kitchener was always splendid when things went wrong. Confident, commanding, magnanimous, he made no reproaches. In a few brief sentences he assumed the burden and declared he would carry the operation through by military force. So here again there was no discussion … No formal decision to make a land attack was even noted in the records of the Cabinet or the War Council.[13]

Churchill's depiction of the events leading to the employment of the army in the operation was another example of his mendacity. To distract from the consequences of his earlier press release, he maintained that the land campaign was not the inevitable result of the navy's failure to force

---

9   See p. 100 in this text.
10 Churchill testimony, 26 March 1917, Dardanelles Commission Report, CAB 19/33.
11 Churchill, *World Crisis*, vol. 2, p. 339.
12 Ibid., p. 183.
13 Ibid., p. 254.

a passage through the Straits. He made the following claim: "Naval operations did not necessarily involve military operations. This was a separate decision, which did not rest with me or the Admiralty."[14] According to Churchill the responsibility for initiating the land campaign rested entirely with Kitchener who alone had the power to do so. Let us see if Churchill's charges square with the facts. To begin with, Churchill was insincere when he claimed that the discussion, centering on whether the operation should continue or be terminated, occurred in the wake of the navy's refusal to resume the assault. True enough it was never debated in the War Council. Why? Because it had already been settled at a meeting on 24 February to send in the army if necessary and opinion had not changed when the issue came up again on 19 March. In another duplicitous exercise, Churchill maintained that formal consent to land the army on the Peninsula could not be found among the records of either the cabinet or War Council, an assertion again intended to blame Kitchener for the episode. Churchill knew that minutes were not transcribed at cabinet meetings, that after each session only the formal decisions contained in a letter Asquith sent to the King were available. That piece of information aside, it should be observed that the cabinet did not devise war policy, only confirmed or rejected it. Churchill was also mindful that after 19 March the Prime Minister did not summon the War Council until 14 May. The War Council had already laid down the conditions to initiate a military assault on Gallipoli and so it was not deemed necessary to summon a meeting for that purpose. It was not the first time that a major decision was approved without the official blessing of the War Council. After all the agreement to send troops to the Dardanelles in February had been taken at an informal meeting with only three-fifths of the ministers present and was never confirmed by the entire War Council or the cabinet.

The Prime Minister took it for granted that Kitchener had already received implicit authorization from his colleagues to arrange for a landing on Gallipoli. He saw no need to hurriedly assemble them simply to obtain affirmation of their earlier verdict. Asquith had reasons of his own for not wanting to involve the War Council, apparently preferring to meet with the service ministers and Hankey as he did on 30 March and 6 April – to which we have already alluded.

After 1968 practically all writers of the Dardanelles episode have taken Churchill at his word in his error filled account, or, as we shall see, the often faulty judgement of the Dardanelles Commission, rather than regularly consult the official records. This explains why Kitchener continues to be held responsible for initiating the land campaign, when in fact he was acting in accordance with the wishes of the War Council. From the beginning he had wanted to avoid sending the army to assault the Peninsula. We have seen that time and time again he resisted Churchill's pleas to employ troops to coincide with the naval operation. After the naval attack was repulsed, he backed Churchill's efforts to persuade de Robeck to try again. When that proved unsuccessful, he hoped that Hamilton's men might be spared the ordeal of invading the Peninsula if de Robeck resumed applying heavy pressure against the Turkish forts which the naval commander gave every indication that he would. Kitchener reasoned that there was always an outside chance that the morale of Turkish soldiers might break down, leading to the wholesale evacuation of Gallipoli. But de Robeck never kept his pledge lest he suffer the loss of additional ships and men and be sent home. Consequently the navy did only the bare minimum, that is, cover the landings of the troops, engage in

---

14   Cited in Bell, *Churchill*, p. 361.

desultory bombardment of the forts and transport supplies and ammunition to the Peninsula. It was only because there was no other option to redress the failure of the naval attack and redeem the nation's honour that Kitchener consented to land the army on the Peninsula. Grey's account on the matter is worth quoting:

> We stood publicly committed to the attack on the Dardanelles, as a serious effort from which we could not withdraw, except by admission of a serious defeat. Kitchener was asked to provide troops for land operations in Gallipoli to support the fleet. This was the very thing that he had expressly stipulated that he should not have been called to do; but in face of what had happened, he could not now refuse.[15]

Churchill thoroughly dominated the naval phase of the operation and when the army took over, he remained involved by working relentlessly to ensure that its needs were met even after the creation of the coalition government when he was no longer at the Admiralty. In repeatedly describing his part in the story, he scrupulously avoided any mention of his press release which had been the direct cause of initiating the land campaign, but always pointed his finger at Kitchener as the prime mover. He attributed the failure of the naval offensive, not to the ships' inability to deal with the Turkish shore batteries, but to a host of other factors. He resented de Robeck's about face, implying that he lacked courage. He took umbrage at the members of the War Staff Group for blocking his order to renew the naval attack when, in his opinion, victory was in sight. Asquith came under fire as well. Churchill criticized the Prime Minister for his want of resolve and inability to maintain a firm grip on the decision-making process, though much of his bitterness grew out of a feeling of betrayal for what he perceived was his unjust eviction from the Admiralty. Churchill aimed his heaviest broadside at Kitchener. He claimed that Kitchener had crippled the chances of a victory on two occasions, once when he had held back the 29th Division, and again by denying Hamilton reinforcements from Egypt at a critical point during the army's first landing in April. Although Hamilton received more formations for the second landing than he had requested, Churchill was careful not to cast any blame on his good friend's leadership. He held that Hamilton, whose mistakes he ignored, came perilously close to achieving a victory despite the inexperience of most of his troops and several poor key commanders. Churchill accused Kitchener and the War Office of saddling Hamilton with inferior manpower resources – as if the New Armies consisted of seasoned troops and officers. In the final analysis Churchill was so blinded by his intense conviction that the plan to knock Turkey out of the war was sound and far sighted, marred only by lost opportunities, that he could not admit that the sad ending of the campaign stemmed directly from imperfections in the original conception.

Although Churchill had been hammered by a hostile press during and immediately following the Dardanelles campaign, he had high expectations that he would be absolved from censure once an impartial body was set up to investigate and weighed the evidence. He was delighted when Asquith yielded under intense parliamentary pressure (to avoid a defeat in the House) and consented to the appointment of a commission of inquiry. In July 1916 parliament, through the Special Commissions Act, formally established the Dardanelles Commission to examine the origins and execution of both the naval assault and the military operations on the Gallipoli

---

15   Grey, *Twenty-Five Years*, vol. 2, p. 79.

Peninsula.[16] The ten-man commission was chaired by the highly respected Lord Cromer (formerly Evelyn Baring) who had served as Consul General of Egypt with exceptional skill until his retirement in 1907. At the age of 75, Cromer was already in frail health and died four months after his appointment. He was succeeded by William Pickford, a lawyer and judge. The remaining members consisted of the New Zealand and Australian High Commissioners in London, a barrister (E. Grimwood Means) who acted as secretary, four parliamentarians and two retired service officers, Admiral Sir William May and Field Marshal William Nicholson, a former CIGS.[17]

Since it was no secret that Nicholson was a bitter foe of Kitchener, his selection to serve on the Commission is incomprehensible. He was clearly expected to assail Kitchener's conduct at the least pretext. As he was the only military expert in the group, it is reasonable to assume that he wielded undue influence over the conclusions of the Commission's report.

Hamilton who had no use for Nicholson and would spar with him during his testimony, considered him a trouble maker with an intense dislike of Kitchener. He vented his feelings about "old Nick" in a letter to Braithwaite in mid-August 1916: "Nick's appointment caused me to shiver… He hates K. a great deal worse than he hates me. Not that I think he hates me at all but he has been jealous of me and has always had a mischievous delight in trying to put a spoke in my wheel."[18] On another occasion in 1919 he suspected Asquith's real motive for Nicholson's appointment:

> Who put that bloodhound Nick, K.'s bitterest enemy, on the Dardanelles Commission. What was the use of Asquith saying afterwards in the House of Commons that he wanted to appoint someone with a watching brief for K. K. would have needed no defence if Asquith had not put on Nicholson in order to try & saddle K.'s memory with all the sins of the old gang.[19]

The Commission took evidence from everyone involved in the planning and execution of the Dardanelles operation except Kitchener who had died tragically several months before it began its work. The full results of its year-long investigation were never published but two heavily censored reports became available to the public in March 1917 and December 1919. The first covered the origins of the campaign up to the end of the naval attack and the second, held back for security reasons until after the end of the war, focused on the military operations. Researchers were finally able to gain access to the printed version of the entire proceedings housed at the Public Record Office (now called the National Archives) in 1968.

The Dardanelles commissioners made two observations during their opening remarks. The first assured its readers of the following: "On the whole, we may state with the utmost confidence that we were furnished with all the materials necessary to form a correct and deliberate judgement upon which Parliament had delegated us to express an opinion." That proved to be wishful thinking. As will be seen shortly, the government did not turn over all classified sources and in addition, frequently doctored summaries of the inner councils of war.

16 *First Report of the Dardanelles Commission*, p. 1.
17 Jenny Macleod, *Reconsidering Gallipoli* (Manchester: Manchester University Press, 2004), p. 27.
18 Hamilton to Braithwaite, 17 August 1916, Hamilton papers, 8/1/13.
19 Hamilton to French, 17 May 1919, French papers, PP/MCR/C33.

The commissioners did not seem to be as adamant in discussing their second conjecture. They began by saying: "We are particularly desirous of stating that the witnesses who appeared before us answered all the questions addressed to them with the utmost frankness." A little later they appeared to modify this statement: "Without casting any sort of imputation on the good faith of the witnesses themselves, it is conceivable that, in giving to the Commission an account of the past they may have been to some extent unconsciously influenced by their knowledge of subsequent events."[20] If the commissioners suspected that some of the witnesses were less than candid, it is doubtful that they understood how widespread the problem had been. Many of the key witnesses with a vested interest to conceal their part in the failed operation, colluded and tailored their testimony to avoid incriminating or contradicting one another. They understood that it was injudicious to single out individuals and that they might all sink together if they engaged in mutual recriminations. Hankey worked behind the scenes with former members of the War Council, coaching them individually to avoid targeting one another and to follow guidelines in order to present a united front when answering questions. The cover-up plot explains why no former member of the War Council sought to condemn Churchill, despite his obvious responsibility both for initiating the purely naval assault and for extending the scope of the operation.[21]

In assessing the work of the commissioners, it must be admitted that their task was very difficult. They were not provided with all the official records connected with the Dardanelles campaign, or given access to the minutes of the inner war councils, which naturally militated against arriving at the truth. That said, the result of their year-long investigation falls short in too many instances, lacking in objectivity and basic research and too often reaching conclusions without hard proof.

The Dardanelles Commission held its first meeting on 23 August and interviewed Monro out of sequence because he was about to depart for India. It adjourned for nearly four weeks to allow Hankey to complete the government's case for the inception of both the naval and military operations. Hankey did not relish to act as the defence counsel for the Asquith government which he described as "one of the most dreary tasks that has ever fallen to my lot."[22] Quite apart from the huge amount of work involved, he found it painful to have to distort the truth to protect friends, sometimes at the expense of Kitchener's reputation. His written submission (or memorandum as he referred to it) to the Commission, was based on the minutes he kept and intended to avoid controversy and shed the best possible light on the action of Asquith, whom he admired, and the War Council.

Hankey tried to provide explanations in his memorandum for many of the questions he anticipated the commissioners would ask. On the first critical issue, he gave a summary of the causes that had induced the War Council to favour Churchill's idea of a naval attack on the Dardanelles on 13 January. He dwelled on three factors, namely the urgent Russian request for a demonstration, the deep concern over the growing threat to Serbia and the desire to enlist the Balkan states on the side of the Entente. His purpose, as Professor Bell has observed, was "intended to bolster the impression that, in January 1915, some action in the east had been both essential and

20   *First Report of the Dardanelles Commission*, p. 3.
21   Bell, *Churchill*, pp. 4-6.
22   Hankey, *Supreme Command*, vol. 2, pp. 522-23.

unavoidable."²³ Hankey placed more importance on the Russian appeal than he should have, as a week before 13 January the Turks had been routed at Sarikamish and the immediate crisis, if there ever was one, was over. Hankey was clearly disingenuous when he moved on to explain why the operation was not called off after the naval attack broke down. In his prepared reply, he made no reference to Churchill's press announcement which, he not only acknowledged at the time was an unpardonable blunder, but had to know that it was the principal cause of the military campaign. Instead he repeated the points that had influenced support for the naval operation, adding the importance of maintaining British prestige after the naval setback and the possibility of inducing Italy to keep its commitment to join the war.²⁴ Hankey calculated that he spent a cumulative total of 174 hours putting together the government's case which was forwarded to E. G. Means, secretary of the Dardanelles Commission, on 6 September.

The Commission nursed a grievance against the government which it dropped in Hankey's lap on the first day of his testimony on 19 September 1916. The Asquith administration had turned over to the Commission a sizeable collection of relevant documents but had refused, on constitutional grounds, to produce the minutes of the War Council and its successor bodies. The Dardanelles Commission insisted that it was entitled to see the record of the entire deliberations and threatened those in authority with dire consequences if their refusal persisted. Hankey at first defended the government's position, but after consulting with Asquith, worked out a compromise under which the minutes would be released only to Cromer to allow him to check whether they corroborated Hankey's evidence.²⁵ Strangely enough after Cromer died no one had any more concerns or thoughts about the original minutes and it no longer became an issue. Without accessibility to the War Council minutes, the members of the Commission had no way of verifying the testimony of witnesses.

Apart from the fuss over the War Council minutes, the rest of Hankey's interrogation on that day, and at the next one on the 27th, was conducted in a cordial atmosphere. As Hankey was thoroughly acquainted with the official material, he fielded the flood of questions with ease and to the satisfaction of the Commission. Although he often provided detailed answers, he was careful to avoid saying anything that would injure the Prime Minister or the members of the War Council. No one benefitted more from Hankey's carefully-guarded testimony than Churchill. If Hankey's evidence had contained the real reason for the escalation of the operation, it may be that Churchill's reputation would have been irreparably damaged.

From what Hankey said, it seemed that the commissioners drew the conclusion that the naval operation was largely in response to Russia's appeal for help. When Fisher was interviewed he not only corroborated that observation but went a step further, claiming that Kitchener had been the driving force behind the naval operation. Whether the former First Sea Lord was trying to protect his friend Churchill, with whom he had colluded, or his memory was fading, is anybody's guess. The Commission should have known, as a matter of course, that Kitchener did not possess the authority to induce the Admiralty to undertake a major naval operation. All he did was to suggest a naval demonstration when the Russian commander requested help at the turn of the year. Yet the commissioners initially accepted Fisher's contrived testimony that Kitchener was the real instigator of the naval operation. They paraded his idea during subsequent

23 Bell, *Churchill*, p. 232.
24 Hankey, "Notes for Evidence," September 1916, CAB 19/29.
25 Hankey, *Supreme Command*, vol. 2, pp. 523-24.

interviews with several members of the War Council without receiving confirmation but eventually altered their early impression about the seminal part they had ascribed to Kitchener in initiating the naval attack, though they remained convinced that the Russian appeal had turned Britain's attention eastwards. In clinging to a faulty premise, they did not absolve Kitchener completely, as their following conclusion revealed:

> Lord Kitchener was, without doubt, strongly impressed with both the military and political necessity of acting on the appeal made by the Russian Government. The army he was creating was not yet ready. He had to provide for home defence, to which he attached the utmost importance. He was most unwilling to withdraw a single man from France... Under these circumstances, Lord Kitchener grasped, perhaps too eagerly, at the proposal to act through the agency of the Fleet alone ... but it cannot with justice or accuracy be said that the responsibility for proposing the adoption of this course rested with him. It rested rather on the First Lord.[26]

The former members of the War Council, all of whom were called to testify before the Dardanelles Commission, followed Hankey's advice to avoid, among other things, pointing fingers at anyone. No one mentioned Churchill's press release which had induced all of them to agree to assign the army to invade Gallipoli in the event the naval attack stalled. Churchill appeared before the Dardanelles Commission five times within the first month. As he was well prepared and an excellent speaker, he created a highly favourable impression. He blamed Kitchener for a host of problems that developed during the campaign. He realized that he could not directly criticize Kitchener, a national hero, so soon after his death, but dropped enough hints that the commissioners "might be expected to reach the same conclusion."[27]

As it happened, the commissioners proved to be ultra-indulgent towards Churchill. In several instances they accepted, without crucial evidence or confirmation, his excuses why his transactions had failed to materialize. Additionally they allowed him to question witnesses, a privilege they did not accord to anyone else. They accepted his false contention that he would have preferred "a joint naval and military attack rather one conducted by ships alone."[28] Churchill made an even more blatantly bald-faced lie when he claimed that if he had known that an army of between 80,000 and 100,000 men would be available in April "we could have made perfectly good plans for a surprise amphibious attack" on the Gallipoli Peninsula.[29] As already noted it was no secret that in the spring of 1915 many of the territorial divisions and the first wave of the New Armies would be ready to face the enemy in battle. Yet none of the commissioners even challenged his ludicrous assertion.

Although the Dardanelles Commission was unaware of Churchill's press release and its dire consequences, it did not even hold him accountable for pushing a defective naval plan on the War Council. Hard as it is to believe, he received only a slap on the wrist in the *First Report of the Dardanelles Commission* and escaped without criticism in the *Last Report*. The *First Report* absurdly concluded that Churchill had failed to see that his support within the Admiralty added

---

26   *First Report of the Dardanelles Commission*, pp. 15-16.
27   Bell, *Churchill*, p. 239.
28   *First Report of the Dardanelles Commission*, p. 15.
29   Churchill testimony, 28 September 1916, Dardanelles Commission Report, CAB 19/33.

up to "a certain amount of half-hearted and hesitating expert opinion."[30] The verdict did not seriously damage Churchill's reputation or prevent him from returning to office in 1917.

The Commission did not show the same consideration to Kitchener as it had to Churchill. The defeat in the Dardanelles had produced 250,000 Anglo-French casualties and the public expected that those responsible for the calamity be held accountable. The commissioners were careful to avoid assailing the competence of anyone who still occupied positions of authority in the government. Besides it would have been inappropriate in wartime to reveal that the planning and execution of the operation had been bungled by high-level political and military officials. Kitchener, however, was a convenient scapegoat. He was the sole mouthpiece of the War Office, occupied a position of immense prestige and power and more importantly, was not around to defend his action.

The commissioners were puzzled as to why the naval attack had not included the assistance of military forces which they deemed would have offered a better chance of success. The main obstacle, they determined, had been Kitchener who claimed that he had no troops to spare. They were critical of the War Council for accepting his statement on faith and for its failure to undertake its own investigation. "Had this been done," they remarked, "we think that it would have ascertained that sufficient troops would have been available for a joint naval and military operation at an earlier date than was supposed."[31] It is difficult to understand the reasoning of the commissioners. Hankey, as we have already noted, had conducted an impartial survey which confirmed Kitchener's figures on the dearth of the nation's manpower at the start of 1915. Nevertheless the commissioners chose to believe Churchill who had a huge stake in the outcome of their investigation and they did it without corroborating evidence. It bears repeating that Churchill had never considered a joint campaign and his insistence that he adopted the exclusively naval plan only because the required military forces were considered unavailable was an excuse he made up to lessen his culpability. The number of troops in Britain at the start of 1915 has already been examined thoroughly, but even if a few more divisions had been available the commissioners should have understood that it was not simply a matter of sending the available troops on hand but rather the possibility of a heavy and continual drain that a fresh military enterprise might impose. As General (later Field Marshal) William Robertson pointed out, to force the Dardanelles, dominate Constantinople, open the Bosporous and defeat large enemy forces on their own ground was likely to require many divisions.[32] With the cupboard bare at home, the only option to keep sending reinforcements would have been to draw them from the western front. No responsible government would have embarked on a distant venture and risk weakening the decisive front at a time when allied defences were still in a rudimentary state.

The commissioners maintained that if either Kitchener or Fisher had expressed strong reservations on technical grounds to the naval plan when initially discussed in the War Council, it would have been abandoned.[33] Fisher may be faulted for remaining silent but Kitchener, contrary to the commissioners' inference, was hardly an expert on modern naval gunnery. Besides the operation under discussion was intended to be exclusively in the hands of the navy. Yet the

30 *First Report of the Dardanelles Commission*, pp. 41-42.
31 Ibid., p. 41.
32 Field Marshal Sir William Robertson, *Soldiers and Statesmen 1914-1918*, vol. 1 (London: Cassell, 1926), p. 103.
33 *First Report of the Dardanelles Commission*, p. 20.

evidence is compelling that Churchill arranged to see Kitchener to strengthen support for his naval scheme before the War Council assembled on 13 January. In the beginning Kitchener questioned the idea of a purely naval attack to force the Dardanelles, insisting that he had always been led to believe that it should not be undertaken without the cooperation of a strong military force. Kitchener referred to the prewar investigations conducted by the War Office and Admiralty which had concluded that even a joint operation was to be deprecated. Churchill countered by maintaining that the destructive power of dreadnoughts like the *Queen Elizabeth* had revolutionized naval warfare and rendered a task, once considered impossible, quite practical. Kitchener would later tell associates that Churchill gave the impression that the *Queen Elizabeth* would almost single-handedly demolish the Turkish forts on both sides of the Straits. Kitchener was not completely convinced by Churchill's arguments initially, but he did not think it was his place to throw cold water on a project which was beyond his expertise to assess. Moreover it was his policy not to interfere in matters that concerned the navy alone and he assumed that the concept had the blessing of the experts at the Admiralty. In eventually lending his support, he was comforted by the knowledge that the attack could not lead to a disaster because he was assured that, if the bombardment proved ineffective, the ships would be recalled.

Kitchener's private secretary, Sir George Arthur, drew attention to the details of the private conference at the Admiralty in a memorandum he submitted to the Commission in late November 1916. In it Arthur claimed that Kitchener revealed to him one day that he had been invited to meet with Churchill who raised the issue of an attack by ships alone against the Dardanelles. Kitchener had doubts about the merits of any such undertaking but Churchill replied that the old service methods were no longer relevant in view of the unique destructive firepower of the *Queen Elizabeth*. Kitchener, according to Arthur, remained opposed to the plan.[34] He would have been more accurate if he had said that Kitchener went along but was not absolutely convinced until a month or so later when the Turks showed themselves on a number of occasions to lack training and resolve.

Arthur subsequently appeared before the Dardanelles Commission to elaborate or clarify points he had raised in his memorandum. Nicholson did not miss an opportunity to come down hard on Arthur or anyone who defended Kitchener. Throughout the interview he asked leading questions, went over insignificant issues and expressed skepticism over some of Arthur's answers. Below is an example of Nicholson seeking clarification as to whether it was Kitchener or Churchill who used the expression "like the walls of Jericho" in reference to the Turkish forts crumbling under the firepower of the *Queen Elizabeth*:

> N: Do you consider that Lord Kitchener was a very imaginative man who was led astray by wild statements. Do you think he was so imaginative that in a vital matter he would be led astray by ridiculous statements?
> A: Not by ridiculous statements.
> N: By foolish statements?
> A: Not by foolish statements.
> N: By exaggerated statements?
> A: I should have thought not, so far as he was able to judge of their being exaggerated.

---

34 Arthur Memorandum, CAB, 19/28. See also Arthur, *Life of Lord Kitchener*, vol. 3, pp. 105, 208-9.

N: Would you call a statement that when a gun was fired the walls of Jericho would fall down an exaggerated statement?
A: I am merely illustrating the conversation by an illustration.
N: I am asking you a question. I asked you whether you consider that the statement that when a gun was fired the walls of Jericho would fall down an exaggerated and foolish statement?
A: Do you mean accepting it as a statement or as an allusion in conversation?
N: Accepting it as a statement which bore any approach to reality?
A: I am afraid I must ask you to distinguish between the two. I never said that was a statement that Lord Kitchener said was made by the First Lord. As illustrating the conversation he made a paraphrase and a chance illusion to that. He did not say the First Lord said that when a gun went off the walls of Jericho would fall down.[35]

Nicholson's bullying tactics were intended to trip up Arthur and discredit him in the eyes of his fellow commissioners. Arthur stood up well under tough cross-examination. Unfortunately he could not remember exactly when Kitchener had discussed his encounter with Churchill and he was vague on details about other issues as well, providing the commissioners with a pretext to write off his entire testimony.[36]

After reading Arthur's statement, Churchill asked to be interviewed again. When the subject came up he protested vehemently that no such meeting had taken place, eager as he was to avoid the impression that he had overcome Kitchener's early warning by convincing him of the matchless capacity of the *Queen Elizabeth*. Such a version of the events was bound to add weight to the prevailing idea among the media that Churchill had imposed his plan upon ill-informed or reluctant members of the cabinet. Churchill's access to official records gave him a clear advantage over Arthur. He maintained that Kitchener had supported the naval operation when it was proposed on the 13 January and he had the evidence to substantiate his claim. Moreover there were members of the War Council who could verify Churchill's contention, although they were unaware of the earlier conference between the two men and obviously had no way of knowing what had transpired. Arthur read Kitchener's statement in the War Council on 14 May in which he had accused Churchill of excessively exaggerating the virtues of the *Queen Elizabeth* in order to gain his support. The commissioners took Churchill at his word and did not bother to investigate Kitchener's charges. They chose to believe that Kitchener's anger on that day was in reaction to the withdrawal of the *Queen Elizabeth*.

Since the Commission had judged Arthur to be an unreliable witness, they used the lame excuse that his "evidence has no direct bearing upon the immediate subject of our inquiry, namely the opinions Lord Kitchener expressed during the period of origin and inception, which … we consider to have closed on March 23rd, 1915."[37] If that had been the case, why did they bother to interview Arthur? Their reference to the cut-off date was a pretext to reject his entire testimony. After all their questions dealt with the subject of their inquiry. The commissioners

---

35 Arthur testimony, 1 December 1916, Dardanelles Commission Report, CAB 19/33.
36 Ibid.
37 *First Report of the Dardanelles Commission*, p. 16.

also alluded to the testimony of von Donop and Creedy, but without elaborating, maintained that neither "added any material information to the facts which were already in our possession."[38]

Once it was determined to send troops to the Dardanelles, the Commission maintained that Kitchener was negligent by failing to assign the general staff to prepare a plan for the army's assault on Gallipoli. It concluded:

> When asked by the Prime Minister at the War Council meeting of March 19th whether any general plan and scheme of disembarkation had been worked out, Lord Kitchener said that, though the question had been examined in the War Office, sufficient information was not forthcoming for the preparation of a detailed scheme of landing, which would be undertaken by Sir Ian Hamilton in concert with the Naval Commander-in-Chief. No general plan of operations had been prepared by the War Office. We can see no reason why a general plan or alternative general plans should not have been worked out, and we think that the elaboration of such plan or plans by competent officers of the General Staff would have put the military problem in a clearer light before the War Council."[39]

There are many tasks that the general staff could have carried out that would have benefited the war effort (and lightened Kitchener's crushing responsibilities), but devising a plan or plans for the army's invasion of Gallipoli was not one of them. An indispensable component in preparing an effective blueprint for a military assault was to have access to vital information which was unavailable. When the Dardanelles Commission asked Callwell if he could offer a reason for what it regarded was a grievous omission on the part of Kitchener, he answered that without up-to-date intelligence the general staff would have been operating in the dark. Thus assigning it to work on a plan, in his view, would have served no purpose. The commissioners chose to disregard Callwell's sensible explanation, presumably on the grounds that, under the *King's Field Regulations,* it was among the duties of the general staff to prepare plans for offensive operations. The element of common sense evidently was beyond their grasp. Kitchener was absolutely right in saying that the job could best be done by the commanders on the spot.

The Commission's stand on the matter of the 29th Division was equally baffling. It reproached Kitchener for the delay in sending the 29th Division to the Dardanelles, judging that it had "gravely compromised the probability of success of the original attack made by the land forces, and materially increased the difficulties encountered in the final attack some months later."[40] The Commission had accepted at face value Churchill's spurious argument that the delay in dispatching the 29th Division had allowed a favourable moment for action to lapse. "We think that Mr. Churchill was quite justified in attaching the utmost importance to the delays which occurred in despatching the 29th Division ... from this country," was the Commission's verdict.[41] I need only observe that if it had bothered to conduct a mere superficial investigation on the issue, it would have realized that Hamilton was not ready to undertake an invasion of Gallipoli on arrival of the division; even if he had, the turbulent weather in April ruled out disembarkation of the army on the exposed beaches.

38 Ibid.
39 *Final Report of the Dardanelles Commission.*, pp. 9, 86.
40 Ibid., p. 42.
41 Ibid., p. 34.

In a related matter, the Commission saw no legitimate cause for postponing the dispatch of the 29th Division. If the last regular unit had been held back for three weeks, it was not due to Kitchener's vacillation or indecision, as the Commission seemed to imply, but to the deepening crisis on the Russian front. Hankey, who supported Churchill's position when the debate was raging over the 29th Division in the War Council, later admitted to the Dardanelles Commission that he had been mistaken: "The military situation was such that Lord Kitchener did not like to part with it; he wanted to send it out to France instead. I pressed very strongly that it should be sent to the Dardanelles: daresay he was quite right. I am not quarrelling."[42]

If there was an issue in which the Commission had reason to question Kitchener's conduct, it demonstrated its prejudice by brushing aside the extenuating circumstances. Hankey had revealed during his testimony that Kitchener entertained strong opinion "as to the absolute necessity of maintaining the strictest secrecy in respect to all matters connected with military operations; and "that some difficulties at times arose owing to Lord Kitchener's unwillingness to impart full information even to the members of the War Council."[43] Hankey also offered an explanation for Kitchener's caution: "If Lord Kitchener decided on an operation he only had one idea in mind and that was to make that operation a success. If he thought it would militate against success to give information, he would not give it, and who can say that it is not right… I can think of operation after operation that has leaked out somehow."[44] The commissioners ignored Hankey's last sentence in making their final judgement. If they had been interested in fair play, they would have revealed Kitchener's motive for withholding vital information from colleagues, and then added that, in their view, he had carried that practice too far.

The Dardanelles Commission relied on telegrams and less than candid testimony of Churchill and other witnesses to determine that Kitchener, on his own initiative, had ordered the army to take control of the Gallipoli Peninsula after learning of Hamilton's on the spot assessment.[45] It will be remembered that Hamilton had contacted the War Office on 19 March to convey his impression that, in view of the failure of the naval attack on the previous day, he doubted that the Straits could be forced by battleships alone as at one time seemed probable.[46] To which Kitchener had replied at once: "You know my views – that the passage of the Dardanelles must be forced, and if large military operations on the Gallipoli Peninsula by your troops are necessary to clear the way, these operations must be undertaken after careful consideration of the local defences, and they must be carried through."[47] The exchange of telegrams between the two men and others that followed were, in the words of the Dardanelles Commission Report, "conclusive proof that Lord Kitchener had by that time wholly abandoned the idea of a purely naval operation, and realized the fact that military operations on a large scale were necessary."[48] The decision made by the Commission continues to this day to be regarded as definitive but it was based only on partial evidence. It lacked access to the minutes of the War Council which

---

42　Hankey testimony, 31 October 1916, Dardanelles Commission Report, CAB 19/33.
43　*First Report of the Dardanelles Commission*, p. 3.
44　Hankey testimony, 19 September 1916, Dardanelles Commission Report, CAB 19/33.
45　*Final Report of the Dardanelles Commission*, p. 7.
46　Hamilton to Kitchener, 19 March 1915, CAB 19/33.
47　Kitchener to Hamilton, 19 March 1915, CAB 19/33.
48　*First Report of the Dardanelles Commission*, pp. 37-38.

would have revealed that on 24 February its members had been unequivocal about sending in the army if the naval attack did not go as well as expected.

The Commission's strong bias against Kitchener undoubtedly would have been offset by Sir Gerald Ellison if he had stayed on as the official historian of the campaign. In 1923 the Historical Section of the CID had selected Ellison to prepare a three-volume study of the Gallipoli campaign. The Historical Section had given Ellison guidelines, directing him to deal only with military operations and to avoid explicitly criticizing individuals for mistakes. Ellison had served on Hamilton's staff as Deputy Quartermaster General and his intimate knowledge of many aspects of the campaign predisposed him to strongly held opinions. Straying well beyond his instructions, he used his position as a vehicle to air his personal views.

Ellison was convinced that the Gallipoli campaign was neither justifiable nor had a realistic chance of success. In his first draft chapters submitted for approval in 1924, he lashed out at Churchill and blamed him entirely for imposing a flawed and reckless scheme on the War Council, adding that when this strategy failed, brought pressure to bear on Kitchener who, against his better judgement, "despatched ground troops before the necessary preparations for a highly hazardous operation had been made."[49] Ellison's intent was to repudiate the charges that Churchill had brought against Kitchener in the second volume of *The World Crisis* which had been published in 1923.[50] Ellison knew he was treading on dangerous ground and wrote to the Historical Section to justify his harsh treatment of Churchill: "The whole trend of Churchill's "World Crisis" is to attribute the failure of the Gallipoli campaign to the vacillation and shortcomings on the part of Lord Kitchener, who is no longer alive to answer strictures on his conduct and to explain the motives for his actions."[51]

The Historical Section, however, deemed that the trenchant criticism of Churchill for ignoring the general staff report in 1906 and imposing an unsound plan on the War Council, were inappropriate for an official history. Ellison was asked to modify the tone and content in his manuscript, but rather than compromise, decided to resign.[52] Ellison's successor on the project was Brigadier General Aspinall-Oglander who, as already noted, believed that the Dardanelles operation could have succeeded but for a succession of errors. Although he did not hesitate to point out mistakes, unlike Ellison, he spread the blame, rather than confining it to one individual and his tone was softer.

Ellison did not remain out of the picture for long. As he was eager to publicize his views, he adopted Hamilton's suggestion that he produce an unofficial history of the campaign.[53] What followed was a brief book (145 pages) published in 1926 under the heading *The Perils of Amateur Strategy: As Exemplified by the Attacks on the Dardanelles Fortress in 1915*. He was adamant that the Dardanelles campaign could not have succeeded and that diverting resources from the western front was a tragic mistake. In his view the crux of the problem was the flawed machinery which allowed strategy to be placed in the hands of a committee dominated by politicians. He took exception to Churchill's statement that policy and strategy were connected and insisted that they

---

49   Andrew Green, *Writing the Great War* (London: Frank Cass, 2003), p. 94.
50   Copies of Ellison's early chapters are available in his modest collection. His notes on the history campaign were written in 1924 and can be found in CAB 45/238.
51   Green, *Writing the Great War*, p. 96.
52   Ibid., pp. 94-96.
53   Bell, *Churchill*, p. 299.

were radically separated from one another. According to Ellison, strategy began where policy left off. His formula would have confined the politicians to work on policy, leaving strategy in the hands of men trained in the study of warfare. He drew an analogy between chess and war strategy with both requiring skill that "comes as the result of much thought and prolonged study."[54] Thus as amateurs, politicians should not be allowed to interfere in matters about which they know practically nothing. To prove his case he referred to the catalogue of bad decisions that occurred in 1915 and castigated the politicians, in particular Churchill, whom he blamed for overruling the naval experts and leading the country into a disastrous operation.

There is no better confirmation of Ellison's thesis than to compare the difference in Britain's military fortune between 1914 and 1915. The quality of Kitchener's leadership during the first four months of the war had been virtually flawless. Britain was totally unprepared for the land conflict. Given free rein, Kitchener's foresight and inordinate capacity to improvise had not only avoided a catastrophe but laid the foundation for the Entente's eventual victory. The decline in the nation's strategic position began during the opening months of 1915 when the politicians, exercising their legal rights, were under the illusion they were better than Kitchener in guiding the nation's war effort. This turned out to be a horrible miscalculation as they knew little about warfare and had no experience in formulating high policy. In planning overseas adventures they paid no heed to such factors as logistics, topography, probable enemy response and whether the requisite number of troops were available. Their decisions, reached after endless discussions and delays, were based on gut instinct, rather than military logic, with the result that they stumbled from one disaster to another. First it was the ill-conceived Dardanelles operation that failed miserably and added a quarter of a million men to the allied casualty roll; followed by the drive to seize Baghdad which ended in the humiliating defeat and the capture of Townshend and his force; and lastly opening a futile sideshow in the Balkans where the size of the Allied army swelled to 600,000 by 1917 and was mostly inactive until the last months of the war, drawing men and supplies from more important areas of operations. Grey was the only member of the Asquith administration to admit that he and his colleagues had followed a senseless and tangled course in 1915 with unfortunate consequences. He wrote in hindsight:

> The chief mistakes in strategy may, in my opinion, be summarized in two Words: "Sideshows." In justice to Kitchener it must be recorded that he disliked them all, and my particular regret is that I did not resolutely support every resistance he made to them... It seems to me to be a true criticism that we did not sufficiently concentrate attention on the one cardinal point: That it was the German Army which had to be beaten, and that this could only be done on the Western Front... Had this been grasped continuously as the central fact of the War, the side-shows – Gallipoli, Baghdad, Salonica – would either never been undertaken or would have been kept within smaller dimensions.[55]

The civilian ministers never understood that there was no alternative to attrition on the western front and that the cost of victory would be high even under the leadership of more competent field generals. Their search for a shorter and cheaper war in secondary theatres was a drain on

---

54 Ellison, *Perils of Amateur Strategy*, p. 2.
55 Grey, *Twenty-Five Years*, vol. 2, pp. 74-75.

men and material that even if successfully prosecuted, would have had no bearing on the final outcome. Yet no one, except Churchill, paid a price for the government's record of dismal failures in 1915. The absence of strategic wisdom turned on its head a celebrated quotation attributed to the former French Prime Minister, Georges Clemenceau, leaving it more accurately as "war is too serious a matter to be left to the politicians."

During and after the war some of the politicians in Asquith's cabinet sought to deflect attention from their support of defective policies by maintaining that Kitchener held arbitrary power and was the only decision maker that mattered. In memoirs, interviews with journalists, and testimony before the Dardanelles Commission, they found ways to slander Kitchener whenever it was to their benefit. No one attacked Kitchener more viciously than Lloyd George. The Welshman despised Kitchener and their exchanges on a number of issues were often sharp and required Asquith's intervention. Outside the cabinet Lloyd George initiated a malicious whispering campaign. In the lobbies of the House of Commons, at private gatherings and in talks with journalists, he painted Kitchener as rigid, unresponsive to new ideas, dogmatic with a military outlook that was too antiquated for modern warfare. Lloyd George continued his assault on Kitchener in his *War Memoirs*, charging that it was his procrastination that had prevented the timely rescue of Serbia; that he had made the decision on his own to commit troops to the Dardanelles (when at the time he had blamed Churchill); that he had failed to provide careful management of the land campaign; and that his dereliction in attending to the army's munitions and equipment needs had resulted in huge manpower losses. Lloyd George was unconcerned if there were no facts to support his claims. As a man without a moral compass, he simply invented them.

Churchill was critical of Kitchener as a means to distance himself from the disaster in the Dardanelles; whereas Lloyd George blamed Kitchener for practically every major military mistake during his tenure as War Minister. Yet, Lloyd George presented himself in his *War Memoirs*, as calm and calculating, as the only person in the cabinet who invariably discerned, with unerring judgement, the correct thing to do. Since official documents were unavailable to scholars when he wrote his lengthy memoirs, (the first volume was published in 1933) no one had any idea that many of his assertions were based on fabricated evidence. The government files for 1915 became accessible to the general public in 1966, but he continues to have a following among writers – perhaps because of his work as a social reformer prior to the war. I view Lloyd George in a much different light. As I have already made it abundantly clear, I consider him a pathological liar, a chronic forger, devious with an inflated confidence in his own judgement and a horrible strategist. Still the publication of the Welshman's often fictional and hateful *War Memoirs* did much to damage Kitchener's posthumous standing among scholars and the general public in Britain and elsewhere.

The members of the Asquith cabinet are long gone but the current accessibility of the official documents for the Great War no longer offers them protection against their inept conduct of the war. They were involved in three disastrous sideshows in 1915, though only Churchill was responsible for both the naval and military operation in the Dardanelles. He had gained the approval of the War Council for his naval attack on condition that it would be abandoned if enemy resistance turned out to be stronger than anticipated. The sequel has been told several times in the course of this study, eliminating the need to repeat it. It is sufficient to say that Churchill's aim at self-promotion had the effect of escalating the operation which was doomed before a single soldier hit the beaches. While his overall culpability is extreme, his colleagues in the War Council, whose trust had been violated, bear collective responsibility only for the failed naval attack.

After everything that has been said and done it is hoped that this investigation has exposed the false accusations against Kitchener by Churchill, Lloyd George and the Dardanelles Commission. In particular much space was devoted to the burning question of whether he had decided on his own to send the army to seize control of the Peninsula. As we have repeated frequently, it was as early as 24 February that the War Council firmly resolved to employ the army if the naval advance was checked. Kitchener shared the belief of his colleagues that to maintain British prestige in the east they could not accept the verdict of March 18 as final.

As we are about to close this chapter on Kitchener's career, it only remains to judge the extent of his blame for the failure of the military campaign. Keeping in mind that when Kitchener supervised the first landing he was acting in accordance with the wishes of the War Council and during the deliberations that led to the second landing, his standing in the cabinet had declined sharply and was not greater than that of the leading lights. Thus when everything is taken into consideration, I would rank Kitchener's liability for the failed military operation to be no greater than that of the other cabinet ministers.

It is evident that my treatment of Kitchener is in stark contrast to the way he has been and continues to be portrayed by military writers. Besides refuting many of the false charges against him, I have taken into consideration that he faced enormous problems, often not of his own making, and for which he had insufficient resources. To make matters worse, he was hampered increasingly as the year wore on by fractious colleagues who were only too eager to prove him wrong. While I have not judged Kitchener harshly for his part in the failure of the military campaign, neither have I given him a free pass.

Bibliography

Manuscript Sources and Departmental Records, National Archives, Kew, London

Cabinet Office
CAB 19/28 Written Statements by Participants in the Dardanelles Campaign
CAB 19/31 Telegrams relating to the Dardanelles Operation
CAB 19/33 Dardanelles Commission Report
CAB 28/1 Anglo-French and Allied Conferences
CAB 37 War Cabinet and Cabinet Memoranda
CAB 41 Asquith to George V, summary of cabinet proceedings
CAB 42 Minutes of the War Council and its successor bodies

Foreign Office

War Office

Private and Archival Collections
* The location is in London unless otherwise indicated
Archives du Ministère des Affaires Etrangères, La Courneuve, Paris
Archives du Ministère de la Guerre, Vincennes
Arthur, Sir George, National Archives
Asquith, H.H., Bodleian Library, Oxford
Asquith/Sylvia Henley, Bodelian Library, Oxford
Asquith, Lady Violet, Bodleian Library, Oxford
Balfour, Arthur J., British Library
Bertie, Sir Francis L., National Archives
Churchill, Sir Winston S., Churchill College Archives Centre, Cambridge
Creedy, Sir Herbert, National Archives
Deedes, Wyndham, National Archives
Delcassé, Théophile, Archives Nationale, La Courneuve, Paris
Ellison, Lieut. Gen. Sir Gerald, National Army Museum
Emmott, Lord Alfred, Nuffield College Library, Oxford
Esher, Viscount Reginald, Churchill College Archives Centre, Cambridge
French, Field Marshal Sir John, Imperial War Museum
Grey, Sir Edward, National Archives

George V, Royal Archives, Windsor
Hall, Admiral Sir William R., Churchill College Archives Centre, Cambridge
Hamilton, Gen. Sir Ian, Liddell Hart Centre for Military Archives
Hankey, Lieut. Col. Maurice, Churchill College Archives Centre, Cambridge
Harcourt, Sir Lewis, Bodleian Library, Oxford
Kitchener, Field Marshal Lord, National Archives
Millerand, Alexandre, Archives du Ministère de la Guerre, Vincennes
Riddell, Sir George, British Library
Wilson, Field Marshal Sir Henry, Imperial War Museum

Official Publications

Aspinall-Oglander, Brig. Gen. C. F. *Military Operations: Gallipoli*. 2 vols. London: William Heinemann, 1929-1932.
Bean, C. E.W. *The Official History of Australia in the War of 1914-1918*. vol. 1. Sydney: Angus & Robertson, 1933.
Coates, Tim (ed.). *Defeat at Gallipoli: The Dardanelles Commission*, Part 1. London: HMSO, 2000.
Corbett, Sir Julian S. *Naval Operations*. vols. 1-3, London: Longmans, Green & Co., 1920-3.
Edmonds, Brig. Gen. Sir James E. *Military Operations: France and Belgium, 1915*. vol. 1. London: Macmillan, 1927.
Falls, Cyril. *Military Operations: Macedonia*. vol. 1. London: HMSO, 1933.
France, Ministère de la Guerre. Etat-Major de l'Armée. Service Historique. *Les armées françaises dans la grande guerre*, tome 8, vols. 1 and 2. Paris: Imprimerie Nationale, 1923.
Great Britain. *First and Final Report of the Dardanelles Commission*. London: HMSO, 1917, 1919.
———. *Report of the Mesopotamian Campaign and Commission*. London: HMSO, 1917.
MacMunn, Lieut. Gen. Sir George and Capt. Cyril Falls. *Military Operations: Egypt & Palestine*. vol. 1. London: HMSO, 1928.
Moberly, Brig. Gen. F. J. *The Campaign in Mesopotamia, 1914-1918*. vols. 1-2. London: HMSO, 1923-1924.

Primary & Secondary Sources

Adams, R.J.Q. *Bonar Law*. Stanford: Stanford University Press, 1999.
Allen, G.R.G. "A Ghost from Gallipoli." *The Royal United Service Institution Journal* 108 (1963): 137-38.
Arthur, Sir George. *General Sir John Maxwell*. London: John Murray, 1932.
———. *Life of Lord Kitchener*. vol. 3. London: Macmillan, 1920.
Aspinall-Oglander, Brig. Gen. C.F. *Roger Keyes*. London: Hogarth Press, 1951.
Asquith, H. H. *Memories and Reflections 1852-1927*. vol. 2. London: Cassell, 1928.
Ballard, Brig. Gen. C. R. *Kitchener*. London: Faber & Faber, 1930.

Barker, A. J. *The Bastard War: The Mesopotamian Campaign of 1914-1918*. New York: Dial Press, 1967.
Barrow, General Sir George. The Life of General Sir Charles Carmichael Monro. London: Hutchinson & Co., 1931.
Beaverbrook, Lord, *Politicians and the War, 1914-1916*. London: Oldbourne, 1960.
Beesly, Patrick. *Room 40: British Naval Intelligence 1914-1918*. New York: Brace Harcourt Jovanovich, 1982.
Bell, Christopher M. *Churchill and the Dardanelles*. Oxford: Oxford University Press, 2017.
Birdwood, Field Marshal Lord. *Khaki and Gown*. London: Ward, Locke & Co., 1941.
Blake, Robert. *The Unknown Prime Minister: The Life and Times of Andrew Bonar Law 1858-1923*. London: Eyre & Spottiswoode, 1955.
Bonham Carter, Victor. *Soldier True: The Life and Times of Field Marshal Sir William Robertson*. London: Frederick Muller, 1963.
Bonham Carter, Lady Violet. *Winston Churchill: An Intimate Portrait*. New York: Harcourt, Brace and World, 1965.
Braddon, Russell. *The Siege*. New York: Viking Press, 1970.
Brock, Michael and Eleanor, (eds.) *H. H. Asquith: Letters to Venetia Stanley*. Oxford: Oxford University Press, 1982.
——. *Margo Asquith's Great War Diary, 1914-1916*. Oxford: Oxford University Press, 2014.
Callwell, Maj. Gen. Sir C. E. *Experiences of a Dug-Out, 1914-1918*. London: Constable, 1920.
Cassar, George H. *Asquith as War Leader*. London: Hambleton Press, 1994.
——. *Kitchener: Architect of Victory*. London: William Kimber, 1977.
——. *Kitchener as Proconsul of Egypt, 1911-1914*. London: Palgrave Macmillan, 2016.
——. *Kitchener's War: British Strategy from 1914 to 1916*. Washington, DC; Potomac Books, 2004.
——. *Reluctant Partner: The Complete Story of the French Participation in the Dardanelles Campaign of 1915*. London: Helion Press, 2019.
——. *The Tragedy of Sir John French*. Newark, DE: University of Delaware Press, 1985.
Charteris, Brig. Gen. John. *At GQG*. London: Cassell, 1931.
Chaussaud, Peter and Peter Doyle. *Grasping Gallipoli: Terrain, Maps and Failures at the Dardanelles 1915*. Staplehurst: Spellmount, 2005.
Churchill, Winston S. *The World Crisis*. vols. 1-2. New York: Charles Scribner's Sons, 1951.
Clews, Graham. *Churchill's Dilemma: The Real Story Behind the Origins of the 1915 Dardanelles Campaign*. Santa Barbara, CA: Praeger, 2010.
Curran, Tom. *The Grand Deception: Churchill and the Dardanelles*. Newport, NSW: Big Sky Publishing, 2015.
Davis, Paul K. *Ends and Means: The British Mesopotamian Campaign and Commission*. Cranbury: Associated University Presses, 1994.
Doughty, R. A. *Pyrrhic Victory: French Strategy and Operations in the Great War*. Cambridge, MA: Harvard University Press, 2005.
Dutton, David. "The Balkan Campaign and French War Aims in the Great War." *English Historical Review* 94 (1979): 97-113.
——. *The Politics of Diplomacy: Britain and France in the Balkans in the First World War*. London: I. B. Tauris, 1998.
Erickson, Edward J. *Gallipoli: Command Under Fire*. Oxford: Osprey, 2015.

———. *Ordered to Die: A History of the Ottoman Army in the First World War.* Westport, CT: Greenwood Press, 2001.
Esher, Oliver Viscount (ed.). *Journals and Letters of Reginald Viscount.* vol. 3. London: Nicholson and Watson, 1938.
Esher, Reginald Viscount. *The Tragedy of Lord Kitchener.* London: John Murray, 1921.
Ellison, Sir Gerald. *The Perils of Amateur Strategy.* London: Longmans, Green and Co., 1923.
Farrar, Marjorie M. *Principled Pragmatist: The Political Career of Alexandre Millerand.* Oxford: Berg, 1991.
Faught, C. Brad. *Kitchener: Hero and Anti-Hero.* London: I. B. Taurus, 2016.
Fisher, Lord. *Memories and Records.* London: George H. Doran, 1920.
French, David. *British Strategy & War Aims 1914-1916,* vol. 1. London: Allen & Unwin, 1984.
Gardner, Nicholas. *The Siege of Kut-al-Amara.* Bloomington: Indiana University Press, 2014.
Gilbert, Martin. *Winston S. Churchill: The Challenge of War 1914-1916.* vol. 3. Boston: Houghton Mifflin Co., 1971; and *Companion* volumes. London: Heinemann, 1972.
Grey of Fallodon, Viscount. *Twenty-Five Years.* vol. 2. New York: Frederick A. Stokes Co., 1925.
Halpern, Paul G. *The Naval War in the Mediterranean, 1914-1918.* Annapolis: Naval Institute, 1987.
———. (ed.). *The Keyes Papers, 1914-1918.* vol. 1. London: Navy Records Society, 1972.
Hamilton, Sir Ian. *Gallipoli Diary.* 2 vols. New York: George H. Doran Co., 1920.
Hamilton, Sir Ian. *The Commander.* (ed) Major Anthony Farrar-Hockley. London: Hollis and Carter, 1957.
Hamilton, Ian B. M. *The Happy Warrior: A Life of General Sir Ian Hamilton.* London: Cassell, 1966.
Hanbury-Williams, Sir John. *The Emperor: Nicholas II As I Knew Him.* London: Humphreys, 1922.
Hankey, Lord Maurice. *The Supreme Command 1914-1918.* 2 vols. London: Allen & Unwin, 1961.
Hazelhurst, Cameron. *Politicians at War, July 1914 – May 1915.* London: Jonathan Cape, 1971.
Hickey, Michael. *Gallipoli.* London: John Murray, 1995.
Hunter, Archie. *Kitchener's Sword-Arm: The Life and Campaigns of General Sir Archibald Hunter.* Staplehurst: Spellmount, 1996.
James, Robert Rhodes. *Churchill: A Study in Failure 1900-1939.* London: Weidenfeld and Nicolson, 1990.
———. Gallipoli. London: Batsford, 1965.
———. *Memoirs of a Conservative: J. C. C. Davidson's Memoirs and Papers, 1910-1937.* London: Weidenfeld and Nicolson, 1969.
———. *Rosebery: A Biography of Archibald Philip, Fifth Earl of Rosebery.* London: Weidenfeld and Nicolson, 1963.
James, Admiral Sir William. *The Eyes of the Navy: A Biographical Study of Admiral Sir Reginald Hall.* London: Methuen, 1955.
Jenkins, Roy. *Asquith.* New York: Chilmark Press, 1964.
Joffre, Field Marshal Joseph. *Personal Memoirs,* vol. 2. New York: Harper and Brothers, 1932.
Jones, John P. *Johnny: The Legend and Tragedy of General Sir Ian Hamilton.* Barnsley: Pen and Sword, 2012.

Keyes, Sir Roger. *The Naval Memoirs of Admiral of the Fleet*. vol. 1. London: Thornton Butterworth Ltd., 1934.
Lloyd George, David. *War Memoirs*. vol. 1 London: Oldhams Press, 1938.
Lomas, David. *First Ypres*. London: Osprey, 1999.
Magnus, Philip. *Kitchener: Portrait of an Imperialist*. London: John Murray, 1958.
Marder, Arthur J. *From the Dreadnought to Scapa Flow*. vol. 2. London: Oxford University Press, 1965.
Millar, Ronald. *Death of an Army: The Siege of Kut, 1915-1916*. Boston: Houghton Mifflin Co., 1970.
Miller, Geoffrey, *Straits: British Policy Towards the Ottoman Empire and the Origins of the Dardanelles Campaign*. Hull: University of Hull Press, 1997.
Moorehead, Alan. *Gallipoli*. New York: Harper & Brothers, 1956.
Morgenthau, Henry. *Ambassador Morgenthau's Story*. Garden City: Doubleday, Page and Co., 1919.
Neilson, Keith. *Strategy and Supply: The Anglo-Russian Alliance, 1914-1917*. London: Allen and Unwin, 1984.
———. "Kitchener: A Reputation Refurbished?" *Canadian Journal of History* 15 (1980).
Nevakivi, Jukka. "Lord Kitchener and the Partition of the Ottoman Empire," in *Studies in International History*, (ed.) K. Bourne and D. C. Watt. London: Longmans, 1967.
Palmer, Alan. *The Gardeners of Salonica*. New York: Simon and Schuster, 1965.
Poincaré, Raymond. *Au service de la France*. vols. 6-7. Paris: Plon, 1930-1931.
Pollock, John. *Kitchener: Architect of Victory, Artisan of Peace*. New York: Carroll and Graf, 1998.
Pottle, Mark (ed.). *Champion Redoubtable: The Diaries and Letters of Violet Bonham Carter, 1914-1945*. London: Weidenfeld and Nicolson, 1998.
Presland, John. *Deedes Bey*. London: Macmillan, 1942.
Prete, Roy A. "Imbroglio Par Excellence: Mounting the Salonica Campaign, September-October 1915." *War and Society* 19 (2001), pp. 47-70.
Prior, Robin. *Gallipoli: The End of the Myth*. New Haven: Yale University, 2009.
Riddell, Lord George. *War Diary 1914-1918*. London: Nicholson and Watson, 1933.
Roskill, Stephen. *Hankey: Man of Secrets 1877-1918*. vol. 1. London: Collins, 1970.
Robertson, Field-Marshal Sir William. *Soldiers and Statesmen 1914-1918*. London: Cassell, 1926.
Royle, Trevor. *The Kitchener Enigma*. London: Michael Joseph, 1985.
Rudenno, Victor. *Gallipoli: Attack from the Sea*. New Haven: Yale University Press, 2008.
Sarrail, Gen. Maurice. *Mon Commandement en Orient 1916-1918*. Paris: Flammarion, 1920.
Simkins, Peter. *Kitchener's Army: The Raising of the New Armies, 1914-1916*. Manchester: Manchester University Press, 1988.
Spender, J.A. and Cyril Asquith. *Life of Herbert Henry Asquith, Lord Oxford and Asquith*. vol. 2. London: Hutchinson and Co., 1932.
Steel, Nigel and Peter Hart. *Defeat at Gallipoli*. London: Macmillan, 1994.
Stuermer, Harry. *Two Years in Constantinople*. New York: George H. Doran 1917.
Tannenbaum, Jan K. *General Maurice Sarrail, 1856-1929*. Chapel Hill: University of North Carolina Press, 1974.
Taylor, A. J. P. (ed.), *Lloyd George: A Diary by Frances Stevenson*. New York: Harper and Row, 1971.

Terraine, John. *Douglas Haig: The Educated Soldier*. London: Leo Cooper, 1990.
Travers, Tim. *Gallipoli 1915*. Stroud: Tempus. 2004.
Wester-Wemyss. Lord R. E. *The Navy in the Dardanelles Campaign*. London: Hodder and Stoughton, 1924.
Wilson, Trevor. The Downfall of the Liberal Party 1914-1945. London: Collins 1966.
——. *The Myriad Faces of War*. Cambridge: Polity Press, 1986.
Woodward, David. Lloyd *George and the Generals*. Newark, DE: University of Delaware Press, 1983.
Woodward, Sir Llewellyn. *Great Britain and the War of 1914-1918*. London: Methuen, 1967.
Wright, Gordon. *Raymond Poincaré and the French Presidency*. Stanford: Stanford University Press, 1942.
Zetland, Marquess of. *The Life of Lord Curzon*. vol. 3. London: Benn, 1928.

Index

Abadan Island, 97, 167
Abdullahi, Ibn Muhammed (Khalifa), xix, xx
Achi Baba, 101, 102, 123
Admiralty War Staff Group, 52n31, 65, 92, 182
Adowa, xx
Ahmed Mohammed (Mahdi), xviii, xix
Alexandretta, 42, 57, 84-85, 161
Alexandria, 92, 96
Amade, Gen. Albert d', 98, 100, 122
Anafarta ridge, 124
Anglo-French withdrawal from Gallipoli, consequences of, 173-74
Anzac front, 123, 155, 171
Anzacs, 57, 66, 68
Arthur, Sir George, 53
   testimony to the Dardanelles Commission, 188-89
Ashmead-Bartlett, Ellis, 94, 117
Aspinall-Oglander, Brig. Gen. C. F., 192
   claims inclement weather inhibited the first landing from taking place earlier, 179
   confirms Hankey's findings, 177-78
Asquith, H. H., 27, 66, 90, 105-6, 135, 138, 141, 143, 146, 147, 154, 169
   appoints Kitchener Secretary for War, 28
   attends conferences in Paris and Calais, 163, 169-70
   character and background, 29
   favours Hamilton's removal, 147
   favours sending troops to aid the navy, 66
   forms coalition government, 112
   forms War Council to oversee the war, 38
   gives controversial speech in Newcastle, 106-7
   insists command be given to Hamilton, 79-80
   and Kitchener, 105-6, 107, 119, 122, 135, 166, 171, 181
   meets informally twice with leading lights in the cabinet, 96-97
   replaced the War Council with the Dardanelles Committee, 113
   supports Kitchener on matter of the 29th Div., 75
   and Venetia Stanley, 58, 77, 92, 96-97, 108
   views on the Dardanelles Operation, 92, 97, 124
   as war leader, 29, 135
Asquith, Margot, 27
Asquith, Violet, 79, 107
Aubers Ridge, Battle of, 106
Augagneur, Victor, 59, 140, 141

Baghdad, 167
Bailloud, Gen. Maurice, 122-23
Balfour, Arthur, 38, 59-60, 77, 110, 112, 113, 120, 141, 154, 158, 163, 166, 168, 169, 172
   replaces Churchill as First Lord, 112
   informs Kitchener that the Bulair plan will not work, 157
Balkans, 58, 59, 60-61, 65, 136, 139, 142, 158, 168, 171
Baring, Evelyn. See Lord Cromer
Basra, 64, 97, 167
Beaverbrook, Lord (Max Aitken), 31
Bell, Christopher, 184
Bertie, Sir Francis, 170
Birdwood, Lieut. Gen. William, 70, 77, 78, 87, 148, 154, 156, 159-60, 161, 169, 174
Bloemfontein, xxiii
Boer republics, xxii-xxiii
Bonar Law, Andrew, 112, 116, 124, 138, 154, 160, 170

calls for an advance on Baghdad, 167
opposed to the continuation of Dardanelles campaign, 143, 155
prefers new front in the Balkans, 143, 170
urges Asquith to dismiss Kitchener, 155
Bouvet, 89
Braithwaite, Maj. Gen. Walter, 80-81
Briand, Aristide, 136, 158
  becomes prime minister, 151
  bows to British pressure at Calais, 169-70
  reneges on his agreement, 170
British army. See British Expeditionary Force; New Armies
British Expeditionary Force, 34, 35
British government, 150, 151
  at the outset cabinet leaves Kitchener to conduct the war, 30-31
  fortunes of the nation take a turn for the worst when cabinet assumes control of the war, 193
  no machinery in place to deal with the war, 30
  unprepared for war against Germany, 30
Buchanan, Sir George, 46
Bulair, 60, 117, 128, 157
Bulgaria, 63, 65, 136, 138, 142, 150
Buller, Gen. Redvers, xxii
Byng, Lieut. Gen. 154, 155, 169

Calais, 27, 120, 132, 140, 149, 169
Callwell, Maj. Gen. C. E., 33, 60, 81-83, 87
  accompanies Kitchener for a meeting at the Admiralty, 105
  does not initially agree with Churchill's plan to attack Gallipoli, 37
  explores possibility of a landing at Alexandretta, 42
  Kitchener is furious at the Admiralty for exaggerating the power of the *Queen Elizabeth*, 54
  testimony to the Dardanelles Commission, 190
Cambon, Paul, 67
Campbell-Bannerman, Henry, 52-53
Cape Helles, 90, 95, 98, 101, 123, 159, 165, 171, 172
Carden, Vice Adm. Sackville, 51-52, 53, 65, 69, 78, 87-88
Carson, Sir Edward, 113, 116, 124, 131, 143
Chamberlain, Austen, 150, 168
Chantilly, 150, 159, 171

Churchill, Winston, 30, 42, 47, 66, 86-87, 96, 109, 115, 124, 127, 135, 147, 174, 195
  advocates vigorous prosecution of the operation, 115-16
  appointed Chancellor of the Duchy of Lancaster, 113
  blames Kitchener for failure of his naval scheme, 177-82, 194
  character and background, 29-30, 52, 57
  consequences of his press release, 72
  convinces War Council of the merit of his plan to force the Dardanelles, 56-57
  criticism of, 33-34, 51, 174
  and the Dardanelles Operation, 50, 59-60, 109-11, 174, 182
  defects in his naval scheme, 50-51, 94-95
  is devastated when navy refuses to resume the operation, 92
  gains control of the Mediterranean from the French, 59
  on Hamilton, 78, 84, 116-118, 147, 182
  and Kitchener, 30-31, 53-54, 66-67, 78-79, 86, 113, 131, 154
  lied and distorted facts to cover up his mistakes, 74, 177, 187
  never accepted that his scheme was seriously flawed, 94
  orders bombardment of outer forts in the Dardanelles, 38
  persuades Kitchener to support his naval plan, 53-54, 188
  breaks faith with his colleagues, 70
  proposes Zeebrugge operation, 48
  removed from the Admiralty, 112-13
  Schleswig-Holstein scheme, 44
  testimony to the Dardanelles Commission, 186, 189
Clews, Graham, 56
Committee of Imperial Defence (CID), xxiv
Constantine, King of Greece, 37, 65, 139,140, 164
Constantinople, 36, 56, 62, 81, 83, 84-85, 133, 136, 141
Cowans, Brig. Gen. Sir John, 53-54
Creedy, Sir Herbert, 53, 190
Crewe, Lord (Robert Crew-Milnes), 110, 120
Cromner, Lord (formerly Evelyn Baring), xix-xx, 182-83, 185
Cronje, Piet, xxii-xxiii

Ctesiphon, Battle of, 167
Cunliffe-Owen, Lieut. Col. Frederick, 82
Curran, Tom, 56
Curzon, Lord (George Nathaniel), xxiv, 135, 138, 166
Cyprus, xviii

Dardanelles Commission, xiv, 53, 83, 87, 187-92, 195
  claims to have been given all relevant documents, 183
    does not pass an opportunity to trip up Kitchener, 185-86, 187, 190-92
    evaluating the work of the Commission, 184
    a list of the members of the body, 182-83
    proves ultra- indulgent towards Churchill, 186-87
    is set up as a commission of inquiry, xiv, 182
Dardanelles Committee, 119, 127, 131, 135, 138, 139, 140, 141, 151, 154
  assessment as an instrument of war, 113
  blames Hamilton for the failure of second offensive, 124
  body is divided over whether to try again, 142, 144
  members opt for a second landing on Gallipoli, 116-17
  replaces War Council, 113
Davies, Lieut. Gen. Sir Francis, 154
Dawney, Maj. Guy, alerts authorities in London about Hamilton's shortcomings, 146
Deeds, Wyndham, 66
Delcassé, Théophile, 63
Digna, Osman, xix
Donop, Maj. Gen. Stanley von, 53, 190
Douglas, Gen. Sir Charles, 33
Duckworth, Vice Adm. Sir John, 50

Edward II, King, xxxiii
Edward VIII, xxxiii
Egypt, xviii, xix, 37, 39, 42, 64, 66, 100, 127, 143, 150, 154, 160
Egyptian army, xx, 64
Ellison, Maj. Gen. Sir Gerald, 80, 95, 119
  resigns as official historian of the Dardanelles Campaign, 192
  wrote a book in which he aired his views, 192-93
Emmott, Lord Alfred, 108

Enver Pasha, 38
Esher, Viscount (Reginald Brett), xxii, 68, 122

Fisher, Adm. Sir John, 38, 58, 60, 61, 66, 72, 87, 194-5
  develops misgivings over Churchill's naval scheme, 60
  resigns in protest against Churchill's method of conducting Admiralty affairs, 112
  testimony to the Dardanelles Commission, 185
FitzGerald, Col. Oswald, 60, 156
French, Field Marshal Sir John, 45-46, 48, 61, 63, 110, 114, 132
  assessment as a commander, 34
  and Kitchener, 34-35, 45-46, 49, 106
French government, 67, 139, 141, 149, 150,
  commits a division for the land operations, 67
  diverts the troops intended for the Dardanelles to the Balkans, 136
  offers to send four additional divisions to the Dardanelles, 129
  sends a squadron to join Carden's fleet, 59
  wants Britain to greatly increase its commitment to the Balkans, 141

Gaba Tepe, 50, 95, 98
Gadkul, xviii
Galliéni, Gen. Joseph, 158, 159
George V, King, 171
Gilbert, Martin, 202
  tries to cover up for Churchill, 52, 72
Girodon, Col. Pierre, 159, 160
Gladstone government, xviii
Gordon, Maj. Gen. Charles, xviii, xx
Gorst, Elton, xxiv
Gouraud, Gen. Henri, 122-23
Greece, 37, 61, 65, 138-40, 151, 163, 165
Grey, Sir Edward, 38, 57, 60, 61, 66, 74, 112, 141, 154, 168
  character, 30
  on the Dardanelles, 57, 110
  insists that the decision to use troops was forced on Kitchener, 182
  refutes Churchill's claim that he would have preferred an amphibious operation, 178
  stunned by Kitchener's prediction of a long war, 31
Guépratte, Rear Adm. E.P., 100

Haifa, 39
Haldane, Richard, 110
Hall, Capt. William Reginald, 86-87
Hamilton, Gen. Sir Ian, 90, 100, 183
  admits his attack has been held up and requests reinforcements, 101-3
  appointed commander of Allied forces in the ardanelles, 78-80
  appraisal of his management of the campaign, 148
  is cleared to assault Gallipoli, 91
  criticism of his leadership is widespread, 146-47
  doubts the navy alone can get through the Straits, 90
  denies French request for a landing in Asia, 123
  elects to strike in the southern half of Gallipoli, 98
  extreme difficulty of his task, 101, 148
  forced to delay his attack, 91-93
  given instructions by Kitchener, 80-82
  government offers heavy reinforcements, 116-18
  overly optimistic about a victory, 115, 118, 175
  qualification for the post, 79
  recalled home, 147
  receives much inside information about the Turks, 83
  the second landing, like the first one, falls short of its objective, 124
  selects Anzac rather than Cape Helles as the focal point of next attack, 124
Hanbury-Williams, Sir John, 46-48
Handub, xix
Hankey, Lord (Maurice Pascal Alers), 96-97, 105, 113, 120, 128, 132, 138, 143, 154, 166
  distorts evidence to protect colleagues in testimony to the Dardanelles Commission, 184-85
  favours an assault against Turkey, 44
  finds fault with Hamilton's military judgement, 146
  and Kitchener, 45, 84, 109, 134
  memorandum identifies only one available division at the start of 1915, 177
  recommends use of troops to support the navy, 65, 77

  sent on a fact-finding mission to the Dardanelles, 122
  talented strategist and secretary of the inner councils of war, 38
Harcourt, Lewis, 90
Hardinge, Sir Charles, 28, 168
Henley, Sylvia, 171
Hickey, Michael, 82
Horne, Maj. Gen. Henry, 165

Indian army, 64, 97, 167
Inflexible, 89
Irresistible, 89

Jackson, Adm. Sir Henry, 112, 142, 156
James, Robert Rhodes, 82
Joffre, Gen. Joseph, 35, 43, 138, 141-42, 159
  applies outdated strategy against Germany, 43
  autumn offensive is a failure, 141
  becomes a late convert to the Balkan enterprise, 142, 150
  finds an excuse to dismiss Gen. Sarrail from his command, 132
  holds a conference with Allied chiefs of staff, 171
  journeys to London to urge the British to send more troops to the Balkans, 151
  tries to block sending French divisions to the Dardanelles, 132-33
  unwilling to adopt an active defence on the western front, 120
Johannesburg, xxiii

Kalid Bahr, 81, 96, 118, 124
Keyes, Commodore Roger, 153, 160, 164, 165, 166
  Admiralty will not sanction a naval attack without army involvement, 157
  Kitchener is attracted to his proposal, 155
  Kitchener tries unsuccessfully to resurrect the idea of a naval attack, 159-60
  pleads for a renewal of naval offensive, 155-56
Khartoum, xviii
Kitchener, Frances Anne, xvii
Kitchener, Lieut. Col. Henry Horatio, xvii, xviii
Kitchener, Field Marshal Lord Horatio

Herbert, 36, 38, 66, 81, 89, 96-97, 102, 112, 141, 152, 154, 159, 172, 174
  accomplishments during first four months of the war, 42-43
  adamantly opposed to withdrawal from Gallipoli, 142, 155
  is allowed to manage the war as he sees fit, 30-31
  appointed secretary for war, 28
  appointed sirdar, xx
  and Asquith, 27-28, 96-97, 126, 162, 171
  Asquith arranges to send him to the Dardanelles supposedly to appraise military conditions, 155
  is attracted to Keyes' plan for a naval attack, 155-58
  and the Balkans, 58-59, 60-61, 63, 138, 143-44, 150, 160, 163-64, 168-70
  and Birdwood, 70, 76, 77, 77-78, 148, 154, 156-57, 159-160, 161, 162
  in the Boer War, xxiii-iv
  cabinet regains control of the war, 43
  campaign to liberate the Sudan, xx
  changing attitude about strength of Ottoman army, 64, 97
  and Churchill, 36-37, 47, 52-55, 57, 61, 66, 73-74, 113, 122, 131, 154
  concerned about rupturing the alliance, 34-35, 49, 134
  at conferences with the French, 121, 132-34, 140, 169-70
  criticism of, 33-34, 51, 174
  and the Dardanelles, 54, 57, 66, 75-77, 84, 90-91, 92, 97, 114-15, 119, 126-27, 130, 154, 148,
  declines Asquith's request that he remain in the east, 165-66
  declining authority in the cabinet, 43, 108, 113-14, 134-35, 154
  disappointed at the results of first landing, 102, 111, 114
  discloses to Wilson his change of policy, 119, 133
  distrusts his colleagues' indiscretion, 108-9
  doubts that the Ottoman front can be broken, 118
  early career, xvii-xix
  engages in lengthy conversations with Briand and Gallieni, 158-59
  explores possibility of an expedition to Alexandretta, 39-42
  and French (Sir John), 35, 45, 49, 63, 106-7
  and general staff, 33, 135, 136, 138-39, 142, 162, 190
  as governor of the Sudan, xxii
  and Hankey, 45, 66, 135, 138
  and Hamilton, 79-83, 90, 93, 97-98, 100, 102, 111, 115, 117-18, 123-24, 127-28, 130, 139, 145, 147
  holds conferences with military leaders and McMahon, 161
  hopes to avoid war with Ottoman Empire, 36
  on imperialism, xxiv
  on invasion fears, 44-45
  and Joffre, 126, 132-33, 138, 141
  and Maxwell, 39, 64, 69-70, 97, 100, 161, 162, 180
  and Monro, 149, 152, 153-54, 157, 160, 161, 163, 165, 166, 171,
  on munitions, 32-33 107-8
  national popularity of, xx, xxiii-iv, 28
  opposes large scale assaults against the western front, 44
  plans to use troops only for mopping up operations, 66, 69, 80
  predicts war will last three years, 31
  as Proconsul in Egypt, xxiv-xxv
  submits final report which advocates withdrawal from Gallipoli, 163
  urges a landing in Ayas Bay to avoid loss of prestige, 162-64
  visits Gallipoli to survey Ottoman defences, 163
  work habits, 28, 31, 33,
  worked tirelessly to provide the nation with the vital tools of war, 32-33
Khartoum, xvii
Krithia, First and Second Battles of, 101, Third Battle of, 123
`Kum Kale, 98, 100
Kut-al-Amara, Battle of, 167

Larken, Capt. Frank and the *Doris*, 42
Lemnos, 66, 90
Limon von Sanders, Gen. Otto, 95, 101
Limpus, Rear Adm. Arthur, 51, 95-96
Lloyd George, David, 57, 66, 107, 110, 135,

146, 160, 163, 169
  and the Balkans, 44, 48, 58, 60, 74, 77, 143, 150, 154, 168, 170
  blames Kitchener for failure to rescue Serbia, 135, 143-44
  character and background, 29
  critical of Churchill, 73, 112-13
  damaged Kitchener's reputation by false accusations in his *War Memoirs,* 194
  fabricated facts in his *War Memoirs* to lend validity to his case, 144-45
  lobbies French politicians on the merits of a Balkan expedition, 63
  as a strategist, 44, 69, 144-45
  wants Kitchener removed from the War Office, 194
Lone Pine, 124
Lyautey, Gen Hubert, 158

Magnus, Philip, 169
Maidos, 98
Marder, A. J., 87-88
Marne, Battle of the, 35
Masterton-Smith, James, 71
Maubeuge, 34
Maucorps, Col. 75-76, 97, 174
Maxwell, Lieut. Gen. Sir John, 97, 140
  considers Carden inept, 69-70
  draws Kitchener's interest in a possible descent at Alexandretta, 39
  favors a landing in Ayas Bay, 161
  reports on an Ottoman assault against the Suez Canal, 64
  warns Kitchener that Gallipoli is heavily fortified, 75, 174
McMahon, Sir Henry, 161, 162, 166
Mesopotamian campaign,
  origins and initial forward movement, 97
  propelling the advance was the lure of capturing Baghdad, 167
Millerand, Alexandre, 58-59, 63, 68, 100-1, 126, 130, 132-33, 140
  requests a landing in Asia to silence Ottoman guns, 122-23,
  urges the British to send more divisions to the Balkans, 149-50
Minto, Lord (Gilbert John Elliot- Murray-Kynymound), xxiv
Monro, Gen. Sir Charles, 152, 153-54, 157, 160, 161, 163, 165, 166, 171, 184
  estimates heavy losses during evacuation, 154
  replaces Hamilton, 149, 161
  refuses to yield under pressure, 169
  visits the Gallipoli Peninsula, 153
Mons, Battle of, 34
Montague, Edwin, 107
Murdoch, Keith, 146-47
Murray, Lieut. Gen. Sir Archibald, 136, 150, 169

Narrows, The, 50, 84, 94, 101, 130, 175
Nejumi, Wad-el-, xix
New Armies, 32-33, 45, 48, 58, 60, 116, 118, 143
Nicholas II, Tsar, 171
Nicholson, Field Marshal Sir William, 33, 188-89
  is a bitter foe of Kitchener, 183
  influential member of the Dardanelles Commission, 183
Nixon, Gen. John, 167

Ocean, 89
Oliver, Vice Adm. Henry, 61, 70
Omdurman, xx
Orange Free State, xxiii
Ottoman army, 61, 97
  attack on Egypt repelled
Ottoman government, 36
  starts the war in the Middle East, 38

Paardeberg, Battle of, xxii
Palestine, 85
Palestine Exploration Fund, xvii
Poincaré, Raymond, 63, 136
Poplar Grove, Battle of, xxiii,

Queen Elizabeth, 53-55, 56, 91, 93, 104-5, 109-10, 188-89
  Fisher insists that the battleship be recalled, 104
  Kitchener protests in vain, 104-6
Qurna, 64, 97, 167

Ralli, Pandeli, 27
Repington, Charles à Court, 106
Richmond, Capt. Herbert, 70
Riddell, Sir George, 71, 119

Robeck, Vice Adm. John de, 165, 166, 181
   attack fails to break though Ottoman defences, 89
   breaks his pledge to assist the army, 93
   changes his mind about resuming the operation, 91
   succeeds Carden, 89
Roberts, Field Marshal Lord Frederick, xxvii-xxviii, 148
Robertson, Gen. (later Field Marshall) Sir William, 172, 187
Rosebury, Lord (Archibald Primrose), 32
Royal Naval Division, 65
Rundle, Sir Leslie, 79
Russian government, 63-64
   gains formal recognition to annex Constantinople and the Straits, 84-85
Russian Grand Duke, 46-47, 63-64

Salisbury, Lord (Salonica, Robert Arthur Gascoyne-Cecil), xix, xx, xxii
Salonica, *see Balkans*
Sari Bahr range, 95, 124
Sarikamish, Battle of, 48, 64, 184
Sarrail, Gen. Maurice, 133-34, 150, 151, 163-64
   removed from command of Third Army, 132
   sent to the Balkans, 149
Selborne, Lord (William Waldegrave Palmer), 113, 135, 150
   advocates vigorous conduct of the operation, 115-16
Seely, Jack, 28
Serbia, 58, 60, 61, 63, 64, 127, 136, 138, 141, 142, 160, 163
Stevenson, Frances, 73, 108, 112
Stopford, Lieut. Gen. Frederick, 146
   charged with conveying new policy to Hamilton, 121-22
Suakin, xix
Suez Canal, xviii, 61, 64, 143, 160
   defenders repel Ottoman attack, 64
Suvla, 124, 138, 139, 171

Talbot, Col. Milo, 37

Thomas, Albert, 170
Times, The, 71, 106
Toski, xix,
Townshend, Maj. Gen. Charles, 167
Transvaal, xxiii
Turkey, See Ottoman Empire
Turkish Army, See Ottoman Army
Turkish government, See Ottoman government

Uskub, 142, 150, 151

Venizelos, Eleutherios, 65, 136, 138, 139, 140
Victoria, Queen, xix
Viviani, René, 141, 150
   ministry falls, 151
   visits London to wrest more divisions for the Balkans, 141

Wadi Halfa, xx
War Committee, 154, 158, 165, 166, 167-68, 172
War Council, 48, 55, 57, 58, 59, 61, 63, 68, 71, 74, 76, 144, 174
   acknowledges Russia's claim to Constantinople and the Straits, 84-85
   defects of, 39
   at first meeting Churchill favours an attack against Gallipoli, 39
   formation of, 38
   at an informal meeting decision is made to send troops to help the navy, 66
   reaction to Churchill's press release, 71-72
War Memoirs, 143, 144-45, 194
Wemyss, Vice Adm. Rosslyn, 91, 168
   replaces de Robeck, 166
   seeks to renew naval assault, 166-67
Wilson, Maj. Gen. Sir Henry, 119, 126, 132-33
Wilson, Trevor, 108
Wolfe-Murray, Gen. Sir James, 33, 38, 60, 136
Wolseley, Gen. Sir Garnet, xviii,
Wood, Field Marshal Sir Evelyn, xviii
World Crisis, The, xiii, xiv, 51, 74, 94-95, 116, 180

Zanzibar Boundary Commission, xix

Also by the same author

The French and the Dardanelles: A Study of Failure in the Conduct of War (London 1972)

Kitchener: Architect of Victory (1977)

The Tragedy of Sir John French (Newark 1984)

Beyond Courage (Ottawa 1985)

Asquith as a War Leader (London 1994)

The Forgotten Front: The British Campaign in Italy (London 1998)

Kitchener's War: British Strategy from 1914 to 1916 (Washington. DC, 2004)

Lloyd George at War, 1916-1918 (London 2009)

Hell in Flanders Fields: The Canadians at the Second Battle of Ypres (Toronto 2010)

Trial by Gas: The British Army at the Second Battle of Ypres (Washington, DC 2014)

Kitchener as Proconsul in Egypt, 1911-1914 (London 2016)

Reluctant Partner: The Complete Story of the French Participation in the Dardanelles Expedition of 1915 (Warwick 2019)

Wolverhampton Military Studies

www.helion.co.uk/wolverhamptonmilitarystudies

Editorial board

Professor Stephen Badsey
  Wolverhampton University
Professor Michael Bechthold
  Wilfred Laurier University
Professor John Buckley
  Wolverhampton University
Major General (Retired) John Drewienkiewicz
Ashley Ekins
  Australian War Memorial
Dr Howard Fuller
  Wolverhampton University
Dr Spencer Jones
  Wolverhampton University
Nigel de Lee
  Norwegian War Academy
Major General (Retired) Mungo Melvin
  President of the British Commission for Military History

Dr Michael Neiberg
  US Army War College
Dr Eamonn O'Kane
  Wolverhampton University
Professor Fransjohan Pretorius
  University of Pretoria
Dr Simon Robbins
  Imperial War Museum
Professor Gary Sheffield
  Wolverhampton University
Commander Steve Tatham PhD
  Royal Navy
  The Influence Advisory Panel
Professor Malcolm Wanklyn
  Wolverhampton University
Professor Andrew Wiest
  University of Southern Mississippi

Submissions

The publishers would be pleased to receive submissions for this series. Please contact us via email (info@helion.co.uk), or in writing to Helion & Company Limited, Unit 8 Amherst Business Centre, Budbrooke Road, Warwick, CV34 5WE, England.

Titles

1   *Stemming the Tide. Officers and Leadership in the British Expeditionary Force 1914* Edited by Spencer Jones (ISBN 978-1-909384-45-3)
2   *'Theirs Not To Reason Why': Horsing the British Army 1875–1925* Graham Winton (ISBN 978-1-909384-48-4)
3   *A Military Transformed? Adaptation and Innovation in the British Military, 1792– 1945* Edited by Michael LoCicero, Ross Mahoney and Stuart Mitchell (ISBN 978-1-909384-46-0)
4   *Get Tough Stay Tough. Shaping the Canadian Corps, 1914–1918* Kenneth Radley (ISBN 978-1-909982-86-4)
5   *A Moonlight Massacre: The Night Operation on the Passchendaele Ridge, 2 December 1917. The Forgotten Last Act of the Third Battle of Ypres* Michael LoCicero (ISBN 978-1-909982-92-5)
6   *Shellshocked Prophets. Former Anglican Army Chaplains in Interwar Britain* Linda Parker (ISBN 978-1-909982-25-3)
7   *Flight Plan Africa: Portuguese Airpower in Counterinsurgency, 1961–1974* John P. Cann (ISBN 978-1-909982-06-2)
8   *Mud, Blood and Determination. The History of the 46th (North Midland) Division in the Great War* Simon Peaple (ISBN 978 1 910294 66 6)
9   *Commanding Far Eastern Skies. A Critical Analysis of the Royal Air Force Superiority Campaign in India, Burma and Malaya 1941–1945* Peter Preston-Hough (ISBN 978 1 910294 44 4)

10 *Courage Without Glory. The British Army on the Western Front 1915* Edited by Spencer Jones (ISBN 978 1 910777 18 3)

11 *The Airborne Forces Experimental Establishment: The Development of British Airborne Technology 1940–1950* Tim Jenkins (ISBN 978-1-910777-06-0)

12 *'Allies are a Tiresome Lot' – The British Army in Italy in the First World War* John Dillon (ISBN 978 1 910777 32 9)

13 *Monty's Functional Doctrine: Combined Arms Doctrine in British 21st Army Group in Northwest Europe, 1944–45* Charles Forrester (ISBN 978-1-910777-26-8)

14 *Early Modern Systems of Command: Queen Anne's Generals, Staff Officers and the Direction of Allied Warfare in the Low Countries and Germany, 1702–11* Stewart Stansfield (ISBN 978 1 910294 47 5)

15 *They Didn't Want To Die Virgins: Sex and Morale in the British Army on the Western Front 1914–1918* Bruce Cherry (ISBN 978-1-910777-70-1)

16 *From Tobruk to Tunis: The Impact of Terrain on British Operations and Doctrine in North Africa, 1940–1943* Neal Dando (ISBN 978-1-910294-00-0)

17 *Crossing No Man's Land: Experience and Learning with the Northumberland Fusiliers in the Great War* Tony Ball (ISBN 978-1-910777-73-2)

18 *"Everything worked like clockwork": The Mechanization of the British Cavalry between the Two World Wars* Roger E Salmon (ISBN 978-1-910777-96-1)

19 *Attack on the Somme: 1st Anzac Corps and the Battle of Poziéres Ridge, 1916* Meleah Hampton (ISBN 978-1-910777-65-7)

20 *Operation Market Garden: The Campaign for the Low Countries, Autumn 1944: Seventy Years On* Edited by John Buckley & Peter Preston Hough (ISBN 978 1 910777 15 2)

21 *Enduring the Whirlwind: The German Army and the Russo-German War 1941-1943* Gregory Liedtke (ISBN 978-1-910777-75-6)

22 *'Glum Heroes': Hardship, fear and death – Resilience and Coping in the British Army on the Western Front 1914–1918* Peter E. Hodgkinson (ISBN 978-1-910777-78-7)

23 *Much Embarrassed: Civil War Intelligence and the Gettysburg Campaign* George Donne (ISBN 978-1-910777-86-2)

24 *They Called It Shell Shock: Combat Stress in the First World War* Stefanie Linden (ISBN 978-1-911096-35-1)

25 *New Approaches to the Military History of the English Civil War. Proceedings of the First Helion & Company 'Century of the Soldier' Conference* Ismini Pells (editor) (ISBN 978-1-911096-44-3)

26 *Reconographers: Intelligence and Reconnaissance in British Tank Operations on the Western Front 1916-18* Colin Hardy (ISBN: 978-1-911096-28-3)

27 *Britain's Quest for Oil: The First World War and the Peace Conferences* Martin Gibson (ISBN: 978-1-911512-07-3)

28 *Unfailing Gallantry: 8th (Regular) Division in the Great War 1914–1919* Alun Thomas (ISBN: 978-1-910777-61-9)

29 *An Army of Brigadiers: British Brigade Commanders at the Battle of Arras 1917* Trevor Harvey (ISBN: 978-1-911512-00-4)

30 *At All Costs: The British Army on the Western Front 1916* Edited by Spencer Jones (ISBN 978-1-912174-88-1)

31 *The German Corpse Factory: A Study in First World War Propaganda* Stephen Badsey (ISBN 978-1-911628-27-9)

32 *Bull Run to Boer War: How the American Civil War Changed the Victorian British Army* Michael Somerville (ISBN 978-1-912866-25-0)

33 *Turret versus Broadside: An Anatomy of British Naval Prestige, Revolution and Disaster, 1860-1870* Howard J. Fuller (ISBN 978-1-913336-22-6)
34 *A Moonlight Massacre: The Night Operation on the Passchendaele Ridge, 2 December 1917. The Forgotten Last Act of the Third Battle of Ypres*, Second Edition, paperback Michael LoCicero (ISBN 978-1-911628-72-9)
35 *The Darkest Year: The British Army on the Western Front 1917* Spencer Jones (ISBN 978-1-914059-98-8)
36 *Ham & Jam. 6th Airborne Division in Normandy: Generating Combat Effectiveness, November 1942-September 1944* Andrew Wheale (ISBN 978-1-915070-85-2)
37 *Stemming the Tide. Officers and Leadership in the British Expeditionary Force 1914,* Revised Edition paperback edited by Spencer Jones (ISBN 978-1-91507-097-5)
38 *Kitchener and the Dardanelles Campaign: A Vindication* George Cassar (ISBN 978-1-915113-75-7)